Tensile Architecture

Tensile Architecture

Philip Drew

Westview Press
Boulder, Colorado

Published in Great Britain by Granada Publishing Limited
in Crosby Lockwood Staples 1979

Published in 1979 in the United States of America by
  Westview Press, Inc.
  5500 Central Avenue
  Boulder, Colorado 80301
  Frederick A. Praeger, Publisher

Library of Congress Catalog Card Number: 79-7357

ISBN 0-89158-550-8

Filmset and printed in Great Britain by
BAS Printers Limited, Over Wallop, Hampshire

Contents

Acknowledgements

I wish to express my gratitude to the many persons who encouraged and supported this research. I gratefully acknowledge my debt to Frei Otto whose ideas and work inspired this study, and to a considerable degree, influenced my interpretation of tensile phenomena. My initial interest in the early development of tensile building was excited by the unsuspected technical parallels between Professor Otto's prestressed tensile surface structures and traditional tents. The large collection of prints depicting nomad and 16–19th century European tents assembled by Berthold Burkhardt of the Institut für Leichte Flächentragwerke (IL) demonstrated that tensile buildings had once existed in the Ancient World.

The translation of a number of important ethnographic works greatly assisted my research. The former Vice-Chancellor and Principal of the University of Newcastle, Professor J. J. Auchmuty, generously agreed to make funds available for the translation of Feilberg's study of the black tent by the Magal Translation Institute Ltd, Tel Aviv, and Ms Keren Bisset translated E. Rackow's *Das Beduinen Zelt* (1938). The translation from the Russian of the section devoted to Siberian dwelling types in M. G. Levina and L. P. Potapova's ethnographic Atlas of Siberia substantially advanced the discussion of northern Eurasian tent groups. Professor G. C. Curthoy volunteered to translate the key terms and later Ms Maggie Kent of the Darwin Museum made a full translation.

I profited from the advice of specialists outside Australia who responded to my request for information, and they include: Peter A. Andrews; Ms M. E. Burkett; Mr Neville Williams; Dr Yigael Yadin; C. B. G. Walker, the British Museum; M. Sheldon Williams, Bodelian Library and Dr Helge Larsen, Danish National Museum.

The cooperation of the library staff at the University of Newcastle in locating books and articles is deeply appreciated. The British Museum and the Bibliotheque Nationale, Paris, supplied microfilms of manuscripts in their collections relating to Renaissance tents. I am indebted to Mr Frank Zabrana of the Department of Metallurgy at the University of Newcastle for his dedication and skill in making the numerous photographic illustrations. He was assisted in this task by Arthur Johnson.

The research has profited greatly by the criticism and suggestions of Ms Jennifer Taylor, and by Dr Harry Woffenden at the School of Architecture, The University of Sydney.

The following sources of illustrations are also gratefully acknowledged. Acta Orientalia Hungarica, Budapest, Hungary. Reprinted by 'Kultura' Hungarian Trading Co. Budapest. Rona-Tas, A. 'Notes on the Kazak Yurt of Mongolia'. *Acta Hungarica Orientalia*. Hungary. 12 (1–3) (1961), p. 102 table IV, 1 and 2, p. 101 table 111, 1 and 2.

Allen, (George), and Unwin Limited, London. Dickson, H. R. P. *The Arab of the Desert.* London 1967, p. 70 and p. 75.

American Anthropological Association, Washington D.C. USA. *American Anthropologist*. (Publisher: G. P. Putnams, New York) 1927. Campbell, N. S. 'The Tipis of the Crow Indians', N.S. (29), p. 91, fig. 2.

American Geographical Society, New York. Musil, A. *Manners and Customs of the Ruwala Bedouins.* AGS Series (6). New York, 1928 p. 63, fig. 3.

American Museum of Natural History, New York. Jochelson, W. 'The Yukaghir and the Yukaghirized Tungus', The Jesup North Pacific Expedition, *Memoir of the American Museum of Natural History*: IX, Pt. 3 (1926) p. 343, pl. XIX, fig. 1, 2. IX,

p. 344, pl. XX, fig. 2. *Anthropological Papers of the American Museum of Natural History*, New York. Jochelson, W. 'The Yakut', **XXXIII**, Pt. 2, 1933, p. 141, fig. 24.

Bureau of American Ethnology, American Museum of Natural History, New York. Boas, F. *The Central Eskimo*. Lincoln, 1888. p. 142, fig. 113, p. 145, fig. 116, p. 143, fig. 115.

AMS Press. (Reprinted, AMS Press, Inc.) New York. Squier, E. G. *Peru, Incidents of Travel and Explorations in the Land of the Incas*. New York, 1877. p. 545, p. 558, p. 559.

American Scandinavian Foundation, New York. Collinder, B. *The Lapps*. Princeton, 1949, pl. XIV.

Architectural Press Ltd, London. Robin Boyd 'Under Tension', *Architectural Review*, **134** (801), Nov. 1963, p. 326, fig. 3. Photographer — Wolfgang Sievers, Melbourne.

Archives Photographiques des Monuments Historiques, Paris. Grube, E. J. *The World of Islam*. London 1966. p. 161, fig. 86.

Arctic Institute of North America, Washington D.C. USA. Okladnikov, A. P. *Yakutia before its Incorporation into the Russian State*. Michael, H. N. (Ed.) London 1970. p. 75 fig. 14—2.

Artemis Verlag, Zurich, Switzerland. Boesiger, W. (Ed.) *The Complete Architectural Works of Le Corbusier 1929—1934*. London 1964. p. 133.

Arts of Asia Publications, Kowloon, Hong Kong. *Arts of Asia* **5** (6), (Dec—Nov. 1975), p. 70 (bottom) p. 65 (bottom).

Bethlehem Steel Corporation, Bethlehem PA. 18016. *Excerpts from Hanging Roofs*. New York, May 1967, BSC Booklet 2319, p. 56, 1 (a) and 1 (b), p. 57 figs. 1 (d) and 2 (d). *Cable Roof Structures*. Booklet No. 2318-A 1968: p. 40 (middle), p. 32 (bottom left).

Black, A. and C. Limited. Webster, G. *The Roman Imperial Army of the First and Second Centuries A.D.* London, 1969, p. 193, fig. 39, pl. XXIV (b).

Braziller, George Inc. New York. Eckardt, W. Von. *Eric Mendelsohn*, New York 1960. p. 10 (bottom), p. 41 and p. 25.
Temko, A. *Eero Saarinen*, New York. p. 54, pl. 14.

Brill, E. J. (Publishers), Netherlands. *International Archives of Ethnology*. **50**, (2) (1966) pl. XIV, fig. 3

British Constructional Steelwork Association, London SW1. Beckett, D. *Bridges*, London, 1969 p. 161.

British Institute of Persian Studies, Surrey, England. *The Journal of The British Institute of Persian Studies* No. XI, 1973, p. 107 pl. 1 (a), pl. 111 (b), pl. V (d), pl. VI (a), pl. VIII (a).

Forlag, A. Reitzels, Copenhagen, Denmark. Steensby, H. P. 'Contributions to the Ethnology and Anthropology of the Polar Eskimos.' *Meddelelser om Gronland*: 1910. (7) p. 328 fig. 19, p. 329 fig. 20, p. 326 fig. 17.

Freer Gallery of Art, Washington, Grube, E. J. *The World of Islam*, London, 1966 p. 145, pl. 83.

du Groupe Expansion, Paris, France. *L'Architecture d'Aujourd'hui*. (78), p. 8, fig. 1, p. 13, fig. 1, p. 40, fig. 4, p. 43 (top left).

Gyldendal Publishers, Denmark © Humlum, J.P.C.N. *La Geographie l'Afghanistan*. Copenhagen, 1959: p. 284, fig. 284, p. 286 fig. 286.

Harvard University Press, Massachusetts, United States. Nervi, P. L. *Aesthetics and Technology in Building*. London, 1966. p. 90, fig. 71, p. 96, fig. 79.

Heinmann William Limited, London and Secker and Warburg Publishers Limited. Sharp, D. *A Visual History of Twentieth Century Architecture*. London, 1972. p. 225 (top).

Heinmann William Limited, Paccagnini, G. *Simone Martini* p. 101, pl. 7.

Hinrichs J. C. (Publishers) Leipzig: Wreszinski, W. *Atlas Zur Altae gyptischen* Kulturgeschichte. Leipzig, 1935. Pt. II, pl. 92 (a) and pl. 81. Pt. III, pl. 107 and pl. 109. Pt. IV, pl. 170 and pl. 177.

Institut des Hautes-Etudes, Rabat, Morocco. Archives Berberes et Bulletin l'Institut des Hautes-etudes Marocaines. Laoust, E. L'habitation chez Les Transhumants du Maroc Central. *Hesperis* **10**, 1930. p. 160. pl. 1, p. 162, fig. 3, pl. XI (top) opp. p. 215, p. 224, pl. XIII.

Institute of Lightweight Structures (IL). West Germany. *Convertible Roofs*. IL. No. 5, Stuttgart, 1972. p. 34 (top left), p. 34 (right) and p. 35. (also my thanks for providing directly all illustrations in the chapter on Frei Otto).

Joseph (Michael) Limited, Botting, D. *Humboldt and the Cosmos*. London, 1973. p. 156, p. 250. Makowski, Z. S. *Steel Space Structures*. London, 1965. p. 195, fig. 219.

Laffont Robert, Publishers, Paris. *The Ancient Art of Warfare*. London 1966. p. 246–7, p. 473, fig. 496.

Loisseau Paul, 1190 Brussels, Belgium. Lejeune, R. and J. S. *The Legend of Roland in the Middle Ages*. Brussels, 1966. **1** p. 172, pl. VI, pl. LIII. **2** fig. 22, fig. 148, fig. 146, fig. 190.

Lund Humphries Publishers, London. Beurdeley, Cecile and Michel, *Giuseppe Castiglione, A Jesuit Painter at the Court of the Chinese Emperors*. London, 1972. p. 85 and p. 110 (top).

Mansell Collection, The. (Incorporating Dorien Leigh), London. Becket, D. *Bridges*. London, 1969. p. 6 (top).

Metropolitan Museum of Art, New York. Museum Excavations 1928–29 and the Rogers Fund, 1930. *The World of Islam*, London 1966. p. 152, pl. 94.

Miklukho, N. N. Maklay Institute of Ethnology, Moscow, USSR. Levina, M. G. and Potapova, L. P. *Istoriko-Ethnografichesky Atlas Sibiri*. Moscow and Leningrad 1961: p. 207 table X, fig. 4, p. 161, fig. 5, p. 167, fig. 1, p. 221, pl. XXIV, p. 163, table 3 figs. 1 and 2, p. 203, pl. VI, figs. 5, 6, 7, 8, 9, 11 and 12, p. 167, table 7, fig. 3, p. 206, table IX, figs. 6 and 7, p. 210, pl. XIII, figs. 9 and 10, p. 214, pl. XVII, figs. 2 and 3, p. 211, pl. XIV, fig. 5, p. 212, pl. XV, figs. 1 and 9, p. 213, pl. XVI, figs. 3 and 7, p. 177, table 17, fig. 2, p. 210, table XIII, figs. 6 and 7, p. 215, table XVIII, figs. 1 and 3, p. 179, table 19, fig. 2, p. 215, table XVIII figs. 4 and 5.

MIT Press, Massachusetts, United States. Wingler, H. M. *The Bauhaus, Weimar Dessau, Berlin, Chicago*. Cambridge, Massachusetts, 1969. Illustration of Marcel Breur's tubular steel chair, 1926.

Mouton & Co. Publishers, The Netherlands. Schurmann, H. F. *The Mongols of Afghanistan, an Ethnology of the Moghols and Related Peoples of Afghanistan*. The Hague, 1961. fig. 6. opp. page 103.

Murray John, Publishers, London. Layard, A. H. *The Monuments of Nineveh — from Drawings made on the Spot*. 1st Series, London, 1853. Series 1, pl. 30 and pl. 77. Series 2 — pl. 23, 24 and 36.

Museum of Modern Art, 'Utica Memorial Auditorium' from *Twentieth Century Engineering*. New York, 1964, pl. 76. © Tranquille Dante, New York also 'Wuppertal Municipal Swimming Pavilion' from *Twentieth Century Engineering* — 1964, pl. 77. © Schmoltz Hugo.

Museum fur Volkerkunde, Leipzig, Germany. Konig, Dr W. *Mongolei*. Leipzig 1967. p. 65, fig. 44, p. 70, fig. 51.

Nationalmuseet, Copenhagen, Denmark, Mathiassen, T. *Material Culture of the Iglulik Eskimos*, 1928. Report of the Fifth Thule Expedition, 1921–24. **6** (1), Copenhagen. p. 132, fig. 80. Nicolaisen, J. *Ecology and Culture of the pastoral Tuareg with particular reference to the Tuareg of Ahaggar and Ayr*. National Museets shrifter Ethnografisk Raekke, **9**, Copenhagen, 1963. p. 352, fig. 264, p. 354, fig. 265 (c), p. 355, fig. 265 (e), p. 376, fig. 278. Feilberg, C. G. *La Tente Noire*, Copenhagen, 1944: p. 29, fig. 1, p. 82, fig. 8, p. 90, fig. 11 (a), p. 87, fig. 9, p. 101, fig. 15, p. 100, fig. 14, p. 101, fig. 15, p. 184, fig. 18, p. 185, fig. 19.

National Palace Museum, Taipei, Taiwan, Republic of China. Willets, W. *Foundations of Chinese Art*. London, 1965. pl. 221.

Niggli, Arthur Limited, Switzerland. Schnaidt, C. *Hannes Meyer: Buildings, Projects and Writings*. Teufen, Switzerland. 1965. p. 20.

Nijhoff (Martinus) Publishers, The Netherlands. Patterson, A. *Assyrian Sculptures: Palace of Sennacherib*. The Hague, 1912. pl. 74–75 and pl. 76.

Olms, Georg. (Publishers), Hildesheim, Hagentorwall 7. Dalman, G. *Arbeit und Sitte in Palästina*. **6.** Gutersloh, 1964 (Reprint: Hildesheim, 1964). pl. 11, pl. 1. p. 3 and 4.

Osterreichisches Nationalbibliothek, Vienna, Austria. Goodwin, G. *A History of Ottoman Architecture*. London, 1971. p. 428. pl 478.

Oxford University Press, London and Jay Gluck Publishers, Ashiya, Japan. Pope, A. U. and Ackerman, A. (Ed.). *A Survey of Persian Art from Prehistoric Times to the Present*. London, 1967. **IX,** p. 907 (b), pl. 910, **IX**.

Oxford University Press, Oxford. Rostovtzeff, M. *Iranians and Greeks in South Russia*. 1922. (Reprinted by Russell & Russell Publishers, N. York, 1969.) pl. XXVIII (top).

Pall Mall Press, London and Phaidon Press, Oxford: Kultermann, U. (Ed.) *Kenzo Tange: Architecture and Urban Design 1946–1969*. London, 1970. p. 202, p. 212, p. 213, p. 216 (b).

Penguin Books Limited, Harmondsworth, Middlesex. Mongait, A. L. *Archaeology In The USSR*. 1961. p. 93, fig. 7. (Reprinted by permission of Penguin Books Ltd.).

Pierpont Morgan Library, The, New York 10016. Bishop. M. *Horizon Book of the Middle Ages*. 1968. p. 65 MS 638 f 27v.

Libraire Plon, Paris. Chapelle, J. *Nomades Noirs du Sahara*. Paris, 1957. pl. opp. p. 263, p. 229, fig. 2, p. 231, fig. 3 and p. 233, fig. 5.

Princeton University Press, United States. Bieber, M. *The History of the Greek and Roman Theatre*. Princeton, 1961. fig. 624. © Alinari, Via Due Macelli 100, Rome, Italy.

Quaritch, Bernard Limited (Publishers), London. Martin, F. R. *The Miniature Painting and Painters of Persia, India and Turkey from the 8th to the 18th Century*. London, 1912. p. 9.

Reimer (Dietrich) Publishers, West Germany. Rackow, E. *Das Beduinzelt*: Baessler Archiv. **XXI**, Berlin, 1938. (Reprint 1968). p. 165, p. 160, pl. 2 (after p. 164), p. 164, pl. 2, pl. 8.

Royal Institute of British Architects, London W1N 4AD. *RIBA Journal*. June 1966: p. 254, fig. 2. 'A Comparison of the Effect of similitude and magnitude in different kinds of bridges.'

Science Museum, Kensington. Hopkins, H. J. *A Span of Bridges*. Newton Abbot, 1970. p. 226, fig. 100. and Beckett, D. *Bridges*. London, 1969, p. 67.

Scientific American Inc., New York. Klein, R. 'Ice Age Hunters of the Ukraine' **230,** (6). (1974) p. 97. Lattimore, Owen 'Chingis Khan and the Mongol Conquests'. **209,** (2). (1963) p. 64.

Spring Books, Hamlyn Publishing Group Limited, Middlesex. Marek and Knizicova. *The Jenghis Khan Miniatures from the Court of Akbar the Great*. London, 1963. pl. 16.

Studio International Publications, London WC1A 1JH. Coulton, G. G. *The Chronicle of European Chivalry*. Studio special Winter Number, London, 1930. p. 20, pl. 11.

Tuttle Charles E. Co., Inc. (Publishers), Tokyo, Japan. Lillys, W. *Persian Miniatures*. London, 1965. pl. 10.

Unesco, Publications de l'Unesco, Paris, France. *IRAN: Persian Miniatures*. © Unesco, 1956. pl. XXVII. Reprinted by permission of Unesco.

United States Steel, New York. Howard, H. S. (Jnr.) *Suspended Structures: Concepts* AD USS 55–1898, 1966: p. 11 (top left). Photograph by courtesy of United States Steel Corporation.

Viking Press Inc. New York. Plowden, D. *Bridges: The Spans of North America*. New York, 1974. p. 104 (centre) pp. 110–111, p. 144 and p. 266. © David Plowden.

Weir, Shelagh, plates 5 and 39 from *The Bedouin* by S. Weir, Assistant Keeper, Museum of Mankind. Published by World of Islam Festival Publishing Co. Ltd. also 3 b/w plates: (1) Woman of Huwaytat bedouin, (2) Tent with tent-dividing wall, (3) Woman weaving strip for a tent roof, Huwaytat bedouin.

Weidenfeld George, & Nicholson Limited, Publishers, London. Yadin, Y. *The Art of Warfare in Biblical Lands*. Jerusalem, 1963: **2.** p. 292. © Professor Yigael Yadin, Jerusalem, Israel.

Whitney Publications Inc., *The Architectural Forum*, New York. **133** (3), (October 1970), p. 29 (top), **97,** (4) (October 1952), p. 136 (top left), p. 139 (top), plan.

Yale University Press, New Haven, United States. Saarinen, A. B. (Ed.) *Eero Saarinen on his Work*. London, 1968. Pages – 7, 62–3, 64, 65, 105, 106–7, 108 (section, top), and 112.

Preface

Early tensile architecture arose among barbarian wanderers and invaders living outside the frontiers of the civilized world. The buildings of barbarian peoples are the antithesis of architecture produced by civilization: they are light instead of heavy; transient instead of permanent; portable instead of static; and demountable instead of immutable. The continual state of flux of barbarian life, especially that of pastoral nomads, deprived their buildings of the sense of permanence which, Kenneth Clark asserts, indicates civilization. The openness and lightness of tensile building creates an immediacy with the surrounding landscape which contrasts with the isolation of heavy monumental buildings. Most important of all, traditional tensile building is relatively adaptable compared with the fixity of the monuments of civilization. The outstanding adaptability of lightweight structures is a recent discovery and partly explains the interest in tensile structures over and above the structural efficiency of their forms.

This outline of tensile building was written to provide an historical perspective for modern tensile architecture in the 20th century, but it became increasingly clear that traditional tensile building is connected with nomadic cultures. The association of traditional tensile building with barbarism partly explains its neglect. It is understandable that architectural historians should have concentrated on the buildings of civilization, since its contribution to human development was much more important than that of barbarism. Nevertheless, this bias has obscured the outstanding technical achievement of the barbarian builders and the relevance of their light portable prefabricated dwellings to modern conditions. The tensile buildings of nomads are the product of a way of life entirely different from that which gave rise to civilization, so it is unfair to assess their achievements by the same criteria. In the final analysis the neglect of barbarian building may come down to a simple prejudice against barbarians.

The emergence of modern tensile building in the early 1950s focused attention on tensile structures as the antithesis of compression loaded vaults and domes. Because of the close identification of compression modes of spanning interior space with historical architecture in the West, tensile buildings quickly acquired a reputation as being entirely new and appropriate to the Modern Age. In a narrow sense, tensile buildings are more 'modern' than much historical architecture, since both the nomadic pastoralist and the modern technologist want to maximize performance per kilogram. The concrete shells of Felix Candela are proof that the search for light efficient structures does not lead invariably to tensile structures.

The sudden appearance of modern tensile building after the Second World War raised a number of questions which could only be answered by a review of traditional tensile building. These questions concerned the origin, early development, character and context of traditional tensile building and its contribution to modern tensile building. Moreover, the history of Western architecture is largely a study of trabeated and compressive masonry construction traditions so it was intriguing to enquire into the existence and character of traditional tensile buildings.

By studying the past it may be possible to determine whether modern tensile building has realized the potential of tensile structures displayed by traditional examples, to establish whether there is any connection between traditional and modern tensile building, and to determine whether the conditions which fostered traditional tensile building are in any way comparable to the factors which promoted modern tensile building.

Traditional tensile building exhibits a much wider range of characteristics than might be inferred from modern applications of tensile building. Architects and designers usually approach tensile building in terms of its novelty and large span capability and this somewhat narrow technical conception of tensile structures has limited the scope of modern applications. Traditional manifestations of tensile building serve as a corrective to this narrow view by demonstrating its adaptability and minimal use of material. Frei Otto stated that 'the structural element is an aid — nothing more — to the fulfilment of a building task. The fewer elements of construction and material needed to fulfil the task, the freer we can be in total conception, in division of space and in adaptation of the building to our daily requirements.'

The interest in light flexible environments in the 1960s in the West and Japan was symptomatic of an increasing disaffection with static formal architecture. The avant-garde's pursuit of a minimal architecture was in response to the need to create adaptable environments capable of responding to changing human requirements. Thus, the light portable shelters of the wanderers and invaders anticipated the light transient environments of the 1960s.

Of the two principal traditional manifestations of tensile building it was the suspension bridge, in the form that it acquired in the 19th century, and not the tent, that served as the basis of modern tensile building. The existence of these two archetypes and their influence on the growth of modern tensile building supplied the leading theme of this outline. This necessitated the documentation of the various tent groups, their geographical distribution, ethnological connections and construction. The scarcity of published work on tents suggested initially that they were a rare phenomenon. Subsequent research soon dispelled this erroneous impression and demonstrated that far from being unimportant, tents had once been widely used over vast stretches of Eurasia, North Africa and parts of North America by hunters, nomadic pastoralists, warriors and princes. Most of the information on nomad tents was obtained from ethnographic sources since there were very few comprehensive studies of particular tent groups or of dwellings found in selected regions. C. G. Feilberg's *La Tente Noire* (1944) remains the only comprehensive study of a major tent group to date. This work is complemented by J. Nicholaisen's (1963) documentation of Tuareg dwellings. M. G. Levina and L. P. Potapova's (1961) monumental survey of Siberian dwelling types was of outstanding service but it lacks the ethnological analysis and interpretative brilliance of Feilberg's study. One of the difficulties in using ethnographic material is that it varies considerably in the detail given. Furthermore, most of the studies concerned the cultures of selected ethnological units and it was necessary to complete the picture of each tent group using several sources.

The origin and early development of the main tent groups has been stressed to a much greater extent than their later development. This is especially true of the treatment of urban tent types. The peoples who use the different tent types have been identified because this seemed the most reliable way of establishing the geographical distribution of each type. The importance of each tent group was assessed in terms of its relevance to modern tensile building. The cylindrical *kibitka* provides striking parallels with modern prefabricated, demountable building systems and the black tent anticipates many of the structural shapes and construction details of Frei Otto's humped membranes. The black tent of the Middle East occupies a central place in this account because it is closest to modern prestressed tensile surface structures. The urban tents revealed the ambivalent nature of heavy and lightweight membrane buildings. Feilberg's study of the origin of the black tent suggests that it developed from an arched hut, while the Ottoman tomb appears to be an instance of ossification of the *kibitka*. The curious influence of masonry architecture on tents can be seen from the manner in which urban tents borrowed the architectural details of palace fenestrations. The ambivalence of heavyweight and lightweight architecture can be observed in some modern tensile buildings.

Tents arose where two conditions prevailed; a shortage of suitable building materials and a need for mobility. The tent required less material to enclose space than most other types of construction and this peculiar advantage made it ideal as a light portable shelter in regions where inadequate resources dictated a nomadic form of economy.

The important lesson of the tent is that of adaptive building rather than its long span capability. Although the tent represents a more appropriate starting point for modern tensile building, the suspension bridge provided the inspiration and technological foundation for its development. Frei Otto's expansion of the tension principle is unique because he started with tent forms and the technology which later developed was related directly to the behaviour and properties of prestressed tensile surface structures. The resemblances between Frei Otto's tents and the black tents of the Bedouin is accidental and result from the solution of similar technical problems.

The shape of nomad dwellings arose from a need for mobility. The outcome of nomadism is a highly functional and uniquely adaptable dwelling. The lightness and flexibility of the tent cloth enabled the tent shape to be modified according to changing conditions or needs. Whereas tents enclose space for dwelling, suspension bridges served mainly as long span linear structures. The tent therefore is closer to modern tensile architecture and more clearly reveals the inherent character and potential of this type of architecture. The rediscovery of the intrinsic adaptability of traditional tensile building offers the prospect of liberating architecture from the stasis of heavy formal architecture.

P.D.

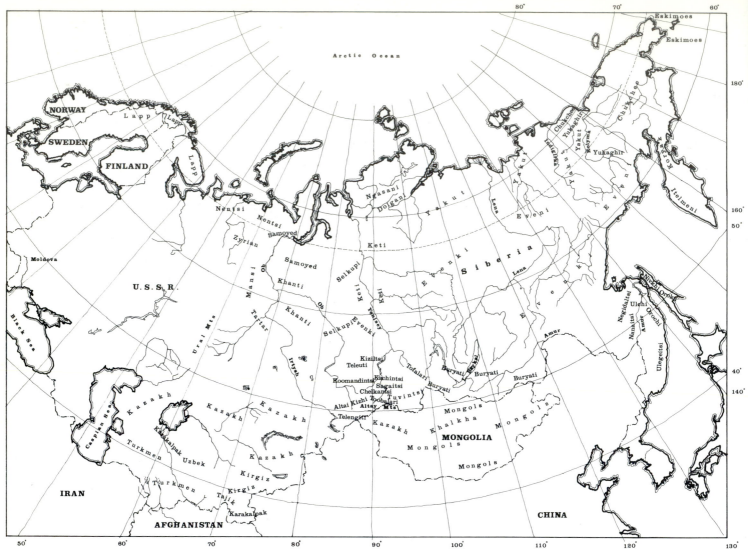

1. Tent dwelling peoples of Northern
Eurasia and Central Asia.

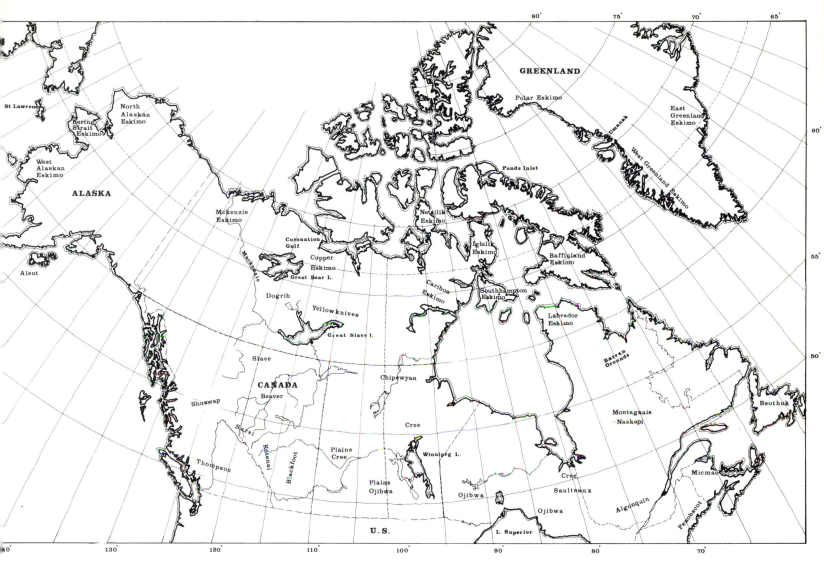

GREENLAND

Polar Eskimo

East
Greenland
Eskimo

St Lawrence

North
Alaskan
Eskimo

Bering
Strait
Eskimo

Umanak

West Greenland Eskimo

West
Alaskan
Eskimo

ALASKA

Mckenzie
Eskimo

Ponds Inlet

Netsilik
Eskimo

Coronation
Gulf

Copper
Eskimo

Iglulik
Eskimo

Baffinland
Eskimo

Aleut

Great Bear L.

Southhampton
Eskimo

Dogrib

Mackenzie

Caribou
Eskimo

Yellowknives

Labrador
Eskimo

Great Slave L.

Barren
Grounds

Slave

Chipewyan

CANADA

Beaver

Montagnais
Naskapi

Beothuk

Shuswap

Cree

Sarsi

Kootenai

Plains
Cree

Blackfoot

Winnipeg L.

Cree

Thompson

Saulteaux

Micmac

Plains
Ojibwa

Ojibwa

Algonquin

Ojibwa

Penobscot

U.S.

L. Superior

2. Eskimo and Indian tent dwellers of
Alaska and Canada.

xix

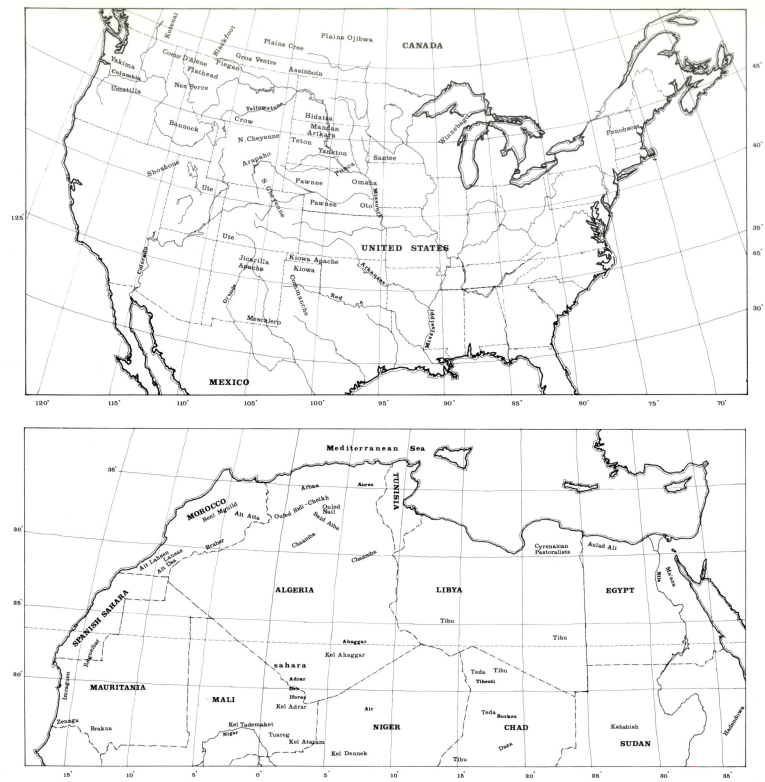

CANADA

Kutenai
Blackfoot
Plains Cree
Plains Ojibwa
Yakima
Coeur D'Alene
Piegan
Gros Ventre
Assinboin
Columbia
Flathead
Umatilla
Nez Perce
Bannock
Yellowstone
Crow
Hidatsa
Mandan
Arikara
N.Cheyenne
Teton
Shoshone
Arapaho
Yankton
Santee
Ponca
Ute
S.Cheyenne
Pawnee
Omaha
Missouri
Pawnee
Oto

UNITED STATES

Winnebago
Penobscot

Jicarilla
Apache
Kiowa Apache
Kiowa
Arkansas
Colorado
Grande
Comanche
Red
Mescalero
Mississippi

MEXICO

120° 115° 110° 105° 100° 95° 90° 85° 80° 75° 70°
45°
40°
125°
35°
65°
30°

Mediterranean Sea

35°
Arbaa
Aures
TUNISIA
MOROCCO
Beni Mguild
Ait Atta
Ouled Sidi-Cheikh
Ouled Nail
Saïd Atba
Braber
Chaamba
Ait Lahsen
Ait Lansas
Ait Usa
Chaamba
Cyrenaican Pastoralists
Aulad Ali
30°
SPANISH SAHARA
ALGERIA
LIBYA
EGYPT
Nile
Maaza
25°
Ragueibat
Tibu
Imraguen
sahara
Ahaggar
Kel Ahaggar
Tibu
20°
Adrar
MAURITANIA
Bes
Iforas
Teda
Tibu
Zenaga
MALI
Kel Adrar
Air
Teda
Tibesti
Brakna
Kel Tademaket
Niger
Tuareg
NIGER
Teda
Borkou
Kababish
Hadendowa
Kel Ataram
Daza
CHAD
Kel Dennek
Tibu
SUDAN

15° 10° 5° 0° 5° 10° 15° 20° 25° 30° 35°

XX

3. Tepee dwelling Indian tribes of the
United States.
4. Tent dwelling peoples of North Africa.
5. Tent dwelling peoples of the Arabian
Peninsula, Iraq, Iran and Afghanistan.
6. Geographical distribution of tent types
in Northern Eurasia.
(1) Hemispherical shaped and barrel-
vaulted tents framed with bent branches.
(2) Ridge tents.
(3) Conical tents.
(4) Cylindrical compound tents with
lattice walls.
(5) Cylindrical compound tents,
unlatticed.
(6) Polygonal compound tents.
(7) Cylindrical-conical tents.

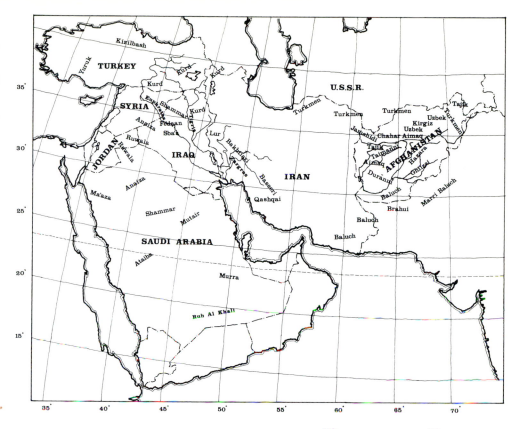

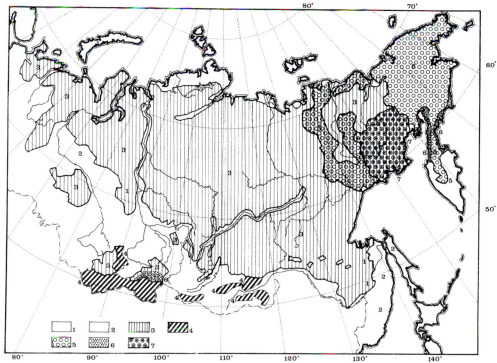

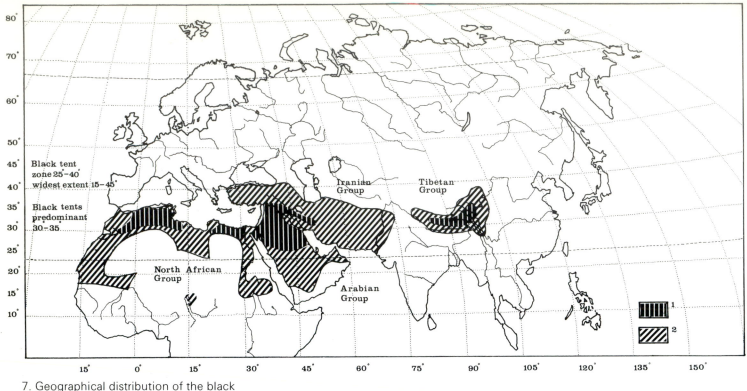

80°
70°
60°
50°
45° Black tent
40° zone 25°-40°
widest extent 15-45°
35° Black tents
30° predominant
25° 30-35°
20°
15°
10°

Iranian Group
Tibetan Group
North African Group
Arabian Group

1
2

15° 0° 15° 30° 45° 60° 75° 90° 105° 120° 135° 150°

7. Geographical distribution of the black
tent in the Middle East.
(1) The tent constitutes the principal form
of dwelling or its use is extremely
widespread.
(2) Widest extent.

Part One

Traditional Tensile Architecture:
The Tents of Nomad Cultures

Tents and suspension bridges are the chief manifestations of traditional tensile building which relate directly to mankind's activities. The modern world discovered suspension bridges almost two centuries before tents began to be seriously considered as a suitable prototype for modern tensile building. The 19th century benefited from advances in metallurgy and the experience gained in constructing large bridges contributed to the prodigious increase in spans in the first half of the 20th century.

The tent was ignored except for military uses, circuses, natural disaster relief, cricket matches, garden parties, and the like, until the 1950s. There are two categories of traditional tents; nomad tents belonging to hunters, fishers and pastoral nomads, and urban tents used by princes and warriors. Nomad tents include the conical framed tent of Northern Eurasia and North America, the cylindrical framed tent having a conical or domical roof of the Central Asian steppelands, and the black tent of the Middle East. A fourth type, the ridge tent, is an ancient form found in cultural resistance regions.

Urban tent types are not unlike nomad tents, the pavilion resembles the ridge tent and the parasol-roof or bell tent is similar to the *kibitka*, except that it has a stressed roof cloth and lacks a supporting framework.

Chapter 1

Tents and Nomads

Nomadism

The tent has been adopted in one form or another, by a large number of peoples living in widely differing environments. Despite some shortcomings it was popular because its lightness, portability, and ease of erection were advantageous in regions in which building materials were scarce and where economic survival demanded mobility. The association of tents with a specific way of life is strong among nomadic pastoralists and, to a lesser extent, among hunters and fishers. The factors which led hunting peoples to adopt the tent were even more compelling in the instance of the nomadic pastoralist.

The tent is commonly found in dry climates.[1] Precipitation rather than temperature is the factor: tents are found in regions subject to extreme heat or cold but rarely in areas receiving abundant rainfall. It seems that this common factor of low and unreliable precipitation, usually less than 254 mm and up to 508 mm, is decisive in the choice of the tent as a dwelling. Although the effect of meagre precipitation is complex, there are two aspects that favour the tent. Firstly, low precipitation results in a nomadic way of life because sedentary agriculture is either impossible or unreliable except at isolated oases, where some form of economy based on hunting or herding of animals adapted to the harsh conditions is probable. Secondly, low precipitation affects the type of vegetation, inhibiting the growth of trees which might otherwise constitute a valuable source of building materials.[2] Low precipitation then not only promotes a nomadic form of economy but also restricts the range of dwelling choices.

Pastoral nomads normally live in portable dwellings of the tent type, which can be readily transported along with the family while the herds migrate.[3] The inclination to live in portable dwellings is a fundamental attribute of pastoral nomadism, and is as much a part of its nature as the herding of animals and the following of regular patterns of movement.[4]

Nomads derive a major portion of their subsistence from large flocks of animals which cause them to follow recurring patterns of movement from season to season in pursuit of suitable grazing and water. Their tents are designed to shelter a single family – the fundamental economic unit – which is the social and political level at which the herds are owned.[5] Five or six tents may be grouped to form a herding unit for the pooling of labour for tasks that can be performed cooperatively, and for additional security from attack. The social, political and economic organization of the tribe need not extend beyond the herding unit.

It has been argued that house form is determined by socio-cultural rather than by physical forces by reason of the low criticality of buildings. Simply stated, 'because physical criticality is low, socio-cultural factors can operate; because they can operate, purely physical forces cannot determine form'. This requires further examination in the case of tents. The low criticality promulgated by Amos Rapoport[6] is modified by the pastoral nomads' attempts to utilize marginal resources in areas too dry, too elevated, or too steep for agriculture to be a viable mode of livelihood.[7] This increased criticality is decisive in the selection of the tent as a portable dwelling in competition with other alternatives. Once the requirements of light weight, demountability, and portability have been met by the adoption of a tent dwelling, then socio-cultural factors come into play. It is the action of socio-cultural factors which causes the diversity of tent details in practically identical migratory regimes.

It might well be found that the association of the major tent groups (the conical skin covered tent, the felt covered *kibitka*, and the black goats' hair tent) with extensive regional cultures in the northern hemisphere indicates the presence of common physical factors. Since the tent velum is normally obtained from animals rather than plants, it is useful to enquire into the influence of herd composition on the distribution of tent types. As the herd type is most often a product of the particular complex of available resources,[8] the choice of the velum material may coincide with certain physical factors. However, herd composition is also affected by cultural factors which modify the impact of available resources. This suggests that physical factors dominate the selection of the tent as the preferred dwelling of nomadic pastoralists, and that physical factors play a role in deciding the distribution of the major tent types. The bewildering diversity of tent types at the tribal level is explained by the operation of socio-cultural factors.

Pastoral nomadism in the Middle East

Pastoral nomadism in the Middle East is a specialized offshoot of agriculture that developed along the dry margins of rainfall cultivation.[9] Some of these agriculturalists increased the numbers of their domesticated animals until the keeping of animals predominated over their farming activities. Once the agriculturalist reached this threshold of pastoral nomadism it only required a series of unusually dry years to cause him to abandon his agricultural pursuits altogether, and concentrate upon the flocks as the major subsistence source. The pastoralist's links with agriculture are never entirely severed as the pastoral economy cannot stand alone, but must acquire agricultural goods to assure an adequate diet and to meet all material needs.[10] The transition from hut to tent was not abrupt and there are many transitional forms in which hut-like frameworks are covered with skins, or reed mats besides goats' hair cloths. The gradual evolution of stressed membrane tents from rigid frameworks parallels the derivation of pastoral nomadism from agriculture. Furthermore, pastoral nomadism is best seen as a continuum between a purely sedentary society on one hand, and a hypothetical 'pure' nomadism that has no contact whatsoever with agriculture on the other.[11] The extent to which the details of permanent and semi-permanent dwellings have been retained, provides an indication of the evolutionary distance of the tent from the hut.

The reindeer herder of Northeastern Asia differs significantly from other pastoral nomads, having passed from hunting to herding wild reindeer. Where the relative dependence of pastoral nomadism on agriculture results in a restrictive form of nomadism or semi-nomadism this is often reflected in mixed dwelling types. Some settled pastoralists have retained the tent while others prefer to exchange it for more convenient permanent quarters.

Nomad tents

Nomad tents may be classified in accordance with similarities of shape and material. Accordingly, there are three principal families of tents, namely: skin covered conical tents, felt covered cylindrical tents and black goats' hair tents. Whilst this classification is based on physical characteristics, common environmental and cultural factors enter into each of the three principal tent groups. In general, the principal groups of tents extend in broad latitudinal bands. Conical tents stretch across the cold northern margins of Eurasia and North America from the Scandinavian highlands to Labrador. The felt tent spreads across the high plateau lands of Central Asia westward into Iran, and the black goats' hair tent is dispersed over the Arabian, Turkish and Saharan plateaux in a band between 15 and 35 degrees North.

Climate

The conical tent is not subject to snow drifts,[12] a factor of some importance in arctic polar and sub-polar climates receiving an annual precipitation of up to 508 mm. The dry highland and semi-arid climates in which the felt tent is found receive from 254 to 508 mm of precipitation, sufficient to maintain large herds of sheep, and horses. The cylindro-conical and cylindro-dome shape is approximately hemispherical and in addition to enlarging headroom this minimal surface also reduces heat loss. The black goats' hair tent occurs in regions of dry-arid and dry-semi-arid climate receiving less than 254 mm of rainfall a year.

Economy

Most of the peoples who live in conical tents belong to tribal societies based on hunting and fishing economies, reindeer herding and specialized hunting and fishing. Both the felt and black goats' hair tent families are found amongst traditional societies sustained by nomadic livestock economies. The similarity of shape and construction of the conical tent and the felt covered cylindrical tents may be explained by contacts between the northern hunters and herders and the pastoral nomads of the steppes. Compound cylindro-conical tents with heavier, cruder walls, such as those found among the tundra Yukaghir, and Okhotsk Tungus, the Chukchee and the Koryak, may represent an intermediate development between the northern conical tent and the Central Asian cylindro-conical felt tent.

Race

Roughly speaking, the conical skin tent and the cylindrical felt tents are found among Mongoloid, Turkic and Americanoid peoples while the black goats' hair tent is connected with Mediterranean Caucasoid peoples.[13]

Language

The conical tent peoples speak a number of Ural-altaic languages, palaeo-Siberian, Eskimo and American Indian, while the cylindrical felt tent dwellers belong to the Ural-altaic linguistic family. The cylindro-conical felt tent is sometimes called the eastern Yurt as its distribution coincides with Mongolian speakers while the cylindro-domical felt tent or western Yurt belongs to the Turkic linguistic sub-family. The black goats' hair tent is used by people within the Hamitic-semitic (Semitic and Berber) and the Indo-European (Iranic) linguistic families.

Culture Realms

With the exception of the Great Plains Indians, the conical tent coincides with the Eurasian Arctic and North American Arctic culture realms. The cylindrical felt tents belong to the Inner Asian culture realms and the black goats' hair tent with the Eastern or Islamic culture realm.

Prestressed and framed tents

There are two classes of tents, depending on whether the structural and enclosure elements are functionally independent or are interdependent and act as a single structural mechanism. The functions of support and spatial enclosure may be provided separately. The supporting system may consist of a three-dimensional arrangement of rigid members subject to a mixture of bending, compressive and tensile stresses. The frame serves as a stable scaffold over which a limp non-prestressed velum is draped and secured. The frame can be and often is erected by itself, a practice which highlights the independent nature of the frame and velum. The integration of support and enclosure so that they behave as a single interdependent structural mechanism differentiates prestressed tension loaded tents from nonprestressed framed tents. The flexible velum is prestressed in tension and supported on light masts, arches or simple frames consisting of beams resting on poles subjected to either bending or compression.

Shape

The classification of tents in terms of shape provides a convenient and easy to follow terminology, especially as the shapes of framed tents approximate to the cone, hemisphere, cylinder, semicylinder, pyramid, cube or combinations of these geometrical solids. Prestressed tension-loaded tents have plane or saddle surfaces curved in two opposite and mutually perpendicular directions (anticlastically curved). Framed tents are predominantly plane or synclastically curved.

Compound forms

Headroom in cylindrical felt tents and hence habitability is increased so that such tents are superior to dome or conical tents resting on the ground. In the *kibitka*, a compound shape is produced by placing a dome or conical roof over a low cylindrical lattice wall. The presence of a wall and its relative importance compared with the roof element provides a further characteristic for distinguishing different types of tents.

Velum material

The remaining outstanding characteristic of nomad tents is the velum material. Bedouin tents in the Middle East are called black tents for the distinctive colour of the goats' hair fabric used in the velum and the Mongolian and Kirghiz tents are commonly referred to as felt tents. The conical tent is covered with a variety of materials such as reindeer, caribou, seal, walrus and bison skins, birch bark or felt. The choice of velum material reflects the local economy. Nevertheless, tent velum materials have been standardized to a surprising degree. The Kalmuck tent is described as a cylindro-conical skin covered tent to distinguish it from the cylindro-conical felt covered or Mongolian tent.

Chapter 2

Ice Age Tents

Ukrainian shelters

During the Ice Age, climatic conditions prevailed in the Siberian steppe far to the south of the present polar zone equivalent to those encountered today in the arctic tundra. Ice Age hunters of the Ukrainian periglacial steppe lived in primitive tent-like shelters whose remains have survived as distinctive oval collections of mammoth bones buried on an ancient terrace of the Dniester River.[1] The oldest of these sites at Moldova 1 is more than 44 000 years old. Further finds at Moldova V indicate that tents were used by late Mousterian and Upper Palaeolithic cultures in very cold conditions. The presence of quantities of charcoal within each tent ring, indicative of hearths, suggests that the tents were heated. Furthermore, the duplication of hearths testifies to the repeated occupancy of each site.[2] It seems that the Ukrainian hunters camped in the river valleys throughout the cold winter, then, with the approach of summer, moved onto the periglacial steppe upland to hunt the great herds of reindeer, wild horse and steppe bison. The Ukrainian hunters would have experienced no difficulty in building tents. In addition to birch bark, the hides of reindeer or steppe bison could have served as tent covers. The method of securing the tent cover varied: for example in the earliest tents the heavy mammoth bones were stacked against the tent, while at a later date large wood pegs and reindeer antlers replaced the bones.

Reconstructions of these Ukrainian shelters depict a low domical shape covered with animal skins and the tent skirt restrained by heaped mammoth bones. Later shelters are crude tepees reminiscent of those used by present day reindeer herders in Northern Asia.[3]

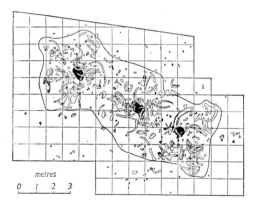

1–3 Three Ice-age shelters built on an ancient terrace of the Dneister river.
1. Mousterian domical shelter comprising a wood frame covered with skins (44 000 years old).
2. Upper Palaeolithic tepee-like shelter (13 000 years old).
3. Tepee-like shelter, 12 000 years old. The skin cover was attached to the wood frame by reindeer antlers.
4. Pushkari 1. Upper Palaeolithic earth house: *1*, plan; *2*, reconstruction.

metres
0 1 2 3

Yakutian shelters

The excavation of dwelling sites in the Ukraine and along the Lena River in Yakutia has yielded evidence consistent with what would be found had these hunters lived in conical skin or bark covered tents. The general absence of forests on the banks of the Angara, Lena and Yenisey[4] caused mammoth and rhinoceros bones to be substituted for timber as the basic material of the dwellings excavated at the Palaeolithic settlement of Buret. Bones were selected according to shape and size for particular constructional tasks. From early Neolithic times until the recent past, Eskimo peoples who inhabited the unforested arctic regions of the Chukchee Peninsula, Alaska and neighbouring islands were compelled by the absence of timber to construct dwellings from the bones of whales, walruses and other sea mammals.[5] Except for the stone foundation wall, the Eskimo stone house is surprisingly similar to the dwellings excavated at Buret.

The Palaeolithic Siberian hunters were forced to abandon their spacious semi-subterranean dwellings for lighter portable shelters by the warming of the climate which called for a more mobile form of hunting. A type of light surface dwelling such as a conical structure covered with tree bark or skins is indicated by the remains unearthed at campsites at the mouth of the Malaya Munku River where it joins the Lena.[6] Neolithic cliff drawings on the Markha River depict cupola-like structures with slightly inclined straight sides surmounted by a gently rounded cupola roof resting on two crossed lines, reminiscent of the ancient summer dwelling or *Urasa* of the Yakut.[7] The remains of dwellings belonging to early Iron Age people who lived by hunting and fishing, demonstrate the wide dispersal throughout the Lena basin of the *Urasa* birchbark covered tent.

The Yakut 'Urasa' tent

The Yakuts were a nomadic horse breeding tribe from the Central Asiatic steppes who eventually settled in the Lena basin. In their language, traces of a former acquaintance both with the smoke hole and with the wooden latticed frame of the steppe nomad's felt tent indicate that the conical birchbark tent supplanted the felt yurt after their arrival in the north.[8] The remarkable inner supporting wall, the *orto kurdu*, of the ancient *Urasa* tent may have been a survival of the Yakut yurt. The ancient Yakut *Urasa* differs from other types of birchbark tents in size and in the heavy and solid construction of the timber frame that made it difficult to transport. These large tent-like dwellings were erected during the summer, some distance from the winter earth huts.[9] They were formerly collective clan dwellings having screened sleeping accommodation around the common clan fire serving many households. According to Yakut legends, the ancient herders, the *Khosuns*, who were chiefs of clans, lived in *Urasa* and in later times they were built only by rich men.[10]

The conical tent is a primitive dwelling type connected with the hunting stage of culture, but many nomadic or semi-nomadic herders and even some sedentary agricultural tribes use it chiefly as a summer dwelling.[11] For the most part the conical tent is associated with hyperboreal peoples in Eurasia and North America. In the southern hemisphere, the Ona Indians of Tierra del Fuego possess elaborate conical huts for ritual purposes[12] and the Vezo, maritime nomads of Madagascar, erect small tilted canvas covered conical tents for stays of short duration.[13]

5. Neolithic cliff drawings of ancient Yakutian cupola-like dwellings.
6. Large Yakut conical birchbark summer tent similar to ancient Yakut *Urasa*.
7. Frame of a Yakut conical dwelling.

CONICAL TENTS OF NORTHERN EURASIA AND NORTHERN AMERICA

Geographical distribution of tent types in Northern Asia

The area of Northern Asia, from the Ural mountains to the Pacific Ocean, to the north of the Sayan mountains and the Amur River and including Siberia is furnished with a great diversity of tent types and houses (Map 6). Domical and barrel-vaulted tents, ridge tents, conical tents, composite conical and cylindro-conical tents, polygonal and cylindro-conical tents having a variety of wall constructions, culminating in lattice frame walls are encountered in Northern Asia.[1] These tents may have provided prototypes for tents in North-Eastern Europe and North America. The conical tent covered with animal skins or birchbark together with a series of transitional forms leading to the fully developed skin covered cylindro-conical tent are the predominant tent genus of the 'taiga' or boreal forest and tundra lands of Northern Asia.

The semi-spherical and barrel-vaulted, and the ridge and pyramidal tent types are much less important in terms of distribution than the conical and cylindro-conical series of tents. The dome and ridge tents are found in association with hunting and fishing economies along the banks of arctic river systems and on the Pacific coast. The ridge tent serves as a temporary shelter over most of the sub-arctic region along with the conical tent.[2] The Yakuts, Mansi, Khanti, Nanaitsi, Udegeitsi and Negidaltsi, Orochi, Oroki and Nivkhi, and all the Finnis-Ugrian peoples including Ostyak, Vogul, Votyak and Zyran also have recourse to the ridge tent.[3] It is the principal dwelling of some Amur and northern Sakhalin tribes. Typically, the ridge tent is found on the outskirts of the boreal region or in places which because of the inhospitable natural conditions and inaccessibility are regarded as 'cultural resistance regions'.[4] It is also found in the central Ob region and among the Tungus-Manchurians. Hemispherical and ridge tents are never far apart. Hemispherical tents are used by Simsk Evenki, the Eloguisk Keti, the Yakuts of Megino-Kangalassk, the Churapchinsk, Fattinsk and Amginsk regions of Yakuts, and amongst the Nanaitsi along the Amur.[5]

The conical tent is dispersed over a vast area extending from Arkhangelsk in the west to the Omolon river in the east. It is found among the mountain peoples of the Sayan region, the independent peoples along the Yenisey, the southern Turkish peoples, the cattle and deer herding Yakuts, Tungus-Manchurian peoples, all the Evenki and Eveni groups and some Palaeo-Asiatic peoples.[6] The conical tent is found in use among tribes who derive their livelihood by hunting or herding reindeer and who live in boreal forest areas for at least part of the year,[7] and while the conical tent is widely associated with the reindeer Tungus, it is shared by Turks, Samoyed, Finn and some Northern Mongolian tribes.[8] Notwithstanding some conical tent dwellers who inhabit the tundra, most of these people live for a part of the year, usually winter, in the 'taiga'.

The tent frame is constructed of numerous long slender wood poles which are easily obtained in the boreal forest areas. The poles are heavy and difficult to transport and so it is not uncommon for the tent frames to be left behind when a tribe moves on.[9] Other materials besides reindeer skins and birchbark are used to cover the conical tent.

The area from the Indigirka River to East Cape, Siberia, including the northern part of Kamchatka, is rich in polygonal and cylindrical compound tents. The cylindro-conical tent is closely identified with Siberian Americanoid tribes who have specialized in reindeer breeding. The southern boundary in Kamchatka is

8. Khanti dwelling made from two single pitched roofed tents.
9. Keti double-hemispherical tent of bent arches.
10. Khanti conical summer tent covered with birchbark.
11. Khanti conical winter tent covered with hides.

defined by the southern limit of reindeer breeding. The maritime Koryaks of Northern Kamchatka possess a primitive octagonal compound tent which is similar to one used by the Chukchee.

The cylindro-conical tent of Northeastern Siberia is unrelated to the Kalmuck and felt-covered Mongolian types. A second group of unlatticed cylindro-conical tents is located in Southwestern Siberia amongst the Tubalari, Chelkantsi, Teleuti, Kachintsi, Sagaitsi, Beltiri, and Kizhi Turkic tribes. Latticed cylindrical tents similar to *Kibitkas* are known to the Altai Kirzhi, Telengiti, Kachintsi, Sagaitsi, Beltiri Kiziltsi and Tuvintsi Turks and to the Mongolian Buryats of Transbaikalia.[10] The omission of the central support structure of the northeastern types and the replacement of the heavy strutted wall by a light lattice wall, indicates that these southern types derive from the felt covered cylindro-conical tent of the Asian steppe. The northeastern cylindro-conical tents developed in isolation and are unrelated to the felt-covered Mongolian and Turkic types of the Asian steppe.[11]

Conical tents of Siberia

The conical tent is essentially a primitive dwelling used by peoples at the hunting stage of culture. It is retained as a summer dwelling by many nomadic or semi-nomadic herders and even by some sedentary agricultural tribes. The tent consists of a conical framework of inclined poles, arranged in a circle with their upper ends secured at the peak. The construction of the pole frame and the material used to

12 Skin tent of the Upper Kolyma Yukaghir.
13 Summer village of the Yassachnaya Yukaghir on the Yassachnaya River.
14. Nentsi conical tent construction: *1*, plan of summer tent; *2*, top fastening of the foundation frame; *3*, plan of winter tent: i, hearth, ii, planking shelf, iii, mat floor; *4*, covers; *5*, raising the covers; *6*, section through tent; *7*, smoke flap.

cover it, but not the form, is exceptionally uniform throughout Siberia. The most significant differences are the types of primary support structure, the method of securing the upper ends of the poles at the peak, the type of frame used to suspend the cooking vessels over the hearth and its degree of integration with the primary support structure, and the material pattern and means of securing the tent sheet to the frame. There are other differences such as the arrangement of the interior, the use of an interior lining, tent furniture, design of openings and decoration of the cover, and whether the tent frame is transported to each new site or is abandoned when the tribal group moves on.

Two, three or four poles are used to construct the primary support or foundation structure. The four-pole structure is thought to have been evolved by combining two two-pole foundations. Two-pole support structures occur in Samoyed, Zyran,

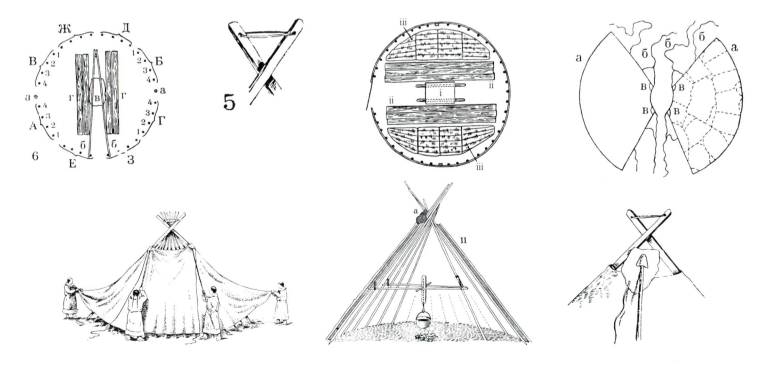

10

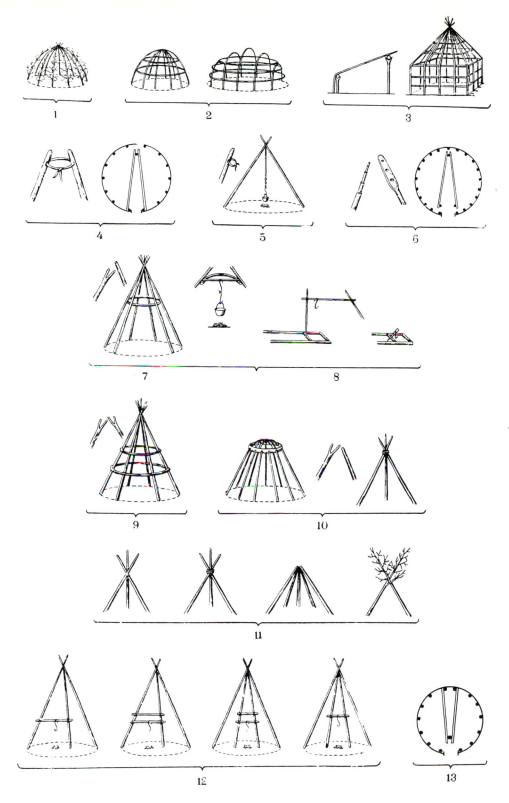

15. Basic features of Siberian conical tents.

1
2
3
4
5
6
7
8
9
10
11
12
13

11

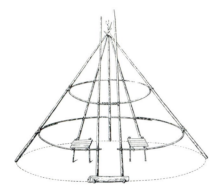

16 Keti conical tent: *1*, frame; *2*, plan: i, hearth, ii, sleeping places, iii, storage for household equipment, iv, storage for cooking utensils.

17 Keti conical tent.

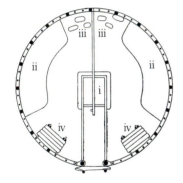

Mansi and Sel'kupi tents; the Ostyak and Vogul use both two and four-pole types. The three-pole foundation is rarely found together with two- or four-pole support structures; it is dispersed among the Northern and Evenki Tungus, Yeniseians, Khanti, Nganasani and the Lapps.[12]

The support structure of the Stony Tungus and Keti is of particular interest because it consists of a two-pole foundation with two additional poles, one on either side of the entrance, a single pole at the back and two rings, one at bench height and another at head height.[13] The entrance and back pole arrangement of the Keti tent frame is reminiscent of the Lapp arch-post conical tent.[14] Intermediate rings are also found in the western type Eskimo tent.[15]

Another important feature of the conical tent is the multiplicity of methods used to secure the upper ends of the poles at the peak (15.9–11). These include threading cord or thong loops through holes in the poles, (15.4) lashing the poles together where they intersect with a cord or thong (15.11), crude mortise and tenon joints (15.6), inserting the pole tips in holes on the outside of a wood hoop (15.10), and tying the poles to a plaited willow ring (15.7) or rings.[16] The weight of poles chosen for the framework and whether or not they are transported is largely determined by geography. The heavy poles used in forested areas are abandoned to avoid their transportation, but on the open steppes, both the light poles favoured there and the tent cover are transported.

The types of tent covers used differ between Northern and Southern Siberia: in the north three separate strips of soft tanned reindeer skins are fastened to the poles with leather thongs[17] and in the south the frame is covered with birch bark softened by boiling before it is sewn together.[18] Skins are used to cover conical tents amongst the Kolyma Yukaghir, the Northern Tungus, the Ostyak, Samoyed, and Lapps. The Amur River Tungus, the reindeer-breeding Soyot and Karagass, and the Southern Ostyak cover their tents with birchbark. Other materials such as bark, felt, sod and snow are sometimes used instead of reindeer skins and birchbark. The Altai Tartar cover their tents with pine or larch bark in forest areas, but substitute felt covers in open country. The Mongolic Kalmuck of Astrakhan and the Kirghiz employ felt covered conical tents as temporary dwellings. Earth and snow are banked against the outside of both the bark and fir covered conical tents to provide insulation in the winter. The smoke from the central hearth escapes through a hole at the apex of the tent which also admits sunlight. This direct sunlight is supplemented by light transmitted through the reindeer hide.

The cooking frame used for suspending kettles and pots over the central hearth is rarely encountered outside Siberia. There are four types of cooking frame (15.12); in the first type, the poles are part of the conical frame, in the second type only one pole is part of the frame, in the third type the two poles are part of the frame and a third pole is freestanding, and in the fourth type two freestanding poles straddle the hearth.[19] The cooking pots are suspended from crossbars lashed to the pole frame and sometimes a second pole is provided above the first to allow for height adjustment. The third tripod type has two cross bars at the same height slung between the three poles. The cooking pot is elevated or lowered by inserting a transverse rod which rests on two cross-bar supports through one of a series of holes in a vertical board from which the pot is suspended. It is significant that the poles in all such cooking frames are lashed to the other poles of the conical frame at their apex and must therefore be considered as part of the tent structure.

Polygonal and cylindrical tents of Northeastern Siberia

The polygonal and cylindrical tents of southwestern and northeastern Siberia are much less well known than the familiar felt-covered cylindro-conical Mongolian *kibitka*. The first group is scattered along the northern border with Mongolia stretching from the Sayan mountains to the Argun River. These tents are related to the Mongolian type, although some of their features have either preserved or borrowed Turkish elements.[20]

The second group is restricted to the extreme northeastern part of Siberia within the area bounded by the Yena River in the north and the Okhotu River in the south, extending east across the Chukchee peninsula into Northern Kamchatka. The foundation of the northeastern cylindrical tent frame is reminiscent of the conical tent foundation. The T-struts which brace the roof poles at mid-span and the wall constructions which range from individual tripod supports to a continuous inverted V-strut framing are features found only in the northeastern tents. The fact that these tents are not only primitive but also isolated from tents of the southwestern type indicates that they were an independent development.[21] Jochelson considered that the cylindro-conical tent was a natural development from the conical tent and regarded it as more advanced.[22] The presence of three- and four-pole foundations in the polygonal and cylindrical types supports his interpretation. Moreover, the Evenki possess a composite tent which is half conical and half cylindro-conical.

More than half of the compound tents in Northeastern Siberia belong to two Siberian Americanoid peoples, the Chukchee and Koryaks, who form a single ethnic group with a common origin.[23] The Tungus, a Mongoloid people who left their home in the valley of the Amur River some time after the 7th century AD and spread over the whole of Eastern Siberia, constitute the third main group of compound tent users.[24] The Tungus borrowed the compound tent from the displaced tribes of Chukchee, Koryak or Yukaghir who stubbornly resisted their slow but constant penetration into Northeastern Siberia. The introduction of deer

18. Chukchee cylindrical compound tent.
19. Chukchee and Asiatic Eskimo cylindrical compound tent.
20. (a) and (b) Heavily framed Koryak polygonal compound tent.
21. Reindeer Chukchee octagonal compound tent.

herding among the Palaeo-Asiatics (Chukchee and Koryaks) by the Evenki, compelled them to develop a mobile compound tent from their immobile dwellings. The resourcefulness of the Tungus is evident in the lightness and simplicity of the frame of their adopted tent.

The compound tent could conceivably have originated at any one of a number of locations in Northeastern Siberia such as Northern Kamchatka or at the mouth of large rivers flowing into the East Siberian Sea. Ferdinand von Wrangel discovered traces of numerous compound tents near the mouth of the Indigirka River at a place still known as 'Yurtowishtche'.[25]

The Chukchee possess two types of cylindro-conical tents, and one octagonal compound tent. In the immobile type of the maritime Chukchee, the upper ends of the roof poles are supported by a central post[26] and their lower ends rest on a cylindrical wall frame consisting of a perimeter ring of poles supported in the forks of upright posts. Slender poles prop up the roof poles in mid-span. The central post is provided with a cross piece, a feature also found in the ridge tent of the Central Eskimo.

The more elaborately framed Chukchee and Asiatic Eskimo cylindro-conical winter-tent, has a central post to which the upper ends of the roof poles are lashed.[27] The roof framing consists of two layers of struts which radiate from the central pole like the struts of an umbrella. The main struts connect the ring beam with the centre pole, while a lower secondary layer of struts thrusts against a second ring midway along the roof poles which assume a slightly convex curvature as a consequence. A similar roof-ring is present in an octagonal Koryak tent. All the Northeastern Siberian compound tents, with the exception of the two Chukchee types already referred to, support the roof apex by means of a foundation frame of three or more poles arranged in a pyramid. The octagonal Koryak tent has a tripod foundation frame and a perimeter wall frame, braced in much the same way as the Chukchee-Asiatic Eskimo example.[28]

The polygonal compound tent is distributed along the east and west coast of Northern Kamchatka, around Penshina Bay, north as far as Khatyrka facing the Bering Sea. It is associated with coastal dwelling maritime Koryaks whose livelihood is derived from fishing and hunting sea mammals and who are therefore less mobile then the reindeer Koryaks. The Chukchee also use an elliptical compound tent in which the roof poles are supported on a tripod foundation structure at the centre and three T-shaped struts.[29] The framing of the Chukchee tent is lighter and more open than the Koryak example. The Chukchee wall framing consists of about eight wall poles which rest on bipod or tripod supports forming an irregular octagon in plan.

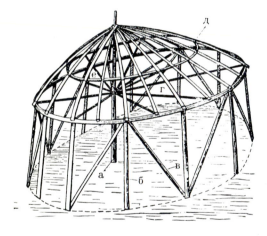

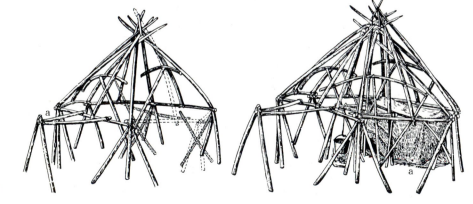

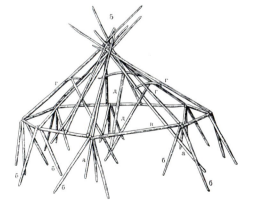

14

22. Portable winter tent of the Eveni: *1*, frame; *2*, plan.
23. Portable cylindrical tent of the Eveni of the Markovsk region: *1*, Frame; *2*, plan.
24. Tent of the Upper Kolyma Tungus.

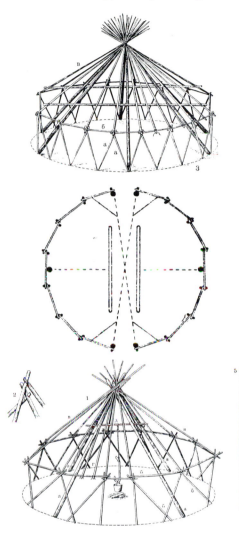

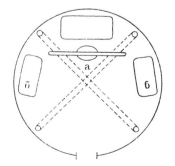

A central foundation structure of from four to six poles is retained in the tents belonging to the Eveni. These are notably more advanced and this is particularly apparent in the rationalized wall framing which anticipates the lattice wall of the Turkic and Mongolian compound tents. Instead of supporting the lower ends of the roof poles on separate bipod or tripod chairs they are secured to the apex of an inverted V formed by two inclined struts.[30] The cylindrical walls of the Eveni tents are divided into triangular facets by diagonal V-struts. These compound tents are not strictly cylindrical because the top wall line consists of straight wall poles which rest on triangulated struts. The Chukchee-Eskimo cylindrical tents unlike the Turko-Mongolian *kibitka*, is constructed on an oval plan, and the apex of the conical roof is therefore shifted from the centre and assumes an assymetric shape.

The cylindrical tent is used by the Okhotsk, Lamut and upper Kolyma Tungus tribes and by the reindeer Yukaghir. The cylindrical Eveni tent has a roof frame of twelve poles supported at their upper ends by a foundation structure of four poles, consisting of two sets of poles joined at the top by mortise and tenon joints with the lower ends planted around inside the wall of the tent.[31] A single cross-beam for cooking is suspended between two of the poles, opposite the rectangular door. Additional poles which have thongs threaded through eyelets in their lower ends for attaching the wall cover are laid upon the basic roof framework. The roof cover is circular with a triangular piece removed to adapt the cover to the conical roof shape.

The Tundra Yukaghir live in a polygonal compound tent similar to that of the upper Kolyma Tungus.[32] Jochelson considered that the Tundra Yukaghir borrowed the compound tent from the Tungus, a supposition borne out by comparison of the two tent types. The sloping roof poles are supported at the central high point by a tripod foundation of heavy poles, and their lower ends rest on inverted V-supports composed of pairs of short struts connected by crossbars.

The Northeastern Siberian compound tents are covered with reindeer skins and occasionally with birchbark, the winter tents of the Chukchee and Koryak are sheathed with heavy reindeer skins, and those of the Eveni and Tundra Yukaghir are invariably covered with dressed skins without the hair.[33] The Eveni of the Okhotsk district cover the lower, cylindrical walls with rectangular pieces of birchbark sewn together with thongs.[34]

Lapp conical tents

The Scandinavian Lapps to the west of Siberia use two types of conical tent. The conical Lapp tent incorporates a three-pole foundation found all over the arctic,[35] but the arched-post conical tent peculiar to the fully nomadic Lapps, has a remarkable support structure consisting of two pairs of curved poles forming arches and connected by a ridge pole and cross braces.[36] Whereas the conical tent occurs all over Lapland, at least as the temporary habitation of reindeer herdsmen and hunters, the distribution of the conical tent with a tripod foundation is confined to forests and well-wooded valleys where long and comparatively straight poles are found. It is still used by the Russian Lapps and by the Fisher Lapps in Finland, and to some extent in Tornio Lappmark, during the summer.[37] The more distinctive conical tent with a double-arch support system occurs in the high mountains and amongst the mountain Lapps.[38]

The framework of the three-pole conical tent consists of twelve or more straight poles, their forked ends secured at the apex which is left uncovered to allow smoke to escape. The tent cover was originally of birchbark in summer and of reindeer skin in winter; today these materials have been replaced by canvas and heavy homespun respectively.

25. Lapp conical tent.
26. The Lapp tent with storage poles in the background.
27. Framework of a Lapp arched-post tent (after Manker).

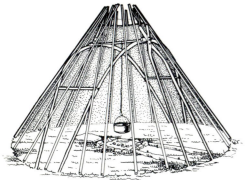

The support structure of the arched-post tent consists of two inclined arches joined by three transverse poles, a ridge or smoke-pole at the top and two other poles at about half the height.[39] Three additional poles, each with a round hole in its upper end, are attached to each end of the ridge pole, where it passes through the two curved birch poles of each arch. Two of these, the door poles, have their lower ends spread apart to form an inverted V and the third pole is attached to the opposite end of the smoke pole. The two halves of the tent cloth are fastened between the rear pole and the door poles. The material of the tent cloth is changed according to the season, in summer it is birch bark and in winter reindeer hides, but today these materials have given way to either sacking or thick woollen rugs according to the season. A large circular opening about 1·2 m in diameter is left above the low tent cloth to let out the smoke, and triangular pieces of tent cloth stiffened by horizontal wooden ribs form triangular door flaps. The floor of the tent is divided into two segmental areas by two parallel logs which run from the door poles to the rear wall enclosing storage for fuel, the hearth or *Arran* ringed by stones and the kitchen and scullery. This arrangement of the tent interior is common in Siberian conical tents.[40]

The earth-lodge of the Coast Lapps has a frame identical to that of the arch-post tent, but unlike the latter, the walls are infilled with closely spaced logs, the outer surface being clad first with birch bark and then with sods.[41] It is possible that the arch-post tent is a combination of both the earth lodge and the conical tent since the arch-post tent resembles the four-pole conical tent found among reindeer herders of the northern tundra. The special frames for supporting a smoke pole from which cooking pots and kettles can be suspended are also featured in Siberian conical tents.

If the Lapps are an off-shoot of the Samoyed or Ugrian tribes of Siberia, then it is likely that their conical tents derived from a Samoyed or Siberian prototype.[42] The conical Lapp tents have many features in common with Siberian tents (three-pole foundation, cooking pole, and division of the interior) and these similarities are particularly marked in the arched-post and Keti conical tents.

Chapter 4

North America

The native peoples of Northern Canada and Alaska and the Indians of the Great Plains of the United States possess two types of tents, an older ridge tent belonging to the Eskimoes and conical tents found among Indians and some Eskimoes. Both the Eskimo and Indian tents have features reminiscent of Siberian types so it is possible that they originated from Siberian archetypes.

Eskimo tents

The variety of Eskimo tents is in marked contrast with the uniformity of Eskimo language and culture. It has yet to be shown whether Eskimo culture is native to North America and was modified by later additions from Northeastern Asia, or whether it was introduced into arctic North America and Greenland by early Eskimoes spreading eastwards from the eastern extremity of Siberia and the Bering Sea.[1] It is significant that all the characteristic methods and implements of the Eskimo of the central area are simpler than elsewhere.

Seasonal specialization of Eskimo dwellings

The extreme seasonal contrasts of the arctic climate promoted two Eskimo cultures; a summer culture marked by the kayak, kayak hunting and the summer tent, and a winter culture typified by the dog-sledge, hunting on the ice and the winter house.[2] The summer cultural elements, including the summer tent, are almost universal, but a more restrictive group of elements and traits connected with the winter culture are found only under truly arctic conditions and slowly disappear towards the south and east.[3] The Eskimoes have developed specialized house types for winter, spring and autumn, and summer conditions, so great is the contrast between the seasons.[4] There are three main types of Eskimo tent: domical, conical and ridged. The Eskimo autumn house (*qarmat*) is a hybrid winter house and summer tent suited to spring and autumn.

28. Eskimo village at East Cape, Siberia.

Whale-rib framed dwellings

Whale-rib framed houses were observed in the late 19th century at East Cape, Siberia, on St. Lawrence Island in the Bering Strait and on the Alaskan coast at Norton Sound and at Point Barrow. The arched whale ribs of the winter houses at East Cape, Siberia spring from the outer wall and converge at a common point over one side of the entrance, where they are propped up by the jawbone of a whale.[5] Tanned walrus hides were laid over this convex fan-shaped framework and secured by lashings and heavy stones or whale vertebrae attached to cords. At the southwestern end of St. Lawrence Island, summer houses in two villages were framed with the jawbone and whale-ribs planted upright in the ground.[6] A semi-oval arrangement of alternating strips sawed from whales' jaws and whale-ribs leant against a jawbone post from which a 50 kg stone was hung to steady the frame. The outside of these summer houses was covered with walrus skins held in place by stone weights, driftwood and bone.

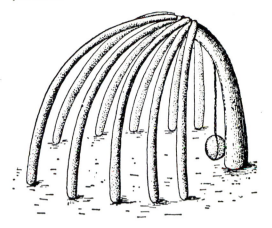

29. House frame of whale ribs and jawbone.

The Eskimo autumn dwelling (qarmat)

At the time of Franz Boas's journey among the Central Eskimo in the 1880s, the Eskimoes built semi-conical skin covered roofs over the low stone walls of earlier semi-subterranean dwellings having a radial system of poles spanning between the outer stone wall and a whale rib arch over the entrance to the passageway. Whilst the Central Eskimo *qarmat* differs from the western whale bone tents in some important respects, the radial framing pattern of the roof is similar.[7] The roof is covered with two layers of sealskins separated by a thick layer of *andromeda* for added insulation. The summer tents of the Polar Eskimoes observed by Steensby at Umanak and Cape York employed the radial framing of the *qarmat*.[8] The nine roof poles sloped upwards from a circle of stones to the crossbar of a gallows frame one metre wide at the front of the tent.

It is significant that a framing pattern of radial elements converging at a high point is found in the construction of Eskimo houses and even tents from the eastern tip of Siberia to Umanak in Greenland. This arrangement is evidently connected with the use of whale bones as a construction material and may well have originated from a type of ancient whale bone framed winter house not very different from those described at East Cape.

The effect of Eskimo migration on the distribution of tent types

The forms of Eskimo tents can scarcely be explained by referring to geographical factors alone, for they are clearly related to comparable types in Eurasia and in other parts of America. The sequence of Eskimo tent development is connected with the timing of Eskimo migrations across the northlands. Moving eastward from Alaska the domical, western conical, eastern conical, and ridge tents are encountered in that order.

The domical tent is confined to the northwest coast of Alaska as far as the Mackenzie River and East Cape, Siberia, by the availability of whale bones. The inland Eskimoes of Northwestern Alaska live in bee-hive tents[9] (*iccellik*) made from caribou hides stretched over a willow frame. The extreme westerly location of the domical whale bone hut does not mean that it arrived late on the North American continent, indeed, it bears a strong resemblance to the winter houses (*qarmang*) of the ancient Thule culture so that it is probable[10] that the domical

30. Central Eskimo summer tent.
31. Iglulik Eskimo sealskin tent, *Ipiutaq.*
32. Frame of a conical summer tent, Hotham Inlet.

form was widespread in ancient times. Ruins of these houses have been found at Northwest Greenland, Southern Labrador, and among the Central Eskimoes.

Ridge tents

There are good reasons for considering the ridge tent to be older than the conical form. The *qarmat* frame perpetuates features of the *qarmang* and domical whale bone hut frames. The differences between the ridge tent and *qarmat* are not so great and it is possible to see a family likeness in the four types of dwelling. The plan of the ridge tent is standard and consists of a trapezium terminated by a semi-circular back across the widest side.[11] The framing of the back portion over the raised sleeping platform is a semi-conical variation of the *qarmat* joined to an inclined ridge piece.

The Ridge tent predominates in Greenland, Baffin Land, and Southampton Island; among the Netsilik, Caribou and Copper Eskimoes it coexists with the eastern conical tent but disappears in Alaska.[12] This easterly diffusion points to the ridge tent's considerable age, moreover, its areal distribution — interrupted in the middle where it is overlaid by the territory of the eastern conical tent — is typical of elements of the Thule culture.[13] Birket-Smith concluded from this distribution that the ridge tent was the particular tent form of the ancient Thule culture.

Interior arrangement of the ridge tent

The relationship of activities and hence the disposition of living areas within the summer tent is much the same as that of the winter snow house. The front part has side platforms disposed about a central passage and the main platform occupies the semi-circular rear section. The intensity of daylight admitted within the tent is controlled by removing the hair from the skins of the front part of the tent and by shielding the rear sleeping platform with hairy skins to exclude light. The ridge tent comprised a simple ridge form terminated at one end by a semi-conical piece. The diversity of ridge tent frames arose because different arrangements of poles were

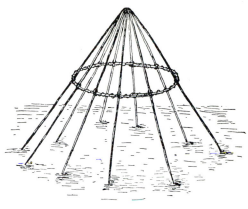

used to support the two high points at either end of the central ridge.

The Eskimo talent for eliminating non-essentials where materials, notably wood, are scarce, is well illustrated by the progressive structural simplification of the ridge tent. The Central Eskimoes of Cumberland Sound, and those from the more southerly parts of Baffin Land and adjacent to Davis Strait, build summer tents with heavy wood frames.[14] The two ridge poles are lashed to the front and central foundation frames formed by two inclined poles a little below the crossing. From six to eight poles are placed against the central foundation frame in a semi-circle around the main platform. The tightly fitting sealskin tent sheets are dehaired to admit daylight and secured by heavy stones.

The summer sealskin tent of the Iglulik Eskimoes is typical of the abbreviated ridge tent type; it has no ridge pole, end poles or side poles.[15] The tent sheet is suspended from a heavy seal thong running from the ridge pole on top of the centre pole to the crossing of two inclined poles at the front, passing over a vertical rod and down to a stone anchor, both some distance in front of the tent. The transverse ridge pole (*sanerutaq*) is characteristic of ridge tents from Southampton Island to Pond's Inlet, and is found at Aivilingmiut, Admiralty Inlet and among the Iglulik Eskimoes.

The western conical tent

The western and eastern Eskimo conical tents whose distribution is confined to Northern Alaska and the central region respectively, are sufficiently different for them to be regarded as two distinct sub-types. The western sub-type has comparatively short poles held together by a wood hoop against which a number of still shorter secondary poles are laid.[16] The short secondary poles and intermediate ring of the western type are present in the Keti conical tent. The tent sheet consists either of several sheets, or are wrapped around the frame in a long spiral terminating at the apex in two pockets which receive the tips of two tent poles. These two pockets may represent an embryonic form of the American Indian tepee's smoke flaps. In common with the eastern sub-type, the western conical tent and unlike the American Indian tepee, it has no smoke hole.

The eastern conical tent

The eastern conical tent, identified by its long poles which project above the top of the tent cover, has a restricted distribution centred in the southern part of the Barren Grounds, and it is unusual to find it outside this area.[17] It is most common among the inland Netsilik Eskimoes of Back River, and is sometimes found among the Caribou Eskimoes in combination with the ridge tent. The eastern type has a two-pole support structure covered by a single tent sheet.

The eastern conical tent was probably borrowed from the Cree Indians who transmitted it to the Caribou Eskimoes, and they in turn passed it on northwards to the tribes of the Northwest Passage, where a shortage of wood restricted its use.[18] The smoke hole was discontinued because the Eskimoes employed a relatively smokeless type of heating and this combined with the natural conditions resulted in its omission from the Eskimo conical tent.

The Indian Tepee
Common features of Asiatic and American tents

The conical tent is a circumpolar trait found in the boreal areas of both North America and Eurasia.[19] The tepee of the Plains Indians is a late modification of this circumpolar type which strayed south over the Great Plains. The tepee has all the essential features of the Eurasian conical tent, the central fire, a smoke hole centring around the crossing of the poles at the top, an eastern entrance, and the place of honour opposite the door, but it is more advanced and incorporates further refinements.[20] For example, the axis of the tepee is tilted backwards to assure an unobstructed smoke hole to protect the opening. Two-, three-, and four-pole foundations, similar to those of Eurasian conical tents occur in the Plains Indian tepee, but whereas the two-pole foundation is widely used in the Eurasian conical type, it rarely occurs in North American tents. Kaj Birket-Smith noted that 'a line seems to run directly from the American to the Asiatic forms of the same type, just as must be presumed with respect to the ridge tent'.[21]

The geographical distribution of tent types

The 19th century conical tent was dispersed throughout North America except for areas lying to the southeast of the Great Lakes and Mississippi where it is noticeably absent.[22] It was rarely used and then only as a temporary shelter on the Pacific coast, having been displaced by the rectangular plank house. Further to the south and away from the coast the conical tent spread as far as Northern California and over the intermontain plateau and the adjacent basin. These areas are directly connected with the vast expanse of grassland west of the Mississippi which stretches unbroken from Northern Alberta and Saskatchewan in Canada to the Rio Grande of Texas. South and east of the Hudson Bay the conical tent extends right to the Atlantic Ocean and Newfoundland.

Development of the Plains tepee

The developed tepee type of conical tent is linked almost exclusively to the horse-bison complex of the nomadic tribes of the Plains. It is worth enquiring how and when this nomadic hunting culture arose and whether the tepee was a part of this culture from the beginning. It is well known that the introduction of the horse which reached most of the typical Plains tribes from three hundred to two hundred years before they lost their cultural independence, greatly affected the life of the Plains tribes.[23] This does not mean that nomadism on the Plains is entirely post-European, inasmuch as the bison provided one of the staple foods of the early post-Pleistocene hunters of the high plains. Similar bands of wandering hunters are known to have followed this mode of life on the eastern and southern Plains throughout the prehistoric period. Many of the techniques used at a later date by the nomadic Plains tribes were previously employed in the eastern Plains area.[24] Wissler indicates that the introduction of the horse merely intensified and caused a more complete diffusion of an already existing nomadic cultural complex based on dog traction.[25] The introduction of the horse inhibited such traits as pottery, basketry, agriculture, and fixed houses, but did not foster any new traits except those directly associated with the horse.[26]

Whilst the introduction of the horse favoured the use and development of the tepee, some form of tepee existed before the acquisition of horses. The true travois developed from tepee poles dragged by dogs in the northern part of the Plains before the advent of horse traction.[27] The tribes of the south placed the load upon the horse and dragged the tepee poles by the horse's sides. Wissler surmised that the tepee originated among a few of the Central Algonkin and that analogous forms found to the eastward originated among the Cree from whence it was diffused over the Plains in some form along with dog traction.[28]

33. Blackfoot travois.

The Plains served as a mixing pot of Indian cultures. Nearly all the tribes within the area drained by the Missouri and Saskatchewan Rivers originated beyond its borders. These tribes shed much of their diversity as a consequence of their respective migrations and assumed instead the same general Plains culture.[29] This new uniformity is reflected in their dwellings.

Primitive conical tents

The conical tent of the Dogrib, Yellowknives and Slave tribes of the western subarctic has a central fire with a smoke hole centring around the crossing of the poles at the top and the place of honour opposite the entrance, features also encountered in Siberian conical tents.[30] The tent frame consists of a dozen or so tent poles covered with skins, the profile being lower and the plan area larger than the Plains tepee. As many as forty caribou skins covered the Dogrib tent while the Slave, who were unable to obtain so many hides, used brush or bark. The tent sides were sometimes covered with snow in winter, a practice also found in Northern Asia.[31] During the bitterest winter weather both Dogrib and Yellowknives preferred to sleep out of doors in skin bags rather than remain inside their tents. Another Asiatic feature, the cross pole support for cooking is found in conical tents in Labrador and the Dene area.[32]

The small bark covered conical tent of the Penobscot in Maine displays a number of primitive traits.[33] The Penobscot are part of the Northern Algonkin area so it can be assumed that this form is allied to the tents of the Ojibway and Cree.[34] The foundation of the Penobscot tent consists of four poles tied together in pairs with cedar rope and erected with one pair superimposed on the other. This inner frame is stiffened by a hoop which is fastened to the inside of the foundation and a further five poles at about two thirds of the height. The conical framework consists of two series of poles, one set inside to support the birch bark cover and one outer series to hold it in place. Pieces of birch bark are lapped and sewn together in strips and then tied to the inner poles. While the smoke hole is located below the crossing of the poles much the same as in Plains tepees, the customary smoke flaps are absent. The primitive construction and small size of the Penobscot conical tent is reminiscent of the Siberian types, as is the use of outer poles to hold the bark cover in place.[35]

Types of foundation frames

Except for a few minor details the southern tepee of the Missouri-Saskatchewan area seems to be of one definite type typified by crossing poles on a three- or four-pole foundation, a one piece cover, an oval door, and two ears beside the smoke hole.[36] Most of the differences in the outside appearance of the various tribal tepees arise from the placement of the poles, since this decides the pattern of the hide or canvas cover.[37] These differences in detail suggest if not the origin, then the centres of influence for the diffusion of the tepee.[38]

The frame of the Plains tepee consists of a foundation of either three or four poles which support the other poles. Whereas the four-pole foundation is common among northwestern tribes, in or close to the mountains, the tribes of the central and eastern Plains prefer tepees with tripod foundations.[39] The Bannock, Yakima and Umatilla tribes in the northeastern basin and southwestern plateau areas appear to have acquired their three-pole tepees from the nomadic buffalo hunters east of the mountains.[40] In general, the northern tribes use tepees with four-pole foundations but the southern and eastern tribes live in three-pole lodges.

Construction

The conical tent developed around the requirements of efficient combustion in a cold windy climate. The tent serves as a combustion chamber, chimney, and wind break for the central fire in addition to functioning as a dwelling.[41] It is essential for

34. Blackfoot tepee and shelter.
35. Crow tepee framework with canvas pole in place. The poles cross and form two apices, one above the other.
36. Patterns of smoke flaps of plains Indian tepee covers: *1*, Blackfoot; *2*, Crow; *3*, Cheyenne; *4*, Sioux.

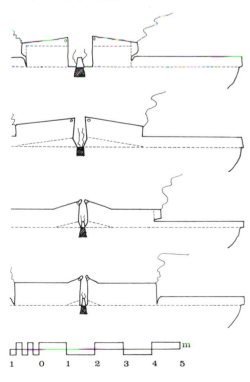

the smoke hole to be located directly above the central fire for effective removal of the products of combustion. This condition is fulfilled in the symmetrical conical tent where the smoke hole centres around the crossing of the poles at the apex. Unfortunately the smoke hole is obstructed by the poles and if the hole is enlarged then it cannot be closed in wet weather. Tepees are invariably tilted cones and this enables the smoke hole to be moved forward of the apex so that the crossing of the poles occurs at the back of the smoke hole which can be closed by means of overlapping flaps. Even so, the smoke hole can become choked by haphazard arrangement of the poles. The poles are usually placed in a definite sequence in order to ensure a neat uncluttered smoke hole.

The disposition of the upper ends of the poles in the crotches of the foundation poles is more critical than the order of placement of their butts on the ground in producing a compact crossing.[42] The three-pole tepee is more effective since a larger proportion of the poles rest in the front crotch than can be accommodated in the smaller front crotch of the four-pole type, and it is plainly more efficient to place the remainder in two crotches than in three. As a consequence, the cover of the three-pole tepee fits more neatly around the back of the tent because the poles are distributed more evenly at the top, and the smoke-hole extends farther down the front of the tent. Two apices or pole crossings are formed in the four-pole foundation: a lower one by the crossing of the foundation poles, and another above it by the crossing of the secondary poles. This results in a shorter, higher smoke hole than that of the three-pole foundation type since the tent cover cannot be raised to the top of the framework. The cover of the three-pole tepee fits better and the smoke hole is easier to close during storms. Gores or triangular pieces are inserted to widen the flaps at the top of the smoke hole; in the four-pole tepees they run the full length, but in the long narrow flaps of the three-pole tepees the gore is much abbreviated, so much so that they are quite small in the Sioux tents.[43] Four-pole tepees are less tilted than three-pole tepees and this difference is reflected in the ground plan.[44] In contrast to three-pole tepees which have an oval plan, the elliptical plan of four-pole tepees approaches a circle as the inclination of the axis is increased.

25

The three-pole tepee is the more stable of the two sub-types because it normally has more poles and they are tied together at the top.[45] Nevertheless, the ability of the foundation frame to resist horizontal overturning moments, which are greatest at the base, is determined by the depth at the base. This is greatest for the tripod foundation which is able to withstand greater horizontal wind loads. Since the four-pole tepee is less stable it frequently has from one to four outside guys, whereas the three-pole type seldom has even one.[46]

37. Setting up a Blackfoot tepee.

The size of tepees is denoted by the number of skins used in making the cover. The maximum size of tepee is determined by the length of poles which could be conveniently dragged by dogs and later by horses when they were introduced.[47] The largest lodges, about 9 m to 12 m in diameter, were never intended to be moved. In contrast, hunting parties used small tepees of about 3·7 m in diameter which were light and easy to transport.[48] In recent times the average tepee was from 5·5 to 6·1 m in diameter with 6·4 m to 7·6 m long poles.[49] The number of poles in Blackfoot tepees ranged from thirteen to thirty two, and Crow tents had from sixteen to twenty two poles.[50] The Crows were noted for their long poles (9·1–12·2 m) which gave their tepees the appearance of an hour glass. Most early single dwelling tepees were 3·7–4·9 m in diameter at the base.[51] Tepee poles tapered from 7·7–10·3 cm at the butts (pointed to prevent slipping) to about 5 cm in diameter at the crossing. The poles lasted for two years at most, and as a result the Plains tribes were regularly obliged to make long excursions to obtain new poles.

Tepee covers were fabricated from soft dressed bison hides with the hair removed. The hides were trimmed and fitted to form a roughly semi-circular shaped

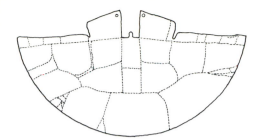

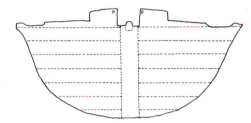

38. Patterns of skin and canvas tepee covers.
39. Plan of a Blackfoot tepee: *1*, fire; *2*, altar; *3*, couch; *4*, back rest; *5*, storage; *6*, door; *7*, foundation poles.

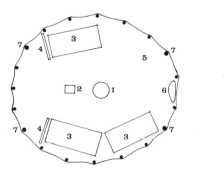

cover and then sewn together with sinew using a bone awl to punch holes. Twelve to fourteen skins were ordinarily needed to make a tepee cover, although the number varied with the size of the tepee.[52] Smaller pieces, such as the smoke flaps, a flap with cords for binding to the back pole used to lift the cover into place, and strips for the flaps and the sides of the door were then added to the leading edge. The curved edge was trimmed after the cover was in position as in a finished tepee. The front seam was secured in place by wooden or bone pins and tied on the inside. The smoke flaps were held open by two poles from behind the tepee.

Most four-pole tribes inserted the smoke flap poles through holes or eyelets in the top corners of flaps, whereas, with the exception of the Comanches and certain extreme northwestern mountain tribes, three-pole tribes always used pockets.[53] The smoke flaps could be adjusted to shield against the wind from all directions other than from the front, usually due east, by manipulating the two poles. The interior was ventilated in hot summer weather by rolling up the lower edge of the tent cover to a height of about 600 mm.

A strip of hide, 1·2 to 1·5 m high was hung from the poles on the inside of tepees for part or all the way round to prevent draughts and discomfort occasioned by excessive condensation. In the north the lining extended all the way round the tepee, but in the south, where the temperatures are mild, the lining sections were hung only over the bed.[54]

Interior arrangement of the tepee

Two of the factors which determine the disposition of living areas within the tepee are head clearance and avoidance of draughts. The area at the back of the tent is least subject to draughts, has greatest head clearance and commands the interior. It is not surprising then to find that it was set aside as the place of honour and as a sacred corner in which ceremonial objects and trophies were exhibited. The front of the tent was low and draughty and consequently was used for storage. The braves' saddlery was stored on the south side of the door and the wives' cooking utensils on the north side. The north and south sides had couches for sleeping, the south being preferred by the brave and his wife, the north being relegated to the children and dependents.

The couches were of dried grass or twigs covered with soft buffalo hides, and at the head, and often at the foot of each, there were back rests for reclining during the day. The location of the fire-place at the centre was subject to small modifications. For example, in the Blackfoot tepee it was moved forward to make room for an altar at which sweet grasses were burnt in rituals while in the Cheyenne tepee it was placed further back.[55]

Seasonal use of the tepee

Some tribes lived in the tepee throughout the year; others, notably the village Indians, used it only occasionally when on the hunt.[56] Most of the groups who utilized the tepee as a secondary dwelling were agriculturalists and their use of the tepee coincided with periodic migrations out across the open country to hunt buffalo. Many primary tepee users tended to use fixed abodes in winter. The Blackfoot, Crow and Assiniboine pitched their tepees in thick timber, invariably in valleys.[57] Other tribes, including the Santee Dakota and Omaha, exchanged their houses for tepees pitched in timber or bush, or deep in wooded ravines in winter.

Chapter 5

The Kibitka of Central Asia

Similarity of the kibitka and modern prefabricated, demountable building systems.

The *kibitka* is one of the most advanced prefabricated and demountable dwellings ever to evolve in a traditional culture. Its form and construction are dominated by the requirements of demounting, transportation, and erection. It consists of an external envelope — usually of felt or reed mats or a combination of both, to keep out the weather and to conserve the heat of the central fire — supported on a sturdy frame assembled from standard elements. The felt covering is of secondary importance since it performs no structural role and is less durable and very much simpler than the frame. The character of the *kibitka* is determined by the geometry and construction of the tent frame rather than by the covering.

The roughly hemispherical shape of the Turkic and Mongolian *kibitkas* offers little wind resistance, reducing drag and permitting the use of a light strong frame. The surface area is a minimum for the space enclosed, leading not only to economies in materials used in the covering, but also reducing heat loss and heat gain. The circular geometry with the framing arranged radially allows the frame elements, except at the entrance, to be simplified into a few standard building components and this in turn makes for economies in their manufacture. Buckminster Fuller used a *kibitka* form for his Wichita House (1944–46), which it is known, was based on a standard type of American grain bin. Beech Aircraft proposed to mass produce the design for housing, for American returned servicemen. The *kibitka* frame is based on a standardised kit of parts whose size and proportions are governed by the strength of the materials used, the method of manufacture, and the system of dimensions.

40. Turkic *kibitka*.
41. Mongol *kibitka*.

Geographical distribution of kibitka types

Throughout the vast area extending from the Volga River and the Anatolian plateau in the west, to the Khingan mountains in the east, the form and details of the *kibitka* are remarkably uniform. For the past four hundred years, *kibitkas* have been built according to the same structural principles, using the same methods, and employed in much the same way.[2] There are two principal types of *kibitka*: the felt covered cylindro-conical type used by Mongol peoples and by some Turkish speaking tribes of Northern Central Asia and the cylindro-domical type found among Turkish speaking tribes of Western and Southern Siberia such as the Kirghiz Uzbeg and Turkmen.[3] The cylindro-conical felt tent is known as the Kalmuck or Mongolian type and the cylindro-domical felt tent is referred to as the Kirghiz or Turkic type. Besides the Kalmuck, the Mongolian type is used by the Mongol tribes,

42. Kirghiz encampment on the Siberian steppe observed by Humboldt, early 19th century.
43. Scene on the Kirghiz steppe *c.* 1893.
44. Unlatticed cylindro-domical *kibitka* of the Central Asiatic Kirghiz, *c.* 1893.

Northern and Transbaikalia Buryat and the Mongols proper. Some of the Turkic tribes in Western Mongolia which have been exposed to Mongolian influences, namely the Bukei-Kirghiz, Altai-Tartar, Kachin Tartar, Kara-Nogai, Khoton, Uriankhai, and Sarts of Northwestern Mongolia also use the cylindro-conical tent. The cylindro-domical felt tent is employed by both branches of the Kirghiz, Kara-Kalpak, Kipchak, Uzbeg, Turkmen, Nogais and the Bashkir.[4]

The *kibitka* is confined to the Turkish and Mongolian peoples who live on the northern steppes of Central Asia. The geographic distribution of the Turkic and Mongolian *kibitkas* reflects ethnographic boundaries with the two main physical types spread along an east-west axis. At the present time Caucasoids predominate in the west and Mongoloids are ascendant in the east with a mixture of the two in between.

The distribution of the two main *kibitka* types is complicated in areas where repeated and lasting contacts between Turks and Mongols gave rise to inter-ethnic borrowings. The Kazak tents in West Mongolia belong to the Turkish type, but some of their features betray strong Mongol influence. Some previously Turkish, now Mongolized tribes, the Khoton and Uriankhai people in Western Mongolia, have borrowed or preserved certain Turkish traits in their Mongolian tents.[5] The intrusion of western Mongols or Kalmucks into the eastern edge of the western zone introduced the cylindro-conical felt tent into a basically Turkic tent area. Nevertheless, the Altai Kalmuck have adopted the same shape and construction for their *kibitka* as those of the Kazak.

Related tent forms

In Western Asia, the distribution of the *kibitka* is less uniform. Turkmen were responsible for extending the domain of the *kibitka* onto the Anatolian plateau, Syria and Northern Iran.[6] The *kibitka* is found in Northwestern and Northeastern Iran, it penetrated Afghanistan to the north of the Hindu Kush mountains[7] and reappears again in Northern Tibet among people of Mongolian background.[8] It should not be inferred from this that the *kibitka* is the only type of tent used by

45. Unlatticed Kiziltsi cylindrical tent. This is a debased form of *kibitka* which nevertheless illustrates the type of construction which may have been employed for early cylindrical tents.
46. Mongol yurts transported on waggons, 13th century reconstruction.

Turkic and Mongol nomads, for, as Rona-Tas points out, the black tent is known to the Mongols and to the Khalkhas in particular.[9] Furthermore, the conical felt covered tent is used as a temporary dwelling by the northern Mongols, the Kalmucks close to Astrakhan, and Altai Kalmucks and by the Kirghiz.[10]

Several related forms occur about the periphery of the *kibitka* zone: in Iran the Yomut *götikme* and the Shah Savan *alachigh* tents preserve the dome-shaped roof of the Turkic type but lack the lattice wall frame. The abbreviated *kibitkas* of the Yomut and Shah Savan tribes provide a link with the Turkmen *kibitka* and the dome-shaped tents of Iran, Turkey, Iraq and Syria.[11] In Northern Afghanistan, *kibitka*-like huts are found alongside true *kibitkas* of the poorer tribesmen. Latticed *kibitkas* with the characteristic roof ring, spread into Southern Siberia where they are found among Turkic peoples (the Altai Kizhi, Telengiti, Kachintsi*, Sagaitsi*, Beltiri*, Kiziltsi*, and Southern Tuvintsi) and among Mongolian peoples (the Buryats of Selenginsk and Aginsk). Degenerate unlatticed *kibitkas* were common amongst several of the Turkic tribes* who have latticed *kibitkas* as do the Tubalari, Chelkantsi and Teleuti Turks.[12]

Early accounts of kibitkas

The *kibitka* might have developed from the covered waggons which served as the early homes of nomadic pastoralists. Pottery models of these covered waggons from Tri Brata on the Kalmuck steppe (*c.* 2000 BC) and Kerch (*c.* 600 BC) depict barrel-vaulted or pyramidal roofs mounted on four wheeled waggons.[13] Strabo[14] refers to Scythians living in felt tents fixed on carts and both William of Rubruck[15] and Marco Polo[16] mention carts surmounted by a tunnel shaped wicker framework covered with black felt. It was customary to transport the *kibitkas* of important persons on carts, for William of Rubruck describes a 9.2 m *kibitka* mounted on a large cart drawn by twenty-two oxen. Sir Henry Howorth based his conviction that the *kibitka* was invented by the Scythians (*c.* 800 BC) on a description by Strabo.[17]

47. Wall painting of a tent on a grave at Kerch (now destroyed) 1st–2nd century AD. The brown felt tent cover is draped over a short ridge pole supported at each end by ridge posts in an arrangement similar to the Tibetan black tent.
48. Drawing by Friar Rubruck of tents which he saw when he visited the Mongol court in 1253.

The use of felt on the northern steppes is ancient. Brightly dyed and embroidered felt lined the walls and floor of a royal Scythian tomb of Chertomlyk on the Dnieper (*c*. 400 BC) and black felt was employed in a similar manner in the second tomb of Pazyryk in the high Altai (*c*. 500 BC).[18] The felt lining of the former burial chamber is thought to imitate the sumptuous interior of the royal tent.

The early use of wattle walls in housing on the western steppes long before the rise of pastoralism, could explain the origin of the *kibitka* lattice wall system.[19] It would have been a simple matter to adapt the wattle house frame to that of a tent covered with felt instead of clay. The use of wattle mats is widespread throughout the domains of both the *kibitka* and the black tent: it is the one feature they have in common.[20]

The Tartar and Mongol tents described by the 13th century travellers Friar John of Pian de Carpini, Friar William of Rubruck, and Marco Polo, closely resemble modern *kibitkas*. Friar John mentions the existence of two types of habitation, a 'fixed' tent transported on four-wheeled waggons and a demountable tent carried on the backs of animals.[21] The fixed and demountable tents must have been similar in external appearance because both Friar William of Rubruck and Marco Polo make no distinction between them but offer a single description for both. By all accounts they had a cylindrical shape constructed of wickers and stakes compactly interlaced and surmounted by rods converging on a ring at the top. The frame was covered by white felt. Although none of the three travellers mention a collapsible lattice wall frame, it may be presumed to exist on the evidence of demountability supplied by Friar John of Pian de Carpini. The wicker framework described by both friars could only have occurred in the fixed tent.

Origin of the kibitka

Two theories have been advanced to explain the origin of the *kibitka*, Jochelson considered that it derived from the conical tent,[22] whereas Feilberg thought that it may have evolved from arched huts.[23] The *kibitka* is closely identified with a form of nomadic pastoral society adapted to the steppes, especially where they do not support agriculture. Pastoralism was preceded by a form of settled agricultural society represented by the Tripolye, Andronovo and Afanasievo cultures which led to limited herding.[24] The slow spread of agricultural communities deriving from those of Western Asia over the northern steppes was followed by the rise of pastoral economies. The later incursion of mounted warriors from Transcaucasia and Northern Iran transformed these early pastoral societies into nomadic societies.[25] This transition from a settled to a nomadic pastoral mode must have been crucial for the emergence of a *kibitka* type of light portable dwelling. The early nomads probably lived in elaborate covered waggons sometimes with two or even three compartments, but at some later stage a lightweight portable tent came into being.

Construction

A *kibitka* is, essentially a limp covering draped over a light demountable wood frame. This frame comprises a low circular wall about 4·6 to 6·1 m in diameter[26] and 1·2 to 1·5 m high assembled from lengths of collapsible trellis, a wood roof-ring or wheel 1 to 2 m in diameter supported some 3·1 m above the ground on a series of radial roof ribs or struts spanning the gap between the top of the wall and the rim of the roof-ring.[27] The ends of the lattice wall are fitted to the posts of a door on the southern side of the tent. The lattice wall lengths consist of rectangular slats held together by camel skin pins inserted in holes where the rods cross, and when extended they assume a rhomboid mesh of about 30·5 cm. The number of lattice hurdles required varies from four for a small tent to six for a large *kibitka* of about 6·1 m diameter.[28] Each 3·7 m long hurdle has approximately 15 heads formed by the V-shaped upper ends of slats to which roof struts are attached. The lattice hurdles are lapped and the slats tied by means of hair cords. The outward thrust of

49. Kirghiz *kibitka*, Afghanistan, with the felt covering removed to expose the light frame.
50. Frame of the Kazak *kibitka* of West Mongolia. Wall framing: *a, kerege; b,* the *čī*-cover; *c, turdoq; d, kösk; f, üzük; g, uq; h, basqur*-rope; *i,* rope; *j, argan; k,* ropes of the *čī* and *turoloq; f,* rope.
51. Kazak lattice wall hurdles, *kerege: a, bas; b, koz; c, ajaq; d, qoq; e, basqur*-rope.

33

52. Erection of a Mongol *kibitka*: *1*, attachment of roof struts to the lattice wall hurdles; *2*, felt cover is lifted onto roof; *3*, tent cover is secured by ropes.

the roof struts is resisted by a tensioning of rope or broad woollen girths encircling the upper parts of the lattice wall.

In Mongol tents the slender roof poles or ribs which radiate from the central ring are straight, but in Turkic tents they are curved towards the lower end. An average tent would need about 50 or 60 poles each 250 cm long.[29] The method of attachment of the roof poles of Kirghiz, Kazak and Turkmen tents differs from that of Mongolian tents.[30] In the eastern types the roof poles are permanently secured to the roof ring, but the lower ends are suspended from the wall heads by means of a string or leather loop inserted through a hole in each butt. The roof poles of western Turkish tents are inserted in holes in the rim of the roof ring, but each lower end lacks a permanent loop and has to be tied to the heads with a separate string.

The roof ring is the most important distinguishing feature of the *kibitka* for it is not found in any other type. It also varies from one ethnic group to another.[31] The roof ring is an ingenious constructional device which overcomes several deficiencies of the conical tent. It eliminates the need for a foundation structure, and avoids obstruction of the smoke hole by the crowding of poles at the apex by distributing the upper ends of the poles around the circumference of the ring. Thus liberated, the roof ring admits light and air to the interior, allows smoke from the central fire to escape, and also serves as a chronometer. The smoke hole prevents great differences of air pressure and so reduces the wind load on the tent frame.

There are two basic types of roof ring. The first is a rigid ring in the form of a wheel with stiff radial spokes, while the second type is a flexible ring braced by transverse tensed arches designed to impose uniform loading on roof ribs throughout the roof system. Whereas the flexure of arched braces of Kirghiz, Kazak and Mongolian roof rings occurs perpendicular to the ring plane, the braces of Yomut and Göklen Turkmen are fixed within the ring and flex in the horizontal plane.

Among Mongols and Turks alike, the tent frame is covered by oblong sheets of felt secured by ropes. The felt is not tailored to the form, and the pattern varies. Thus the Turkmen cover the dome of their tents with two semi-circular pieces while the Kazaks of West Mongolia prefer two trapezoidal sheets.[32] The number of layers used to cover the tent frame depends on temperature. During winter two or even three layers of felt may be added as protection against the cold, whereas in summer the side felts may be raised a half metre or so off the ground to ventilate the interior. Unlike Mongolian tents, the Turkish *kibitkas* have a layer of *čī* grass underneath the felt.[33] In recent times the Mongols have begun the practice of overlaying the felt covering with sheets of canvas or sailcloth as protection against rain, furthermore, certain Mongolian Oirat groups, who have come in contact with Mongolized Turkish tribes, insert a layer of canvas between the felt and the wall in imitation of the Turkish practice. The Yomut and Göklen Turkmen differ from other Turks, for they cover the felt with an outer layer of cane screens.[34]

The roof rings of both Turkish and Mongol tents are covered by rectangular pieces of felt, orientated with their corners pointing to the cardinal points of the compass. This cover is bent back by day, but in bad weather and at night when the fire has died down, the flap is closed.

There are two types of doors, side-hung wooden double doors used almost exclusively by Mongols, and the Turkish felt door which must be rolled upward.[35]

53. Felt cover rope fastenings on a Kirghiz *kibitka*, Afghanistan.
54. Roof fastenings of a Kazak *kibitka* seen from below: *a, canaraq; b, kiskene esik* (made of *čī*-grass decorated with coloured painting); *c,* coloured texture bands; *d,* roof ring ropes; *e,* applicated band (on dark blue ground, red ornament); *f,* applicated band (on green ground, red ornament); *g,* texture bands; *h,* door.

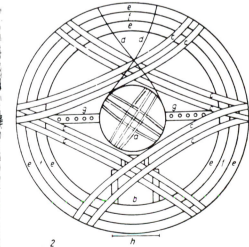

A wide strip of felt is applied around the base of Mongolian tents in winter to prevent draughts.

The *kibitka* is orientated with the door facing south or east in order to give protection from cold winter winds that blow from the north and west in Northern Asia.[36] The door of Mongolian tents face south, while the old Turkish system of orientation demanded that Turkish tents faced east, but in more recent times this requirement has not been strictly met.

Interior arrangement of the kibitka

The arrangement of the *kibitka*'s interior space[38] expresses two principles. First, practical household and work activities are relegated to the front of the tent in the vicinity of the door, and second, social, ceremonial and symbolic functions take place towards the rear of the tent. The rear of the tent is divided into special areas. On the left is the house Master and his couch, while the right side in front of the family's precious objects is reserved for honoured guests. In large *kibitkas* the women's side is screened with reed partitions and serves as a kitchen, although copper cauldrons, wooden platters and leather vessels often lie around the fire pit.

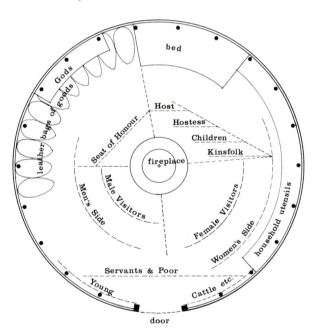

55. Plan of an Altai Tartar *kibitka*.

In spite of their different orientation, the interior arrangement of the *kibitka* is similar to that of the North American Indian tepee. The explanation for these similar layouts is probably physical, the disposition of living areas coinciding with zones of thermal comfort. Other factors are also involved, for example, the area next to the door is most convenient for work activities which require materials to be brought into or taken out of the tent, and the rear of the tent is psychologically dominant since it faces the door. Felt rugs, and among rich people, tapestry carpets from Persia and Turkestan, were used to cover the tent floor of beaten earth or cow-dung. In the past, cooking pots were suspended from iron tetrapods or tripods but most tents are now equipped with an iron fireplace raised above the floor on four legs with a chimney projecting through the roof ring.

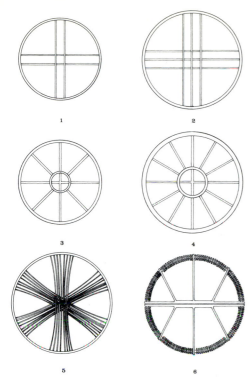

Kibitka sub-types

The *kibitka* tents include a number of sub-types having common structural characteristics which differentiate them from all other tents. These sub-types are distinguished by differences in the shape of the roof-ring, the attachment of the roof poles, the material of the wall cover, the manner and sequence in which wall covers are applied, the disposition of the cover above the roof-ring, the kind of door and the base strip around the outside of the tent. The differentiation occurs along ethnological lines.

The form of the roof-ring is the most important distinguishing feature of sub-types within the family of *kibitka* tents. Rona-Tas recorded eight types of roof rings in Western Mongolia alone and a further three in Southeastern Mongolia.[39] Irrespective of their configuration inside the rim, the braces are more highly arched in Turkish than in Mongolian roof-rings.[40] In the three principal types of roof-rings, the rim is braced by radial spokes, by arched rods placed at right angles, or by groups of spokes gently curved in the plane of the ring.

The Mongols employ roof-rings consisting of radial spokes which can be extremely large and may need to be supported by one or two posts to prevent the crown of the roof from sagging, and are gaily painted.[41]

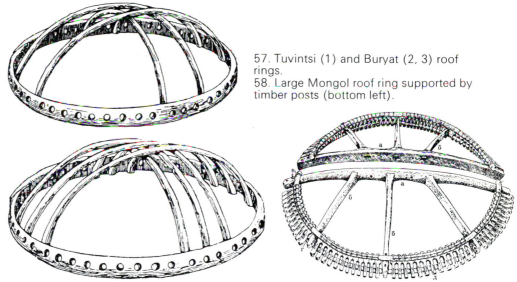

56. Types of *kibitka* roof rings: *1*, Tuvintsi, Torgout, Dzkhachin groups, Western Khalkha groups and some Buryat and Santful groups which have been influenced by the Khalkhas; *2*, Mongols, Kazaks and Transbaikalian Buryat; *3, 4* Mongol; *5*, Shah Savan, Iran; *6*, Transbaikalian Buryat.

57. Tuvintsi (1) and Buryat (2, 3) roof rings.
58. Large Mongol roof ring supported by timber posts (bottom left).

The Uriankhai, Torgut, West Mongolian, Kazaks, Buryat and Mongols incorporate roof-rings braced in the form of a pair of two or three arched struts placed at right angles.[42] The number of struts is determined by the diameter of the roof-ring. Sets of three struts are used in the larger rings.

Among the Turkish tribes, the Kazaks of West Mongolia, the central and western groups of Khalkhas and the West Mongolian Oirats and Buryats, the roof poles are inserted in holes around the outside of the roof-ring. In Eastern Mongolia, the poles are permanently attached to the roof-ring.[43]

The method of attaching the roof poles to the trellis wall differs between the Mongols and the Turkish tribes. The former insert permanent leather loops through holes in the pole butts, and the loops are then slipped over the lattice heads, while the latter lash the roof poles to the heads by means of a separate string.[44] The Turkish practice of inserting a layer of *či* grass beneath the felt wall covering is unknown among the Mongols.

37

59. Latticed Altai Kizhi cylindrical tent covered with felt.
60. Tuvintsi cylindrical tent.

61. Tuvintsi tent frame.
62. Sagaitsi unlatticed cylindro-conical dwelling.
63. Teleuti unlatticed cylindro-conical dwelling.

Cylindrical tents of Southwestern Siberia

A number of tents and tent-like huts similar to the *kibitka* exist in Southwestern Siberia, in Anatolia and Northern Iran. The cylindro-conical tents of Southwestern Siberia differ from those of the northeast in certain respects, notably the replacement of the centre support by a roof-ring and the presence of lattice wall framing. Whereas the weight of the roof of northeastern compound tents is shared equally between the wall frame and the centre support, in the southwestern tents, the roof is carried on the wall frame. Consequently a much stronger wall construction is required to carry the increased wall loading. The existence of roof-rings in the primitive cylindro-conical tents of Southwestern Siberia is significant because this feature is closely identified with the *kibitka*.

The latticed cylindrical tents of the Altai, Khakassi.and Tuvintsi are related to the Mongol *kibitka*. The conical shape and construction of their roofs is similar to the Buryat yurt which follows the Mongol pattern. This suggests that the latticed *kibitka* was adopted by the Turks of Southern Siberia from the Mongols.[45] It is also likely that the unlatticed cylindrical tents derived from the latticed ones.

The Sagaitsi unlatticed tent framework is an odd construction, having an enlarged roof-ring typical of the *kibitka* supported on a crude two-pole foundation which has one of the pole butts resting on top of the wall rail.[46] The roof poles span from the wall ring to the roof-ring. The two-pole foundation is comparable to the centre support of the Northeast Siberian compound tents, and also occurs in a primitive Kirghiz compound tent.

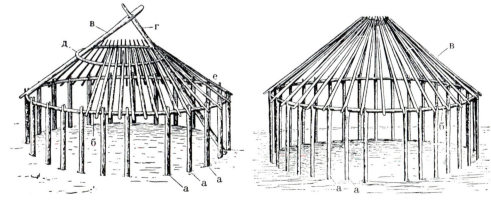

38

Cylindrical tents of Anatolia, Northern Iran and Northern Afghanistan

64. Interior of an Altai yurt.
65. Transport of a single Yomut tent.

Modifications of the *kibitka* form arise in two ways, the complicated lattice system may be simplified, or alternatively it may be eliminated altogether. The *kibitka*-like tent in which a simplified wall of vertical posts or extended roof-ribs replace the complicated lattice occurs in both the North Altai and upper Yenisei region, and in North Iran, North Afghanistan and Turkestan. The *čaparî* tents of the Aimâq Hazâras, Northern Taimannîs, semi-nomadic Tadjiks and some Saikh-âli Hazâras of North Afghanistan are examples of the former process. The *Kötük Götikme* and *Götikme* tents of the Yomut Turkmen, and the *alachigh* tents of the Shah Savan and their neighbours and Qaradagi of North Iran consist of a domical roof frame similar to that of the Turkmen *kibitka*, without the trellis wall. The poorer Shah Savan employ a crudely framed version of the *alachigh* called a *komé*.

Two types of *kibitka* may be discerned in Northern Afghanistan, a true *kibitka* and *kibitka*-like tents in which the lattice wall has been replaced by upright poles planted in the ground.[47] The *čaparî* type of tent prevails over the true *kibitka* wherever semi-nomadism with relatively highly developed agriculture predominates, as in the northern foothills of the Hindu Kush.[48] The poorest elements of the population cannot afford to have the difficult lattice wall lengths made by a specialist so they dispense with them altogether and construct a *čaparî* type of tent instead. The *čaparî* tent is much less mobile than the true *kibitka* and this accounts for the fact that it is found among semi-nomads. In contrast to the *čaparî* the *kibitka* is used by wealthy nomads. There are considerable differences in *čaparî* tent

66. The Yomut tent frame during erection.
67. Lashing of the felt covers to the tent frame.
68. Frame of the Shah Savan *alachigh* tent.

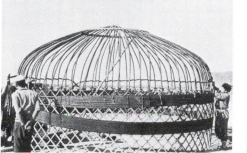

types,[49] those of Aimâq, Northern Taimannîs, and Ĵamšîdîs are all conical. In Turkestan the *kibitka*-like tents and those of the Arabs and Uzbeks are for the most part dome-shaped.

Afghan *kibitkas* are invariably covered with felt mats held in place with ropes, but in *kibitka*-like tents *čî* or *bûryâ* reed mats are used to an increasing extent.[50] Reed matting is sometimes placed around the outside of true *kibitkas* along the walls, and among the northern Taimannîs it usually reaches as far as the roof. The *kibitka*-like tents of the semi-nomadic Tadjiks and Saikh-åli Hazâras are sometimes covered entirely with woven or thatched *bûryâ* mats.

The *kibitka*, or forms very close to it, predominate among the Turkmen peoples of Northern Iran, Syria and Anatolia. In the main there are two kinds of *kibitka* in Iran, the true *kibitka* and *kibitka*-like tents known in Persian as *alachigh*, which lack the complex lattice wall of the *kibitka*.[51] Examples of *alachigh* are to be found among the Shah Savan and their neighbours the Qaradagi and the Yomut. The *topag ev* tent of the Turkmen in Anatolia and the elaborate Turkmen tents of Khurasan are further variants of the *kibitka* type. The *alachigh* tents stand somewhere between the *kibitka* and the domed tents of Iran, Turkey and Syria,[52] the Yomut *kötük götikme* and *götikme* is closest to, and the Shah Savan *alachigh* furthest from, the *kibitka*. The *alachigh* is essentially a *kibitka* with all the usual elements, from which the lattice wall has been omitted.

The roof-ring or 'crown' of the *alachigh* tent of the Shah Savan is anchored to the ground by means of a heavy rope tied to a peg driven into the ground in the centre of the tent.[53] The arrangement of the highly arched braces in the roof-ring is reminiscent of the Kirghiz, and consists of two sets. The main braces span the ring diagonally and a second set of four smaller braces connect between the four points on the rim touched by the main braces.

The poorer Shah Savan construct a primitive dome-shaped tent, *komé*, similar to the *alachigh* but much smaller in size.[54] The tent frame consists of an irregular lattice of bent rods covered by felt mats with an underlay of reed mats around the base.

Although the *kibitka* is well suited to the nomadic existence of the steppe pastoralist, it is far from being an ideal dwelling. Feilberg considered the *kibitka* to be a more recent form than the black tent and speculated that it developed from an ancient type of arched hut with wattle walls from Western Asia.

THE BLACK TENT OF THE MIDDLE EAST

Chapter 6

The Black Tent

These are the black tents which balance in the wind, on the summit of the mountains.

And neither earthquakes nor thunder can manage to uproot their slightest branch, the least piece of wood.[1]

An Arab riddle

The black tent is hardly a primitive form, but rather the most recent product in an evolutionary series. Its prestressed velum is tensed in an aerodynamic shape over minimal wood supports, and is able to withstand the strongest winds. The black tent, unlike the conical tent and the *kibitka*, is a non-skeletal tent with a prestressed velum. Of the major tent types, the black tent is closest in its form and construction to 20th century prestressed tensile architecture. The transformation of the early black tent from a skeletal non-prestressed dwelling to a non-skeletal structure was made possible by the replacement of mats and leather awnings by a woven velum strong enough in tension to be prestressed. The transitory status of the black tent is confirmed by the fact that differences between the tent and huts tend to disappear in primitive dwellings.

Geographical distribution

The geographical distribution of the black tent (map 7) is nearly continuous, extending from Mauritania in Northwestern Africa to Afghanistan, with an isolated Tibetan tent group. The principal zone of the black tent is confined to a narrow belt between latitudes 25° and 40° north and is dominant in a zone between 30° and 35° north.[2]

The distribution of the black tent is best understood in terms of its attachment to a particular way of life adapted to a select range of environments, which in turn limit its spread.[3] Considerations of human geography demonstrate that the black tent is most appropriate in the sub-tropical zone of the desert and the steppes. The latter region was the seat of nomadic peoples and it is significant in this regard that the black tent is typical of Indo-European peoples of Western Asia, and not of the Turks or Mongols.

Evolution of the black tent

A great similarity exists between the various kinds of black tent, surprising for a type spread over such a vast area. A survey of the tents of the different countries reveals the existence of well-defined regional types which can be divided into three main groups — Arabian, Iranian (including Afghanistan) and Tibetan — all in Asia, while only one, that of Arabia, is represented in Africa.[4] The tents of the gypsies of Southeastern Europe form a fifth group, though of lesser importance. The elements of the black tent are of two classes: one class of elements is spread throughout the extensive domain of the black tent, while a second class of elements is only found over a part of this territory.

The unity of the black tent over such a vast domain indicates that the black tent evolved from a common prototype.[5] The fine differentiation of the regional subtypes points to a fairly lengthy evolution. In general the elements having a restricted distribution are localized in two principal groups, one representing the Arab world, the other representing the Iranian and Tibetan peoples. The two are contiguous along the border of the plains of Mesopotamia and Iran. It is probable that the traits shared by the three principal groups are older than those found in only one of the groups. The following elements are common to nearly all the black tents: the velum consists of strips of dark coloured material woven from animal hair, usually goats' hair, sewn together; the velum is prestressed to a greater or lesser extent by means of ropes and supported on poles and stakes; and a distinction is made between roof and wall.[6] The Arab conquests in the second half of the 7th century AD are probably responsible for extending the black tent to North Africa,[7] when black tents similar to Arab tents were first observed among allies of the invaders, the Berbers. By the 12th century, the black tent was established in Morocco as far west as Fez.[8] Historical evidence indicates that the black tent was unknown in North Africa in antiquity and reached there in comparatively recent times. Roman writers in antiquity refer to leather tents similar to those still found in Fezzan, and to portable dwellings of wattles known as *mapalia*. The *mapalia* were widely used especially among the Eastern Libyans and consisted of an arched hut constructed of light stave or wattle walls with a wattle or thatch roof.[9] The largely Arabic origin of the tent vocabulary in Morocco demonstrates that the present extensive distribution of the black tent in North Africa, which it acquired after the 16th century, must be attributed to the Arabs.

Characteristics of the black tent

An examination of the character and functions of the black tent gives a better idea of the impact of physical factors on its geographical distribution. The main climatic function of the black tent is to give protection from the sun, and in doing so, acts as a most effective wind break, reduces glare, and tempers the cold nights.[10] It is, in essence, a well ventilated shade roof whose performance in conditions of wet and cold have at times been accounted inadequate.

The loose woven goats' hair and wool tent velum is a responsive material. In hot dry weather the fabric is relatively open, permitting air to flow through it, but when it rains the fabric shrinks and the weave is denser, thus offering greater resistance to rain penetration.[11] The black colour of the velum gives a distinct advantage over other lighter colours because it is more opaque to sunlight.

Problems arise in the use of the black tent in rainy regions, for unless the velum is well ventilated it will rot; further, after a lengthy period of constant rain, fine droplets are able to pierce the awning.[12] It is interesting to note also that in the extreme cold of Tibet, the *kibitka* was judged to be warmer than the black tent.

The remarkable stability of the black tent in strong winds is achieved by sensible siting, an efficient aerodynamic profile, long slanting anchor ropes, and the variable geometry of the tent form itself.[13] The tent is usually pitched on sheltered sites with the open side facing away from the prevailing wind. The long ropes produce a streamlined aerodynamic profile which offers little resistance to the wind. Since the orientation of the tent is determined by the wind direction, the stability of the tent is threatened by sudden and unexpected changes in wind direction which might dislodge the pegs or penetrate the open front of the tent. If the wind changes, the front poles must be removed to the rear, and the back wall taken down and refixed across the tent front. The geometry of the tent can be varied as required to give it a more efficient aerodynamic shape when the wind gusts. One way of achieving this is to lower the inner wall facing the wind to the ground and weight it with stones and unused poles. In extreme conditions the Arab can lower his tent so that it rises no more than two metres above the ground, increase the number of ropes and drive the pegs deeper into the ground. The long tent ropes have a further advantage in that the tangle of ropes between the tents makes it difficult for thieves or enemy tribesmen to pentrate a Bedouin camp without detection.[14] The portability of the black tent is especially significant in warfare for it can be dismantled, transported or erected again in less than an hour.

Compared with the *kibitka* and the conical tent, the black tent uses the least amount of wood for its size and the space enclosed.[15] The problem of spanning is central to architecture since it affects the creation of interior space, but in dry regions it is critical because the roof and not the walls, is the most difficult structural element to construct in a dwelling. This feature of the black tent's construction assumes even greater significance when related to available resources.

The effect of precipitation and vegetation on the distribution of the black tent

The tent belongs to a zone stretching from Northwestern Africa to Western and Central Asia where the mean annual precipitation is less than 508 mm and in particular to the northern part of this zone. There are however exceptions; for the tent is found in some regions, Central Morocco, Anatolia, Armenia, and Southeastern Europe, which receive more than 508 mm of rain; and yet it is absent from other intermediary regions between the Sahara and the Sudan and in the south of Arabia, which are within the 508 mm isohyet.[16]

The existence of a link between low precipitation and the black tent is supported by a break in the continuity of the tents' geographical distribution in the Northeastern Himalayas where precipitation exceeds 508 mm, even though the region is within the principal latitudinal band between 30° and 35° north. The connection between precipitation and the black tent's geographical distribution is complex because rainfall affects water resources, vegetation, land use and finally the way of life. The northern spread of the black tent was retarded by the cold winters, but this factor has not, as might be expected, excluded it from Tibet. According to Feilberg the spread of the black tent was inhibited by its lack of resistance to rain and its function as a sun shelter, and by two factors of physical geography, a mean annual precipitation exceeding 508 mm and nebulosity higher than 4.[17] Evidently, these factors of physical geography determine the extent of the tent's expansion only in a general way.

The expansion of the black tent is largely confined to bush-covered steppes between the northern edge of subtropical deserts and the scrub.[18] Bush-covered steppes occur in regions where the rainfall will not support forest or tall bushes, but where it is not so deficient as to result in desert; that is to say, in the regions which under these latitudes, receive 254 mm or more of rain annually. In this vegetal zone it is difficult to obtain timber with which to build houses and, under these conditions, the black tent has a distinct advantage over other types of dwellings because it required only a small quantity of timber in its construction. It is significant that the break in continuity of the black tent's distribution between Afghanistan and Tibet occurs in a region rich in forests.

The effect of the dromedary on the distribution of the black tent

The distribution of the black tent is related to the distribution of two animals. The velum is woven from goats' hair, and the tent is, in the main, transported by the dromedary. The effect of this dependence on animal transport, is that the distribution of the black tent is confined to the domains of goats and dromedaries, except for Tibet, where the yak serves as a surrogate dromedary. The distribution of the dromedary approximates to that of the black tent,[19] a conjunction explained in part by the adaptation of the dromedary to those same arid regions in which the tent is widespread, and by the possibility that the black tent and the dromedary both belong to the same stage of evolution among the nomads.

Feilberg thought that the black tent had evolved from a primitive type of arched hut.[20] The tents of the Tuaregs are significant because they provide a link between the primitive arched hut and the black tent. The Tuareg tents are the last surviving examples of a type — widespread in ancient times before the black tent replaced them — which supplied the prototype of the black tent.

The survival of primitive types of tents on the extreme periphery of the black tent domain among the Tuareg and Tibu people, who represent a more ancient cultural layer, is consistent with results obtained by applying the ethnological method of determining the geographical origin of a cultural cycle. The theory states that the oldest elements of an evolutionary series are found on the periphery of the zone, and the youngest elements towards the centre.[21] It is assumed in the ethnological model that the dispersal of the cultural elements occurs in an orderly sequence of concentric waves moving outwards from the centre of generation. The very ancient cultural layer of the Tuaregs survived because the spread of the black tent into North Africa is very recent, even compared with Tibet, and tended to skirt around the northern edge of the Sahara, leaving the home of the Tuareg relatively undisturbed.

The evolutionary series of ridge types provides a clue to the pattern of diffusion of the black tent.[22] The progressive simplification of the ridge support reduces the amount of material, usually wood, used and is accompanied by an increase in the velum prestress needed for stability. Of the four basic types, the ridge pole supported by two poles is the oldest and the circular plate the most advanced. The ridge pole supported on two poles is found in Tibet to the east, in the Atlas region to the west and among the Tuaregs south of Tombouctou. The ridge-bar supported in the middle by a single pole is found in Iran to the east, and from Palestine to Tunisia in the west; the stick sewn into the velum is found in the northern peripheral regions of Northern Arabia; and the circular plate with a hole in its centre, sewn into the velum and placed on a pole belongs to Northern Arabia. It is interesting that the distribution of these ridge types describes a series of concentric waves at certain points moving outwards from a centre in Northern Arabia.

69. Kreda tent frame — Tibu of Hair.

Tuareg tents: Precursors of the black tent

Environment alone cannot account for the complicated development and diversity of Tuareg tents, rather they are the product of historical influences. The Tuareg are a light-skinned, Europid Mediterranean race, who prior to their removal to the Sahara, occupied parts of Libya and the Fezzan. The remoteness of their home in the central Sahara, surrounded by desert, insulated the Tuareg from outside influences and ensured the survival of various ancient features in their culture and the purity of their Berber tongue. Their language is related to languages which were once widespread over much of North Africa.

The actual nomadic pastoralists constitute only a small part of the Tuareg.[23] The increasing adaptation of the Tuaregs to pastoral life finds corresponding expression in the transformation of the dwelling, for, though the tent is now the prevailing type, its construction manifestly derives from a hut of primitive but none the less more permanent type.

44

In spite of their considerable diversity most Tuareg tents are historically related and conform to one of the two basic types; they are either mat tents or skin tents.[24] Whereas skin tents are employed in all Tuareg groups (though there is some doubt that they are used by the *Kel Geres*), the geographical distribution of the mat tent is confined to southern Tuareg groups to the south of an almost unbroken semi-circular line running from Northern Ayr to Tombouctou.[25] This distribution may, perhaps, indicate that the mat tent is of very ancient standing among the Tuareg. There is in fact no boundary between these dwelling types, which are sometimes used by the same people at different seasons, and the two are sometimes combined into one, for mat tents may be covered with skins during the rainy season. It seems that the mat tent is used mainly in areas where dum palm leaves are available for plaiting, and that outside the dum palm area most Tuareg use skin tents for portable dwellings.[26] The mat tent is a true pastoral dwelling type.

The mat tent always has an arched frame while this is true only of some skin tents. The fundamental difference between a mat tent and an authentic skin tent is that the mat covering is fastened to the tent structure, while the skin tent sheet is anchored to poles, pegs, stones or other objects outside the support structure. Tuareg tents could have evolved from a proto dwelling in the following manner; the original barrel-vaulted dwelling was covered with grass mats, but in the rainy season the occasional practice of covering the roof with animal skins led in time to the emergence of a new type, the skin tent, in which the skin sheet entirely supplanted mats for the roof covering.[27] Vestigial mats have survived in skin tents around the open walls.

Except for tents with T-post ridge supports, the transverse arch construction and cross-bars supported on forked poles are present in the majority of Tuareg tents. It is significant that the rudiments of arch constructions occur in skin tents within all Tuareg groups. These two traits together with the use of mats appear to have been inherited from the Tuareg archetype. The investigation of Tuareg tents carried out by Nicholaisen in 1963 provided additional evidence to support Feilberg's (1944)[28] proposal that the black tent stemmed from arched huts.

70. Mat covered Tibu tent:
1–3, construction; *4*, interior.

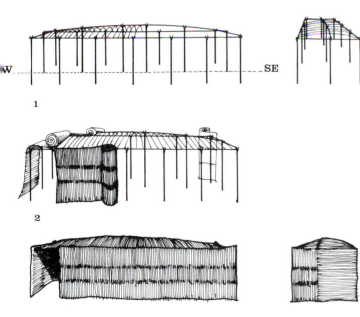

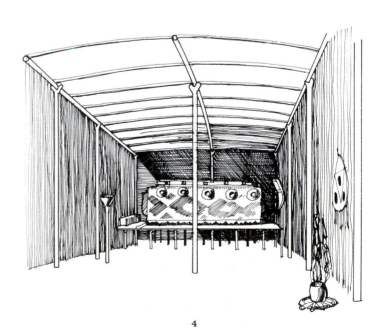

1

2

3

4

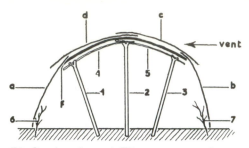

71. Section through Tibu mat covered tent. An awning of skins is placed beneath the mat covers during the rainy season. *a, b, c, d*, mats; *f*, ventilation; *1, 2, 3*, tent poles; *4, 5*, palm leaves; *6, 7*, branch screen.

72. Erection of a Tuareg mat tent in Ayr: *1*, frame; *2*, the frame is covered with oval-shaped and long narrow dum palm mats.

The black tent came into existence when the skin tent sheet was replaced by a woven velum of goats' hair combining the advantages of the mat tent with those of the skin tent. The goats' hair velum is more waterproof than mats but, unlike the skin sheet, allows air to circulate through the covering.

The arched hut is found mainly among cattle breeding peoples in the savannahs and the steppes in Africa.[29] Although they differ from Tuareg mat tents, the Tibu, Teda and Daza pastoralists within the areas of Tibesti, Borku, and Ennedi, and the Hadendowa of Sudan, also cover their barrel-vaulted tents with mats. The area of mat covered dwellings is co-extensive with that of the dum palm and extends from Adrar through Iforas, Air, Kaouar, Djado, Tchiga and Tibesti south of the Fezzan to the valley of the Nile.[30] The mat tents of the Tibu resemble the tent forms depicted in the XIV century Egyptian reliefs of Rameses II's camp. The Tibu tents consist of a rectangular frame of forked upright posts which carry horizontal poles. The central ridge pole is slightly arched, giving the roof the appearance of a depressed barrel-vault, and supported along its length by intermediate forked posts.[31] The roof mats rest on numerous arched rods which span between the two long sides over the central ridge. In the rainy season an awning of animal skins is placed under the roof mats, and the roof itself is given a semi-cylindrical section by inclining the forked wall posts outwards.

The close structural affinities of arched mat tents with other less elaborately supported Tuareg tents indicates that the arched mat tents represent a very ancient type of traditional dwelling, covered originally with mats of grass-stems. The barrel-vaulted dwelling is considered to be the original dwelling type since a similar construction was found amongst the old Libyans and, under the name of *mapalia*, was widespread in ancient North Africa.[32] Two types of mats are used today, the more common one (*asala*) is made from dum palm leaves plaited into long narrow bands sewn together with the strips of the same material, and a second type (*ewerwer*) is made from pieces of straw or similar material which are threaded together horizontally. These straw mats are used under the main covering over the upper part of the Ayr Tuareg and *Kel Geres* tents and in areas where dum palm material is unavailable.

Tuareg arched mat tents

The typical arched mat tent[33] consists of slender curved rods, normally about ten in number, placed over a skeleton of one to four transverse arches between two pairs of crossbars supported by vertical forked sticks, in the longitudinal direction of the tent. The wooden arches consist of two curved pieces of wood fashioned from the very long horizontal roots of *Acacia Radiana*, fixed in the soil and lashed together when the tent is erected. Two pairs of horizontal crossbars set parallel to the arches are supported by vertical sticks placed across the shorter sides of the dwelling at right angles to the longitudinal axis. The completed tent structure is covered by two rectangular *ewerwer* mats placed on the roof first and covered with a combination of oval-shaped and long dum palm mats in strips. The lower part of the tent is enclosed by a narrow dum palm mat when required.

Tuareg skin tents

The skin tent is easier and quicker to erect and less elaborate structurally than the mat tent. The leather tent sheet is heavier than a mat cover and is therefore more difficult to transport. The leather velum is more waterproof than mats but is less

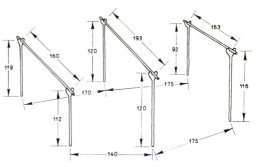

73. Tuareg skin tent.
74. Wood support structure of a *Kel Rela* skin tent, Ahaggar.

comfortable during the hot season. The mat tent is comparatively high and well ventilated, but during the rainy season it is less waterproof than the skin tent. The advantages of both dwellings can be obtained by placing a sheet of skin over the top of the mat in the rainy season. Skin awnings are so ancient that at one time skin covered huts and skin tents were much more widespread all over the world. People at primitive subsistence levels commonly covered their portable dwellings with skins. In Africa, the arched hut is frequently covered with hides and this might be interpreted as indicating that the black tent was preceded by a dwelling covered by hides. The incorporation of an inner layer of *ewerwer* mats over the roof of the mat tent and *afezu* mats for the walls of Tuareg skin tents show that the use of plaited grass mats for covering the true tents precedes the use of skins.[34]

Skin tents are found among all Tuareg groups except for the *Kel Geres* and the *Kel Ayr* among whom they are rare. It is significant that the rudiments of arch construction are present in skin tents of all Tuareg groups. Nicholaisen discerned eight basic types of skin tents depending on the type of support structure employed. These are: skin tents of arch construction; skin tents with semi-arches over horizontal crossbars; skin tents supported by crossbars connected with horizontal sticks; skin tents supported by two pairs of forked sticks with crossbars and a system of cords in the longitudinal direction; skin tents with longitudinal crossbars connected with horizontal sticks; skin tents with pairs of forked poles carrying horizontal crossbars; skin tents with a central T-shaped post; and skin tents with two central oblique posts carrying a short crossbar.[35] The support structures used in skin tents are based on combinations of the three following construction elements: arches, horizontal crossbars resting in forked sticks, and T-shaped posts. These support elements may be inter-connected by semi-arches, horizontal sticks, or a system of cords. The third construction element, the T-shaped post, is foreign to traditional Tuareg dwellings, having been introduced by contact with Arabs who dwell in black tents.[36]

The Tuareg admire richly decorated dwellings and strive to decorate the awning of the skin tent. Blacksmiths are employed to carve the poles. The skin of barbary sheep is preferred to goat skin which is generally used in the awning, otherwise, the skins of zebu-calves, antelope or gazelle may be used. An average Ahaggar tent comprises about 35—40 skins but the large sheets of Tuareg nobles may include 60—80 skins.[37] The skins are depilated, tanned, treated with butter and coloured with red ochre before being sewn together with leather thongs.

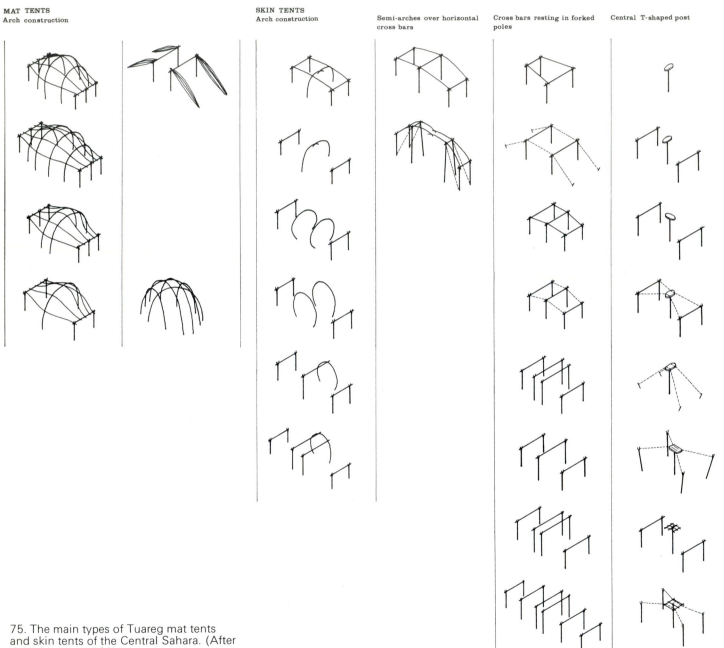

MAT TENTS
Arch construction

SKIN TENTS
Arch construction

Semi-arches over horizontal cross bars

Cross bars resting in forked poles

Central T-shaped post

75. The main types of Tuareg mat tents and skin tents of the Central Sahara. (After J. Nicolaisen, 1963)

Chapter 7

North Africa

The tall transverse ridge that gives the roof a well defined saddle shape, the technically superior construction, stronger side anchorage and richer decoration, differentiate the North African black tent from its Arabian counterpart. The North African tent is typified by a striped awning, a transverse ridge supported by crossed poles, and an awning which falls obliquely almost touching the ground along the short sides.[1] The greater regional variation of the black tent in North Africa may result from the diversity of its landscapes.

An archetype not dissimilar to the tent of the Moroccan hill nomads may be discerned from the geographical dispersal of traits. This form has undergone progressive modification over an extensive area.[2] The prominent ridge results from the use of two types of ridge support, a long slightly curved ridge piece supported by two upright poles, and a short curved ridge piece raised on two crossed poles. The relatively long ridge pole, supported by two other poles, is allied both to a special *triga*, draped over the ridge, and to wattle mat walls in tents in Morocco, West and Central Algeria, and Tripolitania. The short ridge with crossed poles is found in Mauritania, Southwest Morocco, and Algeria-Tunisia.[3]

The dispersal of the T-shaped post is confined to Arabs living in Tunisia and Egypt, and to the *Aulad Nail*. It was first observed in Iran at the beginning of the 16th century. From Algeria to Tripolitania, tents have striped awnings which fall almost to the ground on the shorter sides and are supported by three rows of poles placed across the length of the awning. Curved poles are found across North Africa from Morocco to Egypt. East of Benghazi, the distinguishing traits of the North African tents are suppressed and Arabian features predominate.[4] The tents of the *Aulad Ali* mark the eastern periphery of the North African types, since they combine features from both. The *Aulad Ali* tent appears to be a modified type akin to the tents of the Sba'a in Central Arabia which have retained their Arabian identity.

Certain features are common to tents throughout the Arab speaking territories: narrow bands and fastenings reinforce the awning, and stick fastenings in one form or another are found among nearly all the Moroccan hill nomads, as well as among the *Aulad Ali* and in Northern Arabia and the adjacent regions.

The distinctive keel-shape of the black tent in North Africa is usually explained in terms of the fusion of the West Asian or Arabian form with either a native or introduced dwelling type. Ernst Rackow proposed that the North African black tent was formed from the union of an Asian form with that of a conical tent derived from the Byzantine military tent.[5] The argument for a Byzantine connection centres on Rackow's assertion that the word for the ridge piece *quntâs* which gives the North African tent its distinctive shape derived from the Greek *Kovtŏs*.

The researches of Feilberg and especially those of Nicholaisen suggest that the form of the North African tent resulted from the encounter of the black tent with an indigenous type of mat covered arched hut. The structure of black tents among certain Moors is due to the combination of the black tent which was introduced by the Arabs and a barrel-vaulted portable dwelling thought to resemble the type of dwelling used by the Tuareg in ancient times in those regions conquered by the Arabs.[6]

Mauritania

While accurate information on the Mauritanian tent is lacking, historical reports from the 18th and 19th centuries describe conical or pyramidal shaped tents. This is corroborated by Rackow's sketch of a Bou Tilimit tent depicting a roughly pyramidal shaped velum raised over a square plan.[7] The high central peak is supported by two crossed poles, placed cross-wise to the length of the awning, *49* and capped by a short curved ridge piece similar to that of the Tekna of Southwest Morocco. A main strap passes over the ridge piece and is pulled down towards the sides of the tent in the direction of the tent strips, instead of at right angles as is usual in most North African tents. The pyramidal shaped velum supported on crossed poles and slightly higher front of the Mauritanian tent is similar to other Moorish tents used by the Reguibat and by the Tekna. The Imraguen of coastal Mauritania use large woollen peaked tents supported on a centre pole for temporary camps.[8]

76. Tent of Mauritania and Rio de Oro.

Morocco
Tents of Southwest Morocco

The tents of Southwest Morocco are quite different from those used by the Berber hill nomads of Central Morocco, and by the Arabs in the north. This southern type is used throughout the Noun and the southwest as far south as the Zemmour by the Tekna, and by the Ait Ba-'Amrah, the Ait-Umribet and the Rguibat.[9] Though somewhat smaller in size and more simply constructed, the Tekna tent of Southwest Morocco resembles the tents of the Larbaa and the *Ulad Nail* of Central Algeria, particularly in the arrangement of poles under the ridge.

The striped Tekna roof velum is trapezoidal in shape and consists of seven to eight wide strips bordered by a narrow strip along the front and back.[10] The tent cloths are woven from undyed goats' hair together with varying amounts of wool or camel hair. An extra cotton lining, a tent within a tent, is hung on the inside in winter as insulation against the cold, and for privacy. The tent velum is stretched over a short, curved ridge piece supported on two crossed main poles by four guy ropes attached to each of the short sides.

The structural principle of the Mauritanian and Tekna tents is the same, the crossed poles of the latter are held in place by a pair of guys which stretch the two central roof cloths downwards and outwards on either side of the peak. The two central roof cloths of the Tekna tent serve a similar function to that of the main strap of the Mauritanian tent, but must be renewed more frequently because they are overstressed. Although only two props can be considered as permanent, others are used to brace the front and rear edges of the velum at the middle and at the corners.

The placement of props under the tent awning varies, the two front corner props being permanent while auxiliary props may be introduced under the centre of the front lip, shorter ones may be put in along the back at the corners and in the middle, and sometimes only one prop is provided in the centre rear. The roof is higher at the front than at the rear because the four guys diminish in length towards the rear. The poor development of the girths, or reinforcing straps, in the Tekna tent compared with other tents in Morocco, Algeria and elsewhere, indicates that they are vestiges of much longer girths.[11] The space between the edge of the awning and the

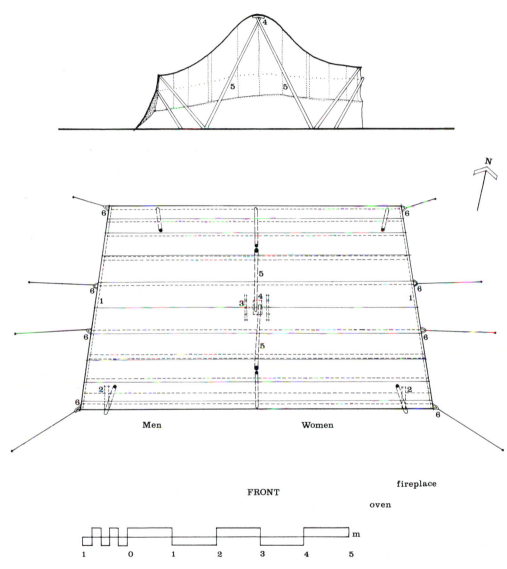

77. Typical Tekna tent of the Lansas, Oulad Bu'Asra, in the area of Taidelt, section (top), plan (bottom). The trapezoidal-shaped goats' hair tent cloth (8 m wide × 4·8 m deep) consists of from 7 to 8 roof widths 40 cm to 70 cm wide with 20 cm to 35 cm wide edge strips at the front and rear: 1, bolt of rope; 2, tag-girths with lifting rings; 3, distinctive crest ornament on peak; 4, 15 cm to 28 cm long wood ridge piece and abbreviated rubbing girth; 5, 2·9 m to 3·5 m long crossed ridge poles with abbreviated rubbing girth 5·5 cm to 6 cm diameter; 6, bent-twig fastenings. (After Andrews)

ground is closed at side and rear with cotton or goats' hair cloths pinned to the velum with iron skewers. The floor is covered with mats made from date palm fibre and esparto stems, while the interior is divided into two sections by a cotton screen suspended from the centre prop at the front and the main poles or a yarn from the velum. The kitchen and women's quarters are placed on the right or east side and the men on the left side. The fireplace, set within a semi-circular courtyard formed by two curved brushwood hedges, is located some distance in front of the tent.

78. Side view of a Lansas tent.
79. Tent of the hill nomads of Central Morocco and the nomads of Western Morocco.
80. Pattern of the hill nomad tent cloth. The 13 m × 12·6 m deep tent cloth consists of a central panel A (eleven 60 cm widths); front panel B (three 120 cm widths); and back panel C (two 120 cm widths). The cloth is made from wool mixed with mohair and dyed black. The poor add quantities of hair from the dwarf palm *chamaerops humilis*: *1*, 2 m long slightly curved ridge pole decorated on its underside with geometrical designs; *2*, 2·5 m to 3 m long cedar wood ridge poles; *3*, 20 cm to 40 cm ridge strap, *triga* 6 m to 8 m long; *4*, auxiliary straps; *5*, narrow reinforcing straps; *6*, bent-twig fastenings. 81. *Triga*.

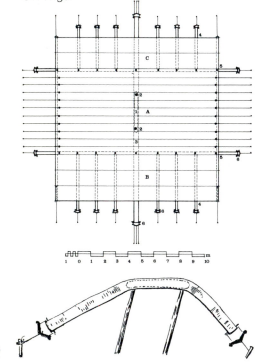

Berber hill tribes of Central Morocco

The tent of the Berber hill tribes of Central Morocco[12] gains its distinctive appearance from the unusual length (200 × 30 cm) of its keel-like ridge piece. The curved ridge piece rests on two slightly inclined cedar poles (250 to 300 cm long) one at each end, and is held in place by the central panel of the awning and a main strap, called the *triga*, stretched over the ridge piece perpendicular to the length of the awning. The *triga*, 20 to 40 cm wide and 6 to 8 m long, is not fastened to the awning but is placed along the topside of the ridge piece and anchored to the ground with wood chevron-shaped beckets. The rectangular awning is made from at least three, but often more than ten strips of material, woven from wool mixed with mohair, though the poor add a large quantity of dwarf palm fibre, on a horizontal loom and dyed black. It is reinforced under the front and back edges and along both sides with narrow straps which cross at the corners. Poles are placed under each of the four strap intersections. The edges of the tent, which tend to droop under their own weight, are raised on stakes sited on the seam lines along the short sides, and under the main and auxiliary straps along the front and back. The long sides are closed in with hanging panels fastened to the front and back edges of the roof with long iron needles or wood skewers. Narrow blankets close the short sides and reed mats 60 to 80 cm high may be added for protection against cold or rain.

The interior of the tent is subdivided by mat screens suspended from the main strap and the central poles under the ridge piece into two parts, the front area of the part which contains the hearth is reserved for the women and given over to domestic activities, while the remaining part is reserved for the men and their guests. The underside of the ridge piece is carved with geometrical designs and sometimes painted green or red. Tribes throughout Western Morocco, as well as the Berber hill nomads, live in tents of this type.

The tent of the semi-nomadic Arabs of North Morocco[13] is not as well developed as that of the Berber hill nomads. Evidence for this is seen in the awning woven from asphodel root or dwarf palm fibres instead of the traditional goats' hair, and in the more rudimentary system of fastenings. The sole feature indicating greater development is the use of narrow 10 cm wide bands to reinforce the seams.

Algeria

The Algerian tent[14] differs from Moroccan tents in several respects: wider strips of material do not appear to be used on the outside as is common in Morocco; the awning is provided with a triangular opening as a smoke vent above the hearth; and the main poles and ridge piece are smaller than those of the tents of the

82. A typical Central Algerian tent.
83. Aulad Nail tent.
84. Typical West Algerian tent from the province of Oran belonging to the Ouled Sidi. Section through tent ridge (top); pattern of tent cloth (bottom). The tent consists of a main panel A (three widths); front panel B and rear panel C (four widths), both form part of the roof cloth. The roof widths, straps, flaps and cards are made from goats' hair with an admixture of wool and dwarf palm fibres: *1*, ridge piece; *2*, ridge pole; *3*, ridge strap, *triga*; *4*, auxiliary straps; *5*, auxiliary poles; *6*, bent-twig fastenings.

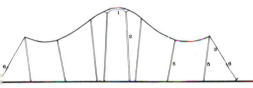

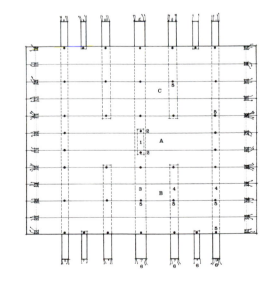

Moroccan hill nomads. Some traits are peculiar to the Algerian tent, thus the front and rear hanging awnings are secured with loops and small toggles to the main roof panel by means of trim, and the tents of each tribe are identified by the distinctive colour of their awnings. In Central and Eastern Algeria the strips of material in the centre of the awning form the actual roof, while the outside strips constitute the front and rear walls.[15] In most cases the ridge piece, which is somewhat shorter than that of the Moroccan tents, rests on two upright main poles but in Central Algeria and Aures the poles may be crossed or abbreviated to a single pole or T-shaped post. The ridge line is frequently lengthened by two additional poles, placed in front of and behind the ridge piece. In addition to the ridge piece there are two lines of poles placed beneath the side straps or *trigas*. And in Central and Eastern Algeria the awning falls quite close to the ground, thus obviating the need for additional wall strips. Towards the east, wattle walls lose their importance and disappear altogether.

There are at least two kinds of tents in Algeria. The main difference between the Central Algerian tent of the *Aulad Nail* and Larbaa and the West Algerian tent in Oran province is the greater depth of the latter. Besides its increased depth, the awning of the West Algerian tent is fabricated on a different pattern; the centre panel which constitutes the actual roof of the Central Algerian tent is much narrower, while the front and back panels are considerably wider. In the West Algerian tent[16] the front and back panels are integrated with the centre panel in the awning and special auxiliary poles have had to be inserted under enlarged back and front panels.

The colours of the narrow and broad stripes proclaim the identity of each tribe. These colours are produced by using predyed warp threads; the weft threads are always uncoloured. The tent widths of the Larbaa near Laghouat are woven with natural warp threads and then dyed a deep black. The colour of the stripes varies from black and brown to yellow-white and black-brown depending on the tribe. The 'red tent' of the *Ulad Nail*, for example, has black-brown inner stripes and red-brown stripes on the outside, sometimes a narrow white and black outside stripe is added as a variant. The weaving material is almost invariably a mixture of sheep's wool and goats' hair. In West Algeria, principally in the province of Oran and also in Morocco, plant fibres such as those of the dwarf palm may be added.

Central Algeria

The Central Algerian tent awning consists of a centre panel which constitutes the actual roof, and hanging panels sewn onto the front and back edges, except, in the case of large tents, where they are fastened by means of wooden pins or by small toggles inserted through loops. The roof awning is reinforced by a broad middle

53

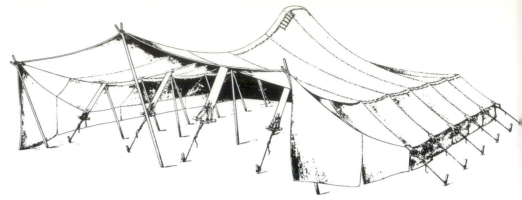

85. Central Algerian tent with the front flap raised. Such tents are typical for the Maghreb.
86. Central Algerian tent. Section through the ridge (top); pattern of the tent cloth, (bottom). The tent cloth consists of a main panel A (five widths), with hanging panels attached to the front B and back C. The roof widths are made of goats' hair strips 60 cm to 100 cm wide in 9 m to 8 m lengths: *1*, ridge piece; *2*, ridge poles; *3*, ridge strap; *4*, auxiliary straps; *5*, auxiliary poles; *6* plaited-loop fastenings.

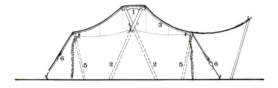

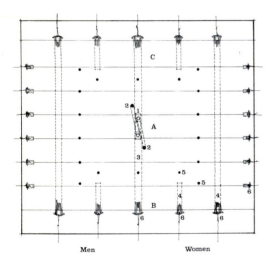

Men   Women

strap and two narrower side straps sewn on the underside of and perpendicular to the tent widths. Short auxiliary straps may be added between the main and side straps in some of the larger tents. They are mostly red, black orange or white. In Central Algeria the front and back walls are formed by the hanging panels which are always narrower than the main roof. The awning itself forms the side walls.[18]

The Central Algerian tent awning is stretched over at least three rows of poles, which correspond to the three straps. The slightly curved 'ridge piece' in the middle, rests on two tall main poles which stand one behind the other and are frequently crossed; a single pole may suffice in smaller tents. Each tent is divided into two parts by a curtain which is suspended from one or both of the two main poles and from the main strap. The seam between the panel and the roof is left open where the women's area is screened by the front hanging panel to allow the smoke from the fire to escape.[19]

Western Algeria

In Central Algeria, only the centre panel of the tent is anchored to the ground. In Western Algeria, in contrast, the front and back panels are also anchored. This difference in the side anchorage between tents in Central and Western Algeria is symptomatic of the increased importance of the front and back panels in Western Algeria, where they are integrated with the narrow centre panel. The arrangement of reinforcing straps and poles is far more elaborate in the West Algerian tent; for in addition to the main and side straps which extend the full depth of the awning, there are four auxiliary straps under the front and back panels on either side of the middle strap and a further four short straps sewn on the leading edge of the panels.[20] The poles are stationed in line with this system of reinforcing straps under the seams, every roof width for the centre panel and every second width for the outside panels. The undulating central *triga* rests upon a ridge piece supported on two main poles tilted inwards and two sets of three poles which carry the front and back panels. Outside panels of at least four strip widths are fastened to a centre panel of only three widths, with wooden pins, but in the south, towards the Sahara, they are buttoned together.

The tents of Tunisia and Algeria are much the same; the roof shape, striped awning and crossed main poles persist in tents throughout Central and Eastern Algeria, and Tunisia.[21] The awning of the Ouled Said of El Hamma is held up by three rows of poles under three corresponding narrow bands or *trigas*,

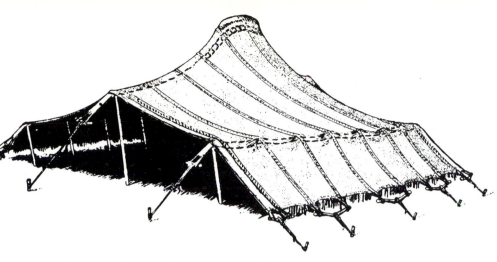

87. Tent of Southern Tunisia.
88. Ridge construction of the tent of the Oulad Sa'id (Tunisia): *1*, ridge piece, *guntas*; *2*, ridge pole, *rhiza*; *3*, ridge strap, *triga*; *4*, auxiliary pole, *omud*.

perpendicular to the length of the tent.[22] The metre long ridge piece is covered with a straw braided cushion which extends over its two ends.

Tripolitania

Whereas the added depth of the West Algerian tent is achieved by attaching large hanging panels to the back and front of the main roof, in Tripolitania the depth of the actual roof has been increased. The roof strips are woven from wool and camel's hair in widths of about 50 cm, whose colour varies from yellow-brown to brown according to the proportion of camels' hair. A white strip a few centimetres wide runs along the edge of the strip.

The three narrow reinforcing bands under the awning are held up by three transverse rows of poles whose numbers increase in proportion with the size of the tent which may be as large as 7 × 10 m.[23] The middle row of the Berber's tent has six poles, the two middle ones of which are tallest and carry a flattened ridge piece.

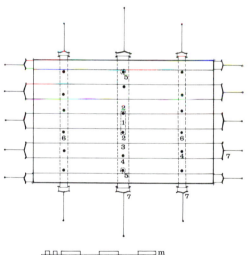

89. Tent of the transhumance Berbers of Djebel Nefousa (Tripolitania).
90. Tent of the transhumance Berbers. Section through the top ridge (top); pattern of the tent cloth (bottom). Camel hair is generally used instead of goats' hair and this gives the Tripolitanian tent its yellow-brown colour. The tent cloth is distinguished by its depth 7 m × 10 m: *1*, ridge piece; *2*, ridge poles; *3*, ridge strap; *4* auxiliary pole; *5*, circular wood bearing disc; *6*, auxiliary straps; *7*, bent-twig fastening.

55

The front and back poles of the middle row are equipped with a small ridge piece or wooden plate to prevent it rubbing through the velum. The short sides of the awning fall almost to the ground and are anchored by edge fastenings consisting of a long piece of curved wood secured by strings at each end to the white stripe of the roof widths. Whereas the stresses acting in the surface of the Moroccan hill nomad's tent are greater in the longitudinal direction, the Tripolitanian tent stresses are greater in the depth.[24] This stress reversal is probably accounted for by the reduction in the number of fastenings along the short sides of the awning.

The Arab tents differ from those of the Berbers; the single central pole which was encountered in Southern Tunisia is prevalent.

Libya

The most characteristic feature of the *Aulad Ali* tent is the placement of the main poles, these stand next to, not behind one another, about 120 to 170 cm apart and support 35 cm long ridge bars perpendicular to the awning length. Two narrow reinforcing bands or *triga* pass over each ridge bar for the full depth of the awning. There is no longer a ridge pole supported by two poles, or an awning which falls almost to the ground on the shorter sides.[25]

The edges of the large rectangular awning are lifted clear of the ground by three stakes on each of the shorter sides, which recall the tents of the Sinai Peninsula and Palestine with their poles grouped in threes. A second feature of the tent is the two extraordinarily deep flaps of fabric, forming a sort of loop which is sewn to the middle of the shorter sides.[26] A sturdy stick is inserted in this loop and a piece of curved wood attached to each end of the stick with ropes. Ropes are stretched from the curved wood to the pegs, about 2 m distant from the tent. As additional anchorage, a further rope is drawn along the entire length of the tent from one of the large fastenings over the ridge bars to the other. The two middle poles press up under the velum and deform it into two gently swelling humps. Frei Otto created a similar form in his humped tent at the Cologne Garden Exhibition in 1957.[27]

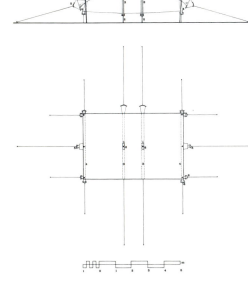

91. Tent of the *Aulad Ali*. Transverse section (top); pattern of the tent cloth, (bottom): *1*, ridge piece; *2*, ridge poles; *3*, ridge strap; *4*, side strap; *5*, special fabric-loop fastening.
92. Tent of the *Aulad Ali*, Libya in the vicinity of d'El Hammam.

93. Special fabric-loop fastening attached to each side of the tent cloth of the *Aulad Ali* tent, Libya.

Egypt

There are two types of tent extant among the bedouin in Egypt. A type similar to that of the *Aulad Ali* predominates in the west,[28] and another, characterised by nine poles arranged in rows of three perpendicular to the length of the tent so that the centre pole is highest, is much in evidence to the east. This second Sinai type is encountered among the Ma'aza in the northern part of the Eastern Desert, to the east of the Nile, and among the bedouin of the Sinai.[29] It is very similar to the type of tent used in Palestine.

Chapter 8

Arabia

The Evolution of Bedouinism in Northern Arabia

Insofar as the dromedary and the black tent are fundamental to the bedouin's way of life, it is temping to assume that they belong to the same stage of evolution among the nomads. The bedouin are both camel herdsmen and rider-warriors whose economic structure is characterized by the maintenance of very large flocks. Their social structure is founded on the notion of descent from common ancestors.

The transformation of the bedouin in Northern Arabia from small herders to militant rider-warriors in charge of large herds has been attributed to the development of dromedary riding technique and gear.[1] Between the 11th and 9th centuries BC the herdsmen of Northern Arabia learned to ride on the dromedary's hump, instead of on the crupper behind the hump. This modest advance in riding technique together with later improvements in riding gear, derived mainly from the horsemen of Central Asia, changed the course of bedouin life in Arabia.

The mastery of this riding position on the dromedary's hump increased the pace and duration of camel journeys, thus enabling large herds to be kept. This change led in turn to more frequent contacts with urban cultures and to a closer economic relationship with the settled population, accounting not only for the presence of many urban elements in both their culture and the black tent, but also for their southward dispersal.

In taking over the principle of the saddle bow from the horse-riders of Central Asia, the tribes of camel-herdsmen received an impulse that facilitated the bedouinization of Arabia.[2] The introduction of the saddle bow suddenly transformed the camel-herdsmen into bellicose rider-warriors.

The common origin of full bedouinization and the black tent, both of which have been traced back to Northern Arabia, suggests that they belong to the same stage of cultural evolution.[3] Feilberg's theory[4] that the black tent is the Indo-European nomadic tent which came to Western Asia after the second millenium with the large migration of Indo-European peoples complements Dostal's theory[5] of the bedouinization of Arabia.

Geographical distribution

The geographical extent of the Arabian group of tents is defined in the west by the Nile valley and in the south by the northern edge of the great sandy desert known as Rub al Khali.[6] Even though they have adopted the terminology of the Egyptian tent, the tent of the Ma'aza, west of the Gulf of Suez is an Arabian type. The northeastern border is poorly defined because the transition from the Arabian to the Iranian types is gradual, and a considerably modified form of Arabian tent is encountered among Kurdish tribes such as the Milli.

Common features of the Arabian tent

There are two notable differences in the pattern of the tents of Arabia and its northern fringe areas, and those of North Africa; the roof of the Arabian tent is supported on three longitudinal rows of poles; the poles of the central row are at the same height and are taller than the front and back poles.[7] There are slight regional variations most evident between the Palestinian tents and those of the desert bedouin, the Sba'a and the Ruwalla. The tent of the North Arab nomads differs significantly from the standard type — its frame consists of only two rows of poles, a front row and a central row. The profile of the awning is not noticeably affected by this modification, inasmuch as the anchor ropes perform much the same function as the absent back pole row. This simplification probably arose from the attempt to lessen the load while travelling. The tents of the Sba'a of the northern part of Syria, and the Ruwalla of Northern Arabia described by de Boucheman and Musil, deviate from the typical Arabian pattern, for they have two tall central poles set side by side along the centre line, with two corresponding stakes in the front of the tent.[8] The placement of the two central poles side by side recurs in the tents of the *Aulad Ali*. The awning of the Swahire Bedouin tent of Syria is exceptionally flat. Notwithstanding these departures from the general pattern, the gable roof of the Arabian tents is unmistakable. The corner poles invariably stand outside the roof. The tent poles and stakes in these regions are usually disposed in groups of threes, and each pole in the central row is provided with corresponding stakes at the front and rear edge of the awning.

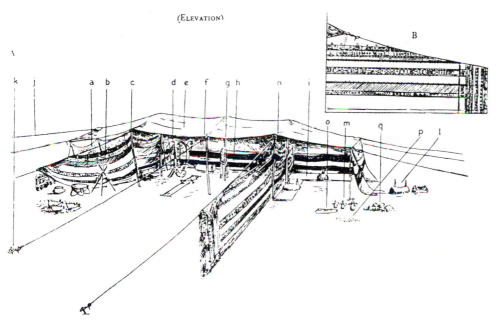

(Elevation)

94. View from the front of a well-to-do three-poled Mutair bedouin tent from the Kuwait area: *a*, kitchen, *Matbakh*; *b*, dividing curtain, *Qata*; *c*, tent-support, *Mijdim*; *d*, women's litter, *Maksar*; *e*, roof widths, *Filjan*; *f*, wooden fastener, *Ritbah*; *g*, tent pole, *'Amud*; *h*, back curtain, *Ruag*; *i*, carpet to sit on, *Frash*; *j*, tent rope, *Tanb*; *k*, tent peg, *Minsab*; *l*, riding saddle, *Shadad*; *m*, coffee pots, *Dallal*; *n*, webbing strap to take strain, *Tarrija*; *o*, fireplace, *Wujar*; *p*, camel-dung fuel, *Jalla*; *q*, brushwood fuel, *'Arfaj*.

Construction of the Arabian black tent

Tent awnings in the Arabian region are predominantly black goats' hair, although camels' hair is used occasionally. The light summer tent commonly found in Northern Syria and Upper Mesopotamia has a velum incorporating hemp, cotton and wool. The length of the roof widths varies according to whether they are produced in villages and towns or by the tribeswomen. In Syria, the Anaiza buy roof widths in lengths of 11·4 to 45·6 m from the villagers, but in Arabia Petraea and Palestine the tribeswomen weave standard 7 m long strips which must be joined end to end for a bigger tent.[9] A medium size Anaiza tent with a central pole, which is somewhat deeper than the tents of other tribes, has at least eight 60 to 70 cm wide strips joined lengthwise. In Arabia the widths may be decorated, but in the north they are, for the most part, plain. The tent awning rests on goats' hair straps named *tarige*. The number of straps is determined by the length of the roof awning and the number of poles in the central row; it is customary to have two side straps in addition to the standard central strap.

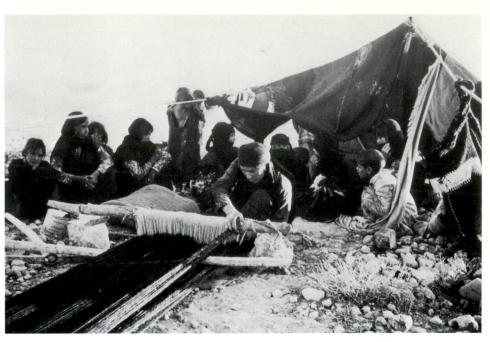

95. Weaving on the bedouin ground loom,
South Jordan.
96. Loom used to weave tent widths.

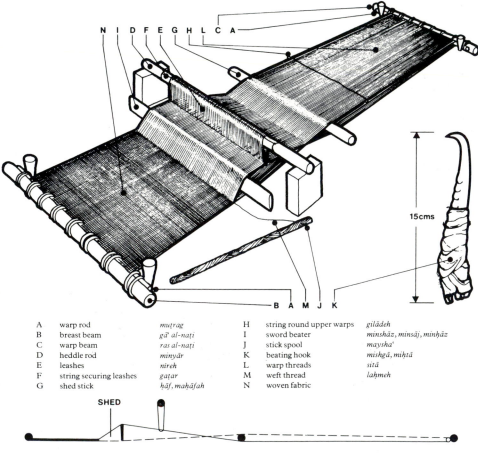

A	warp rod	*muṭrag*	H	string round upper warps	*gilādeh*
B	breast beam	*gāʿ al-naṭi*	I	sword beater	*minshāz, minsāj, minḥāz*
C	warp beam	*ras al-naṭi*	J	stick spool	*maysha'*
D	heddle rod	*minyār*	K	beating hook	*mishgā, miḥtā*
E	leashes	*nireh*	L	warp threads	*sitā*
F	string securing leashes	*gaṭar*	M	weft thread	*laḥmeh*
G	shed stick	*ḥāf, maḥāfah*	N	woven fabric	

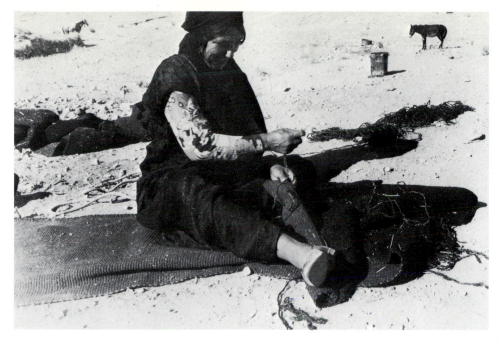

97. Woman of the Huwaytat bedouin, South Jordan, sewing strips for a tent.
98. Tent with a loom, South Jordan.

61

The side walls of the tent may be formed by the awning, by strips of fabric attached to the ends of the awning, or by separate pieces of curtain similar to the back wall. Once past the two outer straps, if these are present, the unrestrained roof awning is allowed to fall to the ground. In other instances, a special thin strip of fabric may be sewn on to the ends of the awning. Tents are often closed on both sides by lowering the poles. The back wall of the tent is made of a lighter material woven in either a yellow ochre monotone, or in brown, white and black stripes obtained by using camel, sheep and goat hair. In winter the back curtain is extended round the sides, and a special curtain similar to the back wall is fastened across the front of the tent. Except for the Syrian tent, scant use is made of wattle walls among the major desert tribes.[10] In Northern Syria and Mesopotamia it is customary to have a wall in the front as well as in the rear of the tent. The Syrian bedouin and the Anaiza make the needles of iron, elsewhere they are of wood which is the material used originally.

The gently rounded outline of the tent awning is produced by the insertion between the top of the central poles and the awning of small wooden planks or ridge bars to prevent the poles from rubbing through the straps of the roof. A roll of tent material may suffice for this purpose, otherwise a piece of wood with an indentation in the centre may be sewn onto the strap. In Upper Mesopotamia, the Fedaan, parts of Syria, Palestine and Central Arabia, a wood billet is sewn into a specially constructed pocket where the two tent widths meet above the central pole.[11]

99. An encampment in South Jordan.

Long tent ropes are a feature of the Arab bedouin tent. Three ropes are attached to each short side by means of short prettily decorated straps (the middle strap is frequently twice as long as the corner straps) sewn onto the topside of the roof velum. The rope is connected to the short straps with a type of hinged fastening tied to a small wooden stick (hem wood) sewn into the ends of the strap at each end. The type of fastening employed varies considerably;[12] in Upper Mesopotamia the hinged fastening is semi-circular in shape, while a bent twig fastening similar to the North African type is encountered in parts of Syria, in Palestine, and in Arabia Petraea. The rope fastening consisting of a plaited camel leather strap tied directly to the hem wood used by the Anaiza is common in Central Arabia. Fastenings for the front and back tent ropes are attached to hem woods provided at the ends of the narrow reinforcing bands or straps, otherwise, the fastenings are the same as on the short sides. In general, the sheep herders use bent twig or forked branch fastenings while the camel herders use rope fastenings. The tribeswomen make the ropes from camel hair or plant fibres as in Egypt, but hemp ropes may be bought.

The bedouin tent is usually divided by one or more long richly decorated curtains suspended from the tent poles, the reinforcing straps or the front tent ropes. The location of the dividing curtains is determined by the placement of the poles in the central row. The tents are designated according to the number of middle row poles, excluding the two outer poles.[13] Apart from the straps, the dividing curtain (qata) is the only part of the Arabian tent which is decorated.

100. Types of black tent fastenings: *1*, rope fastening; *2*, bent-twig fastening, (chevron becket); *3*, forked-twig fastening; *4*, hinged fastening; *5*, narrow split-strap fastening; *6*, plaited-loop fastening; *7*, edge fastenings (a) horse shoe, (b) hooked; *8*, fan-shaped binding cluster; *9*, loop binding.

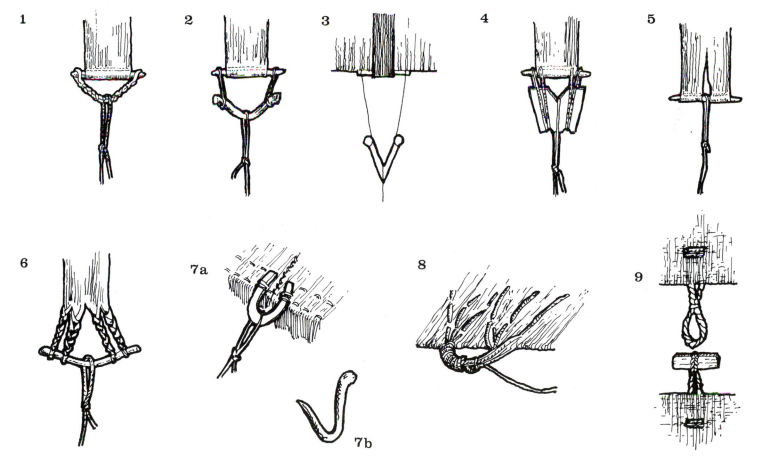

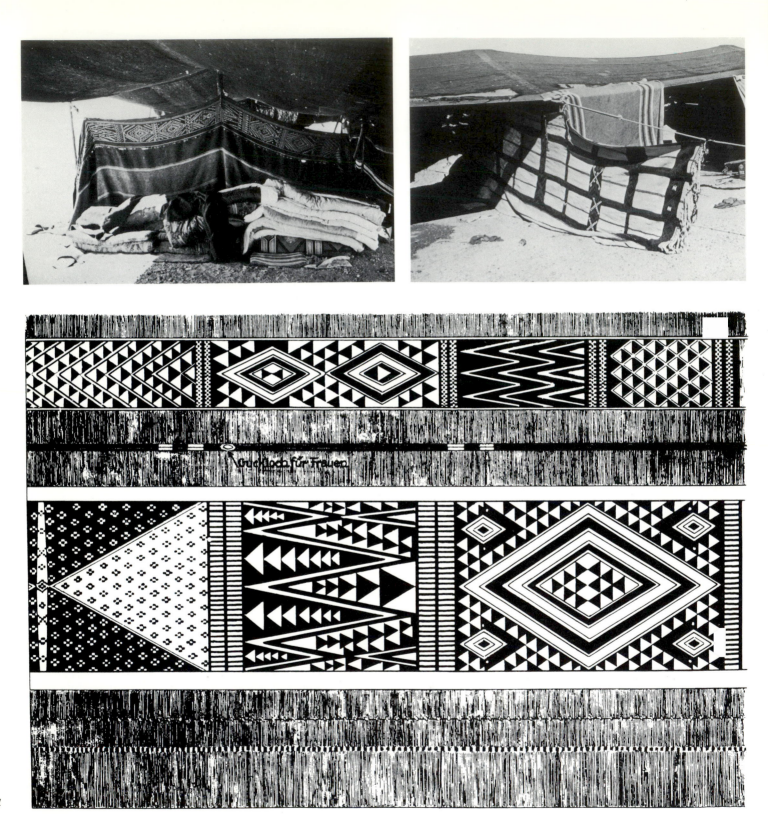

Interior arrangement of the Arabian tent

The *qata* divides the tent into two compartments, sometimes there are more, the right-hand one being for the women and the left-hand one for the men.[14] A small hole is provided in the curtain to enable the women to observe the men on the other side. Guests are received in the men's room which contains a fireplace in the form of a ditch; in the tents of sheikhs from old families it is given a distinctive shape.[15] Besides functioning as a bedroom and a house-keeping room, the women's room is also used as a storeroom for tools and luggage and for the women's sedan chairs. The kitchen is located in the front part of, or in front of, the women's room. In Upper Mesopotamia and elsewhere, individual rooms formed with a special screen made from rush mats permit the women to move about more freely.

In Palestine and Arabia Petraea, the tent usually faces east, and in Iraq, the tents of the Tobe surprisingly, face west. The bedouin site their tents in parallel rows, in family and clan groups, except in Palestine and Arabia Petraea where they are placed in a protective ring or elliptical formation.[16] In the latter, the tents are placed close together so that their ropes and cords intermingle, and the herds are brought into the camp ring at night as a precaution against thieves.

101. Tent dividing curtain with bedding, South Jordan.
102. Dividing curtain, South Jordan.
103. Pattern of a Beni Sahr bedouin dividing curtain.
104. Interior arrangement of Mutair bedouin tent: *1*, two-pole type; *2*, three-pole type.

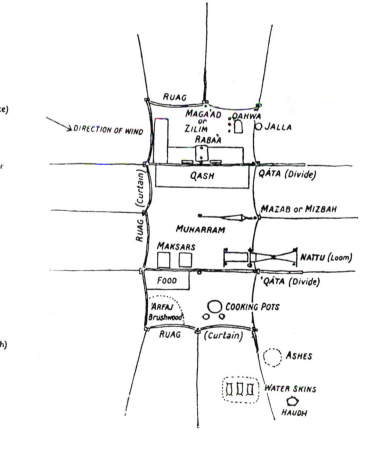

Palestine and Syria

The Swahire bedouin tent is supported on three rows of three poles of which the middle one is tallest; the tent is therefore higher at its centre and over the central part at the front.[17] The roof falls away on either side of the longitudinal ridge above the middle row of poles; the centre poles at the front and short sides are taller than the corner stakes. The central pole is placed off-centre, the women occupying the larger of the two compartments. The awning is reinforced by a goats' hair middle strap 11 cm wide, this strap is sewn to the underside of the awning and passes over the central pole. A small piece of wood is frequently placed on top of the central pole in Palestinian tents. The rear wall and the women's compartment is enclosed by a panel made up of two strips of coarse material secured to the edge of the roof with wooden pins. During the hot season the tent is left open on all four sides. The sexes are separated by a 140 cm high curtain of coarsely woven material suspended from the three middle poles.

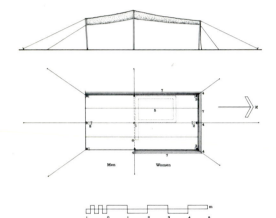

105. Swahire bedouin tent, Palestine and Arabia Petraea. Transverse section (top); plan of tent cloth, 5·65 m long by 2·70 m wide (bottom). The tent cloth is formed of four strips 65 cm to 70 cm wide woven from goats' hair: *1*, 11 cm wide central strap of goats' hair; *2*, 10 cm by 30 cm tag-girths; *3*, 10 cm by 17 cm tag-girths; *4*, forked-twig fastenings; *5*, stone sleeping bench 1·5 m by 2 m; *6*, 140 cm high partition; *7*, walls.
106. Tent belonging to the Adwan bedouin of East Jordan.

The Petraean tent

The three rowed tent extends through Palestine and Arabia Petraea, in these regions the tent is supported by three rows of three, five, seven, or nine poles.[18] Whereas there are only three short straps to each short side in other tents, here there may be as many as five. In winter, which can be quite severe in this highland region, additional auxiliary straps are attached to the front and back edges. The stronger anchorage of the Petraean tent is reminiscent of North African tents.

Northern Arabia
The Anaiza tent

The Sba'a and the Ruwalla belong to a group of tribes known collectively as the Anaiza who control the steppelands of Northwestern Arabia. The Anaiza are a large loosely-knit group of tribes who occupy an area extending from North Arabia to Syria and Mesopotamia. It is necessary therefore, to specify which Anaiza tribe a tent belongs to. Tents with two rows of poles instead of the customary three are prevalent among the Anaiza, especially the Sba'a and the Ruwalla. The arrangement of two tall central poles placed side by side along the middle row with corresponding stakes in the front is peculiar to Sba'a and Ruwalla tents.[19] The improved aerodynamic roof shape and ease of transport which results from the omission of the rear row of tent poles is achieved at the expense of the living space inside the tent. This is not a serious disadvantage since the lower rear portion of the tent is used for storage.

107. North Arabian tent belonging to the Anaiza and Shammar bedouin.
108. North Arabian tent with only two rows of poles. Section through ridge, top; pattern of tent cloth, bottom. The tent cloth is made from 60 cm to 70 cm wide strips woven from pure goats' hair or cotton with small quantities of goats' hair. An average 11·4 m by 4·8 m tent has eight 60 cm wide strips: 1, middle poles under the transverse axis; 2, wooden discs placed on top of the main poles; 3, narrow straps; 4, forked poles; 5, tag-girths; 6, 1·6 m to 1·7 m high dividing curtain; 7, back wall consisting of three strips of goats' hair 1·8 m high.

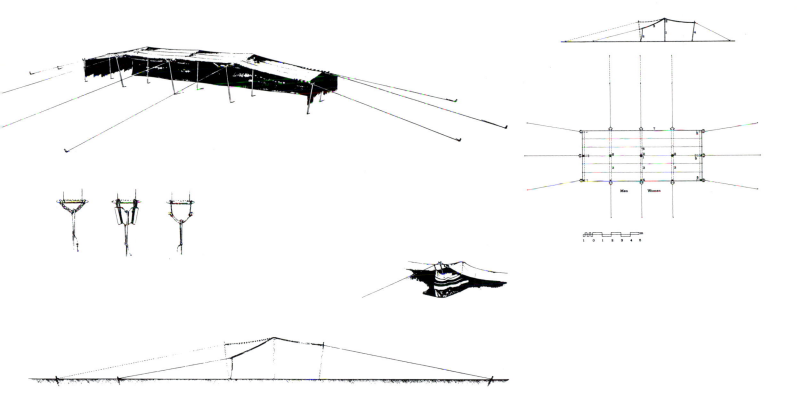

The Fed'an tent

The Fed'an tent awning is supported on two or three rows of five poles depending on whether a low or high rear profile is desired. The Fed'an awning is about 13 m long by 4·2 m deep and consists of six 70 cm wide strips reinforced with three narrow bands placed crosswise to the length of the tent over the central poles; three long tent ropes and their fastenings are attached to each short side by means of tabs sewn onto the topside of the awning.[20] The Fed'an employ a variety of

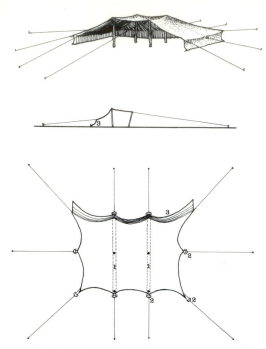

109. Sba'a tent from the northern part of the Syrian desert. View (top); section through the longitudinal axis (middle); pattern of the tent cloth (bottom). The cloth is assembled from 70 cm wide strips of black goats' hair, sometimes camel hair or wool is also included: *1*, narrow reinforcing straps; *2*, stick fastenings supplied with leather thongs; *3*, rear wall.

fastenings to secure the tent ropes to the narrow bands such as rope fastenings, bent twig fastenings and hinged fastenings. The front tent ropes pass over the forked ends of poles which stand in front of the tent edge. The rear and side walls are attached to the edge of the roof with long iron needles and the interior is divided into two compartments by a decorative striped curtain hung from the middle poles and tent ropes.

The Sba'a tent

The Shammar, Ataiba and Gehatan of Central Arabia employ a two rowed tent similar to that of the northern Arabian nomads, examples of which can be found among the Sba'a and Ruwalla. The tents of Northern Syria appear to be longer, they have from four to six poles in the central row, and occasionally the rear part of the awning is pulled downwards. The side walls of Syrian tents are enclosed by wattles made from rushes or papyrus and by low clay walls.[21]

The Sba'a bedouin of the northern part of the Syrian desert live in tents made from 70 cm widths of black goats' hair and, infrequently, of camels' hair and wool. The sheep herders use white widths woven from a type of cotton or hemp, sometimes the entire tent awning is made from this material.

The distinctive shape of the Sba'a tent results from the placement of two tall poles in the middle row and two corresponding poles in the front, the deployment of long ropes and the omission of the rear row of poles.[22] The rear of the tent, facing the wind, is screened by a fabric curtain consisting of three strips, attached to the tent by means of large iron pins threaded on string. Curtains are not provided on the short sides. The awning is reinforced by narrow bands which terminate in rope fastenings with loops made of plaited camel hide at each end where the ropes converge on the tent. The poles are prevented from piercing the awning by small rounded pieces of wood inserted between the pole tips and the reinforcing bands.

The Ruwalla tent

The Ruwalla and Sba'a tents are similar. The Ruwalla tents described by Alois Musil had two rows of poles with anything from one to five or seven poles each.[23] An ordinary tent with one main pole carried an awning 12 m long by 4 m deep consisting of eight 60 to 70 cm wide strips. The roof strips were woven from pure black goats' hair in a heavy or a light weight or from cotton blended with a small amount of goats' hair. The central pole is capped by a small 10 cm diameter disc traditional in Northern Arabia to protect the awning whose edges are bound with a coarse strip of goats' hair. The side walls, and a narrow 50 cm wide back valance of lighter material are fastened to the awning by means of strong pins.

Central Arabia

The Ataiba (Otabeh) is one of the largest tribes of the Nejd in Central Arabia. The awning of a typical Ataiba tent is stretched horizontally over nine poles in three rows of three, the central pole carries a short ridge bar placed lengthwise to the tent.[24] There are exceptions to this general pattern, in some tents the rear middle pole is omitted, while in others, there are only two rows of three poles in which the two middle poles are connected by a bar. Large Ataiba tents have five or seven poles in the front row.

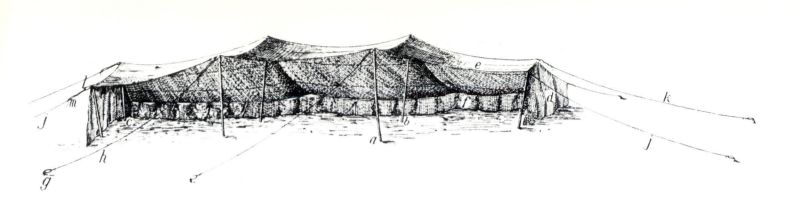

The awning of goats' hair, camels' hair or wool is reinforced by a narrow strap sewn across the awning above the three middle poles. Rope fastenings are provided on the middle and auxiliary straps. Wooden pins are used to attach the side and rear walls to the roof. The interior is divided into two sections (one for men and the other for women), by a fabric partition consisting of three strips of material similar to the walls.

110. Ruwalla tent used by Alois Musil.

Mesopotamia

The tents of the Northern Shammar and the semi-nomadic Tobe indicate that in Iran, tents follow the three-rowed Arabian pattern. Tents in Northern Syria and Mesopotamia normally have walls in the front as well as in the rear. The Shammar tent of Northern Mesopotamia has three rows of poles, the number of inner poles beneath the longitudinal axis varying from two to nine, with each pole in the central row having its corresponding fellows in the front and back.[25] The front poles are forked at the upper ends, and the tent ropes pass through the forks as they do in the Fed'an tent. The goats' and camels' hair strips forming the rectangular awnings are reinforced by narrow straps which also protect them from being damaged by the pole tips. A special fabric wall cloth is hung in the front as well as in the rear of the tent, but it is usually raised over the open front as the ropes are particularly long. In Upper Mesopotamia the women's compartment is ordinarily enclosed with *paravents* made of rush matting.[26] The tent is surrounded by brambles and thorns which thrive in the Euphrates valley.

Primitive tents

Primitive tents are found in many parts of Arabia.[27] The Bani Atiyah and Shararat who inhabit a region west of the Nafud Desert and in the region north of Hijaz have small triangular tents with one main pole. Similar incomplete tents are found among the Murra who live on the northern fringe of the Rub'al Khali. The Ruwalla carry a small travelling tent (*tuzz*) for the benefit of their children during long marches.

69

Chapter 9

Iran and Afghanistan

Primary tent groups

The black tents of Southwestern Asia are divided into two primary groups – an occidental group representing the Arab domain, and an oriental group comprising Iranian, Afghan and Tibetan peoples – along the border of the plains of Mesopotamia.[1] In terms of shape, the oriental group may be divided further into two secondary groups; the tents of Western Iran, the eastern Kurds, the Lurs, and the Qashqai constituting one group and the Tibetan tents another. These two groups are separated by a wedge of dry tropical forest. To the west of Iran, the Yürrüks of Pamphylea and Pisidea, and the Kizilbash in Anatolia have also adopted the black tent. The black tent of Iran is found among the Kurds, Lurs, Bakhtiari, Basseri, Qashqai and Baluch nomads, in an area extending from the Transcaucasus and Caspian Sea in the north to the Zagros Mountains in the south.[2]

The black tent and cylindrical tent culture zones of Afghanistan are separated by the Paropamisus and Hindu Kush. In general, the black tent is found south of these mountains among the Moghôl, Taimannî, Ghilzai, Durānnī, Brahui and Sistan Baluch nomads.[3] The eastern limit of the black tent along the Sulaiman Range is defined by the wanderings of the Marri Baluch in Northern Pakistan and the Ghilzai in Eastern Afghanistan. The most dense expansion of the Tibetan black tent occurs in a zone to the north of a line following the Indus and Tsangpo (Brahmaputra) rivers, in the regions of Koko Nor, Hor and Tsaidam in Northeastern Tibet where they are found among both Mongol and Tibetan nomads.[4]

The chief difference between the Arabian and Iranian tents is the stress placed on the longitudinal direction of the Iranian tent.[5] The longitudinal direction is emphasised by aligning the rows of poles and the ridge bars parallel to, instead of perpendicular to the length of the tent. The highest poles in the Iranian tent are placed underneath the longitudinal axis. Other differences include roof and walls made of one piece, and a roof velum divided along the longitudinal axis.[6] The awnings of Kurd and Lur tents are made in two sections and joined by a system of loops and small wooden sticks. The stick fastenings, or fastenings formed by looped threads with curved or forked pieces of wood, prevalent in Arabian tents, have been replaced in Iran by fan shaped or special clusters of braided loops. The tent awnings of the oriental group have several peculiar features; the roof widths are narrower, vegetable matter is excluded in their composition, and the narrow reinforcing straps, customary in Arabian tents, have been omitted altogether.[7]

The Tibetan tent, geographically isolated from the other major groups of black tents, is a distinct type. Tibetan tents are typified by a roof and walls in one piece, by tent ropes which pass over exterior poles placed some distance from the tent and then divide, so that they can be attached to the awning by several roots, and by a hole in the longitudinal axis of the awning above the ridge pole for the smoke to escape.[8] The tent of the Lurs has a smoke hole high up in each gable under the large gable fastenings.

The tent of the Lurs is a particularly well defined type which shares a number of traits with the tents of the Mukri Kurds and Qashqai.[9] The Lur tent has a large, high, saddle-shaped roof, an awning of black goats' hair, and walls enclosed by reed matting.

The ridge profile of the Kurd and Lur tents betrays an important difference between the two types; whereas the Lur awnings sag slightly between the characteristic horizontal ridge bars, the awning of the Kurd tents is supported at a series of clearly defined points.[10] The T-shaped supports of the Lur tent are found in several places in Iran and among the Durānnī of Afghanistan.

The black tents of Iran and Afghanistan are variations of two archetypes, a ridged roof rectangular tent and a barrel-vaulted or arched form. Of the Baluch, Durānnī and Achikzai barrel-vaulted tents the Durānnī is a transitional form which gradually merges into the Baluch type.[11] There are three main types of black tents in Afghanistan: The Taimannî tent, the east Afghan or Ghilzai tent, and the south and west Afghan or Durānnī tent.[12] The Baluchistan barrel-vaulted tent and its related forms provide an interesting connection with barrel-vaulted huts centred in West Baluchistan.

Walls constructed of wattles, clay and stones are widespread in Iran. The Lurs, Kurds and possibly the Yürrüks surround their tent awnings with wattle walls which appear to be an ancient element in the tent groups of Western Iran.[13] The Manassani of Farsistan throw earthen walls around their tents, and walls made of stone are encountered among the Kurds and the Turkmen, and in Luristan.

Iran
The Kurd tent

The territory of the Kurds, many of whom are not nomadic, extends in an arc from the Turkish Euphrates south of Van Golu to just north of Kermanshah in Western Iran. The black goats' hair awning is carried on three longitudinal rows of poles, the stakes on the sides, however, do not correspond with the tall poles in the middle.[14] Many awnings are divided into two parts along the ridge which are joined with braided loops and small wooden sticks. The poles in some large tents can be taken apart into several pieces.

111. Tent of the Mukri Kurds south of Lake Umria, Iran. Side view (top); plan (bottom). The tent cloth is made of coarse black goats' hair divided into two sections lengthwise and joined by loop bindings: *1*, middle row of poles; *2*, reed and wattle walls and partitions with three parallel strips of interlacings; *3*, men's quarters; *4*, family life and women; *5*, chamber for storing provisions; *6*, hearths.
112. The black tent of Luristan.
113. Lur tent. *a*, pattern of the tent cloth, *b*, two piece ridge pole and ridge piece with mortise.

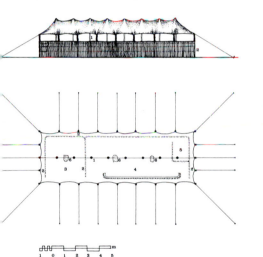

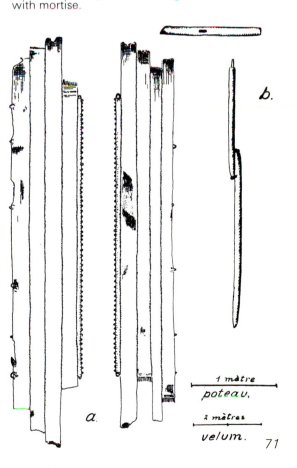

The Lur tent

The tents of the nomadic Lurs who roam the northern Zargos Mountains of Southwestern Iran closely resemble those of the Kurds in that both have a prominent ridge-shaped roof and a black goats' hair awning.[15] The awning of the Lur tent is divided into two pieces which are joined by threading the loops on one side through the loops on the other and securing them with small sticks of wood. The awning is stretched lengthwise by means of large loops at each end of the two narrow strips of fabric along the tent ridge. The longest strips of material which are located along the ridge hang down and close the tent gables.[16]

71

The middle poles dominate the Lur tent. Normally, the poles are assembled from two pieces and support a short ridge bar which lends them the appearance of T-shaped supports. The ridge bar is transfixed on the pole with a mortise and tenon joint.[17] The irregular profile of the ridge results from the placement of the ridge bars side by side forming a sort of sectioned ridge.

Afghanistan
The Afghan and Baluch tent types

Afghanistan is divided into a northern cylindrical tent zone and a southern zone of black tents. The Säbzäk Pass, the Paropamisus Mountains to the east, and the watershed between the Harî Rûd and the Farâh Rûd define the southern limits of the cylindrical tent zone.[18] Cylindrical tents are never seen south of these limits in the black tent zone. The northern black tents, almost without exception, are associated with traditional black tent peoples such as the Afghans, Baluchs and Afghan Moghôls. The northward diffusion of black tents occurred because of the relative mobility of the black tent peoples who are full nomads, compared with the semi-nomadic cylindrical tent dwellers.[19]

There are two basic patterns of black tents: the peaked ridge or Afghan type similar to the Lur tent, and the barrel-vaulted tent of Baluchistan. Barrel-vaulted black tents are found among the Baluchs, the Achikzai, and the Tadjiks of Southern Tadjikstan. In West Baluchistan a tradition of barrel-vaulted construction is reproduced in the form of the black tent, over an extensive area. Although the Baluchistan tents disclose the impact of an ancient tradition of barrel-vault construction based on the form of the black tent, its significance for the evolution of the black tent is slight.[20] The Durānnī and Moghôl tents incorporate arched supports under the ridge which are related to the barrel-vaulted black tent. Whereas the Durānnī tent derived immediately from the barrel-vaulted tent of Baluchistan, it seems that the Moghôls adopted the black tent from southern nomadic peoples and carried it with them into the Ghôrât.[21] The characteristic bent centre bough of the Moghôl tent is also met in the tents of the Afghan nomads. The ridge type is the preferred tent of Afghan nomads, the Ghilzai and the Brahui, and in Sistan. Although the rectangular tent of the Southern Taimannî resembles the ridge type of black tent, it is in reality a singular type which has its origin in the special circumstances of the ethnogenesis of the Southern Taimannî people,[22] and whereas the Moghôl tent is the result of cultural borrowing, it appears that the rectangular Taimannî tent was an independent invention.

Black tents
The Ghilzai tent

The *ghizdi* tents or black tents of the Ghilzai and Durānnī confederations comprising the two main groups of Afghan tribes are distinct types. The black tent of the Ghilzai nomads who inhabit a territory extending from Kandahar to Kabul in Eastern Afghanistan has a black goats' hair roof cloth stretched over three rows of poles placed lengthwise with the help of stays. The Ghilzai tents near Kabul and in the valley of Ghorband have three rows of four poles and the peaks above the two middle poles are higher than the outer poles under the central ridge.[23] A rope is sometimes placed lengthwise under the roof cloth and attached to the fastening rope or may itself serve as the stay fastening, at either end. The sides of the tent are closed with four slanting cloths fastened to the roof with iron needles. The tent

114. Ghilzai tent near Kabul.
115. Autumn encampment of Ghilzai tents in the Ghorband Valley.

interior is extended on the short sides by deep wall cloths which fall gently to the ground. In the Ghorband Valley, the tents are surrounded by a low wall of mud and stones.

The Brahui tent

The Brahui sheep herders of Sistan dwell for five months in high backed, pole-supported black tents made from pure goats' hair and for the remainder of the year in clay village houses.[24] The roof cloth consists of three widths (usually 100 cm or slightly more) but sometimes the middle strip is considerably narrower (40 to 60 cm). The roof shape is defined by the placement and height of the poles. The middle pole is generally highest, and the forked stakes on each side lowest. The central poles are prevented from damaging the middle roof width by placing special cushions with decorative tassels on top of the poles, or by small wooden ridge bars placed across the length of the cloth, bundles of odd rags are used for the same purpose in Sistan.

The four or five forked stakes generally provided on each side of a fully equipped tent are not placed under the stays, but under the loop fastening at the edge which

116. Brahui tent.
117. Pattern of the tent cloth of a Brahui tent consisting of a narrow middle width which is led down to the ground at the rear: *1*, middle poles; *2*, wooden bar or plate 'pole cushions'; *3*, forked front poles; *4*, loops.

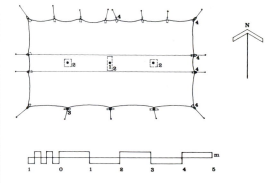

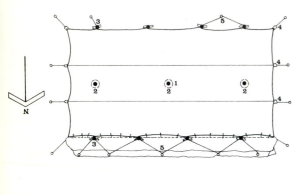

118. The Sistan tent. View from the back with the back cloth raised (top); pattern of the tent cloth (bottom): *1*, middle poles; *2*, wooden discs on top of poles; *3*, forked front and rear poles; *4*, loops; *5*, diagonal stays.

rests directly in the forks. Side cloths consisting of one or two widths of material are usual, although it is customary for the roof to be let down almost to the ground on the short sides and to be without an end cloth. The side cloths are fastened to the upper side of the roof cloth with iron needles threaded onto a thin cord.

The Sistan tent

The Sistan tent is no longer linked to any one tribe, but is a regional type which has come to be associated with a particular mode of life, that of nomadic and semi-nomadic sheep and goat herders.[25] It is the dominant type in a vaguely defined area extending from Birjand in the north to Khash in the south which takes in Sistan and parts of Baluchistan.

Both the Sistan and Durānnī tents have high central sections, an unequal number of cloth widths in the awning, and wooden ridge bars placed at right angles to the tent's length. The high-backed, pole-supported Sistan and Brahui tents are fundamentally similar, but there are some significant differences. For instance, the forked stakes on the long sides are connected to intermediate pegs by short stays in a distinctive zigzag pattern which ensures that each stake is restrained by two diverging stays.[26] The stays, except on the short sides where they are fastened to the edge loops, are lashed round the stake forks and the edge loops. The tent cloth is normally protected by a bundle of rags set on the tips of the central poles. The Sistan tent, unlike its Durānnī counterpart, has a back cloth, but the front is left open except in more permanent encampments or where conditions so dictate.

The Southern Taimannî tent

The hybrid rectangular tent of the Southern Taimannî is unlike the black tents of the Afghans and the Moghôls. The domain of the Southern Taimannî tent in the northern part of the Ghôrât is defined by the limits of Southern Taimannî settlement at the watershed between the Harî Rûd and the Farrâh Rûd.

The Taimannî developed a new type of tent — the Taimannî rectangular tent — when they moved south into the Ghôrât.[27] The new tent retained the skeletal frame of the Northern Taimannî yurt-like *čaparî*, but acquired a new shape, that of the small rectangular houses with the low gabled roofs of the Ghôrât. The *palâs* covering from which the Taimannî rectangular tent took its name (*palâs-i siyãh*) was adopted from either the Moghôls or the Afghans who were adjacent black tent peoples. The absence of any direct line of evolution either from the *čaparî* or from one of the black tent types of the region points to the independent invention of the Taimannî tent in the Ghôrât itself.[28]

The skeletal framework of the Taimannî tent consists of stakes embedded in the ground at regular intervals around a rectangular plan about 6·1 m to 6·7 m long by 3 m to 3·6 m wide. There are seven to eight stakes on the long sides and fewer on the short sides.[29] The longitudinal ridge pole is carried on two poles inserted in the middle on each short side and sometimes the ridge is in two pieces which are joined in the middle where they bestride one or more posts. The stakes which surround the tent on all sides incline inwards and are secured by ropes.

There is no need for the loosely woven *palâs* tent cover to be impervious as there is no rain during the Taimannî tent season. The tent roof is covered by a single large *palâs* or one made up of several pieces sewn together draped over the ridge reaching down to the sides. The walls have single or several pieces of *palâs*

119. Taimannî rectangular tent.
120. Barrel-vaulted black tents of Afghanistan: *1*, Baluch summer tent; *2*, Baluch winter tent; *3*, Durānnī tent; *4*, Moghôl tent.

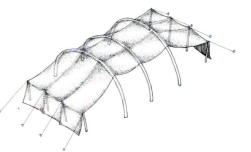

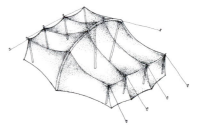

fastened to the top piece around the sides with pointed wooden dowels. The tent is surrounded on all sides, except at the entrance on one end of the long side, by *čiq* matting about two-thirds their height, made of reeds strung together in close parallel rows. The interior is simply provided with felt mats covering the floor, and occasionally it is subdivided with *čiq* mats while the smoke from the fire escapes through the open *palâs*. The contribution of the gable-roofed huts of the Ghôrât to the Taimannî rectangular tent is especially interesting when it is considered in the context of Feilberg's theory that the black tent evolved at the same time as the arched huts and the huts with poles and in doing so borrowed elements from each.

Barrel vaulted tents
Barrel-vaulted Baluch tents and related forms

Barrel-vaulted tents and huts extend in a practically continuous area from Bashakerd and Jiroft along the Halil River in the west to Pakistan Baluchistan. Within the area of the Baluchistan barrel-vaulted tent, the barrel-vaulted reed hut of the Guador people of Humun in Sistan probably supplied the primitive archetype for this development.[30] The evolutionary series of barrel-vaulted forms originated in the primitive mat-covered barrel-vaulted hut and reached a climax in the Durānnī nomad tent which shows signs of becoming a new tent type.[31] The Moghôl type, though not strictly a barrel-vaulted tent, exhibits affinities with the general black tent types prevalent among the southern nomads. In general, cloth tents are confined to groups of semi-nomads and this suggests that the choice of covering is related to mobility. The tent which most resembles the Baluch barrel-vaulted tent belongs to the Achikzai tribe who are also closest to the Baluch area. After the Achikzai tents, the tents of the semi-nomadic Durānnīs come closest to the Baluch type. Related tent forms with several hoops occur amongst village dwellers west of Kandahar, tent dwelling villagers near Obeh in West Afghanistan, and in Qataghan province amongst the Moghôls.[32] Several hoops are present in the winter and spring tents of the semi-nomadic peoples in the Nauzad-Gurz valley in Southern Afghanistan.

75

The Baluchistan barrel-vaulted tent

The distinctive barrel-like appearance of the Baluchistan tent is created by the arrangement of several parallel wooden hoops embedded in the ground at right angles to the longitudinal direction of the extended roof cloth. Although the barrel-vaulted tent is connected with the Baluchs of Baluchistan, it is also found amongst Brahui nomads and as far afield as Quetta. The form of a tent type varies within limits in response to local conditions and to the seasons of the year.[33]

The Baluch tent has at least three different forms adapted to winter and summer and for travelling, and in addition, there is a spring tent which is much lighter than the winter tent. The larger heavier winter tent has normally three transverse wooden hoops, their number varies from between two and four, compared with the summer tent which has from two or three. Each hoop in the winter tent is made of two or three large irregular, curved lengths of wood lashed together. It is significant that the tents of both the Baluch and the Iforas Tuareg tribes of Southern Ayr have transverse arch supports bounded on the short sides by lines of forked stakes. These forked stakes are usually placed under the stay fastening ropes and the fastenings at each corner, but sometimes intermediate stakes are provided at each seam in the roof cloth. The awning of the summer tent is stretched between two or three forked stakes at each short side. The tent awnings are woven from dark goats' hair in strips about 100 cm wide, but in some cases a striped material, possibly wool, is also used, notably for extensions and patches.

121. Baluch barrel-vaulted summer tent near Quetta.
122. Baluch barrel-vaulted winter tent.
123. Tent of the Durānnī nomads has a special portable arch construction.

The roof cloth of the summer tent consists of two strips of material sewn together, each over a metre wide and three to four metres in length. Some tents are fitted with back cloths, but it is more common to find a cloth at one short side. Mostly, however, tattered rags are used for this purpose. These wall cloths may be draped over the inclined stays or hung haphazardly under them.

The winter tent is larger, has more hoops, is fitted with larger roof cloths that often have side and end cloths sewn or pinned on, and has more end stakes.[34] The tent awning is stressed along its length by woollen rope stays anchored to wooden pegs in the ground at the short sides. The roof cloth of the winter tent normally consists of five widths of material, over one metre wide, of which the two outermost act as side cloths. Only four forked stakes are present at each short side, and these correspond to a roof cloth with a main panel of three widths of material. The short sides may be closed by a single width of material fastened to the edge of the roof cloth with small individual wooden sticks. When, as often happens, the end cloth is replaced by the roof cloth the seams are interrupted where the forked end stakes stand under the stay ropes. The tent is surrounded by four or five oval plaited mats lined with a mixture of clay and straw. These mats which stand a little over one metre high, are secured to hoops and end stakes, and to smaller upright sticks driven into the ground. Additional protection is afforded by a low clay wall at the foot of the mats along the short sides and rear.

The careful arrangement of the interior reflects a more settled existence with longer spells in the same location.[35] The tent has a hearth, fuel stove, a clay shelf for churning skins, a sleeping platform constructed of branches, and a sheep stall. The spring tent resembles the summer tent in most respects except that it is supplied with mats and cloths on all sides in recognition of the colder season.

The Durānnī tent

The Durānnī inhabit the arid steppe land of southwestern Afghanistan from Kandahar in the east to Herat in the west, but many Durānnī are also found in northwestern and northern Afghanistan as far as Badakhshan. Two factors, the geographic proximity of the Durānnī and Baluch nomads, and the typological similarity of their tents points to a genetic connection between the two types.[36] The Baluch barrel-vaulted tent and the Durānnī tent have the following common features: hoops perpendicular to the length of the roof cloth; short forked stakes at the short sides; a uniform stay system with stay fastenings and fastening ropes; wall cloths fastened to the roof with small individual wooden pegs; and the

prevalence of plaited mats in the winter and spring tents. The only feature of the Durānnī tent not found in the Baluch tent is the T-shaped ridge support formed by the upper part of the hoop which rests on a main pole with a short cross bar.

The shape of the Durānnī tent awning is governed by the geometry of the main ridge support structure, consequently the simplification of the arch produces tents remarkably different in appearance. The variable geometry of the Durānnī awning illustrates the manner in which the widely encountered T-form might have evolved from arch supports.[37] The lower pieces of the arch are replaced by two smaller forked stakes stationed under a stay arrangement immediately opposite the T-support in summer tents in the Chahar Aimâq area and at times in the spring tent on the steppes of southern Afghanistan. This T-support may be simplified even further in Durānnī travelling tents to a single pole surmounted by a short ridge piece. After such simplification, the form is quite unlike the original barrel-vaulted tent. The simpler ridge support appears to be a more recent development than the use of hoops. Tents with several hoops are associated with semi-nomadic or more settled people who are not inconvenienced by heavier and more stable constructions.

The Moghôl tent

Almost without exception, the Moghôls use a round roofed black tent characterized by a bent centre bough. The round roof form is generated by the profile of the transverse central ridge. The profile of the Moghôl bent centre bough resembles the central arch of the Durānnī winter tent and must be considered, at least typologically, as related in form to the Baluchistan barrel-vaulted tent, but whereas the central arch of the Durānnī winter tent is a complete form, that of the Moghôl tent is incomplete and only enters the ground at the rear, the free end at the front being secured in the bent position by a slanting prop and a stay rope. Two rows of about four poles — the number varies — are driven into the ground parallel to and approximately two metres from the centre bough (120.4). These stakes jut outwards and are held in place by short stay ropes.[38]

A long *palâs*, consisting of one or several pieces of goats' hair cloth sewn together, is suspended between the two rows of side stakes. It extends from the supporting pole at the front to the point at which the bent centre pole enters the ground at the back. The roof takes its shape from the profile of the bent centre bough. Only the sides are enclosed with strips of *palâs* fastened to the roof cloth with wooden needles on the outside of the stay ropes which lead from the stakes to the ground. The entrance is located at the front of the tent, which is mostly left open, beside the front slanting pole. The circles of *čiq̃* or *čapar*, (plaited khinjah twig) matting which surround Moghôl tents are broken only near the entrance. The Moghôl tent, at least externally, bears a certain resemblance to the Lur tent and Schurmann compares it with the neighbouring Taimannî tent.[39]

Chapter 10

Tibet

The cuboid shaped Tibetan tent, unlike other black tents, has its roof awning extended almost horizontally by an unusual system of stays. Abe Huc aptly likened these tents to huge black spiders with long thin legs and gross bodies squatting, unmoving on the ground.[1] This unusual rectangular shaped tent is called *ba-nag* or 'black tent' by the pastoralists who inhabit the high plateau of Central Tibet.

The awning is made of black yak hair, or sometimes goats' hair, woven into narrow strips about 20 cm wide and sewn together with twine made of yak hair. It usually consists of two equal parts joined by means of ropes at the points above the two main poles. The awning is carried on the inside by a longitudinal ridge bar supported at either end by two upright poles.[2] A piece of bone, preferably a rib or knuckle joint, is inserted between the poles and the horizontal ridge bar. A long slit, up to 600 mm wide, is provided along the ridge bar between the two roof cloths to allow smoke from the inside fire to escape and to admit light. The roof is tensed with yak hair ropes which are secured to the edge of the awning at the sides and corners by means of several 'roots'. These cords or ropes stretch almost horizontally, sometimes even slanting upward slightly, then pass over the tip of a stake and continue down to the ground, where they are tied to pegs or even to animal horns. The long ropes resist the frequent wind storms, while the branched stay fastenings spread the wind load more evenly along the edge of the awning and avoid destructive concentrations of stress.

The four sides of the tent are closed by the awning which falls almost vertically or inclines outwards toward the ground where the lower edge is held down by iron pegs or by horns of the *Antilope hodgsoni*. The tent is frequently surrounded by a low wall of clay, grass sods, stones or cow dung, or, when it is large enough, on the inside, as protection from the wind and snow, except in the Koko-Nor area where there is little snow. Piles of leather bags, saddles and innumerable odds and ends set around the walls provide additional protection from the cold.

The interior of the tent is divided into two sections by a stove or by a woollen fabric curtain.[3] The portion of the tent to the left of the entrance is reserved for the family living which is used during the day by the women. To the right is the men's part where guests are received. In the middle of the tent there is a long narrow stove of ingenious design constructed from mud and stones with a hearth at one end and a flue running its entire length so that several pots can be heated simultaneously. The tents vary in size from modest dwellings not much more than 3 to 4·6 m long to huge specimens 15·3 m long and 9·2 m wide; the Dalai Lama's tent is reputed to hold about 300 persons.[4]

The special character of the Tibetan tent was formed by the circumstances of its evolution, and most notable among these was its early separation from the main body of black tents in the west, and its later exposure to influences deriving from the major civilized countries surrounding Tibet. The early separation of the Tibetan tent ensured the survival of archaic forms which were general at the time it reached Tibet.

The use of solid walls made of clay and stones as an integral part of the tent and of a ridge bar supported by two other poles, both of which are archaic forms, attests the primitive nature of the Tibetan nomad tent. The practice of placing a bone between the pole and the ridge bar indicates that the Tibetan ridge form evolved during an ancient period when this arrangement predominated throughout the domain of the black tent.[5] The attachment of stay ropes to the awning by several roots and the use of a type of loom to weave the roof widths common in Mongolia and on the northern frontiers of China, reveal the impact of neighbouring urban cultures on the Tibetan tent.[6]

The common origin of the Tibetan and other black tents is evident from the emphasis of the longitudinal axis and by the placement of the ridge bar underneath

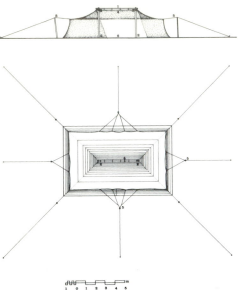

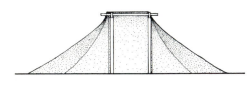

the ridge. Nevertheless the Tibetan tent is a well defined regional type which differs from Afghan and Iranian tents in a number of points; and these include awning and walls formed from one piece; a pole provided in the longitudinal axis of the awning above the ridge bar to let the smoke out; stay ropes attached to the awning by several roots and passing over outside stakes placed some distance from the tent.[7]

The black tent is unsuited to Tibet. Its presence there is explained by the dominance of cultural over geographical factors.

124. Typical Tibetan tent. Section through the ridge, top; plan, bottom. The tent cloth is in two parts: *1*, ridge bar; *2*, ridge poles; *3*, knuckle bone or similar joint, inserted between pole and ridge bar; *4*, 60 cm wide open ridge allows smoke to escape; *5*, Yak hair rope stays attached to roof cloth by several 'roots'; *6*, long narrow stone.
125. Tibetan tent from the Great Basin of Ya-long.
126. Chinese merchant's tent. Section through the ridge, top; pattern of the tent cloth, bottom: *1*, ridge bar; *2*, ridge poles.
127. Tibetan tent south of Tang-la.

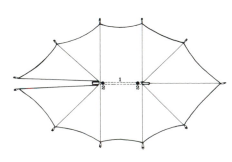

THE TENTS OF URBAN CULTURES
The early development of urban tents

Two types of tent—the parasol-roofed or bell tent and the pavilion tent—are closely identified with urban culture in a large part of the Middle East, and are distributed over a wide area, partially overlapping that in which the black tent is found. The awning of the cylindro-conical parasol-roofed tent is suspended from a single pole under the peak. The tent is made up of four elements, a central pole, a conical roof with a cylindrical wall inserted between the ground and the roof, and radial stays around the periphery of the roof.[1] The roof is tensed from the peak where it is supported at the tip of the central pole by radial stays which run from its lower edge to the ground where they are lashed to wooden pegs. Once the roof velum is erected the wall is suspended between it and the ground.

The 'pavilion', as it was called in the Middle Ages, consists of two semi-cones or parasols connected by a ridge roof. The roofs of the pavilion tent and the parasol tents are based on the cone but in the former tent the conical form is elongated by inserting a ridge between the two semi-cones.[2] Rectangular pavilion tents are covered by a hipped roof. The roof awning is tensed like a parasol by ropes which extend from its lower edge to the ground, while the walls, which incline outwards, are fitted between the roof and the ground.

The parasol and pavilion tents are similar to the black tent in many ways and this is inconsistent with the contrasting character of their respective cultures. The presence of fundamental features common to these two groups of tents makes it probable that there is a primitive connection between the black tent and the parasol and pavilion tents.[3] To begin with, the urban tent and the black tents are a type of non-skeletal prestressed membrane structure comprising a roof awning raised aloft on poles and restrained by stays anchored to the ground. Where they differ is in the material used in the velum and in the method of attaching the stays to the awning. They share a number of features and these include awnings made from woven strips sewn together with separate roof and wall cloths. Ridges are incorporated in the roofs of both the pavilion and the black tent, and awning tension is induced in the velum by means of rope stays. This tension maintains the poles in an upright position and so obviates the need to bury the poles in the ground.[4]

In all those instances where typical elements of urban tents have been detected in black tents, the extent of such borrowings is not confined to a particular regional or ethnic unit. For example, small round bearing plaques are placed on top of tent poles in the tents of North Arabian bedouin, posts divided in two pieces are prevalent in the tents of the Kurds and Lurs, and the characteristic method of attaching stays to the awning by means of several roots is present in the Tibetan black tent.

The degree of geographical and ethnic specialization of the black tent contrasts with the uniformity of the parasol-roofed and pavilion tents. The black tent, on the contrary, is divided into well defined regional types. The regional typification of the black tent is the outcome of its adjustment to particular climatic and geographical conditions, and to a way of life of a certain geographic type determined by the environment and connected to certain groups of people and to certain principal groups of nomads. There is a notable absence of regional differences in the urban tent types whose material configuration is standard and independent of geography.[5]

In spite of their vast extent, the parasol-roofed and pavilion tents present common traits over a large part of their domain. The characteristic stay rope fastened to the edge of the roof by several roots was well known in Mediaeval

Europe, in Morocco, and in Persia where it is depicted in Mediaeval miniatures. The practice of extending the stays across the roof in a nerve-like network existed in Europe in the Middle Ages, in Egypt, Iran, India and even in Central Asia. The use of poles which can be disassembled in two pieces — a distinctive urban trait — was especially widespread and occurred in Morocco, Turkey, Arabia, Iran and India. The tips of tent poles in Morocco, India and Iran were provided with small circular bearing plaques. A further development of this construction detail, the use of balls on top of the central pole to spread the tension in the velum, was popular in Mediaeval Europe, Arabia and Morocco. The practice of providing a diagonally striped border along the edge of the tent roof was current in Morocco and appears in Persian miniatures. The wide extent of these characteristically urban traits gives the impression of a form of tent which spread rapidly from a single centre in relatively recent times.

The late development of the parasol-roofed and pavilion tents, or at least their wide distribution, is attested to by the poverty of evidence prior to the Middle Ages in Europe. This difference in the character of the two groups of tents, the advanced typification of the black tent on one hand and the standardisation of the parasol-roofed and pavilion tents on the other, cannot be explained by reference to the special character of their host cultures because urban cultures are also subject to regional influences.

The uniformity of parasol-roofed and pavilion tents contrasts with the unique character of individual cities in the Middle East. Feilberg supposed that there was once a primitive connection between the black tent and the tents of urban cultures, that the two tent groups had a common origin, and it is this fact which explains the presence of common features in the two groups of tents.[6] He dismissed two other possibilities; that one group derived from the other because, as he contended, the black tent has sustained a series of modifications in the course of its development, and this must also have been the case with the tents of urban cultures. The parasol-roofed and pavilion tents may be defined as interurban archetypes whose universal character transcends regional factors.

The poverty of records depicting parasol-roofed tents and pavilions in the Ancient world is incomprehensible considering that these tents belonged to kings and soldiers. There are only three important series of representations of tents before the 13th century AD, first in 13th century BC Egypt, second in 7th century BC Assyria, but only in the 2nd century AD in Rome do the reliefs portray tent forms which even remotely resemble the pavilion tent. The absence of pictures of tents in the records of the Ancient world may be explained in one of two ways. Either the tents were not shown for some inexplicable reason, or they were not illustrated simply because they did not exist.

The connection between the tent and military activity is emphasised by the observation that nearly all the tents mentioned in the written records of the Ancient world occur in lists of spoils captured from enemy troops. The tardy spread of the tent, which was only introduced into Greece during the invasion by the Medes in c. 500 BC, is significant because it demonstrates that the tent could not have been much older in the parts close to Western Asia since the swiftness of communications would have assured its spread throughout the Mediterranean area much earlier.[7]

The development of the parasol-roofed tent may be followed through time to the opening centuries of our age; the umbrella from which it is thought to have evolved goes back much further to the first half of the third millenium BC in Assyria.[8] The pavilion of the Middle Ages and the military tents depicted on the columns of Trajan and Marcus Aurelius are of the same type. They all have a comparatively low pitched ridge roof and nearly vertical walls. The Byzantines borrowed the Roman army tent known as *papilio*.[9] The tents of the Ancient Persians and of Greece may well have been of an analogous type but this has yet to be proven.

The tents depicted in the Egyptian and Assyrian reliefs are an enigma, neither the material nor the construction is known. The analogous forms of certain nomad tents contain suggestions of how they might have been made. The Egyptian Pharaoh's tent resembles the dum palm mat-covered tents of the Tibu, and the bent centre bough construction of the Moghôl tent of Afghanistan may explain the curious semi-cupola roof forms of the royal Assyrian tents. Whatever interpretation is placed on them, the forms of the Egyptian and Assyrian tents are remote from later urban tents.

The tabernacle of the Old Testament is the earliest example of a pavilion-like form. It is thought that the Sanctuary of Israel had a low-pitched ridged roof and high vertical walls much the same as the Roman army officer's tent. Ingholt's theory that the Sanctuary of Israel developed from a skin-covered cupola-shaped dwelling[10] accords with Feilberg's contention that the black tent evolved from a type of skin covered arched dwelling. The Sanctuary had a goats' hair velum and is the oldest known example of a black tent type.

It would appear that Ancient Persia was an important centre of urban tent culture renowned for the magnificence of its royal tents whose decoration was modelled on the architecture of their royal palaces. In the prolonged warfare which characterised relations between Greece and Persia, the Greeks captured a number of Persian tents, among them being Xerxes's tent which fell into their hands at Plataea in 479 BC, while Alexander celebrated the fall of Susa (331 BC) in the defeated Persian king's tent. The Ptolemies at Alexandria erected large lavishly furnished tents which were presumably modelled after the Persian pattern. Since these tents are described as being round in shape they might well have been a kind of parasol-roofed tent.

Little is known about the Roman tent before the 1st century AD when the leather saddle shaped *papilio* type became the standard legionaries' tent. It is thought that the Romans acquired the tent from the Greek king Pyrrhus about 280 BC.[11] Trajan and Marcus Aurelius used tents of the *papilio* type with saddle roofs which resembled the pavilions of the Middle Ages.

The Byzantine armies appear to have adopted the standard Roman *papilio* army tent and it is interesting to note that Belisarius is described as having set up a rectangular ridge-roofed tent of very coarse cloth referred to as *papilio*.[12] At the end of the 6th century AD the Byzantines acquired round tents with a cupola or perhaps a parasol roof after the Turkish pattern, but there is no reason to suppose that the round tent form was unknown in the Greek Empire before the Turkish era.[13] These later tents were probably made of linen as they are described as being of whitish appearance. Ernst Rackow thought that the Byzantines were responsible for introducing the parasol-roofed tent into North Africa where it was adopted by the invading Arabs.

If we are to take the art of the time as a guide, then we must assume that the full impact of parasol-roofed and pavilion tents was delayed until the late Middle Ages in Europe and Persia. Pictures of parasol-roofed tents begin appearing in Northern Europe about the beginning of the 12th century and were widely used by the 13th century. The earliest representation of tents in Middle Eastern art occurred in Baghdad in the 14th century and by the 15th century, tents of the parasol, pavilion and *kibitka* types were prevalent in the miniature paintings of the Timurids and at Bihzad.

The introduction of tents into the subject matter of European and Persian painting during the late Middle Ages is open to a variety of interpretations. Their appearance may be explained by changes in taste and the rise of new schools of painting, Persian painting emerged only in the 14th century, or equally, it may have been brought about by the sudden appearance of tents, and certainly the effect of the Crusades and of the Mongol Invasion cannot be ignored here. In addition to their felt covered *kibitkas*, the Mongols possessed magnificent tents made either of linen or other fine materials. Parasol-roofed tents are reputed to have existed among the Ogouz nomads, the Mongol and Toughouzghouz princes and among the Fatimids.[14]

Parasol-roofed and pavilion tents appear in Italian and French paintings and abound in narratives on romantic themes such as the 'Legend of Roland' and the life of Charlemagne. The tents of the late Middle Ages are connected with court and military affairs, particularly in paintings of fêtes, tournaments and battles. Perhaps the greatest and most splendid assembly of tents took place at the meeting of Henry VIII and Francis I in 1520 on the 'Field of the Cloth of Gold', so named because of the expensive fabrics used in their construction. Tents in urban cultures were used mainly as portable palaces by warrior-princes, but it was through warfare that their gradual spread from one society to another was accomplished.

Chapter 11

The Ancient World

Egypt

The ancient records of Egypt contain references to the existence of nomad and royal Egyptian tents. The first mention of a tent occurs in the correspondence of a sixth dynasty (2625–2475 BC) Pharaoh, Pepi II[1] and it was not until Tuthmosis III (1501–1447 BC) that written documents indicate that the tent had become a part of Egyptian life.

In the era of Tuthmosis III the word 'tent' was used for both Syrian and Egyptian tents. The Egyptian words for tent are *Jm ȝ w* and *Khen*, the former applying to the Libyan tent.[2] The royal tent of Tuthmosis III is mentioned several times in *The Annals* which provides the first clear and succinct account of a military campaign.[3] During his first campaign (*c.* 1478 BC) against the Syrian coalition at Megiddo, Tuthmosis III captured the son of the king of Kadesh in his tent.[4] Included among the spoils of Megiddo were 'seven poles of (myr) wood, wrought with silver, belonging to the tent of that foe',[5] and a further 'six tent poles, wrought with bronze and set with costly stones' were taken after the fall of the Zahi towns during the ninth campaign eleven years later.[6] Evidently, the richly decorated Syrian tent poles were prized by the Egyptians.

128. Rameses's camp near Kadesh (*c.* 1285 BC) as depicted at the Ramesseum (1), in Luxor (2) and Abu-Simbel (3). 129. Interior of Rameses's enclosure from the Abu-Simbel relief.

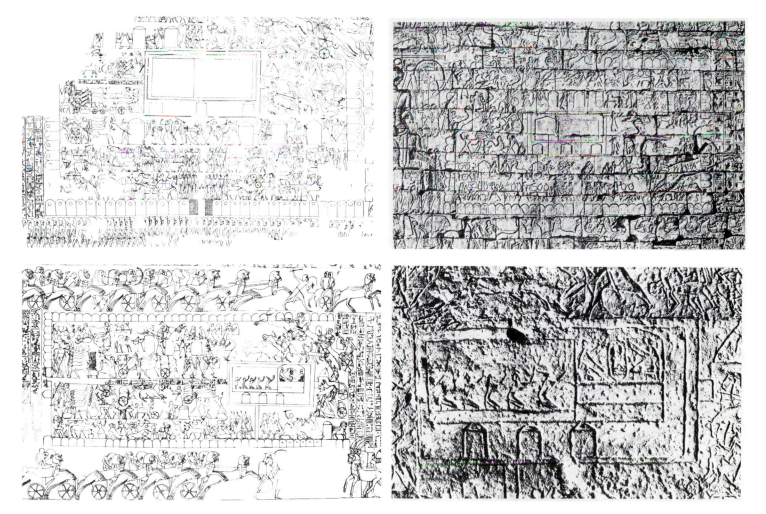

85

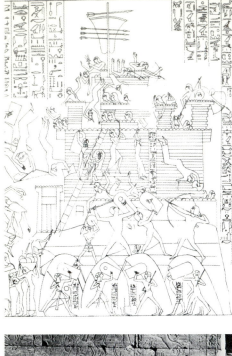

Reliefs at the Ramesseum, Abu-Simbel and Luxor depict Rameses II's advance camp northwest of Kadesh[7] where in *c.* 1285 the young Pharaoh narrowly avoided defeat when the Hittite King Muwatallis surprised him forward of his camp. These illustrations of the Egyptian camp show that it was laid out with two precincts defined by three rectangular barriers, the camp proper being surrounded by an outer palisade of round-topped leather shields and the royal precinct consisting of an outer zone containing three tents and the royal enclosure with Rameses's tent and an adjoining ante-room. The royal enclosure, longitudinal and transverse roads of Rameses II's camp near Kadesh would appear to be equivalent to the *praetorium*, the *via principalis*, and the *via praetoria* of the later Roman marching camp. The form of the tents is conjectural.

A splendid relief at the Ramesseum depicts Rameses's four sons standing in front of four tents while the Pharaoh's forces storm a fortress in the Tabor region during the reconquest of Northern Palestine (*c.* 1282 BC).[8] From the relief which depicts three of the tents in side elevation, and the other in rear elevation, it is clear that they are quite different from those in the Kadesh encampment. The curiously convexly-curved tent sheath is supported by two inclined poles, the whole resembling the upturned bows of a small boat rather than a tent. The openness of the tents on one side is consistent with their function as sun and wind shelters. The tents were probably constructed of light reed or dum palm mats, but the material used for the covering and the method of construction remain unknown.[9]

Palestine
The desert sanctuary

The Israelites adopted the tent as their sanctuary which later became the tabernacle in Christian literature. In Hebrew this tent is called *ohel mô 'ed* which means the tent of reunion, or of meeting.[10] The discovery of a Midianite tent at Timna, the first of its kind, provides a possible connection with the tent-shrine of Israel's desert wanderings, the tent of meeting.[11] Yahweh, who at this time was thought of as being invisible, dwelt among his people in a tent.[12] Indeed the cult of Yahweh may have been of Kenite Midianite origin.

The Midianites returned to Timna for a short time after the Egyptians had ceased mining the copper in the area about the second half of the 12th century BC. They altered the abandoned Hathor temple structure, removed votive gifts, sculptures, inscriptions and Hathor sculptures from the court and converted it into a tent-covered shrine. An investigation of the Hathor temple site uncovered large quantities of a heavy red and yellow cloth consisting of well woven wool and flax decorated with beads.[13] Thick masses of the cloth were found lying on the inside of the low temple walls and also outside the temple court. The presence of this cloth of varying tints of red and yellow puzzled archaeologists until two stone-lined pole-holes were uncovered while clearing the floor. It is thought that these holes were made to secure the poles of a large tent which, during the final phase, had covered the temple court. A tentative reconstruction of the Midianite tent-shrine indicates a bedouin-like tent canopy, supported by four lines of four poles, open at the entrance.[14]

In pre-Islamic times bedouin tribes carried about with them in their wanderings a little sacred tent of red leather (*qubba*) in which the stone idols of the tribe were kept. The *qubba* was carried on the backs of camels in religious processions and in combat; in camp it was set up beside the Sheikh's tent. This pre-Islamic Arab *qubba* itself had semitic antecedents, thus in Carthaginian camps a sacred tent was set up near the chief's tent and a bas-relief from Palmyra dating from the first

130. Rameses's four sons standing in front of arched tents at the storming of the Hittite fortress of Zapur (*c.* 1282 BC): *1*, drawing of a relief in the Ramesseum at Thebes, 1290–1223 BC; *2*, detail of relief depicting the princes' tents.

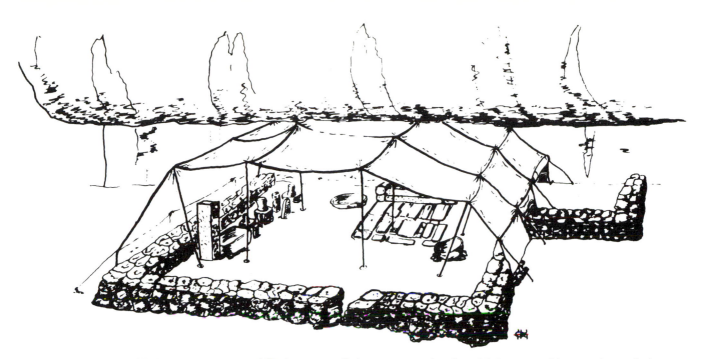

131. Midianite tented shrine, the Hathor temple at Timna, 12th century BC.

century AD shows a religious procession in which a camel is carrying a little tent still bearing traces of red paint.[15]

From the 13th century onwards, caravans making the pilgrimage to Mecca from Damascus or Cairo were led by a camel carrying a *mahmal*, a small cubic tent containing a copy of the Koran. Although it is not certain that the *mahmal* was related to the *'utfa* of bedouin tribes, it is quite certain that the modern *'utfa* is a continuation of a pre-Islamic institution, the *qubba*.[16]

It is reasonable to suppose that during their nomadic life the ancestors of the Israelites had a portable sanctuary, similar in form and construction to their dwellings. The tent of reunion was set up on the plains of Moab for the last time before the Israelites' entry into the promised land and this is the last indisputable mention of it. Much of the description in Exodus is merely an idealization of the desert sanctuary conceived as a demountable temple exactly half as big as the temple of Jerusalem.[17] Even though it was no longer the tent of reunion, the tent under which David is said to have placed the ark in Jerusalem is meant to recall the desert sanctuary. The tent had become such a potent symbol that even after the ancestors of the Israelites had settled in Canaan it continued to serve as a reminder of their former nomadic existence.

Assyria
The house of the plain

Mesopotamia supported a mixture of nomadic types ranging from semi-nomads and sheep- and camel-herders who camped on the steppe and owned land in the valley, to sedentary agriculturalists.[18] Fluctuations in rainfall shifted the boundary — usually taken as the 254 mm isohyet — between the peasant and the nomad, sometimes forcing the latter to leave his traditional lands and seek a settled existence.[19] It is possible that the presence of tents within the walls of Assyrian fortifications and cities in the palace bas-reliefs at Nimrud and Nineveh provides a glimpse of this gradual infiltration of urban life by nomads affected by desiccation of the steppe. The identification of the tent with the steppe by the Assyrians is apparent in their repeated references to the 'house of the plain'.[20] The Assyrian words for tent are *bit seri, kustaru, seru* and *zaratu*.[21] The Temanites, the Aramean tribes who settled in Babylonia, the Elaminites, the Kassites, the Sutu and the Arabian tribes are mentioned in the ancient records of Assyria and Babylonia as possessing tents.[22]

Sargon's royal tent, depicted in a bas-relief with three other tents each supported by a central pole,[23] is set within the oval fortification of his camp which is bisected by a road. This relief introduces the two types of tent used by the Assyrians, the so-called 'royal tent' consisting of a roughly rectangular form surmounted at both ends by two quadrant-shaped bonnets (semi-cupola tent), and the more usual type which has an ogee profile supported by a strutted central pole. The walls of the semi-cupola tent are either vertical or slightly inclined and the two semi-cupola vaults, usually of different dimensions, are depicted in profile — the outer side being part of a circle. The vertical walls of the vaults face each other across a flat roof. An inscription above Sennacherib's royal pavilion in a relief of the king before the city of Lachish declares that it is 'the tent (or *sarata*) of Sennacherib'.[24] Layard justified this interpretation of the inscription by noting that the pavilion is supported by ropes.[25] The lower portion of Sargon's royal tent is covered with ornamental square units similar in pattern to the small metal plates sewn on the leather tunics of archers and cavalrymen. The addition of metal armour sewn on the outside of the royal tent was no doubt intended to discourage assassins and might indicate that the tent cover was of leather.

Sennacherib's tent is illustrated in great detail and there is no indication of metal armour. The wall of his tent is supported by five unevenly spaced posts guyed at right angles by ropes and beneath the smaller of the two semi-cupolas there is a small rectangular opening which may have served as a door. Contenau asserts that the royal tent 'was covered, like a modern perambulator, with a moveable canopy adjustable against wind and sun'.[26]

Devices for promoting ventilation are found in the tents and tepees of the Northern Arabian nomads, the Scandinavian Lapps and the North American

132. Sargon's oval fortified camp.
133. Drawing of the relief *Sennacherib before the city of Lachish,* Nineveh, Palace of Sennacherib (BM No. 124909).

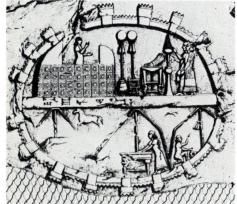

134. The royal tent of Sennacherib, before Lachish.
135. Sennacherib's fortified camp. No. 9 Ch. B, Kuyunjik.

Indians, so it would not be surprising if the Assyrians had used a convertible roof to encourage air circulation within the semi-cupola tent. It is probable that the arrangement of the semi-cupola tent derived from the traditional court house plan and that the semi-cupola vaults cover the living areas which are separated by an open court. The rectangular door gave access to a guard room beneath the small vault while the king's chamber was located at the opposite end of an open court beneath the large vault.[27] The Baluchistan barrel-vaulted tent of Iran may offer a clue as to the derivation of the Assyrian tent.

References to tents proliferate in the reign of Sennacherib (705–687 BC). Several bas-reliefs from Nineveh provide a vivid picture of the organisation and everyday life in Sennacherib's fortified camps. Layard concluded that the Assyrians were accustomed to dwelling in tents within the walls of their cities, a practice he had observed in many Eastern towns.[28] Alternatively, the ground plans of circular or oval fortifications could represent fortified camps rather than cities.

Three semi-cupola tents or 'houses' and seven strutted tents are enclosed within the walls of a captured city in a relief entitled *The King seated on his throne within the walls of a Captured City*.[29] A vizir and two eunuchs holding fans attend the king who sits on his throne in front of the royal pavilion. The secondary bonnets of some semi-cupola tents have been lowered in height so that they no longer project above the roof line and form a continuous curve tangential to the wall and roof lines. The suppression of the secondary bonnet in the semi-cupola tent form indicates that it was not an important functional element and raises doubts about the convertible action of the bonnet structure.

The seven strutted tents consist of a curved envelope supported on a central mast with two branches, each of which terminates in a fork. The thick tent covering forms an ogee profile with a rounded peak, and the steep sides are steadied by guy ropes attached to pegs, the flexible covering material hanging in a gentle curve. The limp covering could be any one of a variety of materials: woven fabric, felt, hide, reed mats, wattles, and perhaps even small branches. The three tents in Sargon's camp are similar in shape to strutted tents but lack the twin struts. The artistic convention of representing strutted tents in profile reveals the interior as it would appear in a sectional view.

Contenau considered that the strutted tents were round in plan with a central stake for a tent pole, not unlike the primitive circular type of Mesopotamian hut.[30] Remains of circular huts found in strata representing the earliest human occupation

89

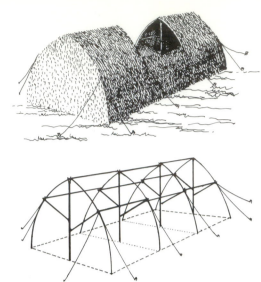

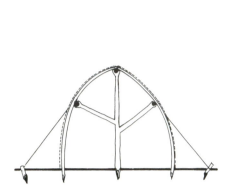

136. Reconstruction of the frame of a composite semi-cupola and strutted Assyrian tent by Max Ringelmann.
137. An Arab tent burning, Nineveh, Palace of Ashbanipal BM No. 124927.
138. Drawing of a relief entitled *Chariots and attendants of Sennacherib and a castle on a mountain.*
139. Camp scene, orderly in a tent.
140. Reconstruction by Charles Chipiez of a pavilion depicted in the relief *The Interior of a Castle, and a Pavilion or Tent*, Nimrud.
141. Detail of relief in 138.

together with vases of much later date indicate that these primitive Mesopotamian huts consisted of a circular exterior wall bent over and fastened to a central post, forming a vaulted framework which was covered with matting.[31] The most likely explanation of the strutted tents is that they represent a primitive form of black tent belonging to Arab bedouin, viewed from the short side, and consisting of a central row of poles with two lines of struts springing from the main poles, or possibly, since the tent profile has been condensed, two rows of front and back poles.

While it must be acknowledged that the two tent forms could merely be the side view and cross section of the same tent form, a thesis which is supported by Herzfeld and Ringelmann,[32] the accuracy of the Assyrian reliefs makes it difficult to believe that they represent the same form. The precise geometry of the semi-cupola tent, composed of straight lines, rectangles and arcs, contrasts with the free curved profile of the strutted tent.

Reliefs from Ashurbanipal's palace (NW) at Nineveh, illustrating incidents in his ninth campaign (644–636 BC) against the Arabs, graphically record the brutal slaughter of Arab tribesmen and the destruction by fire of their tents.[33] The bedouin tents in Ashurbanipal's reliefs are identical with the Assyrian strutted tent, a fact that raises the possibility of the reliefs being a misleading depiction of Northern Arabian tents. The resemblance of the Assyrian strutted tent and the black tent may indicate that the arched hut which Feilberg proposed was the common ancestor of the *kibitka* and the black tent is to be found in the Assyrian strutted tent. The two semi-cupola tents and five strutted tents in the relief, *Chariot and attendants of Sennacherib, and a castle on a mountain*, one of a series believed to represent the siege of Lachish, are not conspicuously different from those already described.[34]

A third type of Assyrian pavilion is illustrated in a relief of Shalmaneser III (858–824 BC) entitled *The interior of a Castle and a Pavilion or Tent*[35] in which he is depicted as installed before a besieged city. The richly embroidered tent canopy is supported by columns probably of painted wood. The pavilion would most likely have consisted of four columns in a rectangular plan, however, the two reliefs show

it with either two or three columns. In all probability the tent canopy would have been stretched over diagonal or transversely bowed wooden members and held together by horizontal ties between the columns.

Persia and Greece

The fabulous tents of the Achaemenid kings and Satraps were probably inspired by royal Assyrian tents, and not by a local nomadic prototype, for at that time the nomads played a relatively unimportant role and were restricted to a much smaller area than they occupy today.[36] The Medes would have known of Assyrian tents from their invasion of Assyria in 614 which culminated in the storming and destruction of Nineveh at the end of the summer of 612.

The Achaemenid kings of the 6th century BC possessed extremely fine Assyrian tents, and this could well have influenced their idea of the type of tentage befitting a great monarch. Herodotus[37] and Xenophon[38] refer to the tents belonging to Xerxes, Mardonius, Cyrus II, Cyazares II, Cyrus the Younger, the Satrap of Sardis Tissaphernes, the Satrap of Lydia Tirabazu, and Artapatas. The fabulous tent of Xerxes captured by the Greeks at Plataea was merely an outstanding example of this tradition.

Very little is known about the form and decoration of ancient Persian tents. They were large and impressive, and imitated Persian palace architecture.[39] The tent of Xerxes was no simple shelter, but an elaborate complex with quarters for his retainers, banquet hall and kitchen. The royal pavilion, at least in its main facade, resembled the permanent palace at Susa.[40] The tents in the camp entrusted to Mardonius by Xerxes before he fled Greece, were adorned with gold and silver and decorated with gaily coloured tapestries. They were furnished with couches and tables, gilded and plated with silver or gold. Even Xerxes's horse was housed in a tent.

The formation of the Greek word for tent, σκηνή and the absence of any word with this specific meaning prior to the Persian invasion in 480 BC could explain the origin of Greek tents. The absence of a word denoting tent in Homer indicates that the Greeks did not have tents at that time and the word σκηνή only became common with the introduction of Persian tents into Greece after the battle of Plataea in 479.[41] The Greek word for tent, σκηνή appears to have originated in the early 5th century, about the time when the tent of Xerxes was a much discussed object of curiosity. At first the word σκηνή may have had an exotic and specifically Persian connotation, but later it was applied to the scene-building of the Odeon theatre and became the name of the theatre *skene*.[42] The few references to tents that do in fact occur in Greek literature are usually found in a Persian context.

The tent used by Alexander for his banquet at Susa is reported to have belonged to the Persian king. This magnificent tent consisted of a sumptuous gold embroidered canopy supported on fifty golden masts.[43]

The royal σκηνή of Ptolemy II at Alexandria, described by Athenaeus who quotes Callixeinus of Rhodes, shows how closely such luxurious tents imitated the details of stone architecture.[44] This vast festive pavilion had a circular scarlet canopy over the middle of the symposium and was decorated with a profusion of motifs.

Even though no formal proof has been found to confirm Broneer's theory connecting the Greek theatre *skene* with the tent of Xerxes, it seems probable that the Persian connection was crucial to the development of the Greek *skene*. Broneer's theory depends on a number of concurrences following the Persian defeat at Plataea in 479 BC.[45] The tent of Xerxes may have been brought to Athens where two new plays by Phrynichus and Aeschylus, *The Phoenician Woman* (*c.* 476 BC) and *The Persians* (*c.* 473 BC) — both of which had scenes in Susa — were about to be performed. Xerxes's elaborate tent imitating Persian palace architecture would have served admirably as temporary scenery for the two plays. Xerxes's tent is supposed to have determined the shape of the odeum, while the facade of the later stone *skene* demonstrates a striking resemblance to Persian Palace architecture. At about this time the name 'tent' came to denote the scene building itself, which constituted the background to the plays. The survival into the 4th century BC of the practice of setting up temporary tents in agoras for the presentation of tragedies strengthens the association of tents with the Greek theatre.[46]

Rome
Military tents

The comprehensive standardization and dimensional coordination of Roman army tents and marching camps further confirms the Roman predilection for order. Three types of Roman army tents, the *papilio* or 'butterfly' tent of the rank and file, a taller officer's tent having a low pitched gabled roof, and a still larger commander's marquee, are depicted in the reliefs on Trajan's column.[47] The method of packing and pitching the legionaries and auxilaries' bivouac tent gave rise to its name *papilio* or 'butterfly' tent. The leather tent membrane was unrolled from a long caterpillar-like roll and pitched by spreading the sides from a central ridge, like a butterfly emerging from its chrysalis and spreading its wings. The tent membrane was fabricated from standard 0·5 m rectangular pieces of calf leather assembled lengthwise in six parallel strips consisting of seven standard panels, three panels on each side with one panel spanning the ridge, thus avoiding a seam.[48] The roof membrane of the small *papilio* tent is suspended at 45 degrees from a central ridge centred on a 3·3 m square base. The *incrementum tensurae*, or additional 0·3 m space for pitching, produced a tent wall or fly 0·3 m high. Some means of rolling up the flies for ventilation would be needed in a tent of this size accommodating eight men.[49] The 2 m high central ridge is supported by at least two uprights within the tent fabric.

The discovery of leather fragments, later identified as constituent parts of Roman tents, at Birdoswald and Newstead yielded detailed information about the pattern and fabrication of Roman tents. Fragments of leather unearthed at Birdoswald in 1931–32 were found to be sections of standard rectilinear panels used in these structures. Leather found at Newstead included a variety of panels resembling those from Birdoswald together with guy-rope fasteners and triangular cross stays from the gable ends with guy-rope fasteners still attached to them.[50] The skin used both at Birdoswald and at Newstead is natural calf approximately 2 mm thick and dressed for a naturally grained surface. Calf skins were preferred for their pliability, workability, consistent thickness and size, and absence of flaws. The leather is always fabricated with the grain or external skin on the outside, and the pile velvet facing inwards. It has been deduced from stitch holes in the surviving leather fragments that six types of stitches were employed and that the panels forming the main tent-cover were joined by a durable and waterproof welted seam.[51]

The tent floor was littered with either new-mown grass or straw, on which the soldiers slept.[52] The Roman troops at Masada, AD 71, pitched their tents on 1·3 m high stone walls which afforded some protection against diurnal extremes of temperature.[53] Traces of three-sided couches or *triclinium* made of earth and stone on which the legionaries slept and dined were found at Camp B.

At Cawthorn, turf screens used to keep Roman tents dry show that the tents of centurions or decurions were about 6·6 m square: and the *de munitionibus castrorum* allots two *papilio* widths to one of these.[54] The centurion's tent-covering of standard leather panels was carried on a rectilinear framework of poles and slats surmounted by a low-pitched gabled roof. This roof had an elaborate

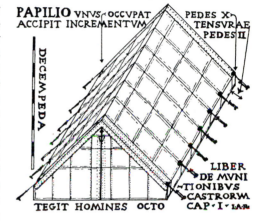

142. Reconstruction of a *papilio* tent.

over-fall, to which loops for guy ropes were attached. These tents were furnished with a dining table and couches and the floor covered with cut turf. They were entered through leather flaps in the front and these are sometimes depicted laced right back to the corner of the tent.[55]

The tent of the Commander (either a tribune or a consul) which is shown as being larger and higher than the centurion's tent on Trajan's column, was lightened by enclosing the walls with side-curtains of cloth. The roof and over-fall were fabricated from the usual standard calf leather panels. Livy gives the dimensions of a similar tent at 65·6 m square.[56] The low pitched roof of the commander's tent caused Josephus, who was probably thinking of the tabernacle, to compare its outline with that of a temple.

The essence of the Roman marching camp is its repeatability. The standardization and comprehensive dimensional coordination of its elements aimed at the creation of a simple memorable pattern which could be repeated on any reasonably flat site within a matter of hours. The standard 0·5 m leather panels served as a module extending from the smallest details in the design of *papiliones* to the layout of groups of tents in maniples and the disposition of sites and streets to accommodate up to two legions. The legionaries' tents were grouped in maniples consisting of sixteen *papiliones* and two centurion's tents arranged in two rows.[57] Since sixteen men were always on guard duty only eight tents were required to house the eighty men in a legionary century.[58] The area allotted to a maniple varied from 33 × 33 m in Republican times to 20 × 40 m, or half an actus, in the Empire.[59]

143. Roman tents depicted in reliefs on Trajan's column.
144. Maniple of double row of tents in a marching camp accommodating two centuries.

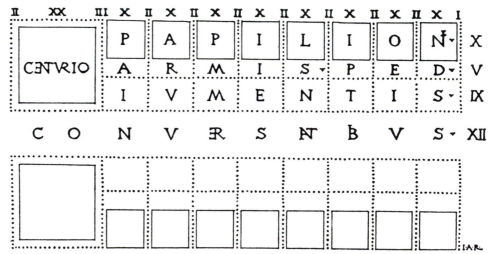

Convertible roofs

Gladiatorial contests were banned from the Pompeii amphitheatre by an outraged senate for ten years following an ugly brawl between rival factions which caused the deaths of many visitors in 59 BC.[60] This event is recorded in a Pompeiian fresco now in Naples which also shows a *vela* or awning suspended over the narrow southwest side of the amphitheatre, where the ladies' boxes were situated, between two towers of the city wall.[61] The *velum* fabric hung from nine parallel spars, which appear to be suspended by means of eyelets from three vertical masts immediately behind the *velum* roof. The generally accepted opinion, one not shared by Rainer Graefe,[62] is that this view of the *vela* is incomplete, because the front portion of the roof seems to have been omitted in order to expose the interior of the amphitheatre.

A comparison of the fresco *vela* with the Pompeii amphitheatre reveals a somewhat naive depiction of the *vela* marred by inaccuracies and distortions. The large theatre at Pompeii has two rows of corbels for fixing the vertical masts from which the *velum* was suspended. Another fresco at Pompeii shows a simple device for transporting a loosely draped cloth along tensioned ropes. [63] The rectangular cloth element, possibly a small sun awning, is suspended from two parallel ropes on rings at each corner. The cloth is pulled along the primary ropes and tensed by means of two additional ropes fastened to each ring. Public inscriptions advertising forthcoming games at the amphitheatre mention the extension of the *velum* with the words 'erunt vela' as a special attraction. [64]

An inscription in Ephesus[65] gives the Greek name 'Petasos', a broad brimmed hat, to the Roman *vela* or *velarium* which are reputed to have originated in Campania.[66] Almost eleven years before the riot at Pompeii, Quintus Catulus is credited with the invention of linen awnings or roofs over theatres in 70 BC.[67] Although no direct evidence exists, the association of fabric structures with the Greek and Roman theatres suggests that the Roman theatre *velum* may have developed from the Greek theatre *skene*. [68]

The occurrence of shade roofs and awnings was much more general than references to theatre and amphitheatre *vela* might indicate. Pliny states that cloth awnings were widely used to shade forums, streets and the inner courts of houses as well as theatres and amphitheatres.[69] Caesar placed sun awnings over the entire Roman Forum and the via Sacra from his mansion and the Clivus to the Capitol.[70] The Roman fondness for ostentatious display reveals itself in the elaborate decoration of brightly coloured cloth *vela*. For example, the Emperor Nero suspended a sky-blue cloth *velum*, decorated with embroidered stars, on ropes over his amphitheatre.[71] On another occasion, he placed purple curtains, embroidered with a representation of himself driving a chariot through the heavens surrounded by golden stars, over a theatre.[72]

The Roman use of coloured linen and their extension and retraction by sailors connects these roofs with seafaring.[73] *Velum* in latin means sail. Margarete Bierber states that sailors manipulated the Collosseum *velum* from a broadwalk on top of the outer wall.[74] Theatres were covered by yellow, red and purple curtain *velum* suspended over poles and beams.[75] White linen was preferred for most purposes, but red awnings were used in the inner courts of houses.[76]

The construction of *velum* roofs remains the subject of academic speculation despite reconstructions by Fontana, Cariste, Choisy and Gaudet, among others. Rainer Graefe undertook (1970) to resolve previous difficulties by applying recent findings on the design and construction of modern convertible roofs to existing evidence.[77] *Vela* roofs are assumed to have consisted of a cloth awning suspended beneath radial or parallel cables. The theatres at Aspendus, Ephesus, Orange, Ostia, Patara, the large theatre at Pompeii, and the Pompey theatre in Rome; and the amphitheatres at Capua, Nimes, Pompeii, Pula and the Colosseum are all thought to have possessed *vela* roofs.[78] Vitruvius cites a tow contrivance for transporting the velum which could be assembled quickly, but 'because of the difficult relationships—required a great deal of mechanical engineering knowledge and design ability of the architect'.[79]

Vela roofs were suspended on ropes from vertical wooden masts mounted on sets of stone brackets which are still to be found on the facades of some theatres and amphitheatres. Examples of stone brackets may be observed on top of the exterior walls of the Colosseum in Rome, and those of the theatres at Orange and Aspendus.[80] The wooden masts were supported by two projecting stone brackets,

145. Fresco of the Pompeii amphitheatre and the riot of AD 59 in which a *vela* or awning is suspended over the narrow south-western side where the ladies' boxes were situated.

146. Stone brackets on top of the exterior wall of the Verona arena for attaching the wooden masts of a *velum* convertible roof.
147. Cozzo's reconstruction of the *velum* roof of the Colosseum, Rome.

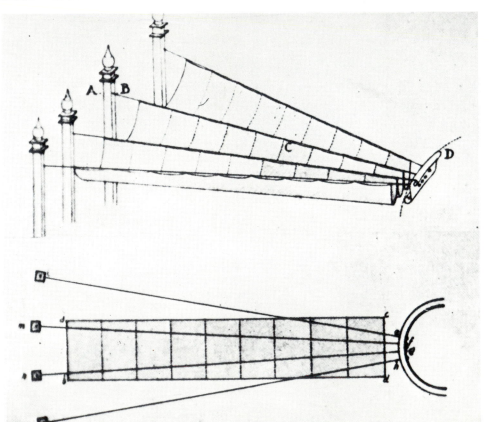

148. The *velum* roof of the theatre at Orange was suspended from timber masts fixed to stone brackets on the rear wall of the theatre.

one above the other. The masts were inserted through a round or rectangular hole, approximately 30 cm in diameter, and rested in a recess of similar size in the lower bracket.

Two types of cable supporting structure — parallel or radial — are usually assumed in reconstructions of Roman *vela* roofs. The *velum* over the Colosseum is thought to have been suspended from a radial system of cables stretched between masts on the periphery and an unsupported annular cable over the centre. The cables were assembled on the floor of the arena and then elevated to the desired height by tensioning the radial cables.[81] These radial cables were hauled over pulleys at the periphery mastheads simultaneously, using windlasses. An oculate opening, similar to the eye in the Pantheon dome, would have been made large to save material and to avoid a too acutely triangular pattern of cables. The Colosseum *velum* probably bunched peripherally. The roof elements were pulled along converging cables towards the inner annular ring where they hung loosely. A radial system of cables was probably adapted to cover theatres by employing a semi-circular edge cable instead of an annular cable. As shown by Cariste in his reconstruction of the orange theatre *vela*, this change in plan shape would have required an elaborate cable construction to anchor the semi-circular edge cable.[82]

The convertibility of Roman *velum* roofs arose from their inability to construct permanent roofs capable of withstanding strong winds and heavy precipitation, rather than from any preference for opening up the amphitheatres during pleasant weather. These remarkable convertible roofs spread throughout the Roman Empire and were unrivalled in size until the advent of modern convertible roofs in the mid-20th century.

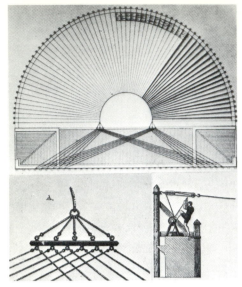

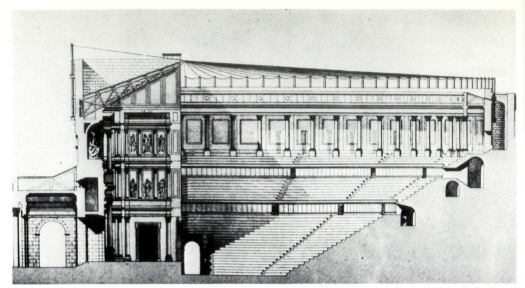

149. Caristie's reconstruction of the *velum* roof of the theatre at Orange.

The Middle Ages and Renaissance

The tents of the Persian miniatures

The accurate reproduction of details in Persian painting is subservient to the decorative scheme; realism tends to be overwhelmed by the imperatives of style. In interpreting such highly stylized painting it is important to recognize the ways in which the artist's processes of composition and technique distort the subject. A considerable amount of the architecture, including tents, depicted in Persian miniatures is fanciful, harmonising in a decorative way with the main subject of the painting, and even when working directly from a model, the Mussulman artist is not especially concerned about realism. The actual shape of the miniature, which is higher than it is wide, results in the lateral compression of the tent profile. This effect is particularly noticeable in the many *kibitkas* that are reproduced. The structural details too are often misrepresented, for even the poles may be wrongly placed or omitted altogether.

Persian painting emerged in the 14th century as a consequence of collision of Chinese influences (which came to Persia with the Mongols) with Ancient Iranian art (which was related in turn to Sassanid art).[1] The oldest school of painting was associated with the Arab milieu of Mesopotamia but spread later to Iran and parts of Turan. To a great extent Persian painting was an art of the court associated with two princely houses in particular; the Timurids of the 15th century, and the Safarids of the 16th century. The best tent reproductions are found in the more ancient original miniature paintings and the works of lesser known local artists who tended to reproduce regional tent types.[2] With more ancient paintings there is less risk that they are copied or traced works.

The *kibitka* is the predominant tent depicted in Persian miniatures where it is identified with princes and the upper classes. They begin to be represented only with the opening of the Mongol period, and appear to be lacking altogether in the oldest miniatures of the Baghdad school.[3] This is to be expected since the *kibitka* is an element of Turan and Central Asian culture. In Rashid-al-din's *History of the World* which has survived in several early 14th century illustrated copies, the *kibitkas* are depicted with narrow bands and trellis walls; similar illustrations occur during the Timurid period.

The *kibitka* of the Mongol Khan was called *Altyn Orda* or 'golden palace' because it was made of particularly rare felt and partly covered with cloth of gold or thin sheets of gold.[4] Indian painters were unable to imagine what the Mongol's gold tent looked like and they therefore painted a large decorated tent, *Khargah*, but whereas the Mongol *kibitka* was simply furnished with several wooden beds covered with furs, a few tables and an open fire, the Mughal painters depicted interiors with red and gold hangings draped in rich folds and luxurious rugs on the floor. Mughal artists transformed the Mongol tent into a magnificent palace hall.

Two trends may be discerned in the Bihzad and Herat schools' rendering of *kibitkas*. Firstly, there are reproductions of magnificent *kibitkas* covered with richly ornamented fabrics, which have an onion shaped cupola which rises abruptly from the perpendicular wall. The bulbous shape of these *kibitka* roofs may have arisen from an analogy with the swollen outline of Persian domes. Reproductions of this kind continued to appear throughout the period of the ancient Safarids. Secondly, the tendency for realistic reproduction of certain details of the *kibitkas* is connected with schools situated on the Turkish border where the *kibitka* is the typical tent.[5] These renderings show the trellis walls, wattle and straw mats and door framing.

Other tent forms reminiscent of the black tents of the Arab Bedouin and the Lurs accompany both types of *kibitkas*. Illustrations of black tents with awnings divided in two parts along the ridge, and a hint of a circular plate on top of the pole occur in the manuscript of *Makamat a Hariri*, Vienna (1334).[6]

150. A magnificent *kibitka* covered with richly embroidered fabrics.

151. Open pavilions and parasol-roofed tents with circular bearing plates mounted on the tent poles appear in illustrations from the *Genghis Khan Miniatures* (c. 1596).

152. Dark brown ridge tents and parasol-roofed tents occur in Mir Sayyid Ali's painting, *Majnun brought in chains to Layla's tent*, 1539–43.

Opposite page

153. *Majnun before Layla's tent*, copy of Jami's *Haft Aurang*, 1556–1565 in Meshed.

154. Parasol-roofed tents and a pavilion in a 13th century miniature of besieging soldiers leaving a fortress to attack an enemy camp.

155. The tents in Muhammadi's sketch *Life in the Country*, Isfahan, AD 1578, possess T-shaped ridge poles.

Certain themes in Persian miniature painting relate to tents: magnificent *kibitkas* abound in miniatures depicting the exploits of Genghis Khan and Mongol princes; sometimes open pavilions with circular plates on top of the two poles occur beside *kibitkas* in the *Genghis Khan miniatures*. Tents with forms suggestive of the black tents of Arab bedouins and the Lurs are prevalent in miniatures illustrating the story of Layla and Majnun and in the 16th century genre paintings depicting scenes from life in nomad camps. Parasol-roofed tents are encountered in 16th century miniatures, particularly those of the Tabriz school.

The enduring popularity of Nizamis's poem of Layla and Majnun is shown by the numerous copies which appeared between the 15th and 17th centuries, and the scene depicting the arrival of Majnun, disguised as a beggar, at Layla's camp was frequently reproduced. A variety of tents appear in the miniatures. The parasol-roofed tent with sloping or vertical walls is often included in the company of the conical tent which has the awning suspended from a single central pole, and a ridge-shaped tent supported at the extremities of the longitudinal ridge by two inclined poles. With the exception of the parasol-roofed tent, the tents have low walls or none at all.

The tent of the Lurs is recalled in two illustrations from the Manuscript of Nizanni in the British Museum (Or 6810)[7]. These tents are depicted with a dark awning draped over a ridge pole indicated by the straight ridge line. Walls are of wattle and large eyelets are provided for the ropes. Both the ropes and pegs are clearly delineated. The conical tents in the second illustration are particularly interesting. In one tent a brief ridge is carried on two crossed poles, and it may be presumed that a short ridge piece rests on the tips of the two poles. In the other tent the single central pole appears to carry a short cross piece.

Both these forms of ridge support can be observed in Tunisia, Southwestern Morocco and Mauritania. Two longish dark brown tents with saddle-shaped roofs

are pictured by Mir Sayyid Ali in *Majnun brought in chains to Layla's tent* from the *Nizanni Khamsa* (1539–43), (BM, Or 2265).[8] Three features may be noted: the entrances are placed at the short ends of the saddle roof, a number of short stay ropes are attached to the lower edge of the awning and there is a suggestion of round plates on the pole top.

In another miniature of *Majnun before Layla's tent*, this time a copy of Jami's *Haft Aurang*,[9] a parasol-roofed tent, a *kibitka*, several baldachins and a conical tent are brilliantly interwoven in a remarkable painting of the Safarid period (*c*. 1565), which brought the Kazvin style to perfection. The painting is a mixture of decorative fantasy and extraordinary realism of detail; the poles and ropes are omitted from the tents, the parasol-roofed tent has a smoke hole covered by a rectangular flap and the central pole is made of two pieces. The exquisite conical tent has a short crossbar on top of the centre pole which sticks out beyond the awning whose edge is finished with a rope.

The earliest representation of a pavilion is a Bihzad miniature dating back to about 1490,[10] but a similar type of military tent occurs in a 13th century miniature. The soldiers of Tamberlaine's army slept at night in tents housing eighteen men, although the elite troops slept five to a tent, and each officer had his own tent.

The placement of openings in the pavilion is not fixed. There are two solutions; the openings may be shown on the long side or at the gable on the short side. The method of supporting each end of the ridge is of considerable interest because these details, which are repeated in many miniatures, are only met in the tents of Arabs and some North African nomads. The two ridge poles are topped by a short bar or circular plate joined to the awning by a decorative cloth or leather reinforcing piece. The poles are raised so that they are approximately perpendicular to the slanting bearing pieces, and the tent is extended longitudinally by long guy ropes running from the tip of each pole to the ground. The two tents in a drawing *Life in the Country*, by Muhammadi (AD 1578),[11] in the Louvre, appear to have much the same kind of T-shaped ridge bars as those in the manuscript of Nizanni. The ridges of ridge tents are rarely supported by a ridge bar and hang in a gentle arc between the two ridge poles, but an occasional straight ridge line suggests the presence of a ridge bar.

Mir Sayyid Ali's *Life in the Camp* (*c*. 1540)[12] depicts a marvellous array of tents in what amounts almost to a compendium of nomad tents. Mir Sayyid Ali was one of

156. *Life in the Country*, by Mir Sayyid Ali, Tabriz, *c.* 1540.

the most able painters of the early Tabriz School, and this masterpiece of genre representation portrays the eight tents in vivid detail. The three perpendicular arches of the roof rings of the *kibitkas* are clearly visible as is the rolled felt door flap. The wall cloth is attached to the lower edge of the parasol roof of one tent by wooden toggles inserted through loop bindings and the smoke hole above the centre pole, which appears to consist of two parts, is covered by a rectangular flap. The three ridge tents have circular bearing plates or bars at the ridge peaks.

The parasol-roofed tents in Mir Sayyid Ali's camp are representative of this type. They are characterised by a large conical parasol roof supported on a central pole. High pyramidal tents are represented in Mongol and Timurid military camps. A hole covered by a square piece of cloth or a large shawl is left at the peak of a radiating trellis to allow smoke to escape. The walls either incline outwards and are fixed by means of short ropes along the bottom edge, or are vertical and can be rolled about the vertical axis around the periphery. The walls are high compared with those of nomad tents and have a broad decorative band or frieze around the lower edge of the roof. The awning and walls are sometimes strengthened with radiating piping in the parasol roof and vertical slats in the wall cloth. The awnings of a parasol-roofed tent and a pavilion illustrated in a Shiraz *Kamseh of Nizanni*[13] from the mid-16th century are stretched by a curious arrangement of pairs of ropes in V-shaped patterns reminiscent of the Sistan tent. The parasol-roofed tent could be related to the parasol (large fixed parasols were fashionable at the time of the Timurids), the parasol being of ancient origin. The occasional practice of joining the roofs of two parasol-roofed tents to create a single shelter is illustrated in a miniature-*Surprise Attack on an Encampment of Rebels by Timur's Forces* from the *Zafar-Nameh*, *c.* 1529.[14]

The radial piping in the roof and the vertical rods in the walls are accentuated in the paintings of the Mughal school. In the first major work of this school, *Assad Ibn Kariba Attacks the Army of Iraj at Night* from the *Hamza-Nameh* (*c.* 1575),[15] these elements are delineated with great care as are the circular plates on top of the tent poles. The walls are gathered up under the roof. These elements are represented in the same manner in *The Genghis Khan Miniatures* which came from the court of Akbar the Great.[16]

The presence of so many tents in Persian miniatures indicates that they were well known in Iran in the 15th and 16th centuries and probably earlier. While the accuracy of these representations is often questionable, certain conclusions appear to be justified.

Elements of the tents of the Lurs, such as braided loops for securing the ropes and ridge bar may be detected in miniatures prior to 1500. Furthermore, traces of the division of the awning along the ridge can be discerned in paintings of the Baghdad school. The Arab tents appear to lack narrow bands and fastenings, while the crossed poles, which are found only in Africa today, seem to have existed in Iran about 1500. The small circular plate that has survived in the tents of the Arab nomads is often depicted in the corresponding tents in Persian miniatures. Another North African element, the T-shaped support, is often shown in the small conical tent.

Perhaps the most interesting aspect of the miniatures is the confirmation that an element known only in Tibet – ropes attached to the awning by several roots – was known also in Iran about 1500. The tents of the Persian miniatures comprise examples from urban and nomad cultures and must be considered among the most exquisite of their kind.

157. *Layla and Majnun unconscious among animals which sympathise with their grief*, from *The Khamsa of Nizami*, Shiraz School, mid-16th century.
158. *Surprise attack on an encampment of rebels by Timur's forces* by Sharaf Ad-din'Ali Yazdi, from the *Zafar-Namah*. Tabriz School, dated 1529.

159. Miniature, *Assad ibn Kariba attacks the army of Iraj at Night*, from the *Dastani-i Amir Hamsa (Hamsa-Nameh)*, India, 1575. 160. *Genghis Khan in his gold tent orders stones strewn on the dusty soil of the camp*, illustration from *History of the Mongols*, Mughal School, Kabul. 17th century.

The Ottoman tent

The Ottoman rulers possessed magnificent military tents or Otaks, which were their real homes.[17] As late as the 15th century the Ottoman capital continued to be wherever the Sultan pitched his tent. The Sultan's quarters consisted of a series of day and night tents surrounded by a cloth screen. The royal tent was frequently lined with cloth of gold since the Altin Oda was as much a symbol of power as was the parasol. The nomadic origin of the Ottomans and their followers may explain the popularity of the tent.[18] The tent had been connected from ancient times with the burial of nomad chieftains of the steppes, as has been noted in the second tomb of Pazyryk. The association was continued by the Ottomans, for upon his death in 1595, Murat III was taken to his tomb and left there inside his magnificent Otak.[19]

The relationship of the tent and the Seljuk tombs (Turbe) has been much disputed, but the Ottomans of the 16th century had no such doubts.[20] This connection can be followed through the Seljuk type and through the Seljuks to the

Iranian Kumbets which closely resemble the fragile Yurt. The Yesil Turbe at Bursa (1421) is nearer to the Seljuk type than that of the earlier Ottoman Sultans.

The royal Ottoman tents are characterised by their magnificence and by the blurring of the distinction between architecture and tents. Architectural elements were frequently incorporated in tents conceived as temporary palaces. Following Central Asian tradition the Ottomans retained the cupola roof as a symbol of sovereignty in the Imperial tent. Selim II is depicted at his enthronement before a cupola-shaped roof of a ceremonial tent.[21] The Otak of the sovereign and the pavilions of the Viziers had painted domes and ceilings as well as tent flaps which, when lifted on poles, formed porticoes. Almet III assembled a fantastic array of 173 tents and kiosks made of lath and plaster to create an imitation Versailles and Marley-le-Roi.[22]

The Grand Signior's tent in a 17th century camp at Davutpasa cost about $180000 and was richly embroidered inside with gold, and had gilded pillars. Rycault states that all sorts of offices, apartments and summer houses of pleasure

161. *Episode from the festivities at Istanbul in September, 1720*, from the Surname-i Vehbi, 18th century. The Ottomans regarded the cupola-roofed tent as a symbol of sovereignty.
162. *Turkish camp before Vienna*, 1529. Drawing by Bartholomaus Behen.

were contained 'within the walls of this tent . . .[23] The arrangements referred to by Rycault are illustrated in a drawing by Bartholomaus Behen of a Turkish camp at the first siege of Vienna in 1529[24] showing an interconnected group of five parasol-roofed tents. The main tent, a tall stepped conical affair, is surrounded by a circular wall straddled by four evenly spaced smaller tents. Two of the outer tents are connected to the centre tent by a transverse gallery and the front tent serves as an entrance for the group. The tents are decorated in imitation of masonry walling and have lights around the lower edge of the roof. The stay ropes are attached to the edge of the roof by two roots. The symmetrical orbicular arrangement of this tent group is remarkably similar to that of Francis I's tents at the Field of the Cloth of Gold nine years earlier.

Vandal, a French ambassador at the Ottoman court in the 18th century, reports that the Imperial war tent in the Atmeydan was made of silk, velvet and brocade and took eighteen months to adorn.[25] Tile panels in the corridor near the Kafes, Topkapisaray, in the reign of Mehmet IV, depict a camp of tents of varying sizes arranged in horizontal bands.[26] The design on the tiles has been so simplified that it is impossible to comment on the accuracy of Behen's sketch beyond noticing the obvious similarity of Behen's tents with European tents of the time. The conical tents on the tiles are depicted as being supported by a tall centre pole with the peak emphasised by four concentric bands of decoration.

The clean and orderly Ottoman camp consisted of numerous tents. The camp at Davutpasa had some two thousand tents[27] laid out in a grid pattern of streets like a Roman town. The royal tents were extremely commodious so that Ahmet I is said to have been better lodged in his tent than he would have been in any available house on the Edirne road. Rycault observed that 'the pavilions of the Great Vizier, and other persons of principal office and quality, may be called palaces rather than tents, being of large extent, richly wrought within, adorned beyond their houses, accommodated with stately furniture, with all the convenience of the city and country . . .'.[28] The Janissaries' tents surrounded the large tent of the *aga* or General, in front of the main body of the camp. A large open space in the centre of the camp was reserved for the five large tents of the Vizier, his chief counsellor, the lord chancellor, the lord treasurer, and the master of ceremonies. Important persons had two tents in order not to be inconvenienced by the move from one site to the next, the second tent being taken a days journey ahead and pitched in readiness. All this entailed a large number of horses, mules and camels and many thousands of attendants.

The soldiery were so accustomed to living in tents that their barracks were divided into groups, or odas, by means of screens which corresponded to the sections who shared the same tent when in the field.[29] In wartime the oda meant a large round tent, presumably of the parasol-roofed type.

The Ottomans retained many of their earlier nomadic habits of mind, and in particular, their love of the open air remained until the twentieth century. The tent was an integral part of the nomadic way of life and when the Ottomans became an urban people, its qualities of openness, lightness, and impermanence infected their architecture. Under the Ottomans, tents came to resemble palaces, and architecture took on some of the qualities of their tents.

China

The geographic proximity of China to the steppes of Central Asia exposed it to the incursions of the Mongol hordes. One of the Mongol contributions to Chinese culture has been the *kibitka*, but the Mongols were not the only peoples possessing

163. Tile panel of a camp near Kafes.

164. *Departure of Wen Chi from the Nomad Camp*, by Chao Meng-fu (1254—1322) dated 1301.
165. Mongol encampment from a 14th century Chinese handscroll, Metropolitan Museum of Art.
166. *The Ch'ien Lung emperor arriving from a victory banquet*, after Castiglione. 18th century.
167. The emperor's throne is placed inside a Mongol yurt.

tents with whom the Chinese had intercourse. Tibetan nobles in the 7th and 8th centuries lived in elaborate tented camps during the summer.[30] The Chinese called the great tents of the Tibetan noblemen 'fu-lu' meaning palace, or military camp. The camps were organized in the style of a fortified enclosure.

The 'golden tent' of the king and his command was erected on a high platform in the centre of the camp and was surrounded by three concentric enclosures. These mobile palaces or cities were thought of as a capital and were used throughout Tibetan history. The camps of the great karma-pa hierarchs from the 12th to the 17th century were extremely large.

The elegant tent in Chao-Meng-fu's painting of a nomad camp has a curious shape, but as the artist had served under the Mongols in 1286 he would have been acquainted with their tentage.[31] The tent is open on the sides and has a sweeping pyramidal awning supported by a centre and four corner poles; one side is screened by a cloth barrier. Rudofsky reproduced an undated Chinese painting of what appears to be a Mongol encampment.[32] The front awning has a transverse ridge bar supported on two main poles. The tents are surrounded by a series of screens forming a rectangular open area. Some of the finest illustrations of *kibitkas*

107

168. View of a Chinese encampment after Damascene. 18th century.
169. *Mu-lan II*. The camp.
170. A royal feast of entertainment for the embassy of the Dutch and British East India Companies, 1695.

and open pavilions in screened nomad encampments belonging to the Hsiung-nu, a Turkic tribe, occur in narrative handscrolls illustrating a cycle of poems known as the *Eighteen Songs of a Nomad Flute* from the 14th century, of which the most complete example is in the Metropolitan Museum.

The *kibitka* was well established with the Chinese by the time of the early Ch'ing. The elaborate camp of the Emperor Ch'ien-lung (1736–95) consisted of *kibitkas* and an impressive array of Chinese tents made of blue cloth supported by two poles and one horizontal bar.[33] The small *mai-han* tents of the ordinary soldiers were arranged in two circles around the royal enclosure which contained a number of large *kibitkas*. The *mai-han* tent was generally used by caravans and George Roerich comments that they are cold and not waterproof.[34] The arrangement of the ropes holding the felt sheets to the roof, and a red tongue-shaped smoke flap are clearly visible in the beautifully drawn *kibitkas*. A hipped-roof pavilion was customarily provided for the Emperor to review the troops. Such hipped canopies served as ceremonial tents, not only in Tibet where they were known as *lding-gur* and used by noblemen, but also in Mongolia. Similar pavilions occur in an engraving of a royal feast of entertainment for the Embassy of the Dutch East India Company in 1695.[35]

Western Europe
Mediaeval tents

The earliest reappearance of tents on the Western European scene cannot be ascertained exactly, but it is unlikely that they were used before the 12th century. It is not clear whether European tents are related to Roman types — after all, St Gregory mentions tents borrowed from the Romans being used on campaigns by the Franks[36] — or whether their emergence was due to the impact of Middle Eastern culture on Europe following the Crusades.

The existence of tents at the beginning of the 12th century is indicated by the institution of the office of Keeper of Tents at the English court in the reign of Henry I (1100–1135)[37] and by an early fresco of Charlemagne receiving Haroun-al-Raschid's gifts in the Roman Church of Santa Maria in Cosmedin,[38] (AD 1119–1124). The art of tent making was sufficiently advanced by the mid-13th century for the kings of France and Hungary to send handsome linen tents as gifts to the great Mongol princes.[39] The tent which Louis IX sent to the great Khan c. 1248 was a wonderful tent-chapel of scarlet cloth painted with Christian themes for the edification of the Tartars.

The uses to which tents were put in the late Middle Ages and during the Renaissance reflect the interests and entertainments of the royal and noble houses of the day. In addition to their function as head-quarters in military campaigns, tents were also deployed at jousts, fêtes, masques and revels, and later they even served as stables. English kings lodged their households in tents when they toured the realm. The Master of the Tents at the English Court, a position which survived for five and a half centuries, was also Master of Revels as well, so close is the connection between tents and the production of royal entertainments. In 16th century France the Grand Master of Artillery was given the responsibility for providing and maintaining the royal tents.

The literature and records of the time rarely give details about the materials, form and construction of the tents, so painting and sculptural reliefs are the principal source for much of the information that follows. The accuracy of these pictures varies considerably because many artists merely followed a pictorial convention and, as a result, their work is of little interest. At the same time, pictures by other artists are closely observed and convey a wealth of detail about tent construction and decoration.

The parasol-roofed tent of *rotundas in modum tentorii* is the predominant type in 13th century painting, the pavilion became important a century later. An illustration in *Res Siculae* or *Liber ad honorem Augusti* by Pierre d'Ebulon shows the Holy Roman Emperor, Henry VI's tent in the top right hand part of the picture above three other less elaborate tents.[40] The picture reveals several important features; among these are the facts that the roof and wall are separate, and that the junction where they meet is covered by a band which has its edge finished in large semi-circular scallops. The bottom edge of the tent is secured to the ground by pegs driven through loops.

The peaks of red and white striped tents in a 13th century Roman-Catalan fresco illustrating an incident in the wars of Jaime of Spain are protected by conical hoods or caps which have balls mounted on them.[41] The profile of the neck joining the cap to the ball continues the line of the roof but becomes progressively steeper in its curvature. This cap and ball termination of the tent peak is extremely common in European tents. A slit in the slanting wall enables a triangular entrance to be formed by drawing the flaps back on either side.

The parasol-roofed tents depicted in the Shrine of Charlemagne in Aachen Cathedral between 1200 and 1207 are the most detailed of these early

171. *Charlemagne receiving Haroun-Al-Raschid's gifts.* Reconstruction by G. B. Giovenale. Santa Maria in Cosmedin, Rome, (*c.* 1119–1124).
172. *The Emperor and the Dukes with the Army* (Holy Roman Emperor Henry VI, 1190–1197), from *Res Siculae.*
173. *Besieging army at foot of fortress.* Wars of Jaime of Spain (1213–1376). Fresco, Roman Catalan Art, 13th century.

174. *Charlemagne, Milo and Roland, Miracle of the Flowering Lances.* Relief on the Reliquary of St Charlemagne 1200–1215, Cathedral of Aix-la-Chapelle, Aachen.

175. *The Siege of Pamplona by the Franks.*
Relief on the Reliquary of St Charlemagne.
1200–1215, Cathedral of Aix-la-Chapelle,
Aachen.
176. A page from the *Maciejowski Bible,*
c. 1256.
177. *The Lady with the Unicorn.* A Mon
seul desir (tapestry detail, *c.* 1500).

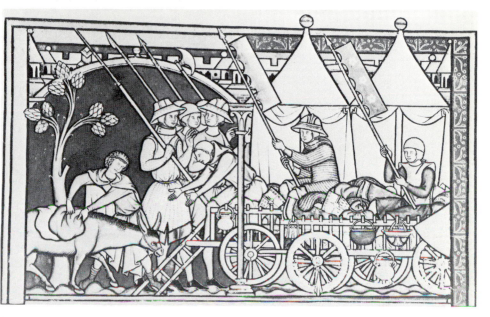

representations. [42] The conical awnings terminate in the customary cap and ball, with the exception of Charlemagne's tent which is surmounted by a royal eagle instead of a cross. The tents stays are shown in the Aachen reliefs attached to the edge of the roof by two short roots or 'crows feet'. This is in itself quite unusual, because most artists leave them out. The roof canopies are given two distinct patterns in *The Miracle of the Flowering Lances* panel where the cloth is either scored with deep curved folds or it is embossed with a chequered pattern. These patterns might indicate a decorative radial or chequer pattern in the roof cloth. Nevertheless, a different interpretation is suggested by the left hand panel depicting *The Siege of Pamplona by the Franks*. The roof canopy has been removed to expose a number of radial ropes which run from the base of the ball on top of the centre pole beyond the edge of the roof and down to the ground. If this interpretation is preferred, then the roof canopy was draped over a series of radial ropes, instead of being itself prestressed by the stay ropes. The parasol-roofed tents illustrated in the *Maciejowski Bible* (*c*. 1256) have tall vertical walls with the usual ball, but no cap on the roof peak. [43]

The gorgeous tent belonging to a series of tapestries known as *The Lady with the Unicorn* in the Cluny Museum in Paris makes the connection between the tent and chivalry clear. [44] The exquisitely rendered slim blue and gold tent has two stays attached to the edge of the parasol roof by twin roots, and the rim is covered by a broad blue band fringed with gold tassels.

The type of parasol-roofed tent which emerges from a survey of 15th century paintings is one which has nearly vertical walls, stays fastened to the edge of the roof by means of several roots, separate roof and wall cloths, and the junction where they meet is covered by a broad ornamental band which is sometimes finished with semi-circular scallops. The peak of the roof is commonly protected by a cap and ball.

Italian tents

Italian painting is more informative than French in the 14th century because, whereas French painters tended to stylize the tent, Italian paintings are more realistic and make detailed observations of the subject. Whilst various types of tents including the Captain General's pavilion were erected, the bulk of mercenary armies encamped in the field in Italy slept beside their horse with no more than their cloaks thrown over the backs of the animals. [45]

Two types of tent, a large pavilion and a parasol-roofed tent, are depicted surrounded by straw shelters in the encampment scene in the Palazzo Pubblico, Sienna (*c*. 1328). [45] The tents in this camp are represented in considerable detail, so that the elaborate system of tent stays and their fastenings can be followed. The seam lines in the tent cloth are clearly indicated so that it is possible to see that the tent cloth comprised parallel strips in the region of the central ridge and segmental elements in the semi-circular ends. The ridge of the pavilion seems to be carried by a horizontal pole which is supported at either end by two main poles on the longitudinal axis. Each of these main poles has three long guys, one in the longitudinal direction and two transverse lines; the centre pole of the parasol-roofed tent is steadied by four perpendicular guy lines. Both tents have two levels of tent stays, the upper series is attached to the edge of the roof at each seam line, and the second lower series is fastened to the wall cloth a short distance above the bottom edge so that a low vertical plinth is formed around the outside of the tents. All the stays are fastened to the tent cloth by means of three abbreviated roots.

An illustration by Giovanni Bettini de Fano of Sigismondo Malatesta's army

178. *A 14th Century Camp*, detail from *Guidoriccio da Fogliano*. Fresco by Simone Martini, the Palazzo Pubblico, Sienna, *c*. 1328.

179. *The Siege of Piombino* (1448). MS illumination by Giovanni Bettini da Fano for the Esperide of Basinio da Parma. The parasol-roofed tents have stays attached to the edge of the roof by two roots and outside guys or storm lines.
180. An armed camp in the early 14th century. Isabel of France and her troops.
181. *An Army Breaking Camp*. MS illumination by Giovanni Bettini da Fano showing parasol-roofed tents in various stages of being struck.

113

182. *Charlemagne and Roland receiving the fatal gifts brought by Ganelon from Saragossa.* MS by Guillaume Vrelaut *c.* 1468.
183. *Maugis stealing the swords of Charlemagne, Roland and his peers. Grisaille* by Tavernier Renant de Montauban in *Croniques et Conquestes de Charlemagne.*

breaking camp in Tuscany, (*c.* 1449) depicts a number of parasol-roofed tents in various stages of being struck, and demonstrates quite conclusively that the roof and wall cloths are separate.[47] These tents have a conical roof and almost vertical walls, the centre pole being held upright by four long guys and the roof being stretched outwards by some eight tent stays fastened to its periphery by twin roots. The roof cloth is crowned by an oval ball and a pennant.

The method of taking the tent down, at least as it is depicted by Bettini de Fano, was extremely simple. The wall cloths were detached first, the pegs at the end of the tent stays were then pulled up, the guys and then the main pole with the roof cloth still fixed to it was rolled up for transport. The main tent pole appears to be in one piece but this may be an oversight on the part of Bettini de Fano.

Tents appear most frequently during the 14th century in miniatures illustrating the Legend of Roland, the marriage of Richard II to Isabella, daughter of Charles VI of France and incidents in the Crusades.

Renaissance tents

By the 15th century, the number of tents included in paintings proliferates and the rectangular pavilion becomes increasingly popular. Nevertheless, the tents are much the same as the earlier examples. 15th century illustrators often went to great lengths to indicate the external decorative treatment of tents. The external decorative treatment featured in 15th century illustrations was strongly influenced at the time by heraldry and architecture. Embellishment of tents with the arms of the owner, with heraldic devices, fleur-de-lis, and with crosses, probably goes back to the need for personal identification in military camps.

The imposition of architectural themes became even more conspicuous in the early 16th century. The roof and wall cloths of the tents were divided into panels with columns, trefoils, quatrefoils and ogee arches borrowed from gothic architecture. The parasol-roofed tent in the miniature, *The Jousts of St. Inglevert*, is an interesting example of architectural transposition in which the roof is adorned with two tiers of small dormer windows.[48] The same detail recurs in a later miniature in the Harley Ms of *The Assault of the Strong Town of Afrique*.[49]

The alien tent was invested with familiar Western decorative themes. The strong connection of the tent with nomad cultures renders it difficult for the Western mind to comprehend its structural and human significance. This is why tensile architecture in the 20th century is conceived almost exclusively in terms of the structural efficacy of the suspension bridge, as an efficient means of spanning, or is interpreted in terms of existing heavyweight aesthetics.

The tents of kings and nobles in the early 16th century were remarkable for their great size, magnificence, wealth of invention, and architectural fantasy. The adoption of the tent as an essential feature of the military and ceremonial life of European courts was a factor in its increase in size, magnificence and complexity. The tent served as a reminder of an earlier age of chivalry and knightly romance. The opulent outfitting, the use of expensive fabrics and decorative enrichment matched the inflated pretensions of these princes. The vertical walls and steep roofs, modelled on domestic architecture, disregarded the most elementary considerations of statics and wind loads.

Two identical pavilions bearing the arms of each monarch have been included in

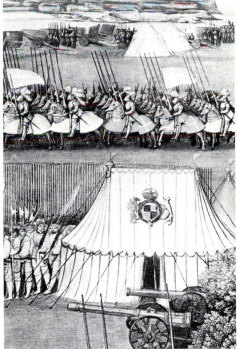

184. Henry VIII's tent, detail from *The meeting between Henry VIII and his ally, the Emperor Maximilian I, in their war with France*, 1513.
185. Two sets of dormers regail the steep conical roofs of the parasol-roofed tents in the miniature *The jousts of St Inglevert*, MS. Harl 4379.

186. A 16th century encampment of the Holy Roman Empire army. *Siege of Rome by the Etruscan Chief Porsena*, painted by Melchior Felsen.

a picture of the meeting between Henry VIII and Maximilian I in 1513.[50] The pavilion consists of two semi-circular ends separated by a rectangular section covered by a ridge roof. The two tall main poles that support each end of the horizontal ridge bar are restrained in the longitudinal direction by long twin guys. Each pole is topped by a ball and a pennant, and the ridge is protected by a chevet fringed coverlet. The steep roof is extended by short stays fastened to its edge by means of two roots. The vertical attenuation of some 16th century tents is corroborated in a painting, *The Siege of Rome by the Etruscan Chief Porsena*, by Melchior Felsen, which shows an encampment of the Holy Roman Empire army.[51] The roofs of an assorted group of pyramidal, conical and pavilion tents are from three to four times taller than the walls. If Felsen's indication of scale is correct then the tents are about 6 to 8 m high.

The Field of the Cloth of Gold

The European idea of the tent was fully realized in the French and English encampments at the meeting between Francis I and Henry VIII in June, 1520. So rich were the costumes and pavilions of both courts that the site of the meeting, between Guines and Ardes, was afterwards known as the 'Field of the Cloth of Gold'.[52] The meeting had many aspects: it was a political conference for bringing about an *entente cordiale* that would foster universal peace; an athletics meeting with jousts, tournaments and wrestling; a festival of music and drama; and a series of state banquets. In some respects it was the forerunner of the modern World Exposition and certainly its creators were beset by much the same problems of planning and administration.

There had been large gatherings of tents before the 1520 meeting. Cellini, when he followed the French court's movement in normal times, states that the numbers to be accommodated were so great that the court set up canvas tents like gypsies.[53] Eleven hales (pavilions) and five round houses (parasol-roofed tents) were required for James I's progress.[54] The number of tents assembled in the two encampments has been variously estimated at 400 in the English camp, Hall puts the figure at 820, and 300 to 400 in the French camp.[55] No previous Western encampment can compare with the magnificence, size or number of tents desported. The dissimilarity of the two camps reflected national differences in some degree. For example, the French set about creating a magnificent array of tents but the English concentrated on buildings. The tents and pavilions in both the French and English camps were constructed of timber masts and hard-wearing canvas subsequently covered with the sumptuous materials which gave the meeting its name.[56]

The more elaborate interconnected tent clusters were assembled from basic tent forms, that is from ridge-roofed galleries, pyramidal and conical-shaped tents and pavilions. These elements have been combined in a manner which reflects the characteristic differences between French and English ecclesiastical architecture. The French tents are extremely high and compact, with individual elements subservient to the whole. By contrast, the English tents are spread out and display an additive quality. It is possible that tent designers had architectural prototypes in mind when they designed the tent cluster. The French love of rich and extravagant forms is evident in the choice of materials for covering the canvas as they used great quantities of cloth of gold and cloth of silver, of velvet and satin, and innumerable heraldic devices, fleur-de-lis, ermines, and white crosses all made of the same materials.[57]

The formidable task of making and transporting the 300 to 400 French tents and

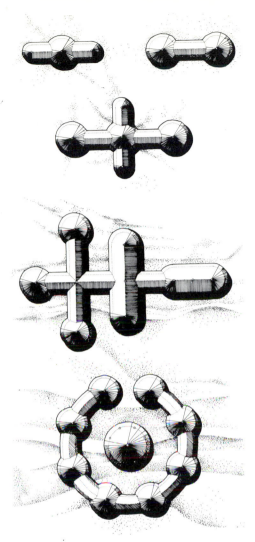

187. Renaissance tent groups: *1*, single parasol-roofed tent penetrated by a pavilion; *2*, two parasol-roofed tents linked by a gallery; *3*, tent group depicted in the English camp at the Battle of the Spurs, 1513 (three parasol-roofed tents intersected by two pavilions); *4*, English tent group from Richard Gibson, 1520; *5*, French tent group depicted in the *Field of the Cloth of Gold*, 1520.

pavilions in time for the meeting fell to Galiot de Genoillac, chevalier, royal councillor and chamberlain, and Grand Master of the Artillery. The tents and pavilions were fabricated at the Archbishop's palace and castle at Tours and then erected on the Isle of S. Gracian on the Loire prior to their transport to Ardes. Some 35,143 aunes of hard wearing canvas was used in the tents, the canvas then being covered with sumptuous materials. These enrichments were the most costly item, amounting to £159 890, 12s, 6d Tours out of a total of £195 546, 11s, 5d.[58]

Included in the 'ville de merveilleuses tapisseries flottantes',[59] as the impressive array of French tents was later described, were Francis I's pavilion and three ancillary pavilions for his use, fifteen smaller pavilions grouped around the central cluster, a special banqueting pavilion, and tents and pavilions for the Queen of France and the Queen Mother. The tents of the great nobles, decorated in their own colours, completed the array. Except for a manuscript in the Bibliotheque Nationale of Paris, which gives a detailed account of the French preparations, there is no full description or pictorial record of the scene at Ardes.[60]

Not much is known about the form and construction of Francis's grand tent, save that it was extremely tall and circular in plan. Eyewitness estimates seem to have exaggerated the tent's height, but it cannot be doubted that the great pavilion of St Michael was exceptionally tall by contemporary standards. The failure of the main mast of Francis's grand pavilion in a storm which devastated the French tents and pavilions only four days after they had been pitched confirms this impression. As the height of a tent increases, the stiffness of the supporting mast decreases, but the wind load on the tent itself increases, in short, tall tents are structurally unsound, as can be seen from the fate of the French pavilions.

An item for the two 17·7 m masts in the Artillery accounts may relate to the great pavilion of St Michael especially as a height of 17·7 m would be more in keeping with a structure which is said to have measured 16 paces across in the central area, and to have been surrounded by a gallery 8 paces wide. The description of the king's tent as being 'as high as the tallest tower', '60 paces high' and that it was supported by masts lashed together and tall enough for a ship of 400 butts, is much too high for a pavilion little more than 32 paces in diameter.[61]

The great pavilion consisting of thirty-two walls with four galleries around it in the accounts might possibly refer to the king's tent.[62] It was covered in cloth of gold with three lateral stripes of blue velvet 'powdered' with golden fleur-de-lis, and with toille d'or. The peak of the tent was capped by a gold ball or 'pinot' which carried a life-size statue of St Michael, patron saint of France, carved in walnut and painted blue and gold. 'False' pavilions or divisions were formed within the great pavilion by screens of cloth of gold. The three medium sized ancillary tents, a chapel or secret chamber, a wardrobe, and a chamber de conseil, about 20 paces in diameter, were to stand near the great pavilion.[63] They had cloth of gold covers fringed in black, white and violet. Fifteen smaller pavilions stood at some 50 paces from this central group. All the pavilions had windows and lights covered with linen or cotton cloth and were decorated with golden apples, and with banners painted with the royal arms.

The great pavilion of St Michael is represented in the Hampton Court painting of the Field of the Cloth of Gold by the golden parasol-roofed tent in the upper part of the picture behind Guines Castle.[64] Francis I is shown greeting Henry VIII at their first meeting in front of a resplendent tent having a golden figure on its peak and surrounded by eight or nine smaller gold and blue striped parasol tents arranged in a circle about the king's tent and all interconnected by a ridge-roofed gallery of similarly striped cloth. The most outstanding aspect of the Hampton Court painting is its indication of a radial composition of tents interconnected by a circular gallery with the king's tent as the centrepiece.

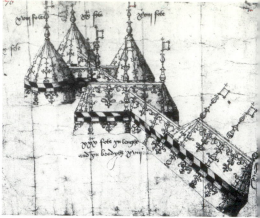

188. *The Field of the Cloth of Gold.*
Narrative painting possibly by Hans Roest.
189. Design for a tent. Cotton MS
Augustus 1 (ii) No. 76.
190. *The Battle of the Spurs,* August 1513.

A second dumb-bell shaped pavilion comprising two conical parasol-roofed tents joined by a ridge roofed gallery is illustrated on a hill overlooking the king's tent. The cloth of gold cover suggests that it was occupied by an important personage such as the Queen of France, but equally, it might have been intended for banquets because it resembles a nearby tent in which a banquet is seen taking place.[65] After the meeting Francis used the three pavilions, but also the chapel and the chamber of the king in his wars. Several of his nobles did in fact buy their tents for later use.

The bulk of the English party had to be accommodated in tents, halls and pavilions since it had never been intended to lodge more than a fraction of their number in the temporary palace and the castle. The English tents were scarcely fewer than the French, as each side strove to outdo the other in splendour.

191. Design for a crimson and gold pavilion painted in connection with the meeting of Henry VIII and Francis I. The tent poles are surmounted by a set of eighteen royal beasts, and the tent cloth is decorated with fleurs-de-lis, and Tudor roses. Cotton MS Augustus (iii), f. 18.

Richard Gibson, the Sergeant of Tents, was largely responsible for the pageantry and arrangement for the Field of the Cloth of Gold on the English side. Gibson's career illustrates the close connection which had grown up between the role of Master of Tents and Revels at the English Court; he began as a player in the interludes at court, then held office in the Wardrobe before being made Sergeant of the Tents in 1518.[66] Fortunately, a marvellous drawing firmly annotated in a contemporary hand, which seems to have been intended for use by Richard Gibson and his craftsmen, has been preserved.[67] The drawing depicts an elaborate cluster of tents comprising three tall parasol-roofed tents and two pavilions inter-connected by low galleries in the form of a latin cross. The three short arms end in tall parasol-roof tents while the long arm is intersected halfway along its length at right angles by a pavilion and terminates in a second pavilion aligned in the same direction as the long arm of the cross. The masts are capped by ornately carved finials with painted pennants and the cloth of gold cover is embellished by an ornate floral motif. A painting in the Cotton MS Augustus (iii, f. 18) depicts a brilliant crimson and gold group of four pavilions linked by galleries and flanked on either side by two lines of five parasol-roofed tents. Eighteen 'royal beasts' derived from the badges and supporters of King Henry and his ancestors are set on the tent poles and the tents are further decorated with fleurs-de-lis, Tudor roses, and the royal motto: *DIEU ET MON DROIT!*

The Hampton Court painting depicts the English tents in much less detail, although the large cloth of gold tent behind the palace may be the replacement for the banqueting house which was never completed. A counterpart of the tents depicted in the Cotton Augustus manuscript occurs in the array of English tents before Therouane in a painting of the Battle of the Spurs between Henry VIII and the French in August 1513.[68] In the midst of the gable-roof and parasol-roofed tents and pavilions is an interesting looking tent-cluster not unlike the ones in the Cotton Augustus manuscript. The group consists of three parasol-roofed tents with lanterns interconnected by two galleries on the longitudinal axis. The centre tent is intersected at right angles by a pavilion with rounded ends. The galleries are distinguished from the cloth of gold parasol-roof tents by vertical blue stripes. The mast tops sport the usual finials and pennants.

The development of elaborate interconnected clusters of tents in the early Renaissance satisfied the need to relate social functions within a single complex. The cluster pattern of the tents expresses the social order much as the arrangement of rooms does in a building. This is achieved by additive groups of tents.

The extravagant flowering of the tent in the early Renaissance was prompted by its association with mediaeval pageantry, romance and chivalry; once this withered then the tent was destined to decline. The magnificence of the tents on the Field of the Cloth of Gold was intended to evoke the chivalry and romance of an earlier age. In England the office of Master of Tents continued on throughout the reigns of Elizabeth I, James I and Charles I; it was interrupted for a time by the outbreak of the Civil War but recommenced with the Restoration.[69] The use of tents declined, except for military purposes, with the cessation of Royal progresses and tournaments following the Revolution when the Court settled permanently at Westminster. The office of Master of Tents was afterwards discontinued. Illustrations of military camps from the Napoleonic, Crimean and First World Wars show that traditional ridge-shaped and parasol tents continued to be commonly used. This lack of innovation ensured the survival of traditional tent types well into the twentieth century as can be seen from the British War Office *Handbook of Tentage* of 16 August, 1946. The advent of travelling circuses in Europe and the United States (*c.* 1815) led in 1828–30 to the adoption of large parasol tents and pavilions with secondary outer rows of poles. The variety of uses for tents multiplied in the nineteenth century where they are recorded at fêtes, fairs, cricket grounds and all manner of temporary outdoor functions.

192. Primitive vine bridge, Amazon basin.

Part Two
Suspension bridges

The connection between indigenous or early suspension bridges and modern suspension bridges is difficult to establish though it may well exist. Native catenary bridges arose in tropical regions around the world where there was a plentiful supply of large vines, but only in two regions, the eastern Himalayan massif and Peru, where this spontaneous development was contiguous with civilization did any notable development of the suspension bridge occur. The suspension bridge is important because the technical challenge of constructing large span bridges created a modern tensile technology and inspired tensile building at a time when there was little awareness of the significance of tents.

Early Suspension Bridges

The Eastern Himalayas and China

Fearful of step, on the flying ladder one advances,
Woven of iron, a lonely thread running straight through the sky
Yang Shen, AD 1540[1]

The concentration and diversity of traditional suspension bridges in the eastern part of the Tibetan massif, places the focus of origin of this type in the Old World somewhere in this region. In historical times the suspension bridge was almost a pre-condition of social intercourse between the people of China and those of Tibet, Afghanistan, India, Burma and Thailand.[2] Many of the early accounts of Himalayan suspension bridges were provided by Chinese Buddhist pilgrims making their way to India along roads such as those that linked Yarkand and Gilgit. Bamboo suspension bridges are still commonly found in the mountainous parts of Yunnan, Szechwan, Sikang, Sikkin, Tibet and Nepal, but they are also found in Burma, the Celebes, Borneo and Sumatra.[3] The Nagas, Nung and Abor tribespeople on the Assam-Tibet and Burma borders construct impressive bridges with various combinations of ropes.

The suspension bridge may well have descended from the practice of attaching cords to arrows so that both prey and arrow might be recovered.[4] This in turn led to the technique of shooting a pilot-cord across a river, after which successive heavier ropes could be pulled over and secured. The earliest Chinese reference to bamboo suspension bridges occurs in a text written about AD 90.[5] Suspension bridges, similar to the Chinese type but with cables of maguey fibre and hide instead of bamboo, are encountered in Peru, where the Incas constructed them as part of their extensive road system. The most famous of these, the Apurimac Bridge, was constructed in *c*. AD 1350.

The forms of primitive catenary cable bridges of the eastern Himalayas illustrate the development of the suspension bridge from the simplest form of all, that of the single suspended cable. They comprise, in order of increasing complexity: the single cable, two cables one above the other, three cable V-shaped, four cable tubular, and catenary deck bridges.

In the single cable system used in the old Nakhi kingdom in Western Yunnan, passengers are carried in various kinds of cradles suspended from a bamboo tube which travels along a declined cable.[6] I and V forms are produced by suspending one or two hand ropes above the tread rope; in the latter, the hand-rails on either side are attached to the tread rope at short intervals. The V-type is improved by introducing a fourth overhead rope to the hand-rails and plaiting the whole together to form a continuous tubular structure 1 to 1·6 m in diameter.[7]

Tubular catenary bridges with spans up to 260 m have been built by the Abor tribespeople on the Assam-Tibet border.[8] The practice of constructing decks by laying transverse planks or lengths of bamboo on as many as half a dozen bamboo cables was firmly established long before the Sung. The modern form of suspension bridge having a flat deck suspended from cables instead of resting on the cables probably arose out of the hypertrophy of the hand-rails.[9] The advantage of this form is that the traveller moves horizontally instead of along the curve of the supporting cables.

The cables of the catenary suspension bridges of West China were made by plaiting the outer layers of bamboo, which have a rupture strength of 182 MPa around a centre core made of the inner part of the culm so that the outer strips grip the core more tightly with increasing tension.[10] Three or more of these ropes which are about 5 cm in diameter are twisted together to form one of the bridge cables.

The majority of catenary suspension bridges in West China have single spans of from 40 m to 80 m supported on 6 to 12 cables.[11] The An-lan bridge at Kuanksien (pre-Sung) consists of no less than eight major spans, the greatest of which is 65·6 m and has a total length exceeding 344 m. The bridge deck is 2·95 m wide and is supported on ten bamboo cables each 16·5 mm in diameter.[12]

Bamboo cables tend to relax in time, and consequently require tightening at regular intervals. They also deteriorate and have to be renewed. The main bridge cables are tightened by rotating vertical columns arranged in two rows inside

193. V-shaped catenary footbridge.
194. A Nung single-cable catenary bridge, Northern Burma.
195. Tubular catenary bamboo bridge, Brahmaputra River.
196. Nung U-shaped bamboo-strand catenary bridge, Northern Burma.

123

197. The Kuanksien An-lan catenary bridge.

houses at each end of the bridge. In China, bamboo cables were superseded by hand forged wrought iron chains with welded links, between the 1st and 6th century.[13] Chinese travellers on their way to India at the beginning of the 6th century remark on the existence of iron-chain suspension bridges. A new problem arose with the elimination of tightening arrangements, that of anchoring the iron chains. The Chinese iron-chain suspension bridges were built with single spans of from 65 m to about 110 m. They are found predominantly in South Western China in the provinces of Yunnan, Szechwan, and Kweichow.[14] Sometimes, long iron

198. The deck of the Kuanksien An-lan bridge is supported on ten 1.65 cm diameter bamboo-strands.

199. The Chi-Hung iron-chain catenary bridge over the Mekong River, *c.* 1470. Span 74 m.

bars connected by pins were employed instead of chains, in bridges with spans of up to 98 m.

Aerodynamic instability was a serious problem then as it is now, and the early Himalayan bridges swayed wildly in strong winds. The large tubular bridges of the Abor tribespeople are reported to sway 15 m from side to side. The terror of these crossings is recounted by Fa-Hsien, AD 399 'Then one passes fearfully across suspended cables to cross the river. . . .[15]

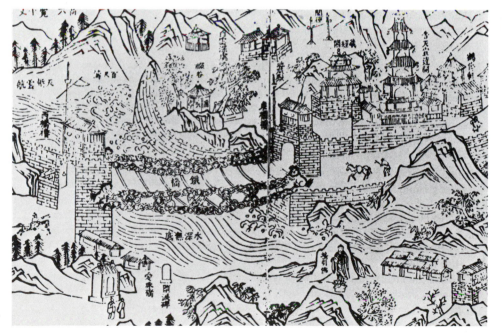

200. An illustration from the *Thieh Chhiao Chih Shu* (Record of the Iron Suspension Bridge), depicting the Kuan-Ling bridge in the gorge of the Northern Phan Chiang in Southwest Kweichow.

201. The thick maguey-ropes are clearly delineated in an etching of a catenary bridge over the Rio Chambo River near Penipe, Peru *c.* 1800.
202. Bridge of the Apurimac River, *c.* AD 1350. Span 48·5 m.
203. Catenary bridge over the Rio Pampas River. Span 43 m. The cables were suspended from high stone towers.
204. View across the Pampas River bridge deck.

205. A contemporary Inca type *Keshwa Chaco* on the upper reaches of the Apurimac River.

Peru

Whereas the Himalayan suspension bridges were constructed along pilgrimage routes and caravan roads, the Inca bridges of Peru were vital links in an extensive network of military roads connecting their empire. The military significance of the suspension bridge is well illustrated by the Apurimac River whose deep gorge halted the northward advance of the Inca armies until a way was found in *c*. AD 1350 of spanning it with a catenary bridge.[16] The great period of Inca bridge construction began about AD 1290 and lasted until AD 1450, and was concentrated at sites on the Apurimac, Pampas, and Urubamba rivers to the northwest of Cuzco.[17]

The similarity between Inca and Chinese catenary bridges led Needham to propose that the two types are related, yet their geographic isolation makes this unlikely, particularly in view of the fact that the hammock is a characteristic Amerindian device.[18] Both the Chinese and Inca bridges had porches and abuttments on each side of the river but the Peruvian type had lacked the capstan-like arrangement for tightening the cables.

Thick rope cables made of hand-twisted fibres from the maguey plant were suspended from high stone towers and anchored to a number of large wooden beams fixed under the masonry platform.[19] The Apurimac bridge had five or six beams arranged each one higher than the other in steps. The wood deck was suspended from the main cables by means of other cables which served as wind bracing. The curve of the deck followed that of the main cables. Estimates of the length of the Apurimac bridge vary from 82 m to 106 m, but Squier's measurement of 48·5 m is probably correct.[20] The bridge over the Pampas River at Paramba was about 44 m long. V-shaped catenary bridges having six main cables anchored to rock bollards are constructed over the Apurimac by local farmers to this day.[21] The eastern Himalayan and Peruvian regions have several factors in common that are worth noting in passing, both regions are characterised by high mountains with deep impassable gorges and areas of rainforest nearby, in which large vines were to be found. The development of these indigenous bridges was facilitated by their proximity to advanced civilizations.

Western Europe
Transmission of iron suspension bridges to Europe

It is likely, but not certain, that European suspension bridges were inspired by Chinese iron-chain suspension bridges. The earliest known European descriptions of suspension bridges were published by Faustus Verantius, a former bishop, in his *Machinae Novae* in *c*. 1617.[22] Verantius's sketches of a portable rope suspension bridge and a metal-stayed bridge anticipated the modern suspension and the cable-stayed bridge. The portable suspension bridge had a horizontal floor slung from the cables by means of hangers which passed over pulleys. The horizontal deck of the rope suspension bridge could be adjusted horizontally and vertically using rope hangers suspended from pulleys. The design probably represents a refinement of rope military bridges then being used by the French army which are mentioned as early as 1515.[23] The metal-stayed bridge is a logical extension of Verantius's studies of truss design as it has a flat deck supported from two stone towers by a system of metal eye-bars. These remarkable designs, which appear to have been conceived without knowledge of the Chinese bridges, anticipated modern types of suspension and cable-stayed bridges.

Descriptions of Chinese bridges began to appear in the second half of the 17th century; the Lan Chin bridge near Ching-tung in Yunnan was described by Martin Martini in the sixth part of the Blaeu *Novus Atlas Sinensis*, 1655, and also in Athanasius Kircher's *China Monumenta Illustrata* in 1667. J. B. Fischer v. Erlach illustrated the same bridge several times in his *Historia Architectur* of 1725.[24]

By the early 19th century the West was able to match and later surpass Chinese achievements in iron-chain suspension bridge construction. The early European iron-chain bridges are unremarkable structures with narrow curved decks of the catenary type, suited only to foot traffic. the first of these was built across the Oder River by the Saxon Army in 1734,[25] and was followed in 1741 by the Winch Bridge over the Tees River at Durham. The latter had both metal suspension members and a rigid deck.

The construction of true suspension bridges is more difficult than that of the catenary type because the lengths of the cables and the hangers which produce a flat bridge deck must be determined beforehand. The problem was solved by a West Pennsylvanian judge named James Finley who built the first true suspension bridge, capable of carrying vehicular traffic over Jacob's Creek, Pennsylvania, in 1801, and who obtained a patent for his invention in 1800.[22] He went on to build some forty bridges between 1808 and 1816, the largest of which was a footbridge across the Schuylkill River at Philadelphia in 1809 with a span of 101 m.

206 Design for a bridge of linked-rods, by Faustus Verantius, *c.* 1617.
207 Drawing of the Lan-Chin bridge near Ching-tung in Yunnan, over the Mekong River. Span 82 m.

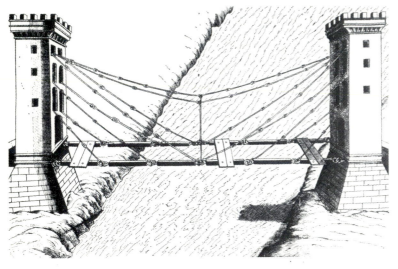

Modern Suspension Bridges

The effect of magnitude on spanning

The critical effect of self-weight in long span structures is explained by the principle of similitude which states that of two geometrically similar bridges, the larger is the weaker of the two.[1] This suggests that the difficulties of engineering design would intensify with greater suspension spans, and while this happened with the bridge deck, the towers, and the anchorages, it was much less so with the suspension system. This is because the efficiency of tensile structural systems is largely independent of the size of the structure.[2] The rate of increase of self-weight with increasing span of tension-loaded structures is appreciably less than that of structures subject to compression and bending. The low self-weight of long span tensile structures is a product of two factors: the superior strength of steel cable in tension and the ability to utilize the entire cross-sectional area at the maximum permissible stress.[3] Since the towers and the bridge deck are subject to compression, bending and torsion, and increase of their self-weight with increasing size is greater than that of the suspension system.

The outstanding feature of suspension bridges throughout history has been their susceptibility to destruction by wind. The unsatisfactory behaviour of most of the 19th century suspension bridges which were frequently damaged, if not wrecked, by wind resulted from the use of light decks with little longitudinal stiffening. The weight of bridge decks tended to increase with larger suspension spans and this improved the stiffness of the bridges.

The importance and influence of the bridge weight itself upon the bridge stiffness was first realised by John A. Roebling at the time of the construction of the Niagara Falls Bridge. Roebling noted that 'weight is a most essential condition, where stiffness is a great object'.[4] Sir Alfred Pugsley adds that Roebling had evidently gained an intuitive understanding from his Niagara experience, of the stiffness of a heavy suspension bridge of long span due to gravity forces. The crucial factor is that of 'cable gravity stiffness associated with long spans'.[5]

The comparative aerodynamic stability of long span suspension bridges enabled 20th century bridge designers to construct bridges with spans of between 525 m and 1380 m, without a knowledge of aerodynamics and of dynamic vibrations. The Tacoma collapse was a harsh reminder that aerodynamic stability was not assured by weight alone. Nevertheless, it is clear from the development of 19th and 20th century suspension bridges, that the advantage, insofar as aerodynamic stability is concerned, lay with long span rather than with short span suspension bridges.

This raises the question of the proper size or appropriate magnitude of suspension bridges. D'Arcy Thompson writes that, 'the effect of *scale* depends not on a thing in itself, but in relation to its whole environment or milieu; it is in conformity with the thing's "place in Nature", its field of action and reaction in the Universe. Everywhere Nature works true to scale, and everything has its proper size accordingly.'[6] The 19th century experience suggests that the appropriate magnitude of the suspension bridge is in excess of spans of 500 m and possibly ranges from 650 m to 1650 m.[7] It was the misfortune of 19th century bridge designers to come upon the suspension bridge long before a technology became available which would have permitted bridges to be built at the appropriate scale.

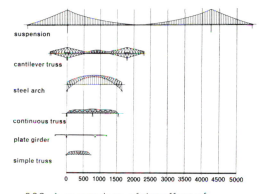

208. A comparison of the effect of similitude and magnitude in different types of bridges (spans in feet).

19th century suspension bridges

The typical form of suspension bridges was established in England by 1826, almost half a century before a suitable technology was perfected, which would have enabled the construction of bridges with long spans. The comparatively short

129

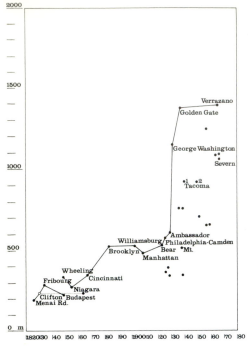

209. Rate of increase of suspension bridge spans since 1820. The vertical scale shows the unsupported span in metres and the horizontal scale shows the year of completion.

spans of the early 19th century bridges deprived these structures of the natural stiffness which is a concommitant of great size and weight. The importance of these early 19th century bridges lies in the creation of a technology appropriate to long span suspension bridges and in the formation of a body of suspension bridge theory. The main elements of this technology were the investigation of means of stiffening, the replacement of weaker cable materials with stronger ones and the development of improved methods of elevating cables to their final position. Bridges were designed with inclined suspension rods, radiating stays, and deep heavy girders, or a combination of these so as to give the desired stiffness. The replacement of chains made of wrought iron eyebar links with iron wires, and later with steel wires, was accompanied by substantial increases in the tensile strength of the suspension members. The use of iron wire cables led in turn to the development of improved methods of assembly and of lifting the cables to their final position culminating in the technique of aerial spinning.

The evolution of the suspension bridge over the past 150 years, measured by the increase in spans, has been fitful. It dominated the first half of the 19th century, but after the late 1840s riveted wrought iron, and later steel, made other forms practicable for even the largest spans.[8] The suspension bridge lost so much ground in the second half of the 19th century that it only regained its lead in the 1930s. The reasons for the decline of the suspension bridge lay in the new needs of the railway age combined with the unsatisfactory behaviour of most of the early suspension bridges.[9] It is hardly surprising in an age dominated by rail transport that most engineers avoided suspension bridges and sought some stiffer form for their long spans. By the mid-1930s the suspension bridge had surpassed its rivals in spanning capacity and the crucial problems appeared to have been beaten. From 1883 to 1929 the span length of suspension bridges remained comparatively modest, increasing only 84 m from 523 m in 46 years. Then in the following seven years, the suspension bridges built before 1930 were dwarfed by the construction of the George Washington Bridge, 1932, over the Hudson at New York City (1148 m) and the Golden Gate Bridge, 1936, at San Francisco (1378 m).[10] After this, spans increased a mere 19·7 m in the 28 years which separate the Golden Gate from the Verrazano Bridge. These graceful modern giants were the progeny of a new age in transportation, that of motor vehicles.

Britain, France and the United States were centres of suspension bridge development in the 19th century, and each country made a distinctive contribution. Britain crystallized the modern suspension bridge form, but France led the way in theory and in the new type of wire cable bridge. Advances in both Britain and France enabled designers working in the United States to perfect wire bridge techniques which enabled stable spans in excess of 320 m to be built. In the 1830s, the French overtook the early British lead in suspension bridge construction and this coincides with the beginning of the 'golden age' of French wire bridges in the period 1830 to 1850. Out of a total of 147 bridges completed between 1825 and 1842, 114 were French compared with 17 British.[11] The future of the suspension bridge lay with the French development of wire cable technology, not with the use of wrought iron chains.

The French led the way in the development of suspension bridge theory, the use of iron wire for cables, aerial spinning, and the protection of the cables. Modern suspension bridge technology has its origins in the advances made in France in the first half of the 19th century. From about 1850 until the mid-1960s almost all credit for the development of the suspension bridge must go to the United States.[12] What is more, in the late 1920s their actual experience of building was far ahead of that in any other country. It is, therefore, hardly surprising that modern tensile architecture began in the early 1950s in the United States. The historical link between the suspension bridge and the development of modern tensile architecture is confirmed by the important contribution of France.

England

The form of the modern suspension bridge is English. Othmar H. Ammann testified that 'engineers, in designing the longest modern suspension bridges, have returned or adhered to the simple, naturally graceful forms which are characteristic of the early bridges of this type'. The qualities of the early English bridges Ammann most admired were '. . . their general simple appearance, their flat catenary, light, graceful suspended structure and their plain massive and therefore monumental towers'.[13]

English suspension bridges were first built soon after the final defeat of Napoleon. Telford designed the Menai bridge, in 1817–18 and Captain Brown's Union Bridge at Norham Ford was opened in 1820. The eminence of Telford and Brunel as engineers has tended to obscure the achievements of others such as Captain Brown and James Meadows Rendel, a pupil of Telford's. Tierney Clark would surely be better known had his masterpiece, with a main span of 218 m, been built in England instead of over the Danube below Vienna.

The English approach to suspension bridge design was essentially empirical. The beginnings of the Menai Bridge can be traced to Telford's experiments to prove the tensile strength of malleable iron and the subsequent proposal for a wrought iron chain bridge at Runcorn in 1814 with a main span of 328 m.[14] Later, Telford collaborated with Brown on a $\frac{1}{10}$ scale model of the Runcorn bridge which served as the basis for the design of the Menai Bridge. Suspension cables were invariably made of flat wrought iron eyebar links which replaced round and square rods after Brown's patent in 1817.[15] The chains were normally assembled away from the bridge and then lifted into position.

The Menai Bridge is the first great suspension bridge, its record span was not exceeded till 1834. It was designed in 1817–1818, at about the same time as Brown's Union Bridge which had a main span of 147 m. The bridge embodied Telford's unrivalled experience of iron acquired both in experiments and in construction. The 9·2 m wide bridge deck incorporated two carriageways and was suspended from four sets of chains made of plate eyebars, having a main span of 190 m. Telford contrasted the delicate iron cables with the solidity of the tapered stone towers in an expressive dichotomy of tension and compression.[16] Navier, the French bridge expert, visited the Menai Bridge while it was under construction in 1823 and was impressed by the audacity of its engineering. The bridge was damaged repeatedly by the oscillation of the deck and chains during storms.[17]

The brilliance of Brunel's proposals for the Clifton Bridge in 1830 was diminished by the long delay in completion. Much of the importance of Brunel's Clifton Bridge designs lay in his proposal to exceed Telford's maximum safe span of 197 m, the span at Menai was 190 m, with spans varying from 285m to 300m.[18] The designs conform both technically and aesthetically to the early English tradition of suspension bridges. The controversy over the maximum safe span for suspension bridges was settled by Chaley whose Fribourg Bridge was finished in 1834, four years after Brunel made his designs. The Fribourg Bridge had a main span of 285 m, equal to that of Brunel's Clifton designs,[19] but instead of using chains made from flat eyebar links as proposed by Brunel, Chaley employed wire cables fabricated on the ground then lifted into place. Wire cables had been suggested for the Clifton Bridge by Mr West of the Clifton Observatory, but the idea was rejected because his scheme lacked the architectural appeal of Brunel's monumental Egyptian towers.[20] Brunel emphasised the elegance of his suspended structure by

210. Menai suspension bridge designed by Thomas Telford, completed in 1826. Span 147 m.

211. Menai iron-chains made of plate eyebars.

212. The Menai bridge, Bangor, North Wales.
213. Brunel's design for the gateways to the suspension bridge over the Avon, Clifton.
214. Clifton with the proposed suspension bridge.

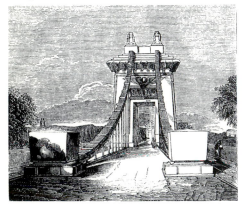

215. The Clifton suspension bridge, completed 1864.
216. The completed Clifton bridge deck was suspended from three sets of chains on each side, instead of two sets as originally proposed by Brunel.

contrasting the slender chains and suspension rods with the monumental towers. The deep Avon Gorge provided a marvellous site for a suspension bridge, and the clean lines of Brunel's bridge effectively dramatised its setting. Floating suspension forms are quite different from the stable forms of landscape, and this contrast enhances the character of each. The special relationship of the suspension bridge with landscape is most keenly experienced in the Clifton and in the Golden Gate bridges.

In his investigation of the failure of the Montrose Bridge in 1838, James Meadows Rendel, a former pupil of Telford's, first differentiated between longitudinal wave motion which he called undulation, and transverse sway, which he called oscillation.[21] Before this, designers had merely regarded the decking as a beam like structure hung from the cable member. Rendel's analysis of deck behaviour led to the recognition of the need to stiffen the deck and give it adequate strength in torsion. Even though Montrose was Rendel's only suspension bridge, the importance of his discoveries justifies his title as the reformer of suspension bridge construction.

The plain catenary and stiffened roadway of Tierney Clark's first suspension bridge at Hammersmith, which was completed in 1827 and had a span of 145 m, reveals his debt to the American James Finley.[22] Clark constructed his greatest bridge over the Danube below Vienna. It was the first permanent bridge erected

133

there since Roman times. The bridge was begun in 1838 and took ten years to complete. The centre span of 218 m was suspended from four flat eyebar chains in conformity with English practice.[23]

France

There were two schools of suspension bridge design in the early 19th century, one English, the other French. While French engineers were impressed by the early English bridges, particularly that at Menai, they nevertheless followed a quite different approach. The theory of suspension bridges developed in France where engineering analysis was more strongly mathematical. Telford actively disliked mathematics and was scarcely acquainted with the elements of geometry. In general, it might be fairly said that English engineers had little interest in structural theory.[24] The French contribution was more original: Navier developed the theory of the behaviour of suspension bridges, Marc Sequin built the first wire suspension bridge with Gabriel Tame in 1824–26, and Louis Vicat invented the method of 'spinning' cables at the bridge site in 1829.[25] As a result of Charles Ellet's visit to France in 1831 to study French suspension bridge design and construction, early American bridge designers are indebted to French methods.

Navier visited England in 1821 where he saw a number of Brown's bridges, and on a second visit in 1823 he observed Menai under construction. His *Rapport et Memoire sur les Ponts Suspendus* (1823) was much more than a report on English achievements for it not only proposed a way of suppressing undulation, but also recognised that the cable shape is a parabola and not a catenary and, in addition, gave a comprehensive method of calculating cable tension.[26] Unfortunately, Navier was more successful as a theoretician than as a builder, and his suspension bridge (Pont des Invalides: main span 189 m) slid into the Seine in 1826.

French thinking about the relative merits of bar iron and iron wire was conditioned by the problems created by a large programme of suspension bridge construction.[27] The level of construction after 1825 was greater than that achieved in any other country. Eight bridges alone were built between 1825 and 1830, and a total of 114 had been constructed in France by 1842.

The Rhone bridges are much less attractive than their English counterparts. Instead of a single large span, French engineers employed two discontinuous spans with a centre tower in the middle of the river. The use of short discontinuous spans of less than 131 m might have been justified technically by a desire to prevent the transfer of vibrations from adjacent spans but it destroyed the purity of the suspension form.[28]

Louis-Joseph Vicat considered the properties of bar iron and iron wire in his report on the Rhone bridges and concluded in favour of iron wire. His judgement on the question was based not so much on a condemnation of bar iron but on recognition of the advantages of iron wire.[29] An important factor in Vicat's judgement was the difficulty of detecting flaws in bar iron and the ease with which iron wire could be protected from corrosion using sheet metal envelopes.

The procedure of aerial spinning developed from a systematic analysis of iron wire cable construction. The Seguin brothers had constructed the Tain Bridge in 1825 with straight cables of parallel wires, but they found that the problems of handling and erection caused unequal tension in individual cables.[30] This occurred because when the straight cables were lifted into position the change in shape resulted in uneven stressing of the wires. Their solution was to pre-shape the wires by spinning them between two temporary towers to give them the same curvature as in the finished bridge. The cables were then taken down and

217. Saint-Andeol iron wire suspension bridge consisting of three discontinuous spans of 92 m. M. Plagniol, 1830.

transported to the bridge where they were lifted into position.[31] Vicat saw that the temporary towers and abutments could be eliminated by using the flying fox or transporter cable to spin the iron wires between the towers of the bridge.[32] The aerial spinning method was born from a process of elimination. The Seguin method of spinning the cables away from the bridge was generally favoured in France and the method of aerial spinning was only used in two bridges constructed in 1840, both of which had long spans.

The United States

Suspension bridge construction in the United States after 1840 was dominated by Charles Ellet and John A. Roebling. Ellet introduced French methods to America and built the first really large spans but he was unable to resolve the fundamental problems of stability. John Roebling made the suspension bridge safe and laid the basis for the modern suspension bridge.

Ellet visited France in 1830–32 during the great period of suspension bridge building and was responsible for introducing French methods to America.[33] He built the first successful wire suspension span in America, the Fairmount Bridge of 1842. The ten iron wire cables were manufactured on the bank because Ellet was unfamiliar with Vicat's method of aerial spinning.[34] Ellet completed the Wheeling Bridge over the Ohio River with a record span of 331 m in 1849. He took the precaution of inclining the suspenders slightly and stiffened the deck with longitudinal timber trusses, but these measures proved inadequate and the bridge was completely destroyed in a storm in 1854. The Wheeling Bridge disaster illustrates how little the principles of aerodynamic stability were understood, except by Roebling.[35]

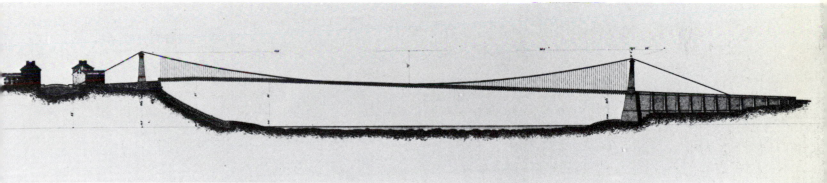

Besides being the greatest suspension bridge builder of the 19th century, John A. Roebling has been acclaimed as the creator of the modern suspension bridge. His Niagara Bridge (1855) was the first modern bridge of its kind. Roebling grew up in Saxony, was trained in engineering and architecture at the Royal Polytechnic Institute in Berlin and at about the same time as Ellet was in France, left for America. Roebling's interest in suspension bridges began with his thesis on a small chain span across the Rednitz at Bamberg. His mastery of the suspension bridge was founded on a profound appreciation of the properties and behaviour of iron wire, and it was this knowledge that led him to advocate 'aerial spinning' and later to recommend the use of steel wires instead of iron wires.[36]

The accident that caused Roebling to become the first manufacturer of wire rope in America gave him a special insight into suspension bridge materials and

218. The Wheeling Bridge, Ohio River, Wheeling, West Virginia, 1849–54.

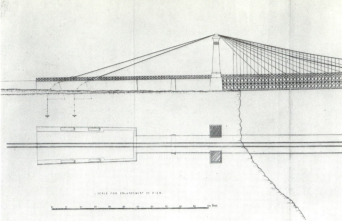

219. The Niagara suspension bridge, 1855. John A. Roebling's first large span, 269 m.
220. The Niagara suspension bridge.
221. The Brooklyn Bridge, East River, New York. Wire-cable suspension bridge, main span 523 m. 1869–83. John A. Roebling.

behaviour. Roebling recognized that the crucial problem of suspension bridge design was that of stability. He perceived that the instability of the suspension bridge could be overcome by giving it adequate stiffness and concluded that no single measure could be relied on to give the required degree of stiffness. Roebling developed a comprehensive strategy combining several actions to defeat bridge instability. Although weight was an essential factor, it was not by itself a sufficient condition for stiffness. Roebling's structural thought was profoundly affected by his analysis of the mechanism of the Wheeling Bridge collapse. He concluded that far from assisting, weight could become the very means of destruction if it was not restrained by stiffness. His philosophy of bridge stability is clearly expressed in a statement that 'the greatest stiffness with the least weight of material'[37] should be the goal of design. Roebling sought to immobilize the suspension bridge through the combined action of weight, stays and counter-stays, as well as by stiffening girders. He considered that a surprising degree of stiffness could be obtained by the united action of girders and trusses without adding much to the weight of the structure.[38] His thinking at this point is essentially modern and closely accords with the principles of prestressed tensile structures. The consequence of Roebling's comprehensive attack on bridge instability was a hybrid suspension bridge form, which was a mixed suspension and cable-stayed structure. His work has been criticised for its conservatism, but it should be recalled that Roebling succeeded where many before him failed.[39]

Roebling's career as a suspension bridge builder began in 1845 with the construction of suspension aqueducts, and in 1846 he built his first real suspension bridge over the Monongahela River. It had diagonal stays which later became his trademark. Ever since Robert Stephenson had pioneered the Britannia Tubular Bridge, engineers considered the suspension bridge to be too light and too flexible to carry railway traffic. Roebling contended that the suspension bridge could be made just as stiff as it needed to be and proved his point by constructing the first stable rail and road suspension bridge at Niagara in 1855, with its record span of 269 m.[40] He used some 64 radiating stays, 56 counterstays, and a deep timber truss between the decks.

Niagara proved Roebling's method and established the pattern for his later bridges. Pugsley's observation that Roebling gained an intuitive understanding of the stiffness of a suspension bridge of long span due to gravity forces is borne out by the progressive structural simplification of his designs with increasing span.[41] Roebling provided only nominal counterstays or underbracing to the Pittsburg

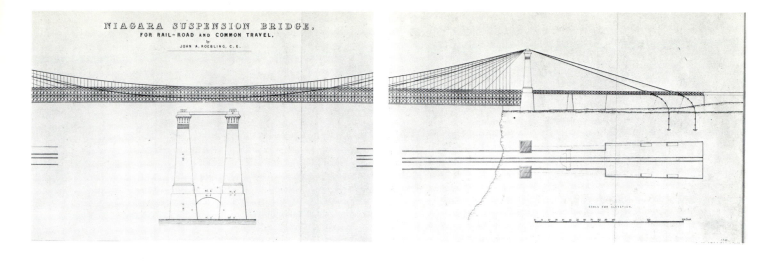

NIAGARA SUSPENSION BRIDGE,
FOR RAIL-ROAD and COMMON TRAVEL.
by
JOHN A. ROEBLING, C.E.

222. The stiffness of the Brooklyn Bridge was provided by the stiffening girders rather than the system of stays and counterstays.
223. The Golden Gate Bridge, San Francisco Bay. Wire-cable suspension bridge, main span 1378 m. Joseph B. Straus, chief engineer, 1937.
224. The Severn Bridge, Severn Estuary, main span 1063 m. Messrs. Mott, Hay and Anderson, Freeman Fox and Partners consulting engineers, 1966.

Bridge (span 347 m), while in the Brooklyn Bridge (span 523 m) he relied less on radiating stays than before, and dispensed with counterstays. The stiffness of the Brooklyn Bridge was provided by the stiffening girders rather than the system of stays and counterstays.[42] The stays served more as stabilisers for the cables and suspender rods than as props for the platform. There is a trend towards a reduction in the number of stays and counterstays and an increasing reliance on the stiffening girder with longer spans. This points towards the structural concept of the modern suspension bridge. The Pittsburg Bridge in 1860 marked the first use of travelling sheaves to spin the cables, and the Brooklyn bridge was the first to have steel wire cables.

20th century suspension bridges

The development of the suspension bridge is characterised by rapid advances followed by lengthy periods of consolidation. Roebling's bridges put construction well ahead of theory and it required almost thirty years before suspension bridge theory was ready for the next great increase in spans after 1929. Considerable advances in the understanding of suspension bridges followed the translation of J. Melan's work on *deflection theory* and *elastic theory* by D. B. Steinman in 1913 and its use in the computations for the Manhattan Bridge in 1909.[43] These advances formed the background to the great expansion in suspension bridge activity in the 1920s and 1930s.

The first distinctly modern suspension bridge on a grand scale was completed in 1926, this was Modjeski's Benjamin Franklin Bridge with a main span of 574 m.[44] The George Washington Bridge in 1931 doubled this span and the Golden Gate with a main span of 1378 m followed soon afterwards (1937). By the mid-1930s not only had the suspension form far outstripped its rivals in spanning ability but all the crucial problems appeared to have been solved.

The Tacoma trauma

It seems astonishing today that the problem of aerodynamic instability should have been ignored for so long. Engineers had formed the rather convenient assumption that bridge decks were now always heavy enough to exceed any known wind uplift.[45] By then, wind forces which had caused havoc on the early suspension bridges were no longer thought dangerous. It is curious that in the late 1930s dynamic wind effects were still being ignored and no one had considered stiffening a suspension bridge against torsion. First, the Bronx-Whitestone 6, gave minor trouble and then on November 7, 1940, the slender Tacoma Bridge tore itself apart

225. The slender Tacoma Bridge tore apart in a steady 18·8 m/s wind on November 7, 1940.
226. Collapse of the Tacoma Narrows Bridge in 1940.

in a steady 18·8 m/s wind.[46] The span failed, not because it had been incorrectly designed, but because engineers neglected to combine and apply in time, the knowledge of aerodynamics and of dynamic vibrations.

There is a critical range of wind speed in which the rate of vortex shedding roughly coincides with the natural vibration of the structure. This might not have proved fatal but the Tacoma bridge was much narrower than other bridges and had long side spans, flexible towers and little vertical stiffening.[47] The susceptibility to deflection and flexibility in torsion resulted in a bridge which was especially vulnerable to the effects of aerodynamic instability. The solution generally adopted in recent years has been to reduce the drag by providing open trusses for stiffening, and to reduce the lift by equalising the air pressure above and below the roadway deck, usually by providing openwork spaces across it.

The loss of confidence following the Tacoma trauma inhibited new thinking to such effect that the next advance in suspension bridge design occured in Britain (1966) with the design of the Severn Bridge. The Severn road deck is a streamlined box of stressed-skin construction suspended by inclined lacing which has a dampening effect, absorbing the oscillatory energy by hysteresis.[48] The streamlining reduces the static pressure on the box section, and thus the lateral load on the towers, to about a third of that on a more conventional deck. The Severn Bridge illustrates the impact of the Tacoma tragedy on engineering thought. In structures where movement is inevitable, damping, streamlining and the avoidance of resonance together with strength, rather than stiffeners, are becoming the goals.[49]

Part Three

Modern tensile architecture

The triumph of suspension bridge builders in the late 1920s and 1930s made tensile architecture inevitable and the Second World War merely postponed the event until 1952. The sporadic essays at tensile architecture after 1840 failed to generate wide support for the principle. Shookhov's series of pavilions in the 1890s very nearly overcame the general mistrust of tensile structures. Modern architects in the 'twenties identified tension as specifically modern because it was seen as the opposite of compressive historical architecture. The interest in spatial tension and efficient structure as an expression of Rationalism attracted the avant-garde whose enthusiasm was not matched by their knowledge of tensile form.

Two kinds of tensile architecture emerged in the 1950s: engineer's tension which was technically motivated, and architect's tension which sought to exploit the novelty of the new tension forms. Some architects were, it is true, attracted to tension because of its technical advantages, but they were in a minority. The choice of the tent as a prototype of tensile building by Frei Otto enabled him to reconcile structure and form. The unity of form, structure and expression in his best work is proof of Frei Otto's mastery of the tensile medium.

Chapter 15

Early Tension

The suspension bridge and modern tensile architecture

Modern tensile architecture need not have developed as it did. The adoption of the suspension bridge and the neglect of the tent as a prototype of the new tensile architecture was neither inevitable nor, as it turned out, the most fortunate of choices. In choosing the ready-made technology of the suspension bridge, the creators of modern tensile architecture committed it to the limited vocabulary of structural forms implied in the suspension bridge. These were not sufficiently varied or flexible to meet the needs of the new tensile architecture.

The early tensile architecture of the 1950s was afflicted by an inability to match structural form with the appropriate technology in a way which was adequate as architecture. The disparity between technology and structural form, since the two are closely linked, arose because the forms derived from suspension bridges had only limited application to architecture, whereas tent forms were much more suitable. Efforts aimed at deriving a modern tent technology from that of the suspension bridge met only limited success. The confusion between form and technology which underlies much early modern tensile architecture was not fully resolved until the emergence of a modern tent technology at Montreal in 1967.

Modern architecture was based on late 19th century technology but it was not until the 1950s that engineers and architects began to take an interest in tensile architecture. The architectural implications of the 19th century development of the suspension bridge were largely overlooked until the 1950s. The increased awareness of the aerodynamic behaviour of tension-loaded structures which flowed from post-Tacoma research prepared the way for modern tensile architecture.

The suspension bridge and the tent are tension-loaded structures which differ in their spatial character and usage. The former is a tensile linear system whose chief function is that of a long span structure. By contrast, the tent is a tensile surface system which has been widely used by nomadic peoples as a lightweight portable dwelling. Of the two, the tent is most closely identified with shelter. Primitive forms of suspension bridges and tents abounded in traditional cultures prior to the industrial revolution but whereas the suspension bridge acquired a modern technology, the tent remained relatively undeveloped until recently.

Early tensile architecture, 1824/1952

Tensile architecture developed late and was preceded by a number of isolated experiments, the work of engineers for the most part, extending as far back as the nineteenth century. The earliest examples of tensile building in the nineteenth century are the roofs by Bederich Schnirch in Czechoslovakia, (1824–26), and the central span of the roof of the Naval Arsenal at Lorient, France, in 1840, both of which illustrate the close connection that existed between the suspension bridge and tensile building, at least in the early phases.

The proposals by the Bohemian engineer and suspension bridge builder Schnirch (1791–1868) which have only recently come to light,[1] represent an ingenious adaptation of early nineteenth-century suspension bridge technology to the requirements of constructing fireproof roofs for theatres, churches, riding schools and warehouses. Schnirch designed and built a chain suspension bridge having a span of 27·43 m (90 ft) and deck width of 4·27 m (14 ft) over the lesser arm of the Morava River, near Strazniche, Czechoslovakia, in 1823–24. When excessive deflection was detected in the suspension chains, Schnirch inserted masonry struts between the pylons and anchor blocks – a precaution that might have saved Navier's Invalides bridge in 1826, thus preventing the anchor blocks from slipping. Following a fire that extensively damaged the nearby town of Strazniche shortly before his bridge was completed, Schnirch conceived the idea of replacing the heavy timber roof framing then in use, with an incombustible roof using malleable iron chains on the same principle as chain bridges. He published his proposals 'Ueber Dachstuehle aus Schmiedeeisen ... Nach dem Princip der Hängenden Kettenbrücken' (About roof structures of malleable iron ... In accordance with the principle of suspended chain bridges) in the Brno *Mittheilungen*, in December 1824 and January 1825. Schnirch described three schemes for roofing a theatre and suggested a simple chain rafter arrangement to replace king-post and other strutted roof structures for domestic construction. In the saddle back roof proposed for a house 18 m deep, the rafter chains are suspended from a ridge wall with ogival openings. The outside walls were stiffened by buttresses and the gable walls to prevent them from overturning. Of the six roofs that Schnirch is known to have constructed in Moravia, Bohemia and Slovakia, one saddle back roof has survived in Banska Bystrica.

The three schemes suggested for roofing a theatre show an interesting structural evolution that begins with a direct transposition of suspension bridge construction to the spanning requirements of a hipped roof, then moves by degrees towards a synthesis of the tensile and architectural factors. In the first scheme the straight ridge and hips are supported from a system of exposed main chains and hangers. The rafter chains in the second proposal are attached directly to the main chains giving the roof a suspended form. Schnirch produced a horizontal ridge in the third scheme by supporting a slender ridge bar off two chains that are held apart by short struts, thus forming a triangular ridge section. The rafter chains are suspended from the main ridge and hip chains as in the second scheme. This third scheme is particularly interesting because it embodies a structural system that approximates the roof structure for the main swimming stadium at the Tokyo Olympics in 1964.

Two aspects of Schnirch's achievement deserve to be emphasised. First, that his approach is original and highly innovative; second, that it demonstrates the strong link between nineteenth-century tensile building and suspension bridge technology. The Naval Arsenal at Lorient, France,[2] in 1840 confirms this connection. The roof with a span of 42 m was formed by supporting transverse roof trusses between two parallel suspension structures that resemble suspension bridge spans. The ends of the roof trusses rested on horizontal members and were supported by vertical hangers from catenaries between towers at either end.

The preeminence of the suspension bridge as a prototype of tensile architecture is demonstrated by the inventor, William Vose Pickett's proposals for suspended roofs. In 1847 Pickett submitted a scheme incorporating the suspension bridge principle for the Army and Navy Club competition, and a year later, he suggested the use of suspended canopies for colonnaded porticoes in Nash's Regent Street Quadrant. Pickett advocated the spanning of vast halls, such as auditoria and churches with suspended roofs, justifying his schemes with the explanation that it would be sufficient merely to provide a light frame to support the suspension chains of the roof.

The 19th century counterpart of Frei Otto is an English Captain of Her Majesty's 94th Regiment, Godfrey Rhodes, who devloped an advanced design for a cupola field tent formed of flexible ash ribs and a larger hospital tent. Rhodes surveyed the tentage of the major European powers (France, Austria, Prussia and Sweden) in 1858 and wrote the first serious history of tents, *Tents and Tent Life, from the Earliest Ages to the Present Time*, (1858)

The outstanding example of early tensile building is unquestionably V. G. Shookhov's four steel tents at the All-Russian Exhibition in Nijny-Novgorod in

1896.[3] Two years earlier, Shookhov had roofed several workshops of the Bary Boilerworks in Moscow with a suspension system of nets made of steel strips covered by thin steel membranes which he later patented. Shookhov chose tent shapes for his pavilions at the Nijny-Novgorod Industrial Fair in 1896: the circular pavilion is a steel *kibitka* with the roof suspended from an elevated inner ring, and the oval shaped pavilion has a steel girder ridge supported on two lattice masts at each end in the manner of the pavilion tent. The two rectangular pavilions have hip roofs and long ridges supported by about ten square lattice masts. Shookhov's understanding of tensile surface structures is advanced for the time and nothing comparable was attempted before the 1950s. The nets of steel strips stiffened the suspended roofs and the heads of the steel masts were enlarged to spread the stresses in the roof. The central section of the circular pavilion was covered by a thin saucer-shaped steel membrane not unlike the one used by Bernard Lafaille in the French pavilion at Zagreb. Daylight was admitted to the interior through hexagonal and diamond shaped lights in the roofs. Shookhov's pavilions are seminal structures.

In 1927 Buckminster Fuller envisaged multi-storey buildings with their floors suspended from a central mast.[4] The concept was projected for a ten storey building at the North pole and his Dymaxion House, 1927–9. The roof and first floor were suspended from a central mast which also served as a service core. At the same time, Heinz and Bodo Rasch, in Wuppertal, Germany, published a sketch of multi-storey housing suspended from a linear series of masts.[5]

During the early 1930s, simply suspended steel sheets were used to cover large grain silos at Albany, St. Louis, and at Memphis, both in the United States.[6] The suspension principle was employed, somewhat clumsily, for the roof of the locomotive roundhouse pavilion at the Chicago World Fair in 1933.[7]

The classical drum of Bernard Lafaille's French Pavilion at Zagreb in Yugoslavia in 1935 concealed a steel suspended roof.[8] The shallow 2 mm sheet metal saucer-shaped roof rested on a single layer of radial cables anchored to a steel compression ring mounted on columns. The comparatively modest diameter of 36 m apparently protected the roof from the destructive effects of flutter. Lafaille's interest in tension-loaded sheet-metal roofs developed from the construction of sheet-metal shell structures. A year earlier, Eugene Beaudouin and Marcel Lods had envisaged a suspended steel cable roof with a diameter of 430 m.

In remote Java, a Dutch engineer, H. McLaine Pont (1885–1971) constructed a church, at Pohsarang in 1936 which incorporated a wire roof suspended between four diagonally arranged arched hips. The principle of the roof may have been suggested to McLaine Pont[9] by the *ruman adat* house of West Sumatra which has a distinctive pyramidal roof of thatch, open and unsupported on all sides. The roof rests on four closely spaced central posts.

227. Erection of the circular (68 m dia)
and rectangular pavilions at the Nijny-
Novgorod Industrial Fair in 1896.
228. Interior of the circular pavilion.
229. Interior of the oval pavilion.
230. Interior of the rectangular pavilion.

231. Simply suspended sheet metal and cable roofs for grain storage, designed by Carghill, Inc.
232. French Pavilion at Zagreb, Yugoslavia, 1935. Bernard Lafaille.
233. Competition project for an exhibition hall with a diameter of 430 m, Paris, 1934. Eugene Beaudouin and Marcel Lods.

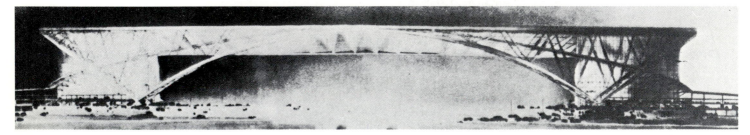

'Tensionism' in the 1920s

The opening of the era of tension in 1952 marked the beginning of a wider discovery of pure force structures and coincided with the outbreak of structural expressionism in the 1950s. Its sudden appearance was not an aberration, but rather the reassertion of a significant current in the Modern Movement which had been repressed in the 1920s following the triumph of the Functionalist view. This impulse has been condemned as a lapse of discipline and as a straying from the central ideals of Modern architecture. It is true that some architects jumped from one form to another, for no better reason than that they were new and exciting, but this playboy approach, as it has been termed, was not typical of the more serious work.[10] Another aspect of the problem was that exploration of the new structural systems was essentially a healthy phenomenon, because it resulted in an enlarged and enriched vocabulary of architectural forms.

The denial of Expressionism and the subsequent domination of Modern architecture in the mid-1920s by Rationalism albeit one heavily burdened with symbolic and aesthetic connotations, profoundly affected the International Style. It resulted in an emphasis on function and logical process at the expense of expressiveness and plasticity. The advent of shell concrete and tensile structures in the 1950s made available a range of structural forms of extreme plasticity and great economy of means. This unusual combination of shapeliness and structural efficiency offered an opportunity for reconciling Expressionism with Rationalism. Concurrently, feeling began to reassert itself in architecture, and this manifested itself in an increase in the expressive threshold of Modern architecture.

The first wave of tensile buildings in the early 1950s was designed not by architects but by engineers, and appeared in the traditional centres of suspension bridge technology — the United States and France. A predisposition towards tensile structures can be discerned in the Rationalist, machine oriented and more extreme anti-Art currents which made up the Modern Movement. The Rationalist view attempted to explain form as a logical consequence of technique and invoked Gothic architecture because it was seen to represent the culmination of logical method in structure. The strand of mechanical determinism permeates the Rationalist arguments of Violet-le-Duc through Choisy to Le Corbusier.[11] The action of a structure in tension is a perfect example of mechanical determinism because it adjusts itself to approach optimum performance.

The consciousness of tension in the 1920s was associated with spatial tension or with the surface tension of plastic forms; only rarely did it refer explicity to structural tension. Sant 'Elia called for a new architecture of maximum elasticity and lightness in the *Messaggio* of 1914,[12] but the earliest visualization of a structure in tension is Mendelsohn's 1914 sketch of a car-body factory, and an imaginary drawing, 1917.[13] Mendelsohn's sketches reveal how unfamiliar tensile forms were. They were conceived in the simplest terms, as straight tensioned systems. His dynamism is an expression of the internal stresses in a building and these happen to be tension stresses in the instance of the car-body factory.[14]

Tensile structures held little interest for architects even after World War I, let alone in 1914. Only in Russia, after the Revolution, was there much enthusiasm for tensile structures.[15] Kiesler's 'Space City Architecture', 1925, exploited the spatial tension, 'a system of tension in free space', engendered by a construction of suspended wooden rails and flat planes, but this was not structural tension.[16] The Italian Mario Fortuny, a brilliant scenographer, fabric and costume designer, and photographer, revived the association of the tent and theatre scene which originated in ancient Greece, with his invention of a convertible scene-tent structure between 1901 and 1929 for the indirect projection of photographic

images. In his semi-cupola shaped scene building, Mario Fortuny stretched the fabric material from a radial arrangement of semi-circular ribs which rotated to allow the membrane to bunch. The suspension details for the fabric were particularly advanced for the time. Undoubtedly the most successful application of tensile structures in the 1920s is Mart Stam's and Marcel Breuer's tubular chairs which had backs and seats of fabric stretched in tension.

Although the Rationalist temper of Constructivism encouraged a kind of constructional expression to develop, it is difficult to find any instances of tensile structures. Thus, while Constructivism failed to produce a tensile architecture of its own, it did inspire two entries for the Palace of the Soviets Competition in 1932. Le

234. *The City in Space*, Paris, 1925. Frederick Kiesler.
235. The Dynamism sketches of Eric Mendelsohn. Sketch for a Motor Car Chassis Factory, 1914.
236. Imaginary sketch, 1917.
237. Marcel Breuer. Tubular steel chair, 1926.
238. Le Corbusier. Palace of the Soviets Competition, Moscow, 1932.
239. Hans Meyer. Perspective sketch of preliminary study for Peter's School, Basle, 1926.

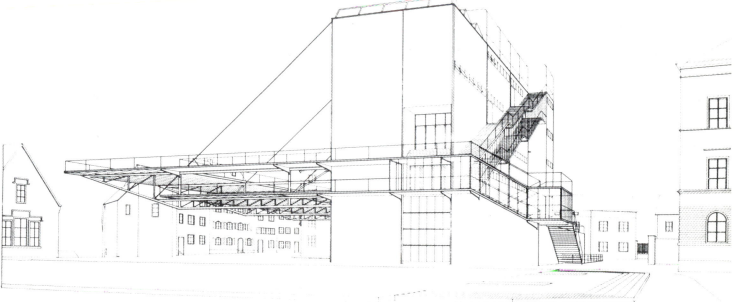

149

Corbusier suspended a series of radial roof beams over his main auditorium by means of vertical hangers attached to the underside of a great parabolic arch,[17] and Simon Breines and Joseph van der Kar pioneered the architectural theme of suspended flexible cables in their entry.[18] Le Corbusier's suspended auditorium roof is more notable for its Constructivist interpretation of structure than its advancement of the tensile principle, though the idea proved influential after World War II. Hannes Meyer's design for Peter's School, Basle in 1927,[19] is by comparison, of much greater intrinsic interest. Meyer intended to sling two 27 m deep steel decks from one side of the school building using four cable stays. The cantilevered decks were to serve as elevated playgrounds.

The Paris World's Fair of 1937 elicited two minor works in tensile architecture by Le Corbusier and Jose Luis Sert. The modest box-shaped tent with simply suspended roof that Le Corbusier designed for the 1937 Exposition Internationale de L'Habitation[20] inspired Renzo Zavanella's pavilions at the Milan Sample Fair of 1948. The light roof was stretched between two walls supported on cigar-shaped open web masts which tilted outwards slightly and were guyed to the ground. The tensile cable frame was covered by a light translucent membrane of canvas. At the same fair, Jose Luis Sert provided a movable awning over the patio-auditorium of the Spanish Pavilion.[21] It consisted of a light membrane stiffened by rods and suspended from parallel wires strung between the main building and the stage.

The concept of tension was associated by the more tough-minded Functionalists with mechanical technology, mechanical determinism and the 'Machine Aesthetic'. It was seen as being, in a vague sort of way, the antithesis of formalism and historical architecture based on heavy masonry structures loaded in compression. Although Werner Graef referred to 'the technology of tensions',[22] and Mario Chiattone included a steel suspension bridge in a 1914 town planning study,[23] the connection was in fact never examined closely or made explicit. Tension was one of the symbolic properties of the Functionalists and remained latent until the early 1950s.

Post-war Tension

The role of the Second World War in the course of the modern movement in architecture is seldom examined, most often it is seen merely as an unfortunate interruption that delayed cultural advances. It needs to be emphasised — and I am grateful to Professor Reyner Banham for drawing my attention to this[24] — that there is a connection between pre- and post-war developments. The continuity of ideas, in spite of the interrruption caused by the war years, is confirmed by Oscar Niemeyer's proposal in 1945 for a National Stadium for Rio de Janeiro. Le Corbusier, in his Palace of the Soviets competition, 1933, introduced the concept of suspending roofs from a free standing arch. The roof beams in Le Corbusier's scheme were to be suspended over the main auditorium by means of vertical hangers from the underside of a great parabolic arch. Niemeyer employed a similar suspension-arch arrangement to support the roof of the National Sports Stadium. This usage, in a modified form, recurs in the station gate to the Festival of Britain. In 1946, another South American, the Argentinian architect, Amancio Williams, applied the suspension principle to the problems of the skyscraper.[25] In Williams's proposal the office floors were to be hung by cables from a deep concrete beam at the top of the tower. Undoubtedly, the strongest line of connection between pre- and post-war developments is to be found in Renzo Zavanella's use in his Transportation pavilion at the Milan Sample Fair, 1948, of Le Corbusier's Paris pavilion of 1937.[26]

It is possible that simple cable-stayed roofs attracted some interest during the years immediately following the war because of the earlier proposals by Fuller and Eero Saarinen. Of these schemes the work of Bruce Goff shows the most consistent commitment to this type of structure. Cable-stayed roofs appeared in a variety of projects: Bertrand Goldberg designed a service station for Standard Oil in 1945 with a roof suspended from two masts, and in 1946 Timber Structures, Inc., advertised their Aero Quad — a small hangar for private aeroplanes — that had a single central mast and six cables.

The early post-war buildings of the mid-western American architect Bruce Goff are of interest because they reveal the impact of wartime thinking and technology, something that was widespread for a time immediately following the war. His Chapel for the Seabees is an excellent example of the architectural exploitation of the Nissen Hut form of construction. Cable-stayed roofs offered similar opportunities for a stripped-down structure, thus it is not in the least surprising to discover Goff employing cable roofs in two projects: the Ledbetter summer lodge, Texoma, Oklahoma in 1947, and the Donald Leidig 'Lilly Pad House' at Hayward, California.[27] The 'Lilly Pad House' represents an interesting adaptation of the cable-stayed principle, comprising a longitudinal beam supported at each end by masts, with the roof suspended from this beam by a system of perpendicular and radial cables. This ridge support arrangement reappears later in Eero Saarinen's Yale Hockey Rink.

The continuity between pre- and post-war development in Europe is demonstrated in the work of the Italian architect and industrial designer Renzo Zavanella.[28] In 1947–48 Zavanella employed a cable-stayed structure for his Transportation pavilion at the Milan Fair.[29] Reyner Banham contends that Zavanella derived his structural system from Le Corbusier's Paris pavilion of 1937 and these usages were then borrowed by British architects for the Festival of Britain.[30]

Le Corbusier's failure to take into account the requirements of structural form was typical of thinking about tensile structure between the war years. Tensile structures in the 1920s and 1930s were usually conceived as linear or cubic forms and at that time there was little recognition of the need to give these surface structures an anticlastic curvature. In his Paris pavilion, Le Corbusier forced the pavilion into the form-mould of the International style, and to a considerable extent Renzo Zavanella accepted this treatment of tensile structure. That is why Matthew Nowicki's Raleigh Arena, with its saddle shaped roof, is such an important turning point in the post-war development of tensile architecture. As late as 1953, Alvar Aalto designed a Sport and Concert Centre for Vienna with a comparatively flat single curvature cable roof that relied on counter-stays for stiffness.

Within the limited pre-Raleigh Arena concept of tensile form, Zavanella developed a cable supported structure of extreme clarity, and indeed brilliance. Zavanella's Transportation Pavilion at the Milan Fair, 1948, was outstanding for several reasons. Zavanella showed a greater knowledge of the structural requirements than did Le Corbusier; moreover, the pavilion possessed a clarity, elegance, and the uncompromising use of modern industrial technology in a structure that was superior to anything else attempted at that time.

Zavanella's enormous competence as an industrial designer can be readily appreciated from the Transportation pavilion, Milan. By comparison, the derivative Festival of Britain structures are much less impressive.[31] The Transportation pavilion consisted of an extremely thin steel brise-soleil roof suspended by cables from six cigar-shaped lattice masts. The thin timber slats used for the roof and platform gave the structure a quality of lightness and precision. In the Transportation pavilion, Zavanella exploited the potential of tensile structure to achieve an open minimal construction that has been reduced to its simplest skeletal elements.

The Festival of Britain served as a joyous national celebration, at a time when the British people wanted to relax and put aside the grim memories of the war and post-war austerity. The design of the outdoors spaces with their emphasis on the unexpected and the picturesque reinforced this intention, even though the majority of buildings consciously pursued a tough engineering aesthetic.

Most prominent among the tensile structures at the Festival, and intentionally so, was Powell and Moya's 100 m high aluminium 'Skylon'.[32] The 'Skylon' was intended not only as a landmark to help visitors to the Festival site to orient themselves but also as a piece of tensile sculpture. The slender cigar-shaped mast of the 'Skylon' was supported on a cradle 13 m above the ground by cables from three outward jutting lattice masts. The 'Skylon' mast was prevented from toppling over by cables from these outer lattice masts to the sides of the 'Skylon'. It is impossible to assess the success of 'Skylon' other than to comment that its gravity-defying structural acrobatics must have been impressive. As a structure the 'Skylon' is rather gimmicky in its exploitation of the novelty of tensile structure, yet to say this is perhaps to seek too serious an interpretation of an object that was after all intended as part of the fun.

It is much more difficult to be kind about the two cone-shaped aluminium porticoes on the main concourse opposite the station gate. These two crude structures, one marking the entrance to the Land of Britain and the other on the opposite side on the upper platform of the main concourse, provided suitable points of focus on the main concourse. In fairness, they should probably be assessed in terms of their role in the streetscape and less as structures. The cones were formed by a radial system of cables running from a central mast to the concourse deck. The cone form was strengthened by wrapping a crescent-shaped aluminium sheath around the rear part of each cable cone. The cones are quite primitive structurally and show no advance over ancient tent forms, many of which are, in these terms, much more ingenious.

Another example of the conscious use of tensile structures at the Festival of Britain, and one that for associational rather than for structural reasons must be considered to have been more successful than the aluminium cones, is provided by the lookout platforms on the seaside section of the Royal Festival Hall terrace. The choice of a 'Nautical Style' by the architects Eric Brown and Peter Chamberlain was especially evocative, particularly since cable and mast structures have long been connected with ships.[33] The observation platforms were carried on a light steel framework suspended from a mast by a system of cables — much in the fashion of a ship's gangway — which were then carried back to support the canvas roof of the displays behind.

Whereas the Festival tensile structures were modern, at Battersea Park a number of traditional tents had been assembled for the Festival Pleasure Gardens. Of these the most interesting was the dance pavilion by James Gardiner and Roger K. Pullen.[34] The dance floor and band platform were enclosed by a large brown and yellow striped parasol tent with an inner tent. The tent was raised into position on a central steel mast and vertical lattice girder stays set in concrete to avoid the need for guy ropes. The edge of the roof was enclosed with metal windows. A large pavilion tent of the traditional pattern was located next to the lakeside stage and a further tent sheltered the Ranelagh beer garden. The Battersea tents reinforced the mood of relaxed gaiety of the Festival Pleasure Gardens. They were entirely traditional in form except for the dance pavilion in which some modern improvements of a very questionable nature were attempted that revealed a superficial appreciation of tent structures.

Chapter 16

Linear Tension

The season of tensile architecture

Matthew Nowicki's livestock pavilion at Raleigh, North Carolina in 1952 announced the opening of the season of tensile architecture. At the outset it introduced the principle of prestressed anticlastically curved tensile surface structures at a time when most designers were thinking in terms of simply suspended roofs. Nowicki's pavilion did not initiate the new tensile architecture, but provided a focus for the rising wave of structural experimentation in the 1950s. There were other factors in the background, but it is difficult to assess their relative importance. The collapse of the Tacoma bridge drew attention to tensile structures and emphasised the need for better understanding of their aerodynamic behaviour.

The greatly increased understanding of aerodynamics and the use of sophisticated techniques of structural analysis which developed during, and immediately after World War II, brought the prospect of a radically new economy in building.[1] With the arrival of so many leading European architects, America became an important international centre of Modern architecture. The holding of the 1947 CIAM Congress at Bridgewater reflected this shift in the balance of architectural influence to the other side of the Atlantic.

America had long led the way in suspension bridge construction and for this reason it was to be expected that this technology would sometime be redirected towards architecture. Besides this readymade tensile technology, America possessed engineers who were experienced in the design and analysis of tensile structures. The curious fact is that several leading exponents of tensile architecture, for example Nowicki, Severud and Zetlin, had only recently arrived in the United States. It will be recalled that the great pioneer of American suspension bridges, John A. Roebling, was also an immigrant.

Modern tensile architecture developed in three phases. In the first phase, from 1952 to 1958, the emphasis was on the solution of technical problems, but by 1958, at the commencement of the second phase, architects were deeply engaged in exploring the sculptural and expressive implications of the new tensile forms. Throughout these phases, designers worked with a modified tensile technology suited to planar rather than surface tensile systems. In the third phase, the constructional means were only properly matched to the structural forms of surface systems with the completion of the German Pavilion at Expo '67 in Montreal.

The first phase was dominated by engineers who directed their attention to conquering the structural and economic complexities of tensile constructions, and to defeating flutter. Engineer's tension was commonly based on the repetition of planar spanning systems over rectangular, circular and oval plans. Their work was frequently dull and inarticulate, though correct. The inflexibility of the plan shapes restricted their use to large span spaces of simple shape.

Sources of planar spanning systems

The engineer's planar systems were derived from three primary sources: the suspension bridge, the cable-stayed bridge, and trusses. Roofs were formed by repeating these spanning systems in parallel or radial series. They were not genuine surface systems but an arrangement of planar spanning systems to form a roof. And even when engineers set out to design prestressed surface systems these are often no more than two superimposed layers of cables of mutually opposed curvature and not flexible, developable cable nets. Rene Sarger, a French engineer who trained with Bernard Lafaille, came closest to realizing the principle of surface systems.

The idea of using cables or stays to support a girder was proposed by C J Loscher in 1784, and in 1821, a Frenchman named Poyet, designed bridge decks supported by radiating wire stays.[2] Hartley designed a harp-shaped suspension system in 1840, and a suspension system stiffened by wrought-iron flat stays was employed in the Albert Bridge over the River Thames (1873). The cable-stayed bridge was revived in Germany in the 1950s for spans in the range of 165 m to 500 m.[3] A number of hangars and a few airport terminals were constructed in the United States with roofs supported by cable-stayed cantilevered beams.

240. The Albert Bridge over the Thames, completed in 1873.

The bicycle-wheel roof was anticipated by Sir George Cayley's invention, in 1803, of the tension spoke wheel. The engineer's attempts at stabilizing the simply suspended dish-shaped roof produced a series of modified forms: first the pre-loaded catenary, then the bicycle wheel form consisting of a prestressed double layer of independent cables, which in turn was succeeded by the double surface bicycle wheel form with pretensioned linked cables.

David Jawerth developed a system of cable trusses made of prestressed cables and struts not so very different from Lev Zetlin's bicycle wheel of pretensioned linked cables.[4] The Jawerth system has two suspension cables or membranes which are tensed against each other by a zig-zag configuration of struts. The profile of the upper cable is concave and that of the lower cable, convex. The spanning elements are usually arranged parallel to each other.

The language of tension

The interest of architects in tensile structures centred on the problem of form. The challenge of the new structures was to perfect the language of tension. This does not mean the formalisation of the tension idea, but rather an understanding of the nature of tensile structures and the way that this is communicated.[5] The problem is to relate structure, form, and expression in a self-consistent manner. Architectural tension, in contrast to engineering tension, was self-conscious. The architectural deployment of any type of structure involves the problem of expression, and this raises the possibility of an imposed formalism. In this case, the danger was exaggerated by the peculiar eloquence of tension. It was soon realised that the first aesthetic rule of the genre is that structural tension need not be translated into emotional tension.[6] An exposed tensile member communicates its task with remarkable eloquence compared with heavy compressive members because of the identity of force and form. In short, the aesthetic qualities depend on the unhindered revelation of structure, the sort of exhibited structure that Mies van der Rohe referred to in 1921.[7]

The language of tension was ideally suited to conjuring up the 1920s illusion of weightlessness and of dynamic plastic form. Tensile structures provided the technical means for realising an optically immaterial, almost hovering, appearance.

The architect's understanding of tensile structures was extremely limited and this showed itself in the form vocabulary and in the inability to relate form to structure in a logical way. The logic of tensile structures was abused because of the primacy of formal ideas and the imperative of expression. In spite of these shortcomings, architects made a real contribution because their awareness of tensile form led them to consider its aesthetic as well as its technical implications.

The repetition of a few favourite themes sets the architect's idea of tension apart from the engineer's technical approach. They comprise simply curved suspended roofs, simple saddle surfaces consisting of cable systems curved in two mutually opposed directions, and traditional urban tent shapes. This range of types reflects a taste for surface systems and a somewhat elementary notion of tension that did not encompass either the diversity and richness of tensile forms or their technical complexity. Architects were attracted to shapes whose structural behaviour was, at least superficially, easy to understand. Their interest in surface systems, especially tent shapes, stemmed from the recognition of their flexibility and appropriateness for vaulting interior space. The simple catenary surface was a recurrent theme, perhaps because it is so closely related to the familiar planar system of the suspension bridge, but also because of the simple elegance of the catenary curve.

The tent as a prototype of modern tensile architecture

Eero Saarinen and, to a much greater extent, Frei Otto, popularised the tent as a prototype of modern tensile architecture. Kenzo Tange's monumental steel tents for the Tokyo Olympics in 1964 are the climax of a line which Saarinen initiated at Yale in 1956. Saarinen led the way in exploiting the formal aesthetic and expressive values of tensile architecture. His compulsive expressionism is less evident in his tensile buildings but the structural principle is, nevertheless, subservient to the formal idea.

Frei Otto's contribution to modern tensile architecture is important and, in a sense, unique, because he sought to develop tensile form and technology concurrently.[8] He did not treat tensile form as separate from the technical problem but adopted an integrated approach which recognised their interrelatedness. The disadvantage of the engineers' and architects' treatment of tensile structures is that they did not consider them as a whole, nor see that tensile form, and the means of making it, are aspects of the same problem.

Frei Otto devoted his researches to cataloguing and analysing the various families of tensile surface structures, and simultaneously, to perfecting the means for making them.[9] He began by designing modest tents with membrane awnings, and from this experience of the behaviour of prestressed woven membranes, he devised developable cable nets. The importance of this structural evolution cannot be overstated since it explains the success of his later structures. Otto could afford to experiment and to take risks with the design of his small membrane structures, whereas engineers designing large span structures had necessarily to be more cautious. Telford also began by constructing a $\frac{1}{10}$ scale model of a suspension bridge to test the principle. Because Frei Otto relied on models to simulate tensile behaviour, he was not inhibited by the complexities of mathematical analysis to the same degree as engineers. The use of models gave him an early advantage in investigating complex tensile forms which were difficult to analyse mathematically in the 1950s.[10] The German Pavilion at Montreal in 1967 was the first truly modern tent, in which form and means were properly matched. The 1972 Munich Olympic stadia are much less satisfactory because the spans are too large for the roof curvature, and there was a failure to relate the architectural and structural solutions satisfactorily.

Suspended roofs

The use of suspended roofs was largely confined to architects who were attracted by the elegant and subtle geometry of the catenary. Engineers avoided simply curved suspended roofs in their search for self-damping cable systems that did not rely on the weight of the construction for stability.

The two most notable examples of engineer's suspended roofs are the aircraft hangar in Kempten and the Wuppertal Municipal Swimming pool with a span of 65 m. Both were completed in 1957.[11] The cables of the latter were embedded in concrete as protection against corrosion and for this reason the roof is more accurately described as an inverted short shell.

Nervi's Paper Mill at Burgo is a displaced suspension bridge.[12] In no other building is the suspension bridge-building metaphor stated more explicit as in this attenuated mill. The choice of a suspension structure was dictated by production requirements that called for a continuous column-free hall over 147·6 m long. The prefabricated truss roof deck is suspended between the window mullions from twin 52·5 m high concrete towers on four flat-steel chains. The window mullions are fixed to the floor slab of the machinery room and have no connection with the roof.

The Healy Summer House (1947–48) was built too early to be affected by the rigor mortis of Paul Rudolph's later formalism. It exhibits freshness, sensible planning and is, at the same time exceedingly economical in the use of materials.[13] The use of a suspended roof over such a short span (6·6 m) has been criticised as being structurally inappropriate, but in defence, it should be pointed out that desert nomads also choose to build tents for much the same reason that Rudolph did; both want light and economical forms of construction.[14] The roof deck was simply suspended on steel flats between wooden posts which were guyed back by steel rods to the ends of protruding floor beams. The small span immunized the roof against the effects of wind, buffeting and uplift, and therefore no stabilizing devices were provided. The roof deck was protected with material similar to that

156

241. Wuppertal Municipal Swimming Pavilion, Germany, 1957. Span 65 m. F. Leonhardt and F. H. Hetzelt.
242. Paper Mill at Burgo, Mantua. View from the south. Pier Luigi Nervi.
243. Twin concrete towers.
244. Longitudinal section.
245. The window mullions were fixed to the floor slab of the machinery hall and had no connection with the roof.

used by the US Navy to 'mothball' its ships. Hence its name, the 'cocoon house'.

The impact of this smart little summerhouse was extraordinary and out of all proportion to its size. It drew attention for the first time to the aesthetic quality and structural novelty of tension, but also showed that the suspended roof possessed a peculiarly classical quality. Saarinen's great gateway to Washington D.C., the Dulles Airport (1963) is founded on Rudolph's discovery. An ever watchful Kenzo Tange used and abused the suspension theme in his Golf Club at Totsuka, completed in the same year. Both buildings have extroverted interior spaces which focus on the activities outside. The spatial extroversion of the hammock roof form is useful for blending interior space and landscape.

246. Paul Rudolph incorporated double suspended roofs in his 1951 cottage for Mrs Kate Wheelan, Siesta Key, Florida.

Saarinen's interest in tensile structures was of long standing. He designed a radial cable-stayed structure for a community centre in 1941,[15] and later on, in 1949, he devised a large tangerine and white 'big top' to house the Goethe Music Festival at Aspen, Colorado.[16] The structural significance of the Dulles Airport influenced its expression, and in consequence, the blatant and wayward formalism of Saarinen's earlier work is held in check. The result is a convincing symbol of flight which avoids the literal expressionism of the TWA terminal. Saarinen transposed the Roman triumphal arch into the inverted-arch form of the singly curved suspended roof to create a fitting gateway to Washington.

The Dulles Airport terminal is spanned by a 191 m long rigid sheet of concrete draped between edge beams supported by two rows of outward thrusting concrete pylons, higher on the arrivals side. The roof is a rigid, inverted concrete shell whose weight and rigidity eliminates the danger of flutter.[17] Precast concrete panels were placed between each set of 25 mm diameter strand cables which were then pre-loaded and encased in reinforced concrete ribs.

The links between the Dulles building and the suspension bridge are strong. Its structure was designed by a leading firm of bridge consultants, Ammann and Whitney. Bridge strand assemblies were employed for its meagre clear span of 52·8 m, and even the structural expression reflects Ammann's admiration of the early English suspension bridge. Saarinen consciously contrasted the apparent weightlessness of the roof span with the heavily wrought concrete pylons much as Telford had done at Menai. Saarinen was not content to allow the structural members to perform their tasks unnoticed, he insisted that they must be seen to do their work. The pylons slice through the roof, curl over and, finger-like, grasp the edge beam. The convex curvature of the glass walls further emphasises the thrusting action of the pylons. Both Saarinen and Tange unconsciously subverted the radicalism of the tension aesthetic by supplying it with traditional references.

Interest in weight-stabilised, singly-curved, suspended roofs revived in the mid-sixties, but it was not till 1968 that Frei Otto was given the opportunity of

247. Community Centre project, Eero
Saarinen, 1941.
248. Music tent, Aspen, Colorado Eero
Saarinen, 1949.
249. View from arrivals side, Dulles
International Airport for Washington, D.C.
Chantilly, Virginia. Eero Saarinen and
Associates, 1958–62.

250. The rigid concrete sheet was draped
between two rows of unequal concrete
pylons.

251. Construction of the suspended roof.
252. View of roof edge beam and pylon
from underside.

collaborating with Rolf Gutbrod on a suspended roof for the Hotel and Conference complex at Mecca, Saudi Arabia.[18] The Mecca roofs mark a new stage in the plastic expression of the suspended roof. The Dulles roof is a uniform sheet of draped concrete, whereas the roofs and walls of the Mecca auditorium and seminar rooms are integrated sculpturally.

There are two kinds of tensile structures; those stabilised by prestressing and those stabilised by self-weight. Frei Otto's interest in heavyweight suspended roofs might appear inconsistent with his devotion to the principle of lightweight structures, but non-prestressed simply suspended surfaces provide a link with lattice grid shell structures stressed purely in compression. The Hotel and Conference Centre at Mecca, Saudi Arabia (1968–74) provided Frei Otto with his first real opportunity to build a heavyweight single spanning roof. Le Corbusier's dictum, 'the plan is the generator',[19] has been reversed at Mecca where the roof, not the plan, is the generator. The heavyweight single spanning roofs over the Mecca auditorium and seminar rooms are composite cable and strut net configurations comprising transverse 75 × 75 mm double angles laid every 500 mm on 26 mm strand cables suspended in one direction.[20] The rigid double angles transfer asymmetrical loads and ensure a more uniform cable action. The wall tees are suspended from the roof and podium edges. The plastic unity of the sharp-edged crescent-shaped auditorium and seminar rooms is enhanced by extending the aluminium sandwich roof deck down the wall surfaces.

It is worth comparing the sculptural expression of the Mecca Conference Centre roofs with Saarinen's Dulles roof: whereas Saarinen's roof is a two-dimensional sheet of concrete suspended above and visually isolated from the floor podium, the roof and walls of the Mecca auditorium and seminar rooms are a sculptural unity. This has been achieved by allowing the outline of the roofs to define the wall surfaces and by covering both with the same aluminium decking.

Bicycle wheel roofs

The circle is an appropriate shape for tensile structures because the compression ring ensures that the outer anchorage is uniformly stressed in compression under symmetrical loading. This advantage has been realized in a number of traditional types of tensile architecture, namely the *kibitka*, and the parasol-roof tent. The *vela* over the Roman amphitheatres are thought to have had radial cable systems, and the earliest instances of modern tensile buildings, Shookhov and Lafaille's pavilions, were both dish-shaped suspended roofs. Eugene Beaudouin and Marcel Lods's proposal to span 430 m, the diameter of the exhibition hall, in their entry for the OTUA competition, in 1934, with a star-shaped, undulating, suspended roof of steel cables, is an extraordinary visionary projection of the tension idea.[21] By comparison, Lev Zetlin's claim, made two decades later, that his patented roof system would span from between 66 m and 590 m sounds conservative.[22]

Saucer-shaped or synclastically curved single cable roofs are closely related to simply curved suspended roofs with the difference that instead of the cables being parallel, they are usually arranged radially. Both types suffer from a serious defect: they are unstable when subjected to dynamic loads.

Problems of movement and flutter are minimized by pretensioning the main cables: this may be achieved by either increasing the dead weight of the roof construction, as in weight-stabilised suspended roofs, or by introducing a set of secondary pretensioned cables. Double cable systems are in fact planar versions of pretensioned saddle surfaces. The use of dead weight to improve the dynamic stability of tensile structures runs counter to the most attractive feature of tensile structure — that is, lightness. Engineers have therefore tended to attack movement and flutter by devising self-damping configurations of pretensioned cables.

Methods employed to prestress saucer-shaped suspended roofs were at first crude, as can be seen from the example of the 101 m diameter roof over the Municipal Stadium in Montevideo, Uruguay, (Mondino, Viera and Mille) which was converted into a slightly compressed suspended concrete shell by the simple expedient of preloading the cables.[23] Precast slabs were placed on the flexible radial cables and then loaded with thousands of bricks so that when the joints between the slabs had been grouted and the load removed, the roof was left in a state of slight compressive prestress.

Tensile architecture was well represented at the Brussels Fair in 1958; there were Rene Sarger's pavilions, Edward D. Stone's US Pavilion, and Le Corbusier contributed an ambiguous hard-edged and thin-skinned essay in hyperbolic paraboloid surfaces. The lid of Stone's candy jar at Brussels had a new cable geometry capable of being prestressed.[24] The roof (span 99 m) consisted of a double layer of independent cables radiating from the upper and lower rim of a central tension drum to an outer compression ring. The secondary cables have different tension than the primary cables and this assists in eliminating flutter by raising the natural frequency of the system. This bicycle wheel system of double independent cables has several advantages: it is a rigid triangulated structure with a conical roof surface that allows rainwater to drain to the outside. Mesh was draped over the two sets of offset cables to create a star-shaped undulating ceiling. An interesting aspect of modern tensile architecture is the way that research has confirmed the functional fitness of certain constructional features in traditional tents. The wind tunnel tests of the US Pavilion revealed that the opening in the centre greatly reduced the effect of wind on the roof, so that the smoke hole in the *kibitka* must also have performed an important aerodynamic function.[25]

About the same time, Lev Zetlin improved the double layer system of prestressed cables by inter-connecting the unequally prestressed cable pairs with vertical strut

253. Bicycle wheel roof structure for the Utica Memorial Auditorium, New York, 1960.

or tie spreaders. This produced a remarkably rigid cable structure which was virtually immune to flutter.[26] Each cable layer has a different vibrational frequency and this results in a self-damping mode. The first building to incorporate Zetlin's roof principle was Gehron's undramatic circular arena at Utica in 1959.[27] Its roof cables were strung from a central metal tension ring in mid-air to an outer reinforced concrete compression ring, and the cables were prestressed by jacking apart the two central steel tension rings. The space between the two layers of cables was utilized for the auditorium's mechanical and air conditioning equipment.

The usefulness of the bicycle wheel roof is restricted to circular or oval plan shapes. Le Ricolais explored the application of interconnected double layer systems of prestressed cables for a variety of plan geometries in 1958 and arrived at triangular and rectangular grid systems of cables without central tension rings.[28]

Cable-stayed roofs

Cable-stayed roofs and bridges are so closely linked in their development that they may be considered to be products of the same technological advance. They were designed, often enough by the same people, and constructed with much the same technical means. Ammann and Whitney's early cable-stayed hangars at Philadelphia and New York International Airports were completed in 1956, the same year in which the first German-designed cable-stayed bridge across the Stormund, Sweden, was completed.[29] Another noted bridge consultant, Professor Riccardo Morandi, designed a cable-stayed hangar for Alitalia at Rome International Airport. The growth of commercial aviation in the 1950s fostered the application of cable-stayed roofs to airport hangars and, to a lesser degree, to terminal buildings.

With the increasing size of aeroplanes, cable-stayed cantilever designs gradually supplanted arches or end-supported trusses.[30] Spans of up to 52·5 m were achieved with balanced double cantilevers, and of about 43 m with single cantilevers. These hulking sheds — unaffected works of engineering — are the modern counterparts of Freyssinet's Airship hangars. Hangar 17 at John F. Kennedy International Airport (1959) is the most impressive structure of this type, having 52 m long steel plate girder double cantilevers supported from 8·9 m high masts by four 63·4 mm diameter bridge strand cables.[31] This elegant and economical structure lacks the flair of Riccardo Morandi's Alitalia hangar roof. Professor Morandi sloped the graceful upturned roof beams and the pairs of inclined struts so that they are no longer passive, but animated structural members.[32]

254. Pan American Hangar, John F. Kennedy International Airport, New York, 1959. Amman and Whitney.
255. Pan American Terminal, John F. Kennedy International Airport, New York, 1959.

The Pan American Terminal at New York's John F. Kennedy International Airport was the first to use cable-stayed roofs in a prestige building, but unfortunately the cables are concealed behind the broad brim of the elliptical roof.[33] Previously, cable-stayed roofs were relegated to the service areas of airports. The roof consisted of an oval ring of radially arranged cable-stayed double cantilevers whose inner ends were secured to a central hexagonal ring opening. The steel plate roof girders were supported on each side by three radial cables. The elliptical roof canopy soared 36 m beyond the columns to provide a weather-protected area around the terminal for embarking passengers.

The Blyth Arena for the 1960 Winter Olympics held at Squaw Valley, California, is the most attractive of these early cable-stayed roofs. In this instance the cables and their tilted mast supports were fully exposed.[34] The 98 m span pitched roof was supported by two rows of inclined cantilevers, back stayed and anchored at their outer ends. Cable-stayed roofs were used for the Tulsa Exposition Centre and the Nicholson Pavilion, Ellensburg, Washington.[35]

The concept of suspending platforms from a central mast which Fuller initiated in 1927 was realized in a cluster of five interconnected cable-stayed platforms over Lake Ontario at Toronto in 1972.[36] The pavilions stand knee deep in the lake and resemble a large modern version of a Swiss 'Lake Dwellers' village. Ontario Place (architects Craig, Zeidler and Strong) consists of a series of square decks suspended by twin cables secured to each corner from a central tower of four large tubular masts rising from the lake bed. The Cinesphere's geodesic dome on the southern edge is a reminder of Fuller's influence on the conception of this pleasant lake village.

256. Ontario Place, 1970.

Double layer cable system

The principle of dampened suspension systems comprising two inter-connected prestressed cables can be embodied in planar or surface constructions. The advantage of anticlastically curved surfaces is that the two layers of cables of mutually opposed curvature intersect at points on the same surface, thus avoiding any need for linear connectors. The two sets of cables are merely laid over the anticlastic surface and clamped together at their intersections. In the example of planar double cable systems the two cables of opposed curvature must be interconnected with ties or struts depending on whether a concave or a convex lens shape is assumed.

Planar double cable systems were used first in bicycle wheel roofs, but in 1959 a Swedish engineer, David Jawerth, patented a system for covering rectangular areas with parallel arrangements of the spanning elements.[37] The cable trusses must be connected by rigid transverse members to stiffen the roof deck against asymmetrical loading. Variations in temperature affect the prestress force in the cables so that it is important to ensure that fluctuations in the thermal environment of the roof structure do not result in the cables being either overstressed or understressed at any time.

After 1960 Jawerth built a series of roofs using his system in France and Germany and Sweden with spans ranging from 24 m to 83 m. The earliest was a factory at Lesjofors (1960) which had a longitudinal series of five concave lens-shaped trusses (5 × 16 m) interlaced with diagonal ties. The wave-like profile of the roof was accentuated by triangular transverse skylights. The largest of Jawerth's roofs was constructed over the ice stadium at Stockholm-Johanneshov. Jawerth employed a single lens-shaped cable truss to span the 83 m wide stadium.

David Jawerth's roofs are extremely pure tensile structures whose lightness has not been compromised by the imposition of an extraneous formalism. They are extremely attractive because they have been shaped by tension alone.

Chapter 17

Surface Tension

Structural Expressionism

Architects were drawn to tensile architecture for no better reason, sometimes, than that it offered an escape from the tyranny of the box. The plasticity of the Expressionists was of a largely superficial kind since the forms expressed theoretical or sculptural ideas with little regard for material. The new structures of the 1950s, shell concrete and tensile structures, offered a legitimate means of creating highly plastic forms without forcing or distorting structure. In the 'fifties, architects wanting to extend the manipulation of interior space beyond freely disposing walls, began to take an interest in the roof. The inherent shapeliness of purely stressed structures offered a means of breaking out of the box and of increasing the plasticity of architectural forms.[1]

One of the disappointments of the new structural expressionism is that architects often failed to understand the structural principles governing the new shapes, and their cultural baggage — an obdurate heavyweight aesthetic reflex — kept on getting in the way. By far the most common fault with architects' tensile architecture was failure to observe the appropriate scale of each structural form. Architects tended to assume that basic prestressed tensile shapes were improved by being enlarged, perhaps because the history of the suspension bridge showed that its stability improved with increasing size once a certain span had been reached.

Another casualty of architects' tensile architecture was lightness, both visual and material. There is a fundamental difference between architects' tensile architecture and the work of Frei Otto aims at optimal forms. Because architects approached tensile architecture with a view to creating a more sculptural expression, they often missed the really radical aspect of tensile structures — the structural efficiency of lightweight. The chief difference between conventional and tensile architecture is largely a matter of shape. Frei Otto's involvement with tensile structures arose from his pursuit of a lightweight architecture. Consequently, not only are his buildings extremely light, but they possess a visual weightlessness which easily distinguishes them from architects' tensile architecture.

Mathew Nowicki: the Raleigh Arena

The Raleigh Arena, North Carolina (1952) is a germinal structure whose classic saddle-shaped roof supplied the prototype for later prestressed cable roofs. The combination of two sets of cables, one suspended between two compression arches, a second set stretched at right angles to the first and curved in a mutually opposite direction, initiated an enduring sculptural theme.[2] This arrangement reappeared, suitably modified, in Saarinen's Yale Hockey Rink (1958), Stubbin's Berlin Congress Hall (1959), and Tange's basketball and swimming stadia at Tokyo (1964). Nowicki's Arena marks the beginning of tensile architecture based on surface as opposed to planar cable systems.

The Raleigh Arena suffered from a number of minor structural defects which are worth recording since they recur in later buildings. The upper part of the roof was too flat, and the roof construction was so light (30 kg/m²) that it was subject to unacceptable vibration and flutter under wind load. These flaws were corrected by inserting damping springs at the cable connections and treating them with graphite, and by adding guy wires and acoustical material to the underside of the roof deck. The unstable two-point foundation had to be heavily modified by inserting support columns under the tilted parabolic arches.[3]

The original idea for the roof of the Berlin Congress Hall (1959) was that of a prestressed cable network stretched between two inclined compression arches

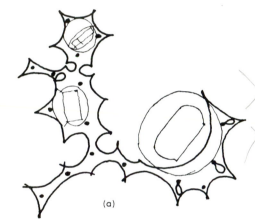

(a)

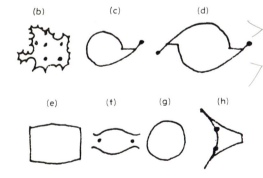

(b)   (c)   (d)

(e)   (f)   (g)   (h)

257. Comparison of the increase in size of cablenet structures since 1952: a, Munich, 1972; b, Montreal, 1967; c, Tokyo, 1964; d, Tokyo, 1964; e, Stockholm, 1960; f, New Haven Yale University, 1958; g, Raleigh North Carolina; h, Melbourne, 1958.

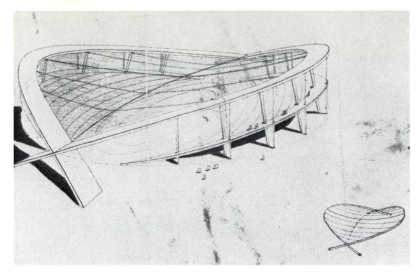

258. Nowicki's original scheme for the Raleigh Arena.
259. Aerial view.
260. Plan.

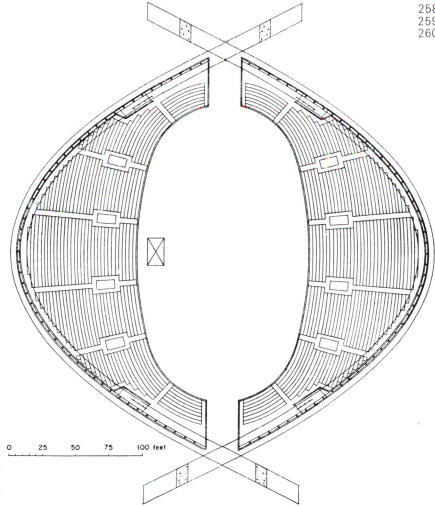

0   25   50   75   100 feet

167

261. Model of the Phillips Pavilion, Brussels. Le Corbusier, 1958.
262. The French Pavilion, Brussels. Rene Sarger, engineer, 1958.

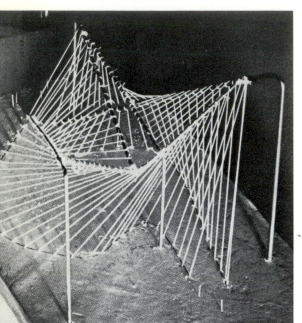

263. Marie-Thumas Restaurant Pavilion, Brussels. Rene Sarger, engineer, 1958. The roof structure.
264. Wave-shaped pavilion.

similar to that of the Raleigh Arena. As it has been realized, the roof is actually a concrete shell, the centre of which is stiffened by means of a heavy ring beam. The arches are connected to this beam for stability. The basic structural principle has been compromised by not allowing for peripheral columns, asymmetrical loads and the acoustical isolation of the auditorium.[4]

Apart from the circular compression rings at each end, the roof of the Rio Grande do Sul Exhibition Hall in Brasilia (1954) consisted entirely of cables acting in tension.[5] The shape accords perfectly with the principle of a prestressed roof: the main longitudinal cables between the two transverse arches are restrained by circular transverse cables. Spiral clamps prevented the transverse cables from sliding down the main cables. The precise semi-catenoid geometry of the roof lacks the expressiveness of the saddle shape.

Rene Sarger: The Brussels Pavilions

By 1958 the impetus in tensile architecture had shifted from the United States to Europe and to France in particular. France had once played a leading role in the development of the suspension bridge so it was appropriate that it should once again make an important contribution to tensile structures. The occasion was the Brussels Worlds Fair in 1958. France contributed three tensile buildings, the National Pavilion, The Marie-Thumas Restaurant pavilion and an information centre. Rene Sarger, a French engineer and former pupil of Bernard Lafaille, was heavily engaged in producing all three structures.

The roof of the French Exhibition Hall comprised two anticlastically curved cable systems stretched across twin warped rhomboids joined along a common boundary.[6] The oppositely curved surfaces were prestressed by the weight of the stiff edge members and the walls. This bulky hall (span 100 m) lacked the vitality of the Marie-Thumas Pavilion.

Marie-Thumas is a rather ambiguous work, its unified external form suggests that it is a surface structure, but an examination of the construction reveals that it was assembled from linear tensile elements, with the result that it remains as a planar tensile structure.[7] It had a wave-shaped roof surface formed by alternating ridge and valley cables. The main ridge cables were supported at each end by two internal V-type masts. The ridge and valley cables were infilled with steel joists made of convex lens-shaped prestressed double cables with strut spreaders. The roof and walls of the prestressed cable network were sheathed in heat-sealed plastic sheets — opaque aluminium-coloured on the roof and shades of blue on the sides.

The most outstanding features of the pavilion were its tent-like wave shape and the successful integration of the roof and wall surfaces into a sculptural whole. In the same year, Sarger also designed a simple saddle-shaped cable net roof (20 × 30 m) covered with plexiglas sheets, to serve as a Saharan shelter tent.[8]

Antipodean tension

The tension idea surfaced in Melbourne, Australia, in 1958 for in that year, Robin Boyd, a noted Australian architect and critic, suspended a simply curved roof over his South Yarra home,[9] and Yuncken and Freeman, with engineer Bill Irwin completed the Sidney Myer Music Bowl. The Music shell comprised a vast tent-like roof — open along one side — tensed between a heavy edge cable elevated on two 21 m high masts and anchored to the ground along the sides and behind the

265. Sidney Myer Music Bowl,
Melbourne, Australia, 1958.
266. Myer Music Bowl —
in construction.

orchestra.[10] In addition to sheltering the orchestra and an audience of 2000, the roof reinforced the music accoustically. A further 20000 people could be accommodated on the surrounding grass slopes. There are two types of roof cables, the main longitudinal cables suspended from the heavy edge cable and transverse cables of opposite curvature which tie the roof down. The cable net is clad with long aluminium-faced plywood panels. The soft rounded form of the music shell blended well with the rolling contours of the surrounding terrain.

Eero Saarinen: Yale hockey rink

Eero Saarinen always sought for his buildings an expressive theme indicative of the human context. In the Ingall's Hockey Rink at Yale University (1956–58) he realized the latent expressiveness inherent in prestressed tensile surface structures and, in so doing, gave a lead in the appreciation of the dynamic quality of tensile forms. The hockey rink was the first masterwork of tensile architecture in which structure and expression are united in a coherent sculptural form. Saarinen recognized that the dynamic quality of prestressed tensile forms, the potential energy stored in the tensed sinews of the structure, create a special empathy with sporting activities. The interior of the rink resembles the upturned hull of a viking ship and this evokes a sense of energetic physical movement. Much of the formal unity of the building derives from Saarinen's repetition of the same parabolic profile in the central ridge and the compressive arch anchorages.

It is natural that architects, rather than engineers who lack the architect's awareness of form traditions, should relate tensile surface structures with tents. Saarinen consciously exploited a modified pavilion tent shape for the Yale hockey stadium.[11] The main supporting cables are draped between a lyre-shaped concrete arch spine and two concrete anchorage walls which repeat the profile of the central spine. Longitudinal cables are superimposed on the main cables and prestressed to prevent wind uplift. The purity of this arrangement is spoilt by the presence of three anti-torsion storm cables which brace the central arch against asymmetrical wind or snow loads.[12] The cable network was overlaid with a 50 mm thick wood deck, stiff enough to prevent local flutter and weatherproofed with a neoprene membrane. In order to correct the visual weakness evident in the open ends of the roof, Saarinen gave the roof itself a flared countercurve which effectively terminated the roof and dramatised the entrances. Unfortunately, this countercurve produced a synclastic surface which could not be prestressed.[13] Victor Lundy repeated Saarinen's termination form in his 1960 USAEC pneumatic pavilion.

Kenzo Tange: the Tokyo Yoyogi Olympic stadia

The primitive feeling of the Tokyo-Yoyogi arena roofs is akin to that of early Shinto architecture. These arenas are in reality national shrines rather than mere sports halls, the modern equivalents of Ise. Tensile architecture has an obvious affinity with the subtly curved roof forms of Shinto architecture and Tange reinforced this identity in the detailed grain of the stadia roofs.

Kenzo Tange took the idea of tensile architecture enunciated in Saarinen's Hockey rink and systematically perfected it so that the Tokyo-Yoyogi arenas are superior to the original. His recent emphasis on communications does not seem to have inhibited his form-making in which he seeks to create final sculptural shapes of enormous presence. The arenas are consummate tensile sculptures, probably the

267. Aerial view of David S. Ingalls Skating Rink, Yale, New Haven. Eero Saarinen and Associates, 1953–58. (Model).
268. Transverse section.
269. View of entrance.
270. Interior.
271. Olympic Arenas in Tokyo-Yoyogi. Kenzo Tange with URTEC, architects, 1961–64. View from east of the great stadium.

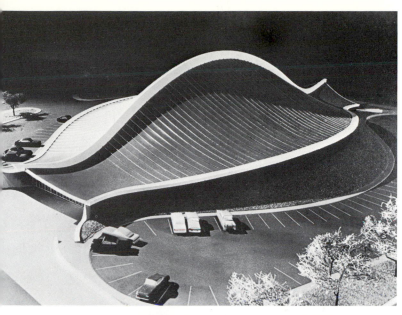

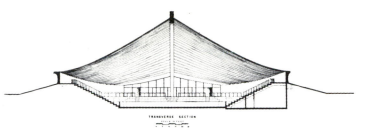

TRANSVERSE SECTION

best this century has produced, but they have been achieved by improperly forcing the structural medium. Tange adopted Saarinen's arched anchorage walls but substituted two ridge cables suspended between enormous concrete masts for the central arch.

These two Tokyo arenas were not Tange's first ventures in tensile form; he employed a rigid saddle-shaped concrete shell for the roof of the Shizuoka Assembly Hall (1955–57); the Totsuka Golf Club (1960–63) had a rigid concrete roof in the shape of a suspended roof reminiscent of Saarinen's Dulles Airport, and a flat hyperbolic paraboloid preloaded cable roof was used to cover the Takamatsu Arena (1962–64).[14]

Tange selected simple evocative tent shapes for his arenas, that of the pavilion or ridge tent for the large stadium and the parasol-roofed or bell tent for the small stadium.[15] The monumental enlargement of these traditional tent shapes paid little regard to their appropriate scale. This meant that the minimal curvature required to ensure the stability of genuine prestressed tensile surface structures could not be maintained throughout the roofs, with the result that they had to be designed as semi-rigid suspended steel shells. The main suspension members are stiff plated steel girders to which 6 mm thick steel plates, painted on the outside and protected by asbestos insulation on the underside, have been attached to form the roof deck.[16] The inadequate curvature of the roof shapes is especially noticeable at their boundaries, and immediately below the heavy louvred ridge of the main stadium. Tensile logic was subordinated to the sculptural intention in the arena roofs and this results in a contrived hybrid structure.

The placement of the two arenas on a common pedestrian platform successfully balanced the sculptural forms of their roofs and seating ramps. The geometry of the arena plans is surprisingly simple, for the seating galleries and the competition areas are contained within great circular amphitheatres. Entrance areas have been created by extending the roofs in wings defined by a tangential arc which continues the curve of the boundary anchorage wall, and the elevated leading edge of the roof which intersects the circle almost perpendicularly. This plan geometry determines the location of the masts and main cable anchorages, each mast is situated at the point where the inside edge of each wing intersects the circular boundary anchorage wall, while the main cable anchorages are situated at the tip of each wing.

The small stadium (seating 3831 people) had one entrance wing on the eastern side, while the large stadium (seating 13 246 people) had two. The roof of the large stadium was suspended in two sections on either side of two main carrying cables draped between two concrete masts on opposite sides of the circular arena, and these cables are continued down to anchorages. The main carrying cable of the small stadium is suspended from a single mast on the boundary of the circular arena and curves back on itself in a tight U before descending to the anchorage.[17] The principal constructional elements – the boundary anchorage walls, the seating galleries, and the masts – have been masterfully integrated in unified sculptural forms. The heavy compressive elements, the anchorages and the masts contrast with the suspended roofs. Skylights have been inserted in the attenuated opening between the two ridge cables of the large stadium and in the space between the main carrying cable and the mast of the small one.

The magnificence of the arena forms tends to obscure the severe structural problems created by their construction. The great size of the roofs magnified the problems of shape, scale and technology which had been largely ignored in this first generation of architects' tensile architecture. Tange was extremely fortunate to have such gifted engineers as Yoshikatsu Tsuboi and Uichi Inoue to solve the structures of his forms.

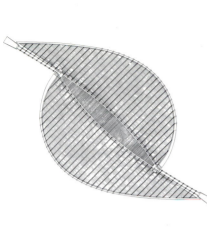

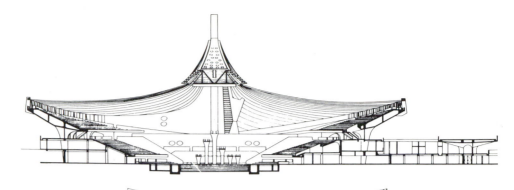

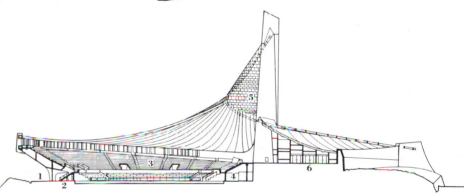

272. Aerial view of the large and small stadiums.
273. Roof structure of the large stadium.
274. Cross section of the large stadium.
275. Longitudinal section of the large stadium.
276. Interior of the large stadium.
277. Roof structure of the small stadium.
278. Cross section of the small stadium.
279. Bracing system of the cable and roof support on the main column of the small stadium.

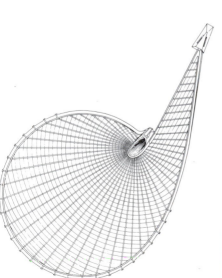

Revival of the Tent

Frei Otto's achievement

Frei Otto's innovations were of outstanding importance for the advancement of tensile architecture because he combined research into the best forms for prestressed surface structures with the development of the technical means for constructing them. He provided a unique bridge between the architect and the engineer, neither of whom seemed to appreciate fully that form and structure were interrelated aspects of the same problem. Despite the fact that Frei Otto has a reputation as a Futurist and as an architectural visionary his quite remarkable achievements in the field of tensile surface structures have been won by the patient application of essentially conservative procedures.

Frei Otto's conservatism, like that of John A. Roebling, grew from an awareness of the dangers associated with constructing tensile structures. In the twelve years that separate the Cassel Bandstand canopy from the German Pavilion at Montreal, the span of his prestressed surface structures increased only from 18 to 46 m. Frei Otto's prestressed tensile surface structures are remarkable not so much because of their spans, which are comparatively modest, but rather because of the quality of their forms and the original means used in their construction.

From the beginning, Frei Otto set out to discover the variety of anticlastically curved surface shapes and the effect of various methods of supporting the prestressed surfaces and also the impact of edge arrangements on the final shape. He did not limit his enquiry to simple saddle surfaces as most other architects tended to do, but extended his studies to encompass undulating surfaces, saddle surfaces between arches, and humped or elastically deformed surfaces.[1] Some of these roof shapes, particularly the humped surfaces, resemble traditional prestressed tent forms, notably that of the black tent. This was, however, largely a matter of structural coincidence rather than imitation.[2]

One of the most general failures in architects' tensile architecture was the choice of simple saddle shapes unsuited to the large scale of the structures. This occurred because the designer's vocabulary of tensile forms was limited to all but the most elementary saddle shapes. Frie Otto's researches disclosed a wealth of forms and this enlargement of the form vocabulary enabled a much closer approximation of the structural and human requirements.

The modern tent

The interpretation of tensile architecture in terms of the suspension bridge is unfortunate, since it tends to obscure other equally interesting and possibly far more significant attributes. The traditional role of the tent in nomadic cultures provides a far better guide to the real nature of tensile architecture than does the modern suspension bridge. Frei Otto's work after 1959 has encouraged a greater awareness of this neglected tensile tradition, especially as it is now more generally realized that the long span capability of prestressed tensile surface structures (about 135 m) is largely illusory. The inherent light weight and flexibility of these structures has a variety of consequences and these may be summarised as: variable geometry, convertible roofs, adaptability to changes in weather and use, demountability, portability, re-use, transience (when desired), empathy with landforms, and unification of interior and exterior space.

Many traditional tent forms are aerodynamically superior to conventional buildings. Frederick Kiesler identified the essence of tensile architecture in his statement for 'Space City Architecture', 1925, when he called for '. . . building that is adequate to the elasticity of the life function'.[3]

280. Multiple exposure photograph of a suspended developable a-priori net.
281. Convertible roof. Hoechst Stadium, Hanover. Frei Otto, 1970.

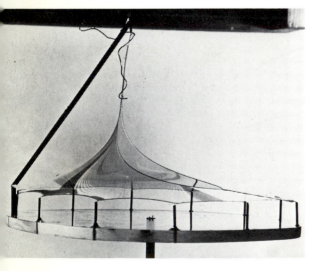

Frei Otto's work on prestressed tensile membranes and cablenets, and convertible roofs is particularly relevant to the present account. His interest in adaptable architecture excluding the development of convertible roofs remains so far theoretical.[4] Although Frei Otto was one of the pioneers of pneumatics, this branch of tensile structures is not considered because it leads to forms which resemble compression loaded vaults, forms in fact, that contrast with the tensile aesthetic.[5]

The 'Neiges et Rocs' Pavilions (max. span 36 m) at the Swiss National Exhibition, Lausanne, in 1964, were the first cablenets constructed by Frei Otto. Prior to this, all his roofs were made of cotton canvas with modest spans from 20 to 30 m.

Form and structure

The experience gained with membrane structures provided a sound technical basis for the development of cablenet structures, and in this sense, the genesis of the XX Olympic Games roofs at Munich in 1972 is to be found in the modest Bandstand at Cassel in 1955. The mechanism of spatial deformation of anisotropic membranes and cablenets is similar, as the surface is deformed, the mutually perpendicular threads or cables are distorted from a square to a rhomboid shape by the angular rotation of these elements. This behaviour served as the basis for Frei Otto's developable a-priori cablenets and prefabricated lattice shells.[6] The special advantages of developable nets with a regular mesh geometry are ease of form determination, prefabrication and erection.[7] Since the net geometry of an a-priori net is known, only the outermost net elements attached to the boundary supporting system are affected by shape. Their length has to be determined by structural analysis of the prestress forces in the cables in order to establish the total unstressed geometry.

The introduction of prefabricated developable cablenets is comparable in significance to Roebling's re-invention of Vicat's method of aerial spinning. It reversed the suspension bridge practice of in-situ assembly of cablenets by prefabricating the cablenet in a factory away from the building site. Frei Otto's method of off-site assembly parallels the bedouin procedure of prefabricating their tent widths from uniform strips of woven goats' hair which are later deformed to the final prestressed geometry. Prefabrication of the cablenet was made possible by the use of developable a-priori nets having equal mesh in both directions.

Special cable clamps were devised in conformity with the principle of developable nets, to permit the cables at each intersection to rotate as the net was deformed.[8] Most of the early cablenet roofs in the 1950s were designed on a quite different basis, simply because there was no accepted method for determining the prestressed surface geometry at that time. It was assumed that the geometry of these projected nets coincided with a parabolic or similar mathematical surface and the cables were clamped together in a way that prevented angular rotation.[9]

Minimal surfaces are nearly ideal prototypes for prestressed tensile surface structures since their anticlastic shape, minimum uniform tension, and uniform mean curvature coincides with the fundamental requirements of static equilibrium in a prestressed membrane or net.[10] Surfaces having these properties can be obtained with soap film, and uniformly prestressed elastic membrane, fabric and wire net models. Professor Otto relies on spontaneous form generating processes, such as those mentioned, to find the forms of his membrane and cablenet roofs because they guarantee that the roof shape is uniformly and highly curved. Highly curved surfaces are preferable because the amount of prestressing required for stability decreases with increasing surface curvature.[11] This avoids flat, soft regions in the surface and ensures a uniform stressing of the surface, essential for a regular mesh prefabricated cablenet.

Frei Otto overcame the problem of giving long span roofs adequate curvature by inserting intermediate point or ridge supports which subdivided the surface into small highly curved elements. He developed a varied vocabulary of forms comprising simple saddle surfaces, undulating surfaces, saddle surfaces formed by arches, hump surfaces, surfaces with interior points of support and a restraint. The introduction of interior points of support and restraint entails the risk of producing stress concentrations if methods are not found for distributing the stresses more evenly in the surface. A number of methods were devised for this purpose in the membrane pavilions. These consisted of umbrella like spreader-heads, bearing-heads of resilient plywood blades which assume a rounded profile and radially arranged 'parachute cable' restraints.[12] In 1964, Larry Medlin, one of Otto's collaborators, discovered that the umbrella support and the parachute restraint could be simplified to a single cable loop for both functions.[13] In addition to cable loops, ridges could be used to supplement loops in transmitting forces to masts or anchorages and also for modifying the roof terrain.

The arch is potentially more efficient as a support system than the cable and mast, the membrane and mast, or the cablenet and mast combination, so Otto introduced a series of saddle surfaces supported between parallel or radial arrangements of arches.[14] Nowicki, Saarinen and Tange also used inclined arches for boundary anchorage of their roofs, but Otto prefers the edge cable stretched between masts because it is lighter and does not obstruct the interior-exterior relationship.

Frei Otto's international reputation is founded on less than a handful of permanent works, and most of these were carried out in collaboration with other architects. The majority of his tensile structures have been transient creations, lasting little more than a single season. This after all, is in the nature of the tent.

The German Pavilion at Montreal (1967–72) was Otto's first durable large scale work. It lasted for little more than five years, when neglect hastened its destruction in a severe winter snowstorm.[15] The Institute for Lightweight Structures, at Vaihingen, is merely the reclaimed test structure of the Montreal Pavilion. The Munich Stadia roofs are the largest and most permanent of the structures with which Frei Otto has been associated.

Membrane pavilions

The early series of light canvas tent structures were built for the Federal Garden Exhibitions at Cassel (1955), Cologne (1957) and Saarbrucken (1958), the Interbau Building Exhibition at Berlin (1957), and the International Horticultural Exhibition in Hamburg (1963).[16] The Cologne and Berlin Exhibitions in 1957 were the most important because they introduced arch-supported membranes, undulating surfaces and humped surfaces. Frei Otto contributed four pavilions to the Cologne Exhibition: an arched entrance, a star-shaped undulating shelter for dancing and two riverside shelters — one a bright red peaked tent, the other a twin humped experimental structure. There were more humped membranes at the Berlin Building Exhibition where the main restaurant consisted of a deformed membrane pavilion raised on eight humped supports, while the Mero space-frame roof over the main hall was covered by a plane deformed membrane. There were both parallel and radial arrangements and the membrane of the humped hall was pulled down at three low points between two rows of four humped supports.

285. Cablenet roof structure viewed from south.
286. Institute Pavilion viewed from south-west.
287. Interior looking north.

288. Peaked tent. Federal Garden
Exhibition, Cologne, 1959.
289. Undulating wave, star-shaped
pavilion, International Horticultural
Exhibition, Hamburg, 1963.

291. Entrance arch. Federal Garden
Exhibition, Cologne, 1957.
292. Sports Centre in Kuwait. Frei Otto in
collaboration with Kenzo Tange and
URTEC, 1969.

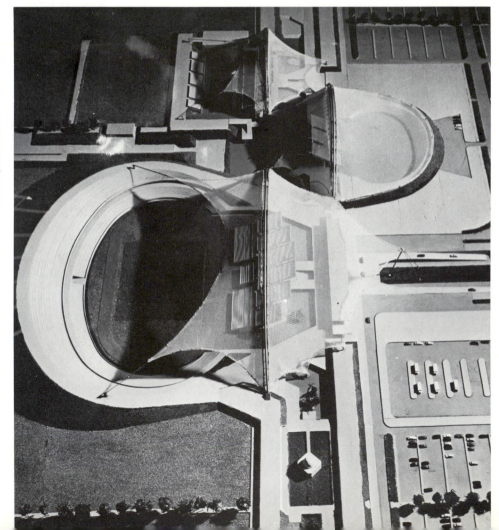

290. Open-air dance pavilion. Federal Garden Exhibition, Cologne, 1957.

293. Humped tent. Federal Garden Exhibition, Cologne, 1957.
294. Humped membrane roof, *The City of Tomorrow*, Exhibition Hall, Interbau International Building Exhibition, Berlin, 1957.

181

Such delightfully unpretentious garden pavilions introduced a variety of structural ideas which recur in Otto's later works. The disposition of internal supports and the grouping of these early pavilions is regular and formal; it is exceptional for them to be given a freer organic roof topography. The principle of arch-supported tents is reminiscent of the barrel-vaulted tents of the Tuareg and the Baluchs. The black tent possesses plane deformed membranes similar to the humped tent and this similarity is particularly noticeable in the North African tents.

The peaked tents at the Lausanne Exhibition (1964) were transitional membrane-cablenet structures.[17] Their simple peaked shape and large scale made it difficult to maintain adequate surface curvature throughout the 8 mm steel wire rope cablenet. A weatherproof membrane sheath was attached directly to the cablenet and the disparity of their behaviour resulted in the formation of wrinkles. In spite of their poor structural shape, the red, yellow and white pavilions formed an exhilarating sculptural composition of dynamic overlayed arcs.

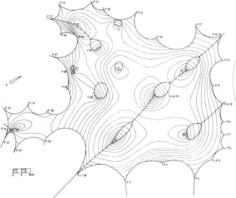

Cablenet pavilions

Modern prestressed tensile surface structures reached maturity with the completion of Rolf Gutbrod and Frei Otto's German Pavilion at Montreal in 1967. For the first time the technical means fulfilled the structural demands of genuine large scale prestressed surface structures. There was a new identity of form, structure and technique which had so far eluded previous attempts to realize an integrated and logical expression of the tension principle.

The Montreal tent consisted of an anticlastically curved prestressed cablenet suspended from masts of varying heights, pulled down at restraining points, and bounded by edge cables which transferred the stresses to perimeter anchor points.[18] The net was constructed of 12 mm diameter steel cables assembled on a 50 cm rhomboid grid so that the planar stresses were transferred to the points of support and restraint by cable loops to avoid excessive concentrations of stress. The asymmetrical roof terrain produced by hoisting the cablenet from eight masts and tugging it down at three low points is varied and interesting and blends with natural landscape forms. The shape of the net was dictated by the site and by the route through the exhibition. The interior space of the pavilion was defined by a PVC coated polyester fabric membrane suspended about 35 to 40 cm below the cablenet on cloverleaf clips.

The Montreal roof form and the use of cable loops at points of support and restraint had been pioneered in earlier studies. The spatial interpenetration of the roof surface at the low points and its freer sculptural topography was investigated in the second scheme for temporary medical accommodation at Ulm University in 1965.[19] The cable loop principle of transferring roof stresses to points of support and restraint developed from studies made in 1964. The shape of the prestressed uniform mesh cablenet was determined using a series of seven complete models together with dozens of part-studies of particularly difficult regions.[20] The cablenet and masts were prefabricated in Germany and shipped to Canada for erection, thus proving the portability of the roof construction. The lightness and flexibility of this highly curved prestressed cablenet roof contrasts with earlier efforts at building prestressed tensile surface structures.

The roofs of the main stadium and arenas for the XX Olympic Games at Munich in 1972 added little of significance to the Montreal achievement. The principal advance was the development of purely mathematical procedures for determining the cable net patterns which supersede Frei Otto's time consuming modelling

295. Peaked tents, *Snow and Rocks* section, Swiss National Pavilion, Lausanne. Frei Otto in collaboration with M. Saugey, 1964.
296. Pavilion of the Federal Republic of Germany. Expo '67, Montreal, 1965–7. Frei Otto with architect Rolf Gutbrod. Plan, Montreal roof topography.
297. Competition model.

298. Interior of roof with membrane skin suspended below the cable net.
299. View of roof.
300. Roofs for the XX Olympic Games, Munich, Germany, 1968–72. Behnisch and Partners Architects, Frei Otto and IL roof consultant. Roof cable net.
301. Site plan.

183

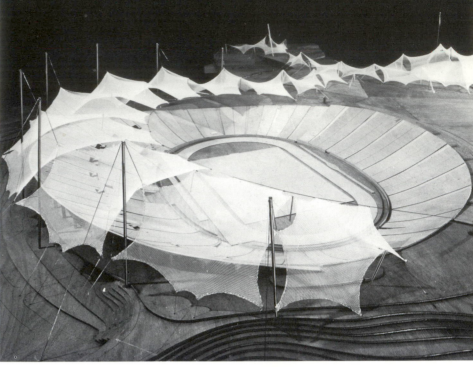

302. Aerial view of the site.
303. Polyester fabric model of the West Grandstand roof.
304. Wire measuring model.
305. Roof of the West Grandstand.
306. Roof of the Sports Arena.
307. Aerial view of the Sports Arena roof.
308. Cast steel system point.
309. Convertible roof for terrace, Palm Beach Casino, Cannes, France, 1965. Frei Otto in collaboration with R. Taillibert.
310. Convertible roof for the open-air theatre, abbey ruin, Bad Hersfeld, 1968. Frei Otto. Convertible roof partly extended.
311. Model

techniques.[21] The Munich Olympic roofs were considerably larger than the German Pavilion (22 000 m² compared with 8000 m²) and the maximum spans increased from about 45 m to 135 m.[22] They compare in scale with Tange's Tokyo Arenas but are quite inferior in the quality of the architectural concept and in the resolution of the subsystems. The architecture of the Munich Arenas is confused and inconsistent and the details fail to sustain the excitement of the roof shapes.

The roof surfaces were divided into separate gently curved saddle-like net surfaces bordered by edge cables.[23] A system of open loop ridges was incorporated in the Munich roofs to create gentle undulating wave surfaces which combine the loop and ridge cable concepts from Montreal. Large radius loops were adopted for the open ridges between the radial system points. The number of high points used to support the roofs was insufficient to assure adequate curvature for stability and this factor combined with the insistence that deflection of the cablenet was to be kept to a minimum resulted in extremely high prestress forces being applied to the roofs.[24] This might not have mattered but the roof forces had to be carried down to the ground and this produced an uneconomical design for the main masts and gravity anchorages.

Convertible roofs

Kinetic enclosures satisfy the need for flexible shelters capable of being physically altered to provide for changing requirements. Despite serious studies of convertible roof systems by Frei Otto in 1960, it was more than five years before the first project was built.[25] Variable geometry enclosures are a natural extension of the flexibility and small bulk volume of tent membranes which enable the built environment to respond to changes in weather and use.

The majority of Frei Otto's convertible roofs were of the converging movement or centrally bunchable membrane type.[26] These consist of a conical shaped membrane suspended from a radial system of cables which converge at a high point. The extended membrane travels inwards from the perimeter towards the mast head on pulleys or self-propelled cable tractors where it is bunched. Several of the early convertible roofs, namely the open air theatre at Cannes (1965), and the swimming pool at Boulevard Carnot, Paris (1966–67), were designed in collaboration with the French architect, Roger Taillibert.[27] A further French convertible roof over the ice rink at Conflans St Honorine, was designed in cooperation with I. Blasco and Girard.[28]

The most successful of Otto's converging movement convertible roofs, aesthetically as well as technically, is the roof over the open air threatre at Bad Hersfeld, Germany (1966–68).[29] A fundamental requirement of the Bad Hersfeld roof, and one which Frei Otto's nonassertive membrane roof admirably fulfilled, was to insert the new structure over the ruined Romanesque cloister without disturbing the historic fabric or interrupting the spatial coherence of the open stage. The hemispherical membrane was restrained at points around the edge and suspended from interior points on cable tractors which travel along fourteen radial guy cables supported on a single 32 m high back stayed steel mast located outside the church nave. The edge cables were stretched between four lattice masts at each corner. The extension and bunching behaviour of the roof membrane was studied in a 1:50 scale model. This also provided values for the variable roof geometry for the static calculations of the roof and support structures. The contrast between the heavy masonry of the Romanesque choir and the lightweight convertible membrane canopy intensified the special character of each.

185

Conclusion

The history of nomad and urban tents dispels any impression that tensile architecture is a modern innovation. Even allowing for the tantalizing incompleteness of present knowledge, it seems certain that tents were used as early as the Ancient World.

Modern tensile technology was created in response to the requirements of constructing long span suspension bridges and it was this existing technology that shaped the opening phase of modern tensile architecture. The use of tent forms and the development of a special technology suited to architectural needs came later. Thus while there is no direct connection between traditional tents and modern tensile architecture, there are fascinating technical, and even visual parallels. It is true that traditional suspension bridges influenced Chinese bridges, but the relationship with Western Europe is difficult to establish.

The unsuspected similarity in the shapes of some black tents and modern prestressed tensile surface structures is evidence of the existence of a 'tensile aesthetic'. The discovery of common visual qualities in nomad tents and tensile architecture came as a genuine surprise as did the technical parallels between black tents and certain modern tensile buildings. These technical parallels are the product of the solution of similar structural and technical problems, and this suggests that the visual affinities also arose from the spontaneous expression of structural form.

The tensile aesthetic is typified by complex anticlastically curved surfaces, flat sweeping profiles, dominant hovering roofs and the suppression of walls. Jørn Utzon identified an important spatial quality of tensile architecture in his discussion of the interplay between roof and platform in Chinese houses and temples and in the traditional Japanese house. The black tent embodied this ideal of hovering roof forms to a considerable degree. The articulation of architectural space in terms of roof and floor elements and the treatment of walls as transparent screens in the 'pavilion' of Modern architecture was prefigured in the tent and finds its most natural expression in the shapely pavilions of Frei Otto. The spatial identity between the roof and the floor platform is increased by giving the floor platform a sculptured terrain.

The value of a survey of traditional tents lies in its demonstration of the intrinsic character of tensile architecture. Such outstanding qualities as light weight, economy, portability and flexibility account for the extensive employment of tents by nomadic hunters and pastoralists. The preoccupation with technological accomplishment, in this instance the construction of long spans, in the 20th century, diverted attention from these qualities. The separation of thinking from feeling — a persistent theme in Sigfried Giedion's account of 19th century European culture — was expressed in the technical approach of engineers and the sculptural response of architects to making tensile architecture. Few designers — and here Frei Otto is an outstanding exception — combined an understanding of the technical problems with sensitivity to tensile form. The goal of long span roofs inspired by the accomplishment of suspension bridge builders distorted the early development of tensile architecture and resulted, in the main, in the neglect of those qualities displayed by nomad tents.

Tents are usually considered to be primitive shelters. The evolution of vernacular dwelling forms shows that the black tent and *kibitka* are comparatively recent developments. Far from being primitive shelters as is sometimes thought, tents are actually advanced and extremely refined structures.

The construction of marvellous tensile pavilions in the second half of the 20th century is hardly unique. These structures represent a continuation of the tradition of magnificent pavilions begun by the ancient Assyrian kings. Saarinen's Yale Hockey Rink, Tange's arenas at Tokyo, and Gutbrod and Otto's pavilion at

Montreal are manifestations of a revitalized tent tradition.

It is tempting to regard traditional tents as the antithesis of monumental architecture. Such a view ignores the inter-dependence of the nomadic pastoralist and the peasant in the Middle East. Tents and monumental architecture are not separate unconnected currents and this is emphasised by the evolution of the black tent. The antithesis, insofar as it exists, is structural rather than cultural. The tents of nomadic pastoralists bear the imprint of civilization. Tents in turn also influenced the forms of monumental architecture so the two architectures cannot be considered as isolated traditions.

The origin and early development of the *kibitka*, black tent, parasol-roof tent and pavilion have yet to be explained satisfactorily. C. G. Feilberg outlined a general theory of traditional tents but he was unable to prove important aspects. Even though Feilberg's theory lacks proof it provides a useful framework for discussion. Feilberg held that the black tent is the Indo-European nomadic tent and the *kibitka* is the Turkic and Mongol tent. The similarities between parasol-roof tents and the pavilions and the black tent point to the two groups having a common origin. This occurred when the Indo-European nomads encountered villages where the black tent was transformed into a pavilion or parasol-roof tent. The *kibitka* of Central Asia in all probability derived from cupola shaped tents constructed of wattles.

The ridge tent was introduced into the Middle East by later migrations of nomads and was transformed into the black tent. It has survived as the black tent of Tibet and appears in Chinese paintings. The ridge tent existed alongside the *kibitka* in Central Asia. The earliest representation of this type was depicted in a wall painting in a 1st–2nd century AD grave at Kerch.

The extraordinary extent and effectiveness of nomad tents demonstrates the flexibility of tensile architecture. The tent, rather than the suspension bridge, is the best guide to the future of tensile architecture. There are two different views of the significance of tensile architecture: it can be dismissed as a useful though limited addition to modern building technology, or alternatively, it can be seen as a valuable means of creating flexible responsive environments capable of being adapted to the flux of life.

Notes

Chapter 1

1. For example, Arctic polar and Arctic sub-polar, dry arid and dry semi-arid, and highland climates all of which are distinguished by their dryness. In contrast to the comparative aridity of these regions the thermal range is great, thus the mid-latitude deserts experience extreme diurnal ranges of temperature caused by continental factors while extremely low temperatures are encountered in Siberia and the polar zone.

2. Tents are found in regions of the following vegetation types: tundra, coniferous forest (Siberia), prairie grasses, semi-arid or steppe grasses and desert shrubs and grasses. It is only in the instance of the Eurasian Reindeer herders and the hyperboreal Indians of North America that we find tent dwelling peoples living in a forested area.

3. D. L. Johnson, *The Nature of Nomadism, a Comparative Study of Pastoral Migrations in Southwestern Asia and Northern Africa*. Chicago, 1969, p. 158.

4. *ibid.*, p. 18.

5. *ibid.*, p. 9.

6. Amos Rapoport, *House Form and Culture*. Englewood Cliffs, N. J., 1969, p. 59.

7. Johnson, *op. cit.*, p. 2.

8. *idem.*

9. *idem.*

10. *ibid.*, p. 11.

11. *ibid.*, p. 12.

12. See M. G. Levina and L. P. Potapova, *Istoriko-Etnografichesky Atlas Sibiri*. Moscow and Leningrad, 1961, p. 131.

13. See Jan O. M. Broek and John W. Webb, *A Geography of Mankind*. 2nd ed., New York, for the distribution of forms of economy, ethnic and linguistic families and sub-families and culture realms. Robert F. Spencer and Elden Johnson in *Atlas for Anthropology*. 2nd ed., Dubuque, Iowa, 1971, give culture areas, tribal groups, and language families of the world.

Chapter 2

1. See Richard G. Klein, 'Ice-Age Hunters of the Ukraine', *Scientific American*. 230 (June 1974), pp. 96–105.

2. *ibid.*, p. 101.

3. *ibid.*, figure p. 97. Klein illustrates three shelters from an ancient terrace of the Dneister River; they include a domical shelter 44 000 years old (Moldova I), a conical tepee shelter 13 000 years old (Moldova V), and a younger conical tepee shelter 12 000 years old (also from Moldova V) in which antlers were substituted for mammoth bones as a means of securing the skin. In his reconstruction of an Upper Palaeolithic earth-house at Pushkari I, A. L. Mongait (1961) assumes that the multiplication of hearths indicates a dwelling form consisting of several cones joined by saddles, (4).

4. A. P. Okladnikov, *Yakutia Before its Incorporation into the Russian State*. London, 1970, p. 28 considers that the presence of the bones of steppe animals, and especially the saiga indicates a general absence of forest in these areas.

5. *ibid.*, p. 30.

6. Besides the two drawings on the Markha, representations of cupola-like dwellings have been found at the cliff Suruktaakh-khaya on the Markha River; on the cliffs on the left bank of the Lena, between Olekminsk and At-Dabagan, 8 km downstream from Olekminsk; between the hamlet of Bestyakh and the cliff of

Mokhsogollokh-khaya, near the village of Pokrouskoye; and near the village of Yelanka, in the Ordzhonikidze *rayon* of the Yakut ASSR. See *ibid.*, p. 74–5, and fig. 14.

7. See *ibid.*, p. 76. The crossed members which form an 'X' within the upper portions of the cliff drawings of the houses may represent supports or frames of the *orto kurdu* of the old-fashioned Yakut *urasa*, while the sticks projecting fan-like above the cupolas obviously represent an openwork funnel.

8. A. P. Okladnikov *ibid.*, pp. 244–5, supplies many examples taken from the Yakut vocabulary which reveal an acquaintance with materials of camel's hair and with the production of felt. Okladnikov concluded from this linguistic evidence that the period of separate existence, when the Yakuts were isolated from other steppe peoples by large tracts of forest and by tribes speaking entirely different languages, was preceded by a time of close association and identity with steppe peoples. In addition, Okladnikov concludes that the ancestors of the Yakuts, with other steppe tribes, created a general pastoral culture in very deep antiquity. If he is correct then this means that the origin of the *kibitka* is much more ancient than might be supposed from the general evidence.

9. See Waldemar Jochelson, *Peoples of Asiatic Russia*. New York, 1928, p. 191.

10. Okladnikov, *op. cit.*, p. 76.

11. Jochelson, *op. cit.*, p. 195.

12. See J. H. Steward (ed.), *Handbook of South American Indians*. **5** Washington, 1949, p. 5.

13. B. Koechlin, 'Abris et Habitations pour Humains et Dieux Chez les Vezo, semi-Nomads Marins de Madagascar', *L'Architectur d'Aujourd'hui*. 175 (Sep/Oct, 1974), pp. 119–20.

Chapter 3

1. See Levina and Potapova, *op. cit.*, pp. 131–60 for a study of the types of tents, their genetic relationships and geographical distribution in Northern Asia. Map 1, p. 224, gives the distribution of ground-based and semi-subterranean framed dwellings in Siberia.

2. K. Birket-Smith, *The Caribou Eskimos*. **2** Copenhagen, 1929, p. 22. The ridge type of tent serves as a permanent dwelling on the outskirts of the boreal region or in places which on account of their inhospitable natural conditions and comparative inaccessibility, must be considered as a kind of 'cultural resistance region'. It is used as a temporary shelter on journeys and hunting trips in the intermediate regions, where, Birket-Smith concludes, it has been replaced by other types, notably by the conical tent which thus reveals itself as being younger.

3. *idem*.

4. See Birket-Smith, 1929, *loc. cit*.

5. Levina and Potapova, *op. cit.*, p. 154.

6. *idem*. The list of peoples who live in conical tents includes the mountain people – Mansi of the lower Ob, the Khanti, to independent peoples – Nentsi, Entsi, Nganasani, Northern Selkupi; the Northern Keti; to the Turkish peoples – Tubalari, Chelkantsi, Kumandinitsi, Altai Kizhi, Telengiti, the Teleuti, Kachintsi, Sagaitsi, Beltiri, Kiziltsi, Tofalari, Tuvintsi, Southern Yakut – cattle herders and Northern Yakut deer-herders; Tungus Manchurian peoples and Dolgani, all the Evenki and Eveni groups, the Negidaltsi Nanaitsi, the Orochi and Oroki and of the Palaeo-Asiatic peoples – the Yukaghir.

7. As delineated in *The Times Concise Atlas of the World*, London, 1972, map 12 (types of natural vegetation) the southern limits of Boreal forest approximate the

southern distribution of the conical tent in Northern Asia.

8. See Jochelson, *op. cit.*, p. 195.

9. *idem*.

10. See Levina and Potapova, *op. cit.*, p. 155.

11. *ibid.*, p. 159.

12. Birket-Smith, 1929, *op. cit.*, table B2, pp. 297–301, lists the distribution in Eurasia and North America of conical tents with two-, three-, and four-pole foundations.

13. See Levina and Potapova *op. cit.*, p. 143, and table ix, p. 206.

14. A Lapp arch-post conical tent is illustrated in K. Birket-Smith, *Primitive Man and His Ways*, London, 1960, p. 129, from a diagram by Manker.

15. The frame of an Alaskan Eskimo conical tent having an intermediate stiffening hoop is illustrated in W. E. Nelson, *The Eskimo about Bering Strait*. New York, 1971, fig. 89, p. 261.

16. The means of fastening the tops of the foundation-poles, and the constructional adaptations for suspending the hearth-hook are the principal features which distinguish the conical tents of one ethnic group from that of another group. Except for these differences, the conical tent in Siberia is remarkably uniform. The variation of foundation pole fastenings is described in Levina and Potapova, *op. cit.*, p. 155 and hearth-hooks on p. 156. See also Jochelson, *op. cit.*, p. 195.

17. The Yukaghir give each strip a name, the upper strip is called *ti'mil*, the middle strip *o'rYolon*, and the lower strip *nu'med a'lgada*. W. Jochelson, 'The Yukaghir and the Yukaghirized Tungus', the *Jesup North Pacific Expedition, Memoir of the American Museum of Natural History*, **IX** part III, New York, 1926, p. 345. See also Jochelson *op. cit.*, p. 189.

18. Jochelson, 1928, *op. cit.*, p. 191.

19. The various types of construction used to suspend hearth-hooks are illustrated in Levina and Potapova, *op. cit.*, plate XIV – 5, 8, 12, 13, p. 221.

20. A. Rona-Tas, 'Notes on the Kazak Yurt of West Mongolia', *Acta Orientalia*. **12** (1–3) (1961), p. 86. The Altai, Khakassi and Tuvintsi use straight roof-ribs similar to those used by the Buryat and this led Levina and Potapova, *op. cit.*, p. 159, to conclude that these tents are related to the Mongol type. Furthermore, they suggest that this seems to point to the latticed cylindrical tent being adopted by the Southern Turks from the Mongols.

21. The different construction of the dwellings of the peoples of the sphere of the mainland culture (the whole of Siberia except for that settled by the N. E. Palaeo-Asiatics) from the dwellings of peoples of the sphere of coastal culture indicates that the contact of the N. E. Palaeo-Asiatics with the southern newcomers (contemporary peoples from the mainland zones) was very late. The lack of great variety of N. E. Palaeo-Asiatic dwellings and their different construction compared with the dwellings of the mainland Siberian peoples seems to indicate an independent development of dwellings in the sphere of coastal culture. Levina and Potapova, *op. cit.*, p. 160.

22. Jochelson, 1928, *op. cit.*, pp. 195–7, considered that the cylindro-conical tent was a natural development of the conical tent, and furthermore, judged it to be a higher type of dwelling. While he conceded that we do not know exactly how the process of transition from the conical to the cylindro-conical tent was affected, he assumed that, 'a casually bent rod may have suggested the idea of allowing the lower part of the poles to remain vertical and the upper part to slope toward the centre of the tent'. The primitiveness of the Chukchee and Koryak tents is evident in the heavier, clumsier construction and less regular shape of their lower wall sections. *ibid.*, p. 197–8.

23. On the basis of their physical, cultural and linguistic affinities with the American aborigines Jochelson *ibid.*, p. 45, groups the Northeastern Siberian Chukchee, Koryak, Kamchadal, Chuvantsy, Yukaghir and Gilyak under the general term Siberian Americanoids.

24. Jochelson, *op. cit.*, p. 241.

25. The remains of Yurts discovered by Von Wrangel seem to have belonged to the Omoki who have since disappeared. The account by Wrangel, *Narrative of an Expedition to the Polar Sea*, London, 1844, p. 181, is cited by Jochelson, 1926, *op. cit.*, p. 347. *Yurtowishtche* means in Russian, village.

26. The immobile cylindrical-shaped tent of the maritime Chukchee is illustrated in Levina and Potapova, *op. cit.*, table 35:3, table XIII:9, p. 210, table 35:3.

27. The immobile winter cylindrical-shaped tent of the maritime Chukchee and Eskimos is illustrated in Levina and Potapova, *op. cit.*, table XIII:10, p. 210.

28. The portable octagonal-shaped tent of the deer-herding Koryak and Chukchee is illustrated in Levina and Potapova, *op. cit.*, table XVII: 4–7, p. 214. The accuracy of the description of the construction provided by N. N. Beretti on which Levina and Potapova based their sketch is open to doubt.

29. The portable winter and summer tent of the deer-herding Chukchee is illustrated in Levina and Potapova, *op. cit.*, table XIV:5, 6, p. 211; table 35:4.

30. The wall framing of the portable winter tent of the Eveni of the Markovsk region is illustrated in Levina and Potapova, *op. cit.*, table XVI:1–7, p. 213. The wall-frame consists of prefabricated tripod elements made of thin sticks, joined together by means of a thong threaded through holes in their tops.

31. The frame of the portable cylindrical tent of the Eveni of the Markovsk region is illustrated in Levina and Potapova, *op. cit.*, table XV:1–9, p. 212.

32. See Jochelson, 1926, *op. cit.*, p. 346.

33. *idem*.

34. See Jochelson, 1928, *op. cit.*, p. 198.

35. Birket-Smith, 1960, *op. cit.*, p. 128.

36. B. Collinder, *The Lapps*, Princeton, 1949, p. 64.

37. *ibid.*, p. 71.

38. Birket-Smith, 1960, *op. cit.*, p. 128.

39. The construction of the Lapp arch-post conical tent frame is illustrated by Kaj Birket-Smith, 1960, *ibid.*, p. 129, after Ernst Manker, in 'Lapsk Kultur vid Stora Lule Alus Kallsjoar', *Acta Lapponica*, IV (1944), Stockholm/Upsala and S. Erixon, 'Some Primitive Constructions and types of Layout, with their Relationship to European Rural Building Practice', *Folkliv*, 1937, fig. 11, p. 137, and pl. XXII, p. 146. B. Collinder, *op. cit.*, p. 64 gives an excellent description of the construction of the tent frame.

40. The disposition of living areas in the conical tent of the Eloguinsk Keti (see Levina and Potapova, *op. cit.*, table IX:6, table 7:3) is remarkably similar to that found in the Lapp arch-post conical tent.

41. The similarity in the construction of the arch-post conical tent and the earth-lodge of the Coast Lapps is readily apparent in a diagram from Birket-Smith, 1960, *op. cit.*, p. 127, based on Manker.

42. This view is supported by the Finnish linguist Eliel Lagercrantz and Björn Collinder. Both Birket-Smith, 1960, (*op. cit.*, p. 106), and B. Collinder (*op. cit.*, pp. 36–37) proposed that the common ancestors of the Finns and the Central Uralic peoples (Mordvins, Cheremiss, Permians) changed their vernacular at some remote time for the Finno-Ugeric language of the ancestors of the Lapps and that the Lapps together with Ugrians (Voguls, Ostyaks, Hungarians) and the Samoyeds are descendants of the people who spoke the common Uralic parent language.

Chapter 4

1. Daryll C. Forde, *Habitat, Economy and Society, a Geographical Introduction to Ethnology*. London, New York, 1952, p. 128.
2. H. P. Steensby, 'Contributions to the Ethnology of the Polar Eskimos', *Meddelser om Grønland*. **VII**, Copenhagen, 1910, p. 284.
3. Forde, *op. cit.*, p. 126.
4. The autumn house (qarmat) is distinct from the old winter house (qarmang), in that it is a purely temporary dwelling covered by a skin roof. The autumn houses consist of an earth, stone, whale bone or ice wall (qarmaq) and a tent sheet roof (ulinga) supported by tent poles. Therkel Mathiassen, *Material Culture of the Iglulik Eskimos*. Copenhagen, 1928, p. 136.
5. See Nelson, *op. cit.*, fig. 85, pp. 257–260.
6. *ibid.*, fig. 86, p. 259.
7. See Franz Boas, *The Central Eskimo*. Lincoln, 1888, fig. 109, p. 140.
8. H. P. Steensby, *op. cit.*, figs. 19, 20, pp. 326–9.
9. The iccellik is confined to a small band of Eskimoes who live in the foothills along the Killik River of Alaska. Robert F. Spencer, *The North Alaskan Eskimo: A Study in Ecology and Society*. Bureau of American Ethnology (bull. 171), New York, 1959, pp. 44–5.
10. Boas, *op. cit.*, p. 139.
11. Typical plans of ridge tents are illustrated in Boas, *ibid.*, fig. 115a, p. 143; figs. 116a and 117b, p. 145.
12. See Kaj Birket-Smith, *The Caribou Eskimos*. **2** Copenhagen, 1929, Table A3, pp. 235–6 for the distribution of the ridge tent.
13. There has been considerable discussion of the relative ages of the ridge tent and conical tent in the northern regions of North America. Birket-Smith, *ibid.*, pp. 20–3, has summarised the range of views in his excellent study of the Caribou Eskimo.
14. See Boas, *op. cit.*, fig. 115, pp. 143–5.
15. Boas, *ibid.*, fig. 116, pp. 144–5, describes a type of abbreviated ridge tent prevalent in Pond Bay, Admiralty Inlet, and among the Iglulik. See also Therkel Mathiassen, *Material Culture of the Iglulik Eskimos*, Copenhagen, 1928, fig. 80, pp. 132–3, for a description of the Ipiutaq sealskin tent of the Iglulik Eskimoes and Jenness, *op. cit.*, fig. 28, pp. 80–81, for the summer tent of the Copper Eskimoes at Bernard Harbour.
16. See Birket-Smith, 1929, *op. cit.*, p. 33.
17. *ibid.*, p. 34.
18. *ibid.*, pp. 35–6.
19. The tepee as a dwelling is not unique to the Plains, and in fact is not the exclusive property of the North American Indian. R. F. Spencer, and J. P. Jennings, *et. al.*, *The Native Americans, Prehistory and Ethnology of the North American Indians*. New York, 1965, p. 353.
20. Vestal, 'The history of the tepee', in R. and G. Laubin, *The Indian Tepee: Its History, Construction, and Use*. New York, pp. 1–2.
21. Birket-Smith, *1929*, op. cit., p. 54.
22. *idem*.
23. C. Wissler, 'The Influence of the horse in the development of plains culture', *American Anthropologist*. N.S., **16** (1) (Jan–March, 1914), p. 25.
24. Spencer and Jennings, *op. cit.*, p. 339.
25. Wissler, *loc. cit.*
26. *ibid.*, p. 18.
27. *ibid.*, p. 12.

28. *ibid.*, p. 11.

29. C. Wissler, Types of dwellings and their distribution in central North America', *Internationaller Amerikanisten-Kongreb.* **II** Pt. XVI, Vienna and Leipzig, 1910a, p. 477.

30. Spencer and Jennings, *op. cit.*, pp. 159–60. See also J. A. Mason, 'Notes on the Indians of the Great Slave Lake area', *Yale University Publications in Anthropology.* (31), pp. 20–1.

31. According to Birket-Smith, (1929) *op. cit.*, p. 133, the covering of tents with snow was common amongst the Chippewa and Cree Indians. It is interesting in this regard, that the Altai Tartar bank snow and earth to about half the height of their felt covered conical tents for additional insulation in winter. Jochelson, (1970) *op. cit.*, p. 195.

32. C. Wissler, 'Material culture of the Blackfoot Indians', *Anthropological Papers of the American Museum of Natural History.* **V** Pt. I, March 1910b, p. 116 refers to Chippewa, Newenot (Labrador), Dogrib and Beaver Indian tepees as having a cross-pole for suspending a hearth-hook above the central fire.

33. For descriptions of the primitive Penobscot tepee see R. M. Underhill, *Red Man's America, a History of Indians in the United States.* Revised ed., Chicago, 1971, p. 59, pl. IV, also Frank G. Speck, *Penobscot Man: The Life History of a Forest Tribe in Maine.*. Philadelphia, 1940, fig. 4, pp. 27–9.

34. Wissler, (1910a) *op. cit.*, p. 484.

35. Conical tents which incorporate external poles are encountered among the following Siberian peoples, Khanti, Keti, Ngasani, Teleuti, Tuvintsi, Yakut, Evenki, Negidaltsi, and Oroki.

36. *ibid.*, p. 114.

37. Walter Stanley Campbell, 'The tepees of the Crow Indians', *American Anthropologist.* N.S. (29), 1927, p. 87.

38. Wissler, (1910a) *op. cit.*, p. 481.

39. *ibid.*, and Laubin, *op. cit.*, p. 163.

40. Wissler, (1910a) *op. cit.*, p. 485.

41. In the tepee, the requirements of human shelter have been subordinated to providing an effective shelter for the central hearth. The conical enclosure of the tepee acts as a multi-directional wind-break and as a chimney for the central fire. The tent is essentially a combustion chamber. Walter S. Campbell, 'The Cheyenne Tepee', *American Anthropologist.* N.S. **17** (4) (Oct–Dec, 1915), p. 691, and Laubin, *op. cit.*, p. 64 also comment on this aspect of the tepee.

42. Campbell, (1927) *op. cit.*, p. 88.

43. *ibid.*, fig. 2, pp. 90–1.

44. *idem.*

45. Laubin, *op. cit.*, p. 22.

46. *ibid.*, p. 172, and Campbell (1927) *op. cit.*, p. 104.

47. Two to three horses were required to transport a large tepee and it seems unlikely, therefore, that dogs could have hauled the large poles in use today. See Wissler, 1914, *op. cit.*, p. 11.

48. Campbell, (1915) *op. cit.*, p. 686, noted that the size of Cheyenne tepees ranged from 10 to 30 ft in diameter. The Crow, in common with many other tribes (Cambell, 1927, *op. cit.*, p. 92), also possessed small light lodges for rapid travel. Laubin, *op. cit.*, p. 155, states that small tepees similar to tepees used on hunting trips were about 12 ft in diameter and required 8 to 10 buffalo hides.

49. The size of tepees was related to the means of transport. With the introduction of horses onto the Great Plains and the replacement of dog traction by horses much larger tepees were possible. Thus, early hide tepees are somewhat smaller than later canvas tepees. Laubin, *op. cit.*, p. 155, gives the average diameter of lodges as

ranging from 14 to 16 ft and adds that about 22 buffalo hides were required for the cover. Spencer and Jennings, *op. cit.*, p. 352, estimated that Teton tepees were 12 to 16 ft in diameter and required 8–12 hides. Underhill, *op. cit.*, p. 179 gives the diameter and height of tepees as 15 ft and 15–18 ft respectively. Wissler, (1910a) *op. cit.*, p. 104, gives 8–15 ft as the diameter of Dakota lodges.

50. See Wissler, (1910b) *op. cit.*, p. 104.

51. Campbell, (1927) *op. cit.*, p. 93.

52. Wissler, (1910b) *op. cit.*, p. 103, describes in detail the shaping and fabrication of Blackfoot tepee covers, and Laubin provides additional information about Sioux, Crow and Blackfoot canvas covers.

53. Campbell, (1927) *op. cit.*, p. 93 and Laubin, *op. cit.*, p. 53.

54. Campbell, (1915) *op. cit.*, p. 691, observed that the air supply to the central fire is drawn under the skirt of the tepee and this causes an uncomfortable draught unless it is deflected upwards between the tent cover and lining. See also Wissler, (1910b) *op. cit.*, p. 106. Laubin, *op. cit.*, p. 64, also comments on this phenomenon and adds that most of the activity is carried on at the rear of the tent where there is more head room, *ibid.*, p. 114.

55. The interior layout of Blackfoot tepees is typical of most Plains tepees with minor exceptions. See Wissler, (1910b) *op. cit.*, pp. 105–6.

56. The list of primary tepee tribes includes Blackfoot, Crow, Assiniboine, Sarcee, Gros Ventre, Plains Cree, Cheyenne, Arapho, Kiowa, Teton, Yankton Dakota, Comanche, and possibly the Wind River Shoshone and some Ute. The following tribes used the tepee as a secondary dwelling: Hidatsa, Kansas, Mandan, Omaha, Osage, Otto, Ponca, Santee Dakota, the Northern Shoshone, Nez Perce, the chief modern divisions of the Cappoan stock, possibly some Cree and some central Algonkin tribes.

57. J. C. Ewers, 'The Blackfoot war lodge: its construction and use', *American Anthropologist*. N.S. 46, 1944, p. 191, comments that the stereotyped conception of the nomadic Plains tribes as living exclusively on the open plains is misleading because they depended on timbered areas for wood for essential articles in their material culture, and for protection in winter from both cold and from enemies. The tepee is basically a cold climate dwelling of forest regions.

Chapter 5

1. Marks, R. W. 1960. *The Dymaxion World of Buckminster Fuller*, Southern Illinois U.P.: Carbondale and Edwardsville, p. 35. Marks relates that the idea of using corrugated steel grain bins as the prototype for the Wichita House (1944) occurred to Fuller in the summer of 1940 while driving through Missouri with his friend, the novelist, Christopher Morely. The striking shape resemblance between Fuller's Wichita House 1944, and the Turkic *kibitka* – both are cylindro-domical – may be explained by the optimization of several factors which have been summarised as: '. . . a cylinder encloses more space than a cube of the same wall area; with proper materials the walls are rigid, requiring no internal supports or bracing; the cylinder produces the most efficient distribution of internal heat; and its inherent streamlining cuts external heat losses to a minimum'. Some of these advantages apply to the conical tent as well, but it seems very probable that the *kibitka* form arose as an optimization of performance. Other factors such as ease of fabrication, transportation, quick erection, concussion resistance, demountability and efficient aerofoil shape must also have been involved in the evolution of the kibitka dwelling type.

2. Peter A. Andrews, 'The White House of Khurasan: The felt tents of the Iranian Yomut and Göklen', the *Journal of the British Institute of Persian Studies*, (XI),

London, 1973, p. 93. Peter Andrews is currently writing a thesis on the central Asian yurt for his Doctorate at London University. This study promises to resolve many of the mysteries of the origin and development of the *kibitka*. I have referred to his publications in the present work and gratefully acknowledge Peter Andrew's assistance and comments.

3. N. N. Kharuzin, (1896) first distinguished the two main subtypes of the central Asian felt tent and subsequent research has added little to his original observations. The central Asian tent was called *kibitka* by the Russians, 'yurts' by the Kirghiz, while the Mongols themselves use 'gar', 'garg', or 'ger'. I have followed Feilberg in this matter and use the Russian term *kibitka* to refer to the cylindrical felt covered tent of central Asia. See also Sir H. Howorth, *History of the Mongols from the 9th to the 19th century*, Pt. 4, New York, 1927, p. 45. Peter Andrews points out that 'yurt' is something of a misnomer since it means 'camping place', 'camp', or 'native country'. See W. Jochelson (1928), *op. cit.*, p. 198, for a discussion of the ethnological distribution of the *kibitka*.

4. See W. Jochelson (1928), *op. cit.*, p. 198.

5. A. Rona-Tas, 'Notes on the Kazak Yurt of West Mongolia', *Acta Orientalia Hungarica.* **12** (1–3), 1961, p. 86.

6. P. A. Andrews, *op. cit.*, p. 198.

7. H. F. Schurmann, *The Mongols of Afghanistan: An Ethnology of the Moghols and Related Peoples of Afghanistan*. The Hague, 1961, p. 336.

8. C. G. Feilberg, *La Tente Noire*, Copenhagen, 1944, p. 164.

9. A. Rona-Tas, *op. cit.*, p. 85.

10. W. Jochelson (1928), *op. cit.*, p. 195.

11. P. A. Andrews, *op. cit.*, p. 94.

12. See Levina and Potapova, *op. cit.*, p. 155.

13. The superstructure on these waggons could in fact consist of a detachable tent. E. H. Minns, *Scythians and Greeks: A Survey of Ancient History and Archaeology on the North Coast of the Euxine from the Danube to the Caucasus*. Cambridge, 1913, p. 51, concluded that the Scyths transported their assembled tents on their carts and later set them down upon the ground when they came to a halt. The representation of a Panticapaen tent in a grave at Kerch (1–2nd century AD) which is set directly on the ground (Minns *ibid.*, fig. 223, p. 313) supports Minns' interpretation. The Panticapaen tent is an enigma since it seems to consist of a brown felt cover suspended from a short ridge pole supported on two posts much the same as the Tibetan black tent.

14. Strabo, *Geographica*, **VII** (3), 254 says of the Scythians, 'The tents of the nomads are of felt, and fixed on carts, and in these they live, . . .' and Aeschylus, *Prometheus Vinctus*, 1.735, observed, 'and thou shalt come to the Scyths, nomads who dwell in wattled huts high in the air upon their fair wheeled wains, equipped with far shooting bows.'

15. William Woodville Rockhill (Ed. and Translator), *The Journey of William of Rubruck to the Eastern Parts of the World 1253–55*. Hakluyt Society, second series, (IV), Nendeln/Liechtenstein, 1967, pp. 55–6.

16. Ronald Latham (Ed. and Translator), *The Travels of Marco Polo*. Harmondsworth, Middlesex, 1958, pp. 97–8.

17. Howorth, *op. cit.*, p. 45.

18. See E. D. Phillips, *The Royal Hordes, Nomad Peoples of the Steppes*, London, 1965, pp. 76, 78, 82, for details of these two tombs.

19. The walls of the houses of the Tripolye Culture (*c.* 3500–1900 BC) were constructed of wattle and clay or compacted earth. Phillips, *op. cit.*, p. 19.

20. See Feilberg, *op. cit.*, p. 164.

21. Pian de Carpine is quoted by Rockhill, *op. cit.*, p. 54: 'They (ie, the Mongols)

have round tent-like dwellings (stationes), made of twigs and small sticks. In the top they have a round opening which admits the light, and by which the smoke can escape, for they keep a fire always in the centre. The sides and roof are covered over with felt, and the doors are also made of felt. Some dwellings are large, some small, according to the importance or poverty of the people. Some of them can be taken down and put up in a moment, and are always carried on pack animals; while others cannot be taken apart, and are carried on carts; one ox hitched to the cart could have the smaller ones: the larger require three, four, or more, according to their size; and wherever they go, either to war or elsewhere, they take them along with them.'

22. Jochelson (1928), *op. cit.*, pp. 195–8.

23. Feilberg, *op. cit.*, pp. 161, 170, noted that the conical hut does not appear in the domain of the *kibitka*, while, on the other hand, the arched hut does. Furthermore arched huts with radial ribs closely resemble the *kibitka* roof. In addition, both the *kibitka* and arched huts use reed mats as a covering for the walls.

24. Phillips, *op. cit.*, p. 50.

25. *ibid.*, pp. 25, 47.

26. The diameter of *kibitkas* varies within narrow limits according to the authority quoted: Howorth — 15 to 20 ft; Andrews — 5·5 m, large 128 strut tents 12 m; William of Rubruck — 30 ft; and Atkinson — 34 ft. Evidently the average *kibitka* was from 15 to 20 ft in diameter, but large *kibitkas* in excess of 30 ft diameter were constructed for important personages.

27. The diameter of the roof ring is related to the number of roof struts which must be inserted in slots around the outside of the rim without weakening it, and hence, ultimately, to the size of the *kibitka*. Forde gives the diameter of the Kazak and Kirghiz rings as from 2 ft to 3 ft, Atkinson mentions a 4 ft ring, while Andrews measured Yomut rings 2·02 to 2·10 m in diameter. This suggests that roof rings varied from about 1 m to 2 m in diameter, the maximum size that could be conveniently loaded on a camel.

28. The numbers of wall lattices, roof struts and the size of the roof ring are all interrelated: the number of lattices determines the number of heads to which the roof struts are affixed, and the number of roof struts, in turn, determines the size of the roof ring. The more roof struts the larger the roof ring has to be to accommodate the struts. In general the number of lattice hurdles ranges from 4 to 6 in small to average sized tents, though tents with up to 8 or 10 lattices have been recorded.

29. The optimum number of roof struts is around 60, Kirghiz tents vary from 30 to 50, and Kazak from 30 to 60. The Iranian Yomut tents have 58 to 64 struts, and the Mongols are recorded as using anything from 60 to 100 struts although the upper figure seems somewhat excessive.

30. See Rona-Tas, *op. cit.*, p. 87.

31. *ibid.*, p. 86.

32. See Andrews, *op. cit.*, p. 99 and Rona-Tas, *op. cit.*, pp. 83, 84.

33. The botanical name for *ci* grass is *Lasia-grostis splendens*.

34. See Rona-Tas, *op. cit.*, pp. 87–8 and Andrews, *op. cit.*, pp. 101–2.

35. Rona-Tas, *op. cit.*, p. 89.

36. For a discussion of orientation see Howorth, *op. cit.*, p. 49.

37. *idem.*, and Rona-Tas, *op. cit.*, p. 88.

38. Rockhill, *op. cit.*, pp. 57–9, based his description of the arrangement of the (Altai Tartar) *kibitka* interior on a description by William of Rubruck and a plan from A. Radloff, *Aus Sibirien*, Leipzig, 1884, i, p. 270.

39. Rona-Tas, *op. cit.*, p. 86, n. 13.

40. The maximum vertical displacement of the Turkish roof ring is from 50 cm to 80 cm compared with 30 cm for standard (1·40 m diameter) Mongolian roof rings.

ibid. p. 86, n. 14.

41. See William O. Douglas, 'Journey to outer Mongolia', *The National Geographic Magazine.* **121** (3) March 1962, pp. 313, 324–5.

42. Levina and Potapova, *op. cit.,* table XVIII: 3, 4, p. 215. The Buryat roof ring (table XVIII: 5) is divided into two semicircular parts with wood keys for attaching the roof struts arranged around the outside.

43. Rona-Tas, *op. cit.,* p. 87.

44. *ibid.*

45. Levina and Potapova, *op. cit.,* p. 158, state that the Altai, Khakassi and Tuvintsi latticed *kibitkas* must be related to the Mongol tent because the roof-struts are straight and conform with the roof-struts of the Buryat (Mongol) *kibitka.* They therefore conclude that the latticed *kibitka* must have been adopted by the Southern Turks from the Mongols.

46. *ibid.,* pl. XIII: 7, Table 16:3, p. 210. The Sagaitsi unlatticed *kibitka* is 4.65 m in diameter and 2·80 m high and is covered by pieces of birch-bark.

47. See Schurmann, *op. cit.,* p. 350. The true *kibitka* is usually known in Persian as *Khargah* and in Turkestan as *Siyah-khana.* The *kibitka*-hut is called *căparî* by the Hazâra and Jaṁsîdî Aimaqs, *kappa* or *kappa-i ghisai* in Turkestan, and *alaciq* in Turkic.

48. Schurmann, *op. cit.,* p. 353.

49. *ibid.,* p. 351.

50. *idem.*

51. Several spellings of the Persian are given for *kibitka*-like huts *alachuq* (pl. *alachiq*), *alaciq,* and *alachigh.*

52. C. Op't Land, 'The admirable tents of the Shah Savan', *International Archives of Ethnography,* **50** (2), 1966, p. 243, rejects Birket-Smith's suggestion that the Shah Savan *Alachigh* is a degenerate form and considers instead, that it has come into being from the refinement and simplification of the construction of the *kibitka.* He considers the Shah Savan *alachigh* is a more advanced form of *kibitka.* In these terms simplification does not necessarily imply a degenerate form.

53. *ibid.,* p. 240, pl. XV: 5, XVI: 7.

54. *ibid.,* p. 238, pl. XVII: 10.

Chapter 6

1. Gustaf Dalman, *Arbeit und Sitte in Palastina,* **VI** Gutersloh, 1939, p. 16.

2. See Feilberg, *op. cit.,* p. 113 f. and Map 2.

3. Feilberg, *ibid.,* p. 131 summarised the distribution of the black tent in the following terms:

> Le resultat de notre examen de la distribution de la tente noire peur etre resume comme suit: Dans les grandes lignes, ce sont des facteurs de geographie physique qui determinent les limites de la distribution de la tente noire; mais si nous examinons en detail ces limites, nous constatons, a maintes reprises, que le facteur decisif de cette distribution est le rattachement de la tente a certains groupes de peuples, ce qui est ulterieurement confirme par le fait qu'en Europe la tente se rattache aux tziganes. Ce sont donc des causes d'histoire culturelle qui sont decisives.'

4. This division of the black tent into groups is based on similarities of shape. The fact that the three basic black tent types spread throughout Asia would appear to indicate that the early evolution of the black tent took place there.

5. *ibid.,* p. 223.

6. *ibid.,* p. 153.

7. Stephane Gsell, *Histoire Ancienne de l'Afrique du Nord*, **V** Paris, 1913, p. 215f. quoted in *ibid.*, p. 202. Also p. 226f.

8. Tents similar to Arab tents are mentioned in connection with the Berber in the 8th century, *ibid.*, p. 193.

9. Oric Bates, *The Eastern Libyans, an Essay*. London, 1914, p. 168.

10. Feilberg, *op. cit.*, p. 112.

11. *ibid.*, p. 111.

12. Charles M. Doughty, *Travels in Arabia Deserta.* (1888) London 1923, p. 225. Quoted in *ibid.*, p. 111, n.4.

13. Feilberg, *op. cit.*, pp. 109–10.

14. *ibid.*, p. 113.

15. *ibid.*, p. 116. If entirely modern constructions are excluded, the black tent uses the least amount of material for space enclosed of any dwelling type.

16. *ibid.*, p. 114.

17. *ibid.*, p. 115.

18. *ibid.*, p. 116.

19. The relationship between the camel and the black tent could be explained by the fact that the dromedary served as a strong pack animal which was well adapted to the transport of large and heavy tent velums. Further east, in central Asia, the Yak served in the same way. *ibid.*, p. 117. See *Koppels Atlas* (Ed. Dr. E. Ambrosius), sheets 15–16. Also, *ibid.*, map. IV.

20. Feilberg, *ibid.*, pp. 169–70, suggests that the black tent could have evolved from arched huts in the following manner: 1. simple vaulted hut covered by hides, 2. the arches forming the barrel vault roof are supported by posts, 3. some of the posts are furnished with ridge bars or alternatively a long ridge pole could be supported by posts. 4. the construction is simplified to an awning of hides stretched on the ridge pole supported by posts, 5. finally the awning of hides is replaced by a woven awning.

21. *ibid.*, p. 156.

22. *ibid.*, p. 155f.

23. See Johnson, *op. cit.*, p. 131.

24. See Johannes Nicholaisen, *Ecology and Culture of the Pastoral Tuareg with Particular Reference to the Tuareg of Ahaggar and Ayr.* Nationalmuseets Skrifter Etnografisk Raekka IX, Copenhagen, 1963, p. 350f.

25. *ibid.*, p. 358.

26. *ibid.*, p. 360.

27. *ibid.*, pp. 360, 386.

28. *ibid.*, p. 388f.

29. Conical huts and beehive huts are believed to be amongst the oldest types of huts known to mankind. Such dwellings are typical of many primitive peoples with a mixed hunting and collecting economy. Nicholaisen, *ibid.*, p. 341, contended that true beehive huts are widely used among many agriculturalists of Northern Africa, while they seem to be less common among pastoralists who tend to use barrel-vaulted huts. Feilberg, *op. cit.*, p. 167, states that the arched hut is found mainly in the savannahs and the steppes in Africa where it is connected with hunting and pastoral cultures.

30. See Jean Chapelle, *Nomades Noirs du Sahara*. Paris, 1957, p. 228.

31. *ibid.*, fig. 2, p. 229, fig. 5, p. 233.

32. Nicholaisen, *op. cit.*, pp. 359, 385–6. Feilberg, *op. cit.*, p. 202, adds that the black tent was not the typical dwelling of the nomads of North Africa in Antiquity.

33. See Nicholaisen, *op. cit.*, figs. 265a–265f, pp. 354–5 and fig. 264, p. 352.

34. *ibid.*, pp. 385–6.

35. *ibid.*, p. 364f.

36. *ibid.*, p. 390. It is interesting to note that the distribution of T-shaped posts further north in Africa seems to indicate that this particular structure in black tents is found among the Arabs, but not among the Berbers. See also Feilberg, p. 155.
37. *ibid.*, pp. 361–2.

Chapter 7

1. Ernst Rackow, 'Das Beduinenzelt', *Baessler-Archiv.* **21** Berlin, 1938, p. 181.
2. Feilberg, *op. cit.*, p. 147.
3. *idem.*
4. *ibid.*, p. 61. The Libyan tent differs from the Mahgreb type of tent in many respects, and in fact is closer to the tents of the Arabs of Northern Arabia and Palestine than it is to the North African tent.
5. Rackow, *op. cit.*, p. 181 states:

> 'Eine solche Vereinigung ist nun gerade in Nordafrika durchaus denkbar: Als die Araber ihre Eroberungszüge begannen, benutzten sie zunächst die ihnen vertrauten Beduinenzelte, später aber übernahmen sie auch für Heereszwecke die Militär-und Prunk-zelte der Byzantiner (und Perser), wie solche schon zuweilen in vorislamischer Zeit von einzelnen Häuptern der Grenzgebiete gebraucht worden sein mögen.'

6. Nicholaisen, *op. cit.*, p. 389. The distinctive structure of black tents among the Western Moors is due to the fact that it contains a barrel-vaulted dwelling covered by canvas.
7. Rackow, *op. cit.*, fig. p. 165.
8. 'Imraguen' in *Family of Man: Peoples of the World, How and Where they Live.* **4** Pt. 46, pp. 1277–1278.
9. Peter A. Andrews, 'Tents of the Tekna, Southwest Morocco', in Paul Oliver, (Ed.), *Shelter in Africa*, New York, 1972, p. 126.
10. *idem.*
11. *ibid.*, p. 133.
12. See Rackow, *op. cit.*, p. 164, and Feilberg, *op, cit.*, p. 39. The hill nomads include the following Berber tribes: Ait-Seghrouchen, Ait-Warain and Marmoucha of the Zenetic group; Ait-Youssi, Beni-Mguild, and Zayan of the Sanhadja group; as well as Ichqern Ait-Sgougou, Ait-Seri and Ait-Chokman. The tent described by E. Laoust, 'L'habitation chez les Transhumants du Maroc Central et la Tent dans l'Afrique du Nord, *Hesperis*, **10** 1930, p. 209 is also used in most of Western Morocco.
13. Feilberg, *op. cit.*, pp. 40–1. These tents are described by E. Michaux-Bellaire, and G. Salmon, 'Les Tribus Arabes de la Vallee du Lekkovs', *Archives Marocaines*. **IV** 1905, pp. 108–10.
14. Feilberg, *ibid.*, pp. 51–2, has summarised the principal differences between Moroccan tents and Algerian tents.
15. Rackow, *op. cit.*, p. 157, and Feilberg, *op. cit.*, p. 52.
16. Rackow, *op. cit.*, pp. 162–3.
17. *ibid.*, p. 153.
18. *ibid.*, p. 157.
19. *ibid.*, pp. 159–60.
20. *ibid.*, p. 163.
21. Feilberg, *op. cit.*, pp. 55–6.
22. *ibid.*, p. 54.
23. *idem.* See also Laoust, *op. cit.*, p. 220f.

24. Laoust, *op. cit.*, p. 218.

25. Laoust, *op. cit.*, p. 220f. and Feilberg, *op. cit.*, p. 61.

26. See Laoust, *ibid.*, fig. 48, p. 221; fig. 51, p. 223; and pl. XIII, p. 225.

27. See Philip Drew, *Frei Otto: Form and Structure*, London, 1976, fig. 91, p. 31.

28. Feilberg, *op. cit.*, p. 64.

29. This second Egyptian type is sometimes called the Petraean tent. See G. W. Murray, *Sons of Ishmael. A Study of the Egyptian Bedouin*, London, 1935, p. 80f, also *ibid.*, p. 62.

Chapter 8

1. See Walter Dostal, 'The Evolution of Bedouin Life' in F. Gabrieli (Ed.), *Ancient Bedouin Society*, Studi Semitici 2, Rome, 1959, p. 16f.

2. *ibid.*, pp. 18–21.

3. Feilberg, *op. cit.*, p. 117.

4. *ibid.*, pp. 224–5.

'Il parait tout indique d'en conclure que ces peuples indo-europeens, plus ou moins nomades, possedaient des tentes noires. La distribution geographique meme des trois formes principales de tente — Arabie, Iran Tibet — semble indiquer que le centre de l'evolution doit s'etre trouve plus a l'Est que l'Arabie. Les circonstances suivantes viennent encore affermir cette suite d'idees. Nous avons vu que le metier horizontal des nomades avec longue chaine tendue etait repandu en une trainee continue de l'Asie occidentale, a travers l'Asie centrale, jusqu'au Tibet. Le genre de vie auquel la tente noire se rattache notamment, est le grand elevage des moutons dans les steppes. . . . Le principal centre de domestication du mouton se trouve dans la Transcaspie et l'Est de l'Iran, d'autres centres dans l'Asie centrale et le Sud de l'Europe.'

5. Dostal, *op. cit.*, pp. 25–7.

6. Feilberg, *op. cit.*, p. 151, and Rackow, *op. cit.*, p. 171.

7. *ibid.*, p. 181.

8. Feilberg, *op. cit.*, p. 76.

9. Alois Musil, *The Manners and Customs of the Ruwala Bedouins*. American Geographic Society, Oriental Explorations and Studies, (6), New York, 1928, p. 61.

10. Rackow, *op. cit.*, p. 173.

11. *ibid.*, p. 175.

12. *ibid.*, p. 176.

13. Albert de Boucheman, *Materiel de la Vie Bedouine*. Documents d'Etudes orientales de l'Institute Francais de Damas III. Damas-Paris, 1934, p. 108f.

14. Rackow, *op. cit.*, p. 176–8.

15. *ibid.*, p. 177.

16. *ibid.*, p. 178.

17. Gustaf Dalman, *Arbeit und Sitte in Palastine*, VI Hildesheim, 1964, figs. 3, 4, and 6, pp. 12–17.

18. Alois Musil, *Arabia Petraea III*, Ethnologischer Reisebericht, Vienna, 1908, pp. 124–32. In Arabia Petraea the black tent is used by the *At-Terabin*, Tijaha, Al-Huretat and *Beni Sahr* Bedouin.

19. Some Central Arabian full nomads such as the Shammar, Otake and Gehatan also use the two rowed tent like the North Arabian nomads. Rackow, *op. cit.*, p. 175, and Feilberg, *op. cit.*, p. 78.

20. See Max Freiherrn von Oppenheim, 'Die Beduinen' in E. Braunlich and W.

Caskel, *Die Beduinen stamme in Mesopotamien* u. Syrien, Leipzig, 1939.
21. Rackow, *op. cit.*, p. 177.
22. Boucheman, *op. cit.*, p. 108f.
23. Alois Musil, *The Manners and Customs of the Ruwala Bedouins*. New York, 1928, pp. 124–32.
24. J. J. Hess, *Von den Beduinen des innern Arabiens*, Zurich and Leipzig, 1938, pp. 108–11.
25. Max Freiherrn von Oppenheim, *Vom Mittelmeer zum Persischen Golf*, **11** Berlin, 1899–1900, p. 44f.
26. Rackow, *op. cit.*, p. 177.
27. *ibid.*, pp. 179–80.

Chapter 9

1. Feilberg, *op. cit.*, p. 152.
2. *idem*.
3. See H. F. Schurmann, *The Mongols of Afghanistan, An Ethnology of the Moghols and related peoples of Afghanistan*, The Hague, 1961 p. 336.
4. Feilberg, *op. cit.*, p. 115.
5. *ibid.*, p. 156.
6. *ibid.*, p. 97.
7. *ibid.*, p. 151.
8. *ibid.*, p. 105.
9. *ibid.*, p. 97.
10. *idem*.
11. Schurmann, *loc. cit.*
12. Klaus Ferdinand, 'The Baluchistan Barrel-Vaulted Tent and its Affinities', *Folk*. **1** 1959, p. 36.
13. Feilberg, *op. cit.*, p. 154.
14. *ibid.*, p. 83.
15. Feilberg studied the tents of the hill nomads at first hand, *ibid*, p. 86f.
16. See *ibid.*, fig. 9, p. 87.
17. *ibid.*, p. 88.
18. Schurmann, *op. cit.*, pp. 336–7.
19. *ibid.*, p. 338.
20. Ferdinand (1959), *op. cit.*, p. 46.
21. Schurmann, *op. cit.*, p. 349. The closest tent to the Moghôl tent is a type of tent used in Luristan and Kurdistan which has a slightly circular transverse bar supported on two upright poles.
22. *idem*.
23. See Klaus Ferdinand, 'Les Nomades', in Johannes P. C. N. Humburn (Ed.), *La Geographie de l'Afghanistan*. Copenhagen, 1959, p. 283.
24. Klaus Ferdinand, 'The Baluchistan Barrel-vaulted Tent: Supplementary Material from Iranian Baluchistan and Sistan', *Folk*, **2** 1960, p. 36f.
25. *ibid.*, p. 41.
26. *ibid.*, p. 40.
27. All signs seem to indicate that some of the ancestors of the Southern Taimannîs must at some time have had tents of the Northern Taimannî type (ie, yurt-type *čaparîs*). See Schurmann, *op. cit.*, p. 348f.
28. *ibid.*, p. 349.
29. *ibid.*, pp. 434–5.
30. Ferdinand (1960), *op. cit.*, p. 48.

31. Ferdinand (1959), *op. cit.*, p. 46.
32. *ibid.*, p. 37.
33. *ibid.*, p. 27.
34. *ibid.*, p. 30f.
35. *ibid.*, p. 34.
36. *ibid.*, p. 38.
37. *ibid.*, fig. 6, 7; pp. 35, 38–9.
38. Schurmann, *op. cit.*, p. 341.
39. *ibid.*, p. 347.

Chapter 10

1. M. Huc, *Souvenirs d'Un Voyage dans la Tartarie, le Thibet et la Chine.* **2** Paris, 1850, p. 156.

'Les grandes tents qu'ils se construisent avec de la toile noire, sont ordinairement de forme hexagone; a l'interieur, on ne voit ni colonne ni charpente pour leur servir d'appui; les six angles du bas sont retenus au sol avec des clous, et le haut est soutenu par des cordages, qui, a une certaine distance de la tente, reposent d'abord horizontalement sur de longues perches, et vont ensuite, en s'inclinant, s'attacher a des anneaux fixes en terre. Avec ce bizarre arrangement de perches et de cordages, la tente noire des nomades Thibetains ne ressemble pas mal a une araignee monstrueuse qui se tiendrait immobile sur ses hautes et maigres jambes, mais de maniere a ce que son gros abdomen fut au niveau du sol. Les tentes noires sont loin de valoir les iourtes des Mongols; elles ne sont ni plus chaudes ni plus solides que de simples tentes de voyage. Le froid y est extreme, et la violence du vent les jette facilement a bas.'

2. Feilberg, *op cit.*, p. 105, summarised the chief features of the Tibetan black tent.
3. Albert Tafel, *Meine Tibetreise,* **1** Stuttgart, 1914, p. 195, and **2** p. 74.
4. The size of Tibetan tents varies according to the authority quoted. A few examples will suffice to give some idea of the variation in size, W. W. Rockhill (1895) – from 10 to 12 ft in depth and up to 30 ft × 50 ft in length: W. Filchner (1930) – 10 to 15 ft in depth and up to 30 ft to 40 ft in length; and A. Tafel (1914) – 12 × 17 m.
5. See Feilberg, *op. cit.*, pp. 149, 155.
6. *ibid.*, pp. 136, 150.
7. *ibid.*, p. 152.

The tents of urban cultures

1. Feilberg, *op. cit.*, p. 132.
2. *idem.*
3. Feilberg, *ibid.*, p. 221, states:

'Quelques petites ressemblances entre les tentes de la civilisation citadine et les types de la tente noire ont deja ete mentionnees . . . poteaux divises en deux, la petite plaque circulaire sur le sommet des poteaux, les cordes qui partent du velum avec plusieurs racines. Ce sont des choses que l'on doit plutot attribuer a des echanges reciproques qui se sont fait valoir plus tard, tandis que, pour les points a—e il s'agit d'une ressemblance dans les elements fondamentaux, dans la conception meme de la tente. L'explication la plus naturelle que l'on puisse donner, c'est qu'il y ait eu primitivement une connexion entre ces deux groupes de tentes.

4. *idem*.
5. *ibid.*, pp. 221–2:

'Malgre leur grande expansion, le pavillon et la tente a toit en parasol presentent des traits communs dans la plus grande partie du domaine de leur expansion . . . Ces nombreux elements communs donnet l'impression d'une forme de tente qui, a une epoque relativement moderne, s'est repandue en partant d'un centre donne'.

6. *ibid.*, pp. 226–7.
7. *ibid.*, pp. 218 and 226.
8. *ibid.*, p. 219.
9. Robert Grosse, 'Das Romisch-byzantinische Marschlager vom 4–10 Jahrhundert,' *Byzantinische Zeitschrift*. **XXII** 1913, fig. 283, p. 603. Cited in Feilberg, *op. cit.*, p. 201.
10. Feilberg, *op. cit.*, p. 209, p. 215.
11. *ibid.*, p. 218.
12. Gertrude Lowthian Bell, *The Desert and the Sown*. London, 1907, pp. 21, 23. Cited by Feilberg, p. 201.
13. Grosse, *op. cit.*, p. 103 n.3.
14. Feilberg, *op. cit.*, pp. 196–7.

Chapter 11

1. Pepi II's instructions to Harkhuf concern the safe delivery of a dwarf – thought to be a pigmy – to the Pharaoh's court. In the Harkhuf inscriptions, J. H. Breasted, *Ancient Records of Egypt: Historical Documents from the Earliest Times to the Persian Conquest*. **1** New York, 1961, § 353, p. 161, Pepi II instructed Harkhuf to place a heavy guard about the dwarf's tent.
2. The word *khen* which signified a light Libyan hut was followed by animal skin and this allows us to conclude that the framework was covered with a hide or skin. See Feilberg, *op. cit.*, p. 202, n.4.
3. Tuthmosis III lived in a heavily guarded royal tent while campaigning, Breasted, *op. cit.*, **2** § 429/1.4, 1.7, p. 183; § 433/1.8, p. 186; § 447/1.14, p. 192.
4. *The Annals* state: 'Behold, there was captured the tent of that wretched for (in) which was (his) son . . .', *ibid.*, § 431/1.4, p. 185.
5. *ibid.*, § 435/1.9, p. 187.
6. *ibid.*, § 490/1.10, p. 205.
7. i. Ramesseum: lepsius, *Denkmäler*, **III** pp. 154, 155, Prisse, *Histoire de L'Art Egyptien*, Battle of Kadesh, pl. 1 Y. Yadin, *The Art of Warfare in Biblical Lands*, p. 107.

ii. Abu Simbel: Champollion, *Monuments*, 30, 31; Champollion, *Notices Descriptives*, 1, 65, 66; Rossellini, *ibid.*, 98–99, Battle of Kadesh, pl. VI; Y. Yadin, *op. cit.*, p. 108.

iii. Luxor: Champollion, *Monuments*, p. 326, 327 (no text); Rossellini, *Monumenti Storici*, p. 106, 107, (no text); Battle of Kadesh, pl. IV; Y. Yadin, *op. cit.*, p. 109.
8. The relief at the Ramesseum, Thebes (*c.* 1290–1223 BC) is illustrated in L. Cottrell, *The Warrior Pharaohs*, London, 1968, pl. 25 and Y. Yadin, *op. cit.*, p. 229.
9. The Assyrians constructed coracles of plaited rushes waterproofed with a covering of skins and the Libyans made portable shelters or *mapalia* from Aspodel-

wattling similar to yurts. O. Bates, *The Eastern Libyans*. London, 1970, p. 168.

10. R. de Vaux, *Ancient Israel, it's Life and Institutions*. London, 1968, p. 294.

11. B. Rothenberg, *Timna, Valley of the Biblical Copper Mines*. London, 1972.

12. de Vaux, *op. cit.*, p. 295.

13. Rothenberg, *op. cit.*, pp. 125–207, describes the excavation in March, 1969, of the Hathor Temple at Timna. The temple was erected by the Egyptians in the reign of Sethos I (1318–1304 BC). A detailed analysis of these textiles was incomplete at the time of publication, *ibid.*, p. 151.

14. The reconstruction in Rothenberg, *ibid.*, fig. 44, p. 152, assumes a Bedouin tent-like canopy, but this is only one of a number of possibilities. A wood framed tent similar to the Tabernacle described in *Exodus* is also likely.

15. See de Vaux, *op. cit.*, p. 296f., for an account of the role of the sacred tent in Arab traditions and its relationship to the Israelite Tabernacle.

16. *idem*.

17. de Vaux, *op. cit.*, p. 296. The Tabernacle and its furnishings are described in Exodus 26:1–32; 36–37, the Court of the Tabernacle 27:9–18; construction of the Tabernacle 36:8–38; and the court 38:9–20.

18. The role of nomads in the ancient history of Mesopotamia is analysed by J. R. Kupper 'Le Role des Nomades dans l'Histoire de la Mesopotamienne', *Journal of the Economic and Social History of the Orient*. II Leiden, 1959, pp. 113–27.

19. *ibid.*, pp. 114, 115.

20. D. D. Luckenbill, *Ancient Records of Assyria and Babylonia*, Chicago, 1927. **1** § 769/1.20, p. 273; **2** § 818/1.10, p. 314.

21. C. B. F. Walker, Assistant Keeper, Department of Western Asiatic antiquities at the British Museum drew my attention to the Assyrian words for tent. References for all these words (except *seru*) may be found in the Chicago Assyrian dictionary.

22. See Luckenbill, *op. cit*:
    Temanite tents – **1** § 368, p. 113;
    Aramean tents – **2** § 39, p. 20;
    Elaminite tents – **2** § 254, p. 128, § 352, p. 156;
    Kassite tents – **2** § 277, p. 135;
    Sutu tents – **2** § 522, p. 210;
    Arabian tents – **2** § 818, p. 314, § 869, p. 338, § 1084, p. 400.

23. Yigael Yadin, *The Art of Warfare in Biblical Lands*, **2** Jerusalem, 1963, p. 292.

24. Layard, *The Monuments of Nineveh, from Drawings Made on the Spot*. Second series, London, 1853, pl. 23 (Kuyunjik).

25. A. H. Layard, *Nineveh and its Remains, A Narrative of an Expedition to Assyria*. London, 1873, p. 151.

26. G. Contenau, *Everyday Life in Babylon and Assyria*. London, 1954, p. 147. None of the reliefs show the semi-cupolas partly rotated so Contenau's theory lacks confirmation.

27. In a letter to the author, C. B. F. Walker stated that it would be worth considering whether there is any relationship between the construction of the semi-cupola tent and the construction of the covered siege engines or battering rams. The military context in which the semi-cupola tent is often depicted and the use of metal armour on Sargon's tent supports this theory.

28. Layard, (1873) *op. cit.*, p. 230, and also *Nineveh and its Remains*, New York, 1849, **2** p. 215.

29. Layard, (1853) *op. cit.*, pl. 77.

30. Contenau, *op. cit.*, p. 147, stated that the semi-cupola tent was used by the Assyrian armies or at least by the officers and notes that cookhouses were always provided.

31. *ibid.*, p. 26.

32. See Feilberg, *op. cit.*, for a discussion of the merits of Herzfeld and Ringelmann's thesis.

33. Reliefs depicting incidents from Ashurbanipal's ninth campaign are illustrated in Yadin, *op. cit.*, **2** p. 450–1, and in R. D. Barnett, *Assyrian Palace Reliefs and the Influence on the Sculptures of Babylonia and Persia.* London, n.d. pl. 114 (BM room L).

34. Layard, (1853) *op. cit.*, series 2, pl. 24.

35. See A. Champdor, *Babylon.* London, 1958, pl. 42, p. 42, and Layard, 1853, *op. cit.*, series 1, pl. 30.

36. W. B. Fisher, *The Cambridge History of Iran.* **1** Cambridge, 1968, p. 411.

37. Herodotus, *History*, recorded that Xerxes was transported past his fleet on a ship equipped with a golden canopy (VII. 100). In the field, a pavilion was provided for Xerxes' comfort while his army camped in the open, (VII.119); Mardonius' tent is mentioned (IX.70); and Herodotus records how Pauxinias captured Xerxes' camp (IX.80–2).

38. The following references to Persian military tents occur in Xenophon: *Cyropaedia* – Cyrus' mess tent (II.i.30), breaking camp (III.iii,21), layout of camp (VIII.v.2–5, 8–14), and Cyaxares II's tent (IV.ii.11); *The Persian Expedition* – Cyrus' tent (I.v. p. 32, I.vi. p. 40), Tissaphernes' tent (II.iv. p. 86), Tirabazus' tent (IV.iv. p. 148), and Artapata's tent (I.vi. p. 42).

39. See Oscar Broneer, 'The tent of Xerxes and the Greek theatre', *University of California Publications in Classical Archaeology.* **1** (12), 1944, p. 311.

40. *idem.*

41. *ibid.*, p. 309. Feilberg, *op. cit.*, p. 198, considered that tents as we know them were not used by the Greeks until about 500 BC.

42. Homer refers to two types of military shelters in *The Iliad*, κλισίης, a substantial hut consisting of a thatch roof supported on walls constructed of wood planks (XXIV.448–55), which are usually mentioned in connection with ships (XII.1–6). The Greeks erected temporary shelters beside their beached ships and sometimes surrounded these with a ditch and a wide wall. These maritime shelters may have been fabricated from sailcloth suspended from the hulls of the ships or on a framework of ship's spars. The word σκηνή first appeared in the play *The Persians* by Aeschylus in 473 BC.

43. The royal Persian tent is described in Athenaeus, *Deipnosophistae*, XII.538d:

> 'Moreover the structure was decorated sumptuously and magnificently with expensive draperies and fine linens, and underfoot with purple and crimson rugs interwoven with gold. To keep the pavilion firmly in place there were columns thirty feet high, gilded and silvered and studded with jewels. The entire enclosure was surrounded with rich curtains having animal patterns interwoven in gold, their rods being overlaid with gold and silver. The perimeter of the courtyard measured four stadia' (about 1000 m). Later XII 539.d–e the pavilion is described as having fifty golden uprights.

44. Athenaeus' description of the royal pavilion of Ptolemy II at Alexandria in *Deipnosophistae*, V.196–7, is vague about the construction of the tent. It is clear that Ptolemy's tent was sumptuously furnished and the reference to one hundred couches is identical to the description of Alexander's pavilion at Susa. It is probable therefore that a large part of the details of the tent are literary inventions.

45. See Broneer, *op. cit.*, pp. 305–11, for a detailed explanation of the concurrences between Xerxes' tent and the development of the *skene* in the Greek theatre in the first half of the 5th century BC.

46. As late as the 3rd century BC Cleomenes of Sparta, 'pitched a theatre'. Plato, *Laws*, VII.817c. and Plutarch, *Cleomenes*, XII.

47. See Conrad Cichorus, *Die Reliefs der Traianssäule*, Berlin, 1896. The three tent types are illustrated in the following scenes:
    the *papilio* – iv, xi, lxi, lxii, lxvi, cii, ciii, cvii, cix, cx and cxiii;
    the officer's tent – viii, xiii, xvii, xxi, xxviii, xliii, lxi, cv, cxiii, cxxv, cxxviii, cxlviii;
    and the commander's tent – vii, xii, xiii, xvii, xxi, liii, ixi, lxii, xcviii, cxxv, cxli, cxlvii.
48. See I. A. Richmond and J. McIntyre, 'Tents of the Roman army and leather from Birdoswald', *Transactions of the Cumberland and Westmorland Antiquarian and Archaeological Society*. **34** 1934, pp. 72–3. Pieces of leather from Birdoswald and Newstead have been identified as calf (Richmond, *op. cit.*, p. 76) but the Valkenburg fragments proved on microscopic examination to be goat leather (*Romeins Lederwerk vit Valkenburg*, 1967, pp. 17–18, cited by Webster, p. 167).
49. *ibid.*, p. 65.
50. *ibid.*, p. 75.
51. *ibid.*, p. 76–7.
52. *ibid.*, p. 64.
53. Yigael Yadin, *Masada, Herod's Fortress and the Zealot's Last Stand*. London, 1966, p. 219.
54. *Archaeological Journal*. **lxxxix** fig. 12, p. 61.
55. Richmond, *op. cit.*, p. 65.
56. Livy, x.38. gives the dimensions as being two hundred feet square.
57. See *De Munitionibus Castrorum*, for a layout of a *striga* or double row of tents.
58. Graham Webster, *The Imperial Army of the First and Second Centuries AD*, London, 1969, p. 168, cites Hyginus as his source.
59. Polybius, VI 28, 3–4, gave the size of a maniple in a Republican camp as 100 × 100 ft while Hyginus stated that the size of an Imperial maniple was 120 × 60 ft.
60. Tacitus in *The Annals of Tacitus*, XIV, XVII, gives an account of the Pompeii riot.
61. Fresco, Pompeii amphitheatre, Naples.
62. See Rainer Graeffe 'Roman theatre velum', *Convertible Roofs*, IL (5), Stuttgart, 1972, p. 29.
63. See Graeffe, *op. cit.*, p. 33 and Maiuri, *Amedo la Peinture Romaine*, Skira-Verlag, 1953, p. 176 (Fresco at Pompeii).
64. *ibid.*, p. 29.
65. *Forschungen im Ephesos*, II, p. 162, (39), 1.4 and (40) 1.6.
66. Valerius Maximus, *Factorum et Dictorum Memorabilium*, II, 4, 6.
67. Margaret Bieber, *The History of the Greek and Roman Theatre*, Princeton, 1961, p. 179, gives 70 BC while Graeffe, *op. cit.*, p. 25, suggests that linen velarium were introduced in 69 BC. These ancient convertible roofs are described by Pliny, *Natural History*, **XIX** (VI), 23.
68. The invention of vela roofs by the Campanians may have been influenced by the Greek practice of deploying cloth theatre *skene* in the nearby settlements of Magna Graecia in southern Italy and Sicily.
69. Pliny, *Natural History*, **XIX** (VI), 23–5.
70. *ibid.*, **XIX** (VI), 23.
71. *ibid.*, **XIX** (VI), 24.
72. Cassius Dio, *Dio's Roman History*, LXII, 6, 2 (AD 66).
73. For example, Commodus Antonius, '. . . gave orders that the Roman people should be slain in the amphitheatre by the marines who spread the awnings.' Lampridius, *Historia Augusta*, Commodus Antonius, XV, 6.
74. Bieber, *op. cit.*, p. 199.
75. Lucretius, *On the Nature of Things*, IV, 76, comments on the light effects on the audience of coloured vela.
76. Pliny, *op. cit.*, **XIX** (VI), 24.
77. Rainer Graeffe gives a brief account of the development of 'Roman Theatre

Velum' in *Convertible Roofs*, IL5, pp. 25–37.
78. *ibid.*, p. 29, n.12.
79. Vitruvius, *Ten Books of Architecture*, X, preface.
80. Graeffe, *op. cit.*, p. 29, and Bieber, *op. cit.*, the colosseum (pp. 198–9) Orange theatre (pp. 290–1) and Aspendus theatre (pp. 208–9), describe the archaeological evidence of *vela* roofs.
81. Graeffe, *op. cit.*, p. 31.
82. Auguste Cariste, *Monuments Antiques a Orange, Arc de Triomphe et Theatre*. **XL**, XLIX, Paris, 1856, fig. 29, 30. p. 76.

Chapter 12

1. Feilberg, *op. cit.*, p. 179.
2. *ibid.*, p. 180.
3. *ibid.*, p. 188.
4. Jan Marek and Hana Knizicova, *The Jenghis Khan Miniatures from the Court of Akbar the Great*. London, 1963, pp. 17–18.
5. Feilberg, *op. cit.*, p. 189.
6. Manuscript of Makamat d'Hariri, Vienne, Bibliotheque Imperiale of Vienna (372), executed in 1334. See F. R. Martin, *The Miniature Painting and Painters of Persia, India and Turkey from the 8th to the 18th century*. **1** London, 1912, p. 9.
7. *Layla and Majnun* and *The Death of Majnun at the Tomb of Layla*, from *Manuscript of Nizami*, British Museum (Or. 6810), probable date *c*. 1480. See F. R. Martin and Sir T. Arnold, *The Nizamis Ms. Illum, by Bihzad, Mirak and Qasim Ali, written 1495 for Sultan Ali Mirza Barlas Ruler of Samarqand* in the British Museum (Or. 6810), Vienna, 1928, pl. XVI and XVII.
8. *Majnun brought in chains to Layla's Tent*, by Mir Sayyid Ali, Tabriz School, dated 1539–43. *The Kamsa of Nizami*, MS. British Museum (Or. 2265). See A. U. Pope, *A Survey of Persian Art from Prehistoric Times to the Present*. **IX** London and New York, 1967, pl. 910.
9. *Majnun before Layla's Tent*, painting from a copy of *Jami's Haft Aurang* ('Seven Thrones') copied for the Library of Adu'l Fath Sultan Ibrahim Mirza, cousin of Shah Ismail II, between 1556 and 1565 in Meshed. Freer Gallery of Art, Washington. See E. J. Grube, *The World of Islam*, London, 1966, pl. 83, p. 145.
10. *Manuscript du Zafar Nameh*, Museum of Fine Arts, Boston. See Sir Thomas W. Arnold, *Bihzad and his Paintings in the Zafar-Namah Ms*. London, 1930, pl. V–VI.
11. *Life in the Country*, sketch for a painting by Muhammadi, Isfahan, *c*. 1578. Louvre, Paris. See E. Blochet, *Musulman Painting XII–XVIth Century*, London, 1929, pl. CXXXVII.
12. *Life in the Country*, by Mir Sayyid Ali, Tabriz, Iran, *c*. 1540. Probably a copy of Nizami's *Khamsa*. Fogg Art Museum, Harvard University, Cambridge, Mass. See E. J. Grube, *The World of Islam*, London, 1966, pl. 83, p. 145.
13. *Layla and Majnun unconscious among animals which sympathise with their grief*. The Khamsa of Nizami, Shiraz School, mid-16th century. See *Iran : Persian Miniatures – Imperial Library*, UNESCO World Art Series, Paris, 1956, pl. XXVII.
14. *Surprise attack on an encampment of rebels by Timur's forces*, by Sharaf Ad-Din 'Ali Yazdi, *Zafar-Nama*, Tabriz School, dated 1529. Library of the Gulistan, Teheran. See Pope, *op. cit.*, **IX** p. 907B.
15. *Assad Ibn Kariba attacks the army of Iraj at Night*, painting from the *Dastani-i Amir Hamsa* (*Hamza-Nameh*), India, 1575. Metropolitan Museum of Art, New York. See Grube, *op. cit.*, pl. 94, p. 152.
16. *Jenghis Khan in his gold tent orders stones strewn on the dusty soil of the camp*, illustration of the *Chronicle of Jenghiz Khan in the years 1219–1227*, from

the *History of the Mongols*, sec. 2, Bk. 2, Pt. 1, Mughal School, Kabul, *c.* 17th century. See Marek and Knizikova, *op. cit.*, London, 1963, pl. 16.

17. Godfrey Goodwin, *A History of Ottoman Architecture*, London, 1961, pp. 107, 429.

18. The early Ottoman rulers were chieftains of a small tribe of shepherds and Gazis (warriors) on the frontiers of the Faith. Their followers were the Kayi clan of the numerous Oguz Turkish people who fled from central Asia into Anatolia before the onslaught of Genghis Khan.

19. Goodwin, *op. cit.*, p. 339.

20. *idem*. It is tempting to associate the concial shape of Seljuk türbes with the tents of the central Asian nomads and the Kurds. A drawing by Friar Rubruck of tents which he saw when he visited the Mongol court in 1253 is reproduced in de Bergeron's edition of his work. These tents may well have served as prototype for the Seljuk mausolea. See Goodwin, *op. cit.*, p. 66.

21. *Episode from the festivities at Istanbul in September, 1720*, from the two volume *Surname-i Vehbi*. 18th century, Topkapi Museum (A III 3594) Istanbul. See W. Lillys, *Persian Miniatures, the Story of Rustam*, London, 1964, pl. 10. Also Miniature (14), 1339, among others, in the Topkapisaray — *The Enthronement of Selim II*, from *Nuzheti-Esrar al-Bahar*, dated 1658, by Ahmet Feridun Pasha shows a splendid example of a royal tent.

22. Goodwin *op. cit.*, p. 373.

23. Sir P. Rycault, *The History of the Turkish Empire from the year 1623 to the year 1677*, London, 1680, p. 30. There were about two thousand tents in no order, but the Grand Signior's appeared to be in the midst and to overtop all the rest.

24. *The Turkish camp before Vienna*, drawing by Bartholomaus Behen, 1529. Bild archiv der Ost, National Bibliotek, Vienna. See Goodwin, *op. cit.*, pl. 478, p. 428.

25. A. Vandal, *Une Ambassade Francaise en Orient sous Louis XV*; la Mission du Marquis de Villeneuve, 1728–41, Paris, 1887, p. 72.

26. See Goodwin, *op. cit.*, fig. 355, p. 356.

27. Rycault, *op. cit.*, p. 30.

28. Sir P. Rycault, *The Present State of the Ottoman Empire*, Bk. 3 London 1687, p. 98.

29. Goodwin, *op. cit.*, p. 322.

30. R. A. Stein, *Tibetan Civilization*, London, 1972, p. 119. An anonymous photograph of the Dalai Lama's Camp in 1939 (fig. 3) is remarkably similar to the arrangement of Chinese tents depicted in a series of 18th century French engravings (1766).

31. *Departure of Wen Chi from the Nomad Camp*, Chao Meng-fu (1254–1322), ink on silk, signed and dated 1301. National Palace Museum, Taichung, Taiwan. See William Willets, *Foundations of Chinese Art, from neolithic pottery to modern architecture*, London 1965, fig. 221, p. 358. Chao Meng-fu was called into service under the Mongols in 1286.

32. See Bernard Rudofsky, *Architecture without Architects*. Garden City N.Y., 1964, pl. 45.

33. See John Warner 'Castiglione and the conquests of the Ch'ien Lung Emperor', *Arts of Asia*, **5** (6) (Nov–Dec. 1975), pp. 62–72.

34. George N. Roerich, *Trails to Inmost Asia, Five Years of exploration with the Roerich Central Asian Expedition*, London 1931, p. 173.

35. *A Royal Feast of Entertainment for the Embassy of the Dutch East India Company, 1695*. Engraving, National Maritime Museum, Greenwich. See A. J. Toynbee, *Half the World*, London, 1973, p. 271, pl. 15.

36. Vesey Norman, *The Mediaeval Soldier*, London, 1971, p. 21.

37. Neville Williams, 'The Master of the Royal Tents and his Records', *Journal of

the Society of Archivists, **11** (2) (Oct. 1960). Reprint supplied by author, p. 2.

38. *Charlemagne receiving Haroun-Al-Raschid's Gifts*, reconstructed by G. B. Giovenale. Santa Maria in Cosmedin, Rome (Central wall, left hand wall, scene 9 of the cycle), *c.* 1119–1120. See R. and J. S. Lejeune, *The Legend of Roland in the Middle Ages*, **2** Brussels, 1966, fig. 22.

39. Manuel Komroff (Ed.), *Contemporaries of Marco Polo*, New York 1928, p. 35; and Christopher Dawson, *The Mongol Mission Narratives and Letters of the Franciscan Missionaries in Mongolia in the thirteenth and fourteenth centuries*. Translated by a nun from Stanbrook Abbey, London and New York, 1955, pp. 94–6.

40. *The Emperor and the Dukes with the Army*, (Holy Roman Emperor Henry VI, 1190–1197). *Res Siculae* or *Liber ad Honorem Augusti*, by Pierre d'Ebulon, Cod. 120, II fo. 109, Berne Bibliothek. See A. Maurois (Ed.), *An Illustrated History of Germany*, London, 1966, pl. 66.

41. *Besieging Army at Foot of Fortress*, an incident in the Wars of Jaime of Spain (1213–1276). Fresco, Roman-Catalan Art, 13th century, Held Museum. See *The Ancient Art of Warfare*, Barrie and Rockliff, London, 1966, p. 246–7.

42. (i) *Charlemagne, Milo and Roland, The Miracle of the Flowering Lances*, and
   (ii) *The Siege of Pamplona by the Franks* reliefs from the Reliquary of St Charlemagne 1200–1215, Aix-la-Chapelle, Aachen Cathedral. See Lejeune, *op. cit.*, i) **1** pl. VI, p. 172, and **2** fig. 148, also ii) **2** fig. 146.

43. *Maciejowski Bible*, MS 638f. 27v. Pierpont Morgan Library. See M. Bishop, *The Horizon Book of the Middle Ages*, London, 1968, p. 65, also Vesey Norman, The Mediaeval Soldier, London 1971, p. 217, pl. 18.

44. The Lady with the Unicorn: A mon seul desir (tapestry detail, *c.* 1500). Musee Cluny, Paris.

45. Michael Mallet, *Mercenaries and their Masters*, Totowa, N.J. 1974, fig. 3(a), p. 54.

46. *A 14th Century Camp*, detail from *Guidoriccio da Fogliano*, a fresco by Simone Martini. The Palazzo Pubblico, Sienna, *c.* 1328, from G. Paccagini, *Simone Martini*, London n.d. pl. 7, p. 101.

47. (i) *The Siege of Piombino* (1448) and
   (ii) *An army breaking camp*. Manuscript illumination by Giovanni Bettini da Fano for the *Esperide*. Bodleian Library, Oxford, MS, Canon, Class. Lat. 81 :i) f. 27, ii) f.49v. See Mallet, *op. cit.*, i) fig. 10, p. 135, ii) fig. 13(a), p. 182.

48. (i) *The Jousts of St Inglevert* (M.clviii), MS Harl. 4379, fol. 23b.
   (ii) *The Tournament of St Inglevert* (M.clxiv), MS. Harl. 4379, fol. 43.
   See G. G. Coulton, *The Chronicler of European Chivalry*, London, 1930, i) p. 30 and ii) pl. 11, p. 20.

49. *The Assault on the Strong Town of Afrique* (M.clxvii). MS. Harl. 4379, fol. 83b. See Coulton, *op. cit.*, p. 401, pl. IV.

50. *The meeting between Henry VIII and his ally, the Emperor Maximilian I, in their war with France, 1513*. Painting at Hampton Court, in the Collection of Her Majesty the Queen. See Neville Williams, *Henry VIII and his Court*, London, 1967, pp. 22–23.

51. *Siege of Rome by the Etruscan Chief Porsena*, a painting by Melchior Felsen, 16th century. See *The Ancient Art of Warfare*, *op. cit.*, p. 473, fig. 496.

52. Williams (1967), *op. cit.*, p. 72.

53. *The Life of Benvenuto Cellini*, newly translated by J. A. Symonds, London, 1889, p. 306.

54. Williams, 1960, *op. cit.*, p. 4.

55. See *ibid.*, p. 2 and Jocelyne G. Russel, *The Field of Cloth of Gold*, London, 1969, pp. 27, 46. Williams (1967), *op. cit.*, p. 78 estimated the size of the English

party at 5172 men and women requiring the services of 2865 horses.

56. Russel, *ibid.*, p. 24.

57. BN MS. Francais 10383 (the original accounts), (f.10^v – 27^r). This manuscript in the Bibliotheque Nationale of Paris gives a full account of the French preparations. It is the record of the accounts of Guillaume de Saigne, Treasurer and Receiver-General of the Artillery, for the making and transport of the tents and pavilions.

58. *ibid.*, f. 172^r – 193^v.

59. Russel, *op. cit.*, p. 30.

60. See Sydney Anglo, 'The Hampton Court painting of the Field of Cloth of Gold considered as an historical document', *The Antiquaries Journal*, **XLVI** 1966, pp. 287–307 for an analysis of the pictorial evidence.

61. Russel, *op. cit.*, p. 27.

62. Bernard de Montfaucon, *Les Monumens de la Monarchie Francaise*, Paris, 1729, 1733, IV, pp. 164–81, cited in *ibid.*, n.2, p. 27.

63. Russel, *op. cit.*, p. 28.

64. *The Field of the Cloth of Gold*. Narrative painting possibly by Hans Roest. Painting at Hampton Court, in the Collection of Her Majesty the Queen. See Williams (1967), *op. cit.*, pp. 74–5.

65. Russel, *op. cit.*, p. 29.

66. Williams (1960), *op. cit.*, p. 2.

67. BM MS. *Cotton Augustus* 1 (ii) (76). British Museum (Or. 42678).

68. *The Battle of the Spurs, August 1513*. Painting at Hampton Court, in the Collection of Her Majesty the Queen. See Williams, (1967), *op. cit.*, pp. 42–43.

69. See Williams (1960), *op. cit.*, p. 4f for a detailed account of the history of the office of Master of Tents at the English Court.

Chapter 13

1. J. Needham, *Science and Civilization in China*. **4** Pt. 3 Cambridge 1971, p. 201.

2. Needham, *op cit.*, p. 189, and L. C. Goodrich, 'Suspension Bridges in China', Sino Indian Studies, **5** (3–4) (1957), p. 53.

3. *ibid.*, pp. 186, 189.

4. *ibid.*, p. 187.

5. *idem.*, in the passage in which the *Chhien Han Shu* refers to the Hindu Kush mountains.

6. *ibid.*, p. 185.

7. *ibid.*, p. 186. See also Paul Popper, 'Cane bridges of Asia', *The National Geographic Magazine*, **XCIV** (2) 1948, pp. 243–50.

8. Popper, *op. cit.*, p. 249, and Needham, *op. cit.*, p. 186.

9. Needham, *op. cit.*, p. 190.

10. *ibid.*, p. 191, n.d. The tensile strength of the outer strips of bamboo of 26000 psi is given by H. Stranb, *Die Geschichte d. Bauingeriewkunst; ein Uberlick von der Antike bis in die Neuzeit*. 2nd ed., Liebing, Wurzburg, 1964, p. 196.

11. H. Fugl-Meyer, *Chinese Bridges*, Shanghai and Singapore, London, 1937, p. 114.

12. Needham, *op. cit.*, p. 192. The Am Lan Bridge over the Min River is certainly pre-Sung and may go back to the 3rd century. The great scholar and traveller Fan Chheng-Ta described it in AD 1177.

13. *ibid.*, p. 193. The invention of hand forged wrought iron chains probably occurred in Southwest China where the two essential preconditions existed: traditional catenary cable bridges and an advanced metallurgy of iron.

14. *ibid.*, p. 210.

15. *ibid.*, p. 188.

16. V. W. von Hagen, *Highway of the Sun*, London, 1956, pp. 107, 113. The Incas expanded their realm to the edge of the Apurimac some time after 1300 and according to their chronicles the bridge was completed by Inca Roca, then chieftain.

17. *ibid.*, pp. 131, 158. The Purcara bridge was built by the sixth Inca *c.* 1290 and marks the beginning of the great period of Inca construction which ended with the Bonbon bridge *c.* AD 1450. Von Hagen refers to the following Inca bridges: Urumbamba bridge, Purcara bridge (166 paces long), Mayoc bridge, Charqui-Saytayoc bridge, Carabaya river bridge, Bonbon bridge (over the Montaro river), and the Apurimac (river) bridge. Squier mentions bridges over the Ollantaytambo and Rio Pampas rivers.

18. Needham, *op. cit.*, p. 190, comments that the relation between the American suspension bridge and the hammock should not be overlooked when considering the origin of these bridges. The discovery of Asian (Chinese or Japanese) stone anchors off the Palos Verdes Peninsula in 1975 raised the possibility that Chinese mariners reached the west coast of America 1000 years ago. The great similarity of ancient ceramics found in South America and China supports Needham's contention that the Peruvian suspension bridge could have derived from a Chinese proto-type.

19. von Hagen, *op. cit.*, p. 113.

20. E. G. Squier, *Peru, Incidents of Travel and Explorations in the Land of the Incas*, New York, 1877, p. 548. The measurements vary so much that it is hard to believe they are of the same bridge. Thus: Garcilasco de la Vega, 200 paces; Gieza de Leon (1543), 85 m (250 ft); Sir Clements Markham (1855), 90 ft, Lieutenant Gibbon (1817), 324 ft; and G. Squier (1864), 148 ft.

21. Besides the Apurimac, Squier measured the Rio Pampas bridge and gave its length as 135 ft, being 45 ft high in the centre. McIntyre discovered contemporary rope suspension bridges constructed over the Apurimac river by local farmers. See *The National Geographic Magazine*, (Dec. 1973), pp. 782–5.

22. W. B. Parsons, *Engineers and Engineering in the Renaissance*, Baltimore, 1939, pp. 490–2.

23. H. J. Hopkins, *A Span of Bridges*, Newton Abbot, Devon, 1970, pp. 175–6. German and Switzers troops built a rope bridge across the Padus river in Italy in 1515, catenary bridges were also deployed by Admiral Coligny (1569) across the Clain river at Poiters, and by 1792 they were standard equipment in the French Army.

24. Needham, *op. cit.*, p. 208, concluded that the engineers of the Renaissance and later Europe were given a stimuli from the publication of the Chinese iron-chain suspension bridges even though there is no proof which directly links Verantius' proposals with reports of Chinese bridges.

25. The iron chain bridge over the Oder river at Glorywitz was more likely to have derived from the general practice of building suspension bridges for military purposes than to the writings of Verantius. David Plowden, *Bridges, the Spans of North America*. New York, 1974, p. 59.

26. *ibid.*, pp. 59–60.

Chapter 14

1. D'Arcy Thompson, *On Growth and Form* abridged edition ed. by J. T. Bonner, London, 1966, p. 18.

2. Conrad Roland, *Frei Otto: Structures*. Translated by C. V. Amerongen, London, 1972, p. 7.

3. Lev Zetlin, 'Elimination of Flutter in Suspension Roofs' in N. Esquillan and Y. Saillard (Eds), *Hanging Roofs*, Amsterdam, 1963, p. 93.

4. Plowden, *op. cit.*, p. 117. Cited from J. A. Roebling, *Final Report of John A. Roebling, Civil Engineer, to the President and Directors of the Niagara Falls Suspension and Niagara Falls International Bridge Companies*, Rochester, New York, 1855.

5. Sir A. Pugsley, *The Theory of Suspension Bridges*, London, 1957, p. 5.

6. Thompson, *op. cit.*, p. 17.

7. Derrick Beckett, *Bridges*, London, 1969, p. 156, states that the cable-stayed bridge acts as useful transition between the continuous girder and the suspension cable and that it is therefore suited to spans in the range of 500 ft to 1500 ft. With the increase in heavy vehicular loading the problem of stability increases for spans less than 1500 ft. Suspension bridges built after the Brooklyn bridge have spans between 1500 and 4260 ft. See also Myron Goldsmith, 'RIBA annual discourse', *RIBA Journal*, June 1966, pp. 253–4, for a comparison of the effect of scale and magnitude in different types of bridges.

8. James Sutherland, 'Long Span Bridges', *The Architectural Review*, **CXL** (835) (Sep. 1966), p. 177.

9. *idem*.

10. Hopkins, *op. cit.*, p. 228.

11. *ibid.*, fig. 98, p. 211. See also A. A. Jakkula, *A History of Suspension Bridges in Bibliographical Form*. Texas, 1941, for the dates of completion of the 147 19th century suspension bridges.

12. Sutherland, *op. cit.*, p. 178.

13. Hopkins, *op. cit.*, p. 227, cites O. H. Amman, 'George Washington Bridge' – 'General Conception and Development of Design', *Transactions of the American Society of Civil Engineers*, (97), (1933), pp. 1–65.

14. *ibid.*, pp. 185–6.

15. *ibid.*, p. 181.

16. Kenneth Clark, *Civilization*. London, 1972, pp. 331–2.

17. Hopkins, *op. cit.*, p. 189.

18. Beckett, *op.cit.*, p. 67.

19. Brunel's designs for Clifton ranged from 870 ft to 916 ft (1830) so it is a striking coincidence that M. Chaley decided on a span of 870 ft for his Fribourg bridge (1832–4) in Switzerland. The four cables (each $5\frac{1}{2}$ in dia.) consisted of some 1056 wires fabricated on the valley floor and hoisted into position.

20. Beckett, *op. cit.*, pp. 67–8.

21. Hopkins, *op. cit.*, p. 190, cites J. M. Rendel, 'Memoir of the Montrose Suspension Bridge', *Proc. ICE*, (1) (April 1841), pp. 122–9.

22. *ibid.*, pp. 191–2.

23. See W. T. Clark, *The Suspension Bridge Across the River Danube*, London, 1852–3.

24. Beckett, *op. cit.*, p. 66.

25. See Plowden, *op. cit.*, p. 72, for a discussion of French innovations, also Hopkins, *op. cit.*, p. 203f.

26. Hopkins, *op, cit.*, p. 202.

27. *ibid.*, p. 206.

28. *ibid.*, pp. 208–9.

29. L. J. Vicat, 'Ponts Suspendus en fil de fer sur le Rhone', *Annales des Ponts et Chaussees*, (Memoires et Documents), (1), (1831) pp. 93–144.

30. The variation in tension in a small cable in which each wire is firmly lashed so

that it maintains its position in relation to the other wires could be as much as 30%. A similar problem arises in prestressed cablenets where the intersecting cables are prevented from rotating by the cable clamps. Hopkins, *op. cit.*, p. 208.

31. *ibid.*, pp. 208–9.
32. *idem.*
33. Ellet published the first of his many pamphlets, *A Popular Notice on Suspension Bridges*, in the spring of 1838.
34. Even though Ellet was in France in 1830–31, he adopted the method of Seguin, and subsequently this method rather than Vicat's superior method became known throughout America as the 'French method'. Plowden, *op. cit.*, p. 73.
35. *ibid.*, p. 76.
36. John A. Roebling was the first (1841) manufacturer of wire rope in America, *ibid.*, p. 73. The first ropes were intended for use on the Pennsylvania Canal.
37. Hopkins, *op. cit.*, p. 216.
38. Plowden, *op. cit.*, p. 117, from J. A. Roebling's final Report to the Directors of the Niagara Bridge Company (1855).
39. Charles B. Bender in commenting on the Niagara Railroad Bridge noted that, 'they are to be appreciated as great works of American enterprise and boldness; but they exhibit nothing commendable in the way of invention . . .' (paper of 18 March, 1868), cited by Hopkins, *op. cit.*, p. 227.
40. Plowden, *op. cit.*, p. 80, from J. A. Roebling's final Report to the Directors of the Niagara Bridge Company (1855).
41. Pugsley, *op. cit.*, p. 5, comments 'Roebling still clung to the radiating inclined suspension rods of his earlier designs, but was clearly becoming more confident of the cable gravity stiffness associated with long spans.'
42. Hopkins, *op. cit.*, Pittsburg, p. 221; Brooklyn, p. 227.
43. Pugsley, *op. cit.*, pp. 6–7.
44. Carl Condit described the Benjamin Franklin Bridge as, 'the first distinctly modern suspension bridge built on a grand scale. It combined and resolved all the principles of suspension bridge engineering in preparation for the next spectacular increase in suspension spans.' Plowden, *op. cit.*, p. 241.
45. Sutherland, *op. cit.*, p. 179.
46. Plowden, *op. cit.*, p. 289.
47. The ratio of depth of stiffening girder to span for the Tacoma Narrows bridge was $\frac{1}{350}$ compared with $\frac{1}{168}$ for the Golden Gate and $\frac{1}{33}$ for the George Washington bridges. Sutherland, *op. cit.*, p. 183. See table 2 for a comparison of Tacoma with other notable suspension bridges of the 1930s.
48. *ibid.*, p. 184.
49. *ibid.*, p. 185.

Chapter 15

1. I am grateful to Professor J. Gero for drawing my attention to I. B. Hruban's excellent paper on Schnirch's chain roof constructions: 'Suspension roofs for ordinary rectangular houses designed and erected in 1824–1828' in proceedings of the *IASS Conference on Lightweight Shell and Space Structures for normal seismic zones.* September 13–16, 1977, Alma–Ata, USSR. MR Publishers, 1977, pp. 97–106.
2. T. C. Bannister, 'Bogardus revisited', Pt. 2 'The iron towers', Journal of the Society of Architectural Historians, **16**, 1957, pp. 11–19, cited in R. J. Mainstone, *Developments in Structural Form.* London, 1971, n.28, p. 238.
3. I. G. Liudkovsky 'On the choice of the optimum types of suspended roofs and

their bearing contours' in N. Esquillan and Y. Saillard (Eds.) *Hanging Roofs*, Amsterdam, 1963, pp. 176–7.

4. James Meller (Ed.), *The Buckminster Fuller Reader*, Harmondsworth, Middlesex, 1970, pl. 2a, 2b, 3.

5. Frei Otto, *Tensile Structures*, **2**, Cambridge, Mass. 1969, p. 17.

6. Z. S. Makowski, *Steel Space Structures*, London, 1965, fig. 219, p. 195, also Laurence Lessing, 'Suspension Structures', *Architectural Forum*, **107**, (6) (Dec. 1957), p. 140.

7. Lessing *ibid.*, p. 135.

8. Robin Boyd, 'Under Tension', *The Architectural Review*, **134**, (801) (Nov. 1963), p. 325.

9. This information was kindly supplied by Hugh O'Neil, Lecturer, Department of Architecture, Melbourne University. Helen Jessup has written a thesis, *McLaine Pont's Architecture in Indonesia.* Courtauld Institute, 1974.

10. Sigfried Giedion, *Space, Time and Architecture* (5th ed.), Cambridge, Mass. 1967, p. xxxii.

11. Reyner Banham, *Theory and Design in the First Machine Age*, London 1970, p. 14.

12. Antonio Sant'Elia/Filippo Tommaso Marinetsi, 'Futurist Architecture' in Ulrich Conrads (Ed.), *Programmes and Manifestoes on 20th Century Architecture.* Translated by Michael Ballock, London, 1970, p. 38.

13. *Sketch for Motor Car Chassis Factory*, 1914, Wolf von Eckardt, in Eric Mendelsohn, New York, 1960, p. 10.

14. Reyner Banham, *op. cit.*, p. 168, noted 'Not the least important revelation of this passage is that it proves to deal with a structure in tension, a concept that seems to have had little interest for architects even after the War, let alone 1914 when this sketch was made'.

15. *idem.*

16. Frederick Kiesler: 'Space City Architecture' in Conrads, *op. cit.*, p. 98. See also Manifesto of of Tensionism 'Organic building, the city in Space, functional architecture' in *Zodiac* 19, Milan, n.d. p. 25.

17. W. Boesiger (Ed.), *Le Corbusier and Pierre Jeanneret, The Complete Architectural Works* II, 1929–34. London, 1964, p. 133.

18. See Marks, R. W., 1960, *op. cit.* p. 87. In 1929 Simon Breines won the Architectural League of New York award with a design for a roadside service station based on Bucksminster Fuller's 4D Dymaxian house of 1927. Marks comments that Breine's design for Russia's Palace of the Soviets used Fuller's 'tensional-structure strategy'. Fuller's pole house concept was applied in the Transportation Building at the Chicago World's Fair of 1933. The idea recurs in several American schemes in the 1940s such as Eero Saarinen's 1941 community centre project.

19. Claude Schnaidt, Hannes Meyer, *Buildings, Projects and Writings*, London, 1965, p. 20.

20. Le Corbusier, *Le Corbusier, My Work.* Translated by James Palmes, London, 1960, p. 129. The connection is a tenuous one since the Paris and Milan pavilions represent two quite distinct types of tensile structure, the former simply suspended, the latter cable-stayed.

21. Knud Bastlund, *Jose Luis Sert*, New York, Washington, 1967, pp. 38–45.

22. Werner Graeff, according to Reyner Banham, *op. cit.*, p. 193, proclaimed: 'Uninfluenced by the methods of mechanical technology, the new and greater technology begins — the technology of tensions, invisible motions, action-at-a-distance, and speeds unimaginable in 1922'.

23. Wolfgang Pehnt, *Expressionist Architecture*, London, 1973.

24. Professor Banham has noted that my account jumps from 1937 to 1952, as though there were no connection between pre- and post-war developments. The work of Renzo Zavanella, and the tensile pavilions at the Festival of Britain continued a conception of tensile structure that ignored the requirements of structural form and tended to force tensile structures into the form-mould of the International style. The importance of Nowicki's Raleigh arena lies in its clear recognition of anticlastic saddle-shaped surfaces as the logical form of tensile surface structures. Of the early post-war developments Renzo Zavanella's contribution was clearly outstanding.

25. See *Architectural Forum*, February, 1947, p. 109.

26. *ibid.*, **88**, no. 3, March, 1948, p. 99.

27. The Lilly Pad House is illustrated in *ibid.*, p. 101.

28. I am grateful to Professor R. Banham for drawing my attention to the work of Renzo Zavanella.

29. See *L'Architecture d'Aujourd'hui* (27), (December 1949) p. 73.

30. Professor R. Banham examined the structural sources of the Festival of Britain pavilions in 'Opinions on the Festival of Britain' in *Architectural Review*, **CXIII**, (673) (Jan, 1953) p. 62–3.

31. The planning of the Festival of Britain site and the design of the individual pavilions and spaces is analysed in a 'Special Issue on the South Bank Exhibition' of the *Architectural Review* **110** (656), August 1951. See also Banham, M., and Hillier, B., 1976, *A Tonic to the Nation, The Festival of Britain, 1951*. Thames and Hudson, London.

32. The 'Skylon' employed Buckminster Fuller's tensegrity mast principal to lift the plyon free of the ground. Fuller began development of his tensegrity system from 1949 on. The first tensegrity mast was erected at North Carolina State College in 1950. See *Architectural Review*, **110**, (656), August 1951.

33. *ibid.*, p. 110, for a discussion of the nautical connotations of the seaside structures along the Royal Festival Hall Terrace.

34. The Festival Pleasure Gardens at Battersea Park are reviewed in the *Architectural Review*, **109**, (652), April 1951, p. 230 on.

Chapter 16

1. Lessing, *op. cit.*, p. 135.

2. Beckett, *op. cit.*, p. 158.

3. *ibid.*, p. 156.

4. See David Jawerth, 'Einige bauten mit Vorgespannter Hängekonstruktion aus Gegensinnig Gekrümmten Seilen', in N. Esquillan and Y. Saillard, *op. cit.*, pp. 117–28.

5. Boyd, *op. cit.*, p. 334.

6. *idem.*

7. Banham, *op. cit.*, p. 268, from Bruno Taut's magazine Frülicht: 'Skyscrapers reveal their bold structural pattern during construction. Only then does the gigantic steel webb seem impressive. When the outer walls are put in place, the structural system which is the basis of all artistic design, is hidden in a chaos of meaningless and trivial forms . . .'

8. See Philip Drew, *Frei Otto, Form and Structure*, London, 1967, p. 28f.

9. *ibid.*, p. 11.

10. *ibid.*, p. 13f.

11. Otto, *op. cit.*, p. 25.

12. Pier Luigi Nervi, *Aesthetics and Technology in Building* translated by Robert

Einaudi, Cambridge, Mass. 1966, p. 90f.

13. See Paul Rudolph, *Buildings and projects*, Stuttgart, London, New York, 1970, also Boyd, *op. cit.*, p. 326.

14. Boyd, *ibid.*, p. 328.

15. Community Centre project, Eero Saarinen, 1941. A. Tempko, *Eero Saarinen*, New York, 1967, pl. 14, p. 54.

16. See 'Music Tent', *Architectural Forum*, **91** (3), September 1949, pp. 88–9.

17. See H. Seymour Howard, *Suspended Structures Concepts*, AD USS 55–1898, Pittsburg, April 1966.

18. See Drew, *op. cit.*, pp. 110–13.

19. See Le Corbusier, *Towards a New Architecture*, translated by Frederick Etchells, 1st paperback ed., London, 1970, p. 44.

20. Mick Courtney 'Mecca Hotel and Conference Centre', *The Arup Journal*, **6** (3), (September, 1971), pp. 12–13.

21. Competition project for an exhibition hall (dia. 430 m), Paris 1934. Architects Eugene Beaudouin and Marcel Lods, *Twentieth Century Engineering*, Museum of Modern Art, New York, 1964, pl. 74, 75.

22. Boyd, *op. cit.*, p. 333.

23. Otto, *op. cit.*, p. 30.

24. Howard (1966), *op. cit.*, p. 21. See also Boyd, *op. cit.*, p. 328.

25. *idem*.

26. See Lessing, *op. cit.*, pp. 138–40, and Lev Zetlin, 'Elimination of Flutter in Suspension Roofs', in Esquillan and Saillard, *op. cit.*, pp. 93–103.

27. Municipal Auditorium, Utica, N.Y., 1960. Gehron and Seltzer Architects; Frank Delle Cese, Associated Architect, Lev Zetlin, Structural Engineer. 'Bicycle Wheel roof spans 240 ft', *Architectural Forum*, **112** (5), (May 1960), pp. 144–5.

28. Le Ricolais 'Bicycle Wheels', *Progressive Architecture*, **42** (Feb. 1961), pp. 144–53.

29. Beckett, *op. cit.*, p. 159.

30. Howard (1966), *op. cit.*, p. 11.

31. *idem*.

32. Rowland Mainstone, *Developments in Structural Form*, London, 1965, p. 238.

33. Cable Roof Structures, *op. cit.*, pp. 32, 33, and Howard, (1966), *op. cit.*, pp. 12–13.

34. Howard, ibid., p. 11.

35. *Cable Roof Structures, op. cit.*, p. 44.

36. 'New World in the Works', *Architectural Forum*, **133** (3), (Oct, 1970), pp. 26–9.

37. Jawerth, *op. cit.*, p. 117f.

Chapter 17

1. Boyd, *op. cit.*, p. 325.

2. Curt Siegel, *Structure and Form in Modern Architecture*, translated by Thomas E. Burton, London, 1962, p. 286.

3. Lessing, *op. cit.*, p. 137.

4. Siegel, *op. cit.*, pp. 288–9.

5. *ibid.*, p. 284.

6. Rene Sarger, 'Valeur Plastique des structures l'Exposition de Bruxelles,' *L'Architecture d'Aujourd'hui*, (78), p. 8f. See also Siegel, *op. cit.*, pp. 292–4.

7. *ibid.*, p. 40f.

8. Howard (1966), *op. cit.*, p. 17.

9. Robin Boyd, *Living in Australia*, Sydney, 1970, pp. 62–5, 108–9.

10. Howard, *op. cit.*, pp. 18–19, see also Boyd, *op. cit.*, 1963, p. 328.

11. Siegel, *op. cit.*, p. 300.

12. Howard, *op. cit.*, p. 16.

13. Siegel, *op. cit.*, pp. 301–2.

14. See Udo Kultermann (Ed.), *Kenzo Tange: Architecture and Urban Design, 1946–1969*, London, 1970, pp. 72, 176, 196.

15. Terrence Farrell, 'Two Tange Tents in Tokyo', *RIBA Journal*, **72** (1), (Jan. 1965), p. 35f.

16. See Y. Tsuboi and M. Kawaguchi, 'The analysis and design of a suspension roof structure', in R. M. Davies, (Ed.), *Space Structures: A Study of methods and developments in three-dimensional construction resulting from the International Conference on Space Structures, University of Surrey*, September, 1966, Oxford, 1967, pp. 925–41. Professors Tsuboi and Kawaguchi explain: 'In the first stage of the design, it was proposed to use ropes to constitute not only the main cables and the bracing cables but also the hanging members with stiffening steel sections attached along them. However, *it was concluded that the sharp roof surface desired by the architects would provide uneconomical results if this shape was attempted only by adjustment of tensions in the cable network*. The hanging ropes were therefore substituted by stiffening members of steel which were designed to function at the same time as hanging members. To be more correct, the steel members designed in this way assumed three combined roles — they are essentially hanging members, *but they have enough bonding rigidity to maintain shapes that differ considerably from catenaries*, and moreover, they act as stiffeners to prevent deformation due to partial loading. These I-shaped steel members, or hanging girders, which have flanges of 22 × 190 mm and webs 12 mm thick, with a depth varying from 500 to 1000 mm. They are set at 4–500 metres centres.' (author's italics). p. 927.

17. See plan of roof structure of the small stadium, Kultermann, *op. cit.*, p. 212, also Y. Tsuboi and S. Kawamata, 'The Design and Construction of a suspension structure — The Minor Gymnasium of the Tokyo Olympic Indoor Stadium', in Davies, *op. cit.*, fig. 3, p. 1008.

Chapter 18

1. See Drew, *op. cit.*, p. 13f.

2. A number of black tent types have similar shapes to Frei Otto's prestressed membranes. For example the Tekna tent (SW Morocco) resembles the peaked tent at the Federal Garden Exhibition 1957 at Cologne, the *Aulad Ali* tent (Libya) is not dissimilar to the Humped tent at the same exhibition, and the Durānnī tent (Afghanistan) is strikingly similar to the Entrance arch at Cologne.

3. Frederick Kiesler: *Space City Architecture* (1926) in Conrads, *op. cit.*, p. 98.

4. The reuse of the West German Pavilion test structure (1967) for the Institut fur leichte Flachentragwerke, Stuttgart-Vaihingen (1967–8) illustrates the potential adaptability of cablenet structures. Frei Otto's interest in adaptability revealed itself in an early publication — Frei Otto, *et. al., Anpassungs fahiges Bauen* (Adaptable Building), EL.6, Berlin, 1959 — produced by the Development Centre for Lightweight Construction.

5. Pneumatic structures are much less important in traditional tensile building than tents so I have limited the scope of this review so as to emphasise the similarities and contrasts between modern and traditional manifestations of tensile building.

6. See *Grid Shells*, Information of the Institute of Lightweight Structures IL10, Stuttgart, 1974, p. 38, and Drew, *op. cit.*, p. 17.

7. Drew, *op. cit.*, fig. 103–6.

8. 'Frei Otto at Work', *Architectural Design* **XLI** (March 1971), p. 151.

9. See Eberhard Haug, *A Method to Define the Stress-free Configuration of prestressed Cable Nets*, Information of the Institute of Lightweight Structures, IL35/70, Stuttgart, w.d.

10. Otto, *op. cit.*, p. 49f.

11. See Gernot Minke, 'Tensile Structures', *Architectural Design*, April 1968, p. 179, for a summary of the structural requirements influencing the development of prestressed tensile surfaces.

12. Drew, *op. cit.*, p. 14.

13. See Larry Medlin, *Prestressed Membranes with Tensile Boundary Members, A Report Given at the Architectural Researchers Conference Houston, Texas – November 1969*, Information of the Institute of Lightweight Structures IL 19/70, Stuttgart, 1970. See also Minke, *op. cit.*, p. 181.

14. Roland, *op. cit.*, p. 53.

15. See 'German Pavilion Expo '67, Montreal' in *Biology and Building*, Pt. 2, Information of the Institute of Lightweight Structures IL 4, Stuttgart, 1972, pp. 74–75.

16. See Roland, *op. cit.*, p. 18f.

17. Edward Happold, *et. al.*, 'Frei Otto at Work', *op. cit.*, p. 144.

18. *Expo '67, Montreal: German Pavilion*, published in co-operation with the Federal Ministry of Federal Property, 1968, pp. 8–15.

19. Drew, *op. cit.*, pp. 80–1.

20. See Minke, *op. cit.*, pp. 179–83 and Expo '67, *op. cit.*, pp. 16–25.

21. The computer determination of the Munich cable nets is described in several papers:
(i) Mick Eekhout 'Frei Otto and the Munich Olympic Games',
(ii) J. H. Argyris, W. Aicher, T. Angelopoulos, 'On the static Analysis of the Olympic Cable Roofs in Munich' and
(iii) Klaus Linkwitz, 'New Methods for the Determination of Cutting Pattern of Prestressed Cable Nets and their Application to the Olympic Roof Munich' in 'Light Structures', *Zodiac 21*, Milan, 1972, i) pp. 44–45, ii) pp. 74–6, and iii) pp. 76–80.

22. *ibid.*, p. 14f.

23. 'The Load-Bearing Characteristics of Pre-stressed Cable Net Constructions', in *Planning of the Buildings and Facilities for the Olympic Games, Munich 1972. Progress of Planning and Construction, Autumn, 1970*, Stuttgart/Bern, Autumn 1970, pp. 17–21.

24. Professor Fritz Leonhardt and Dr. J. Schlaich, 'Structural Design of Roofs over the Sports Arenas for the 1972 Olympic Games: Some Problems of Prestressed Cable net Structures', *The Structural Engineer*, **50** (3), (March 1972), pp. 113–4.

25. An early proposal for a convertible roof to cover the open-air theatre on the Killesberg near Stuttgart (1955), was succeeded in the 1960s by a number of similar projects, the most noteworthy being Bad Hersfeld (1959), Nijmegen (1960–61), and Heppenheim (1964).

26. See *Convertible Roofs*, Information of the Institute of Lightweight Structures, IL5, Stuttgart, 1972, p. 60f.

27. *ibid.*, p. 236f. 242f.

28. *ibid.*, p. 273f.

29. *ibid.*, p. 252f.

Bibliography

Chapter 1

Bacon, E. E. (1946) 'A preliminary attempt to determine the cultural areas of Asia'. *Southwestern Journal of Anthropology.* **2**.

Birket-Smith, K. (1960) *Primitive Man and his Ways, Patterns of Life in Some Native Societies*. Translated by R. Duffell. London: Odhams Press.

Broek, J. O. M. and Webb, J. W. (1973) *A Geography of Mankind*. 2nd ed., New York: McGraw-Hill.

Fitch, J. M. and Branch, D. (1960) 'Primitive architecture and climate'. *Scientific American.* **203** (6), December.

Forde, C. D. (1952) *Habitat, Economy and Society, A Geographical Introduction into Ethnology*. London: Methuen.

Johnson, D. L. (1969) *The Nature of Nomadism: a Comparative Study of Pastoral Migrations in Southwestern Asia and Northern Africa*. Chicago: University of Chicago Press, Department of Geography Research Paper (118).

Murdock, G. P. (1971) *Our Primitive Contemporaries*. New York: Macmillan.

'Nomads and nomadism in the arid zone'. (1959) *International Science Journal*. UNESCO, (2).

Nomads of the World. (1971) The National Geographic Society. Washington, D.C.

Patai, R. (Winter, 1951). 'Nomadism: Middle Eastern and Central Asian'. *Southwestern Journal of Anthropology,* **7** (4).

Rapoport, A. (1969) *House Form and Culture*. Englewood Cliffs, N.J.: Prentice-Hall.

Service, E. R. (1966) *The Hunters*. Englewood Cliffs, N.J.: Prentice-Hall.

Ucko, P. J. Tringham, R. and Dimbleby, E. D. (1972) *Man, Settlement, and Urbanism*. London: Duckworth.

Chapter 2

Klein, R. G. (1974) 'Ice-age hunters of the Ukraine'. *Scientific American.* **230** (6).

Mongait, A. L. (1961) *Archaeology in the U.S.S.R.* Translated by Thompson, M. W. Harmondsworth: Penguin Books.

Okladnikov, A. P.
   — (1959) *Ancient Population of Siberia and its Culture*.
   Russian Translation Series of the Peabody Museum of Archaeology and Ethnology. **1** Harvard: Harvard University Press.
   — (1970) *Yakutia Before its Incorporation into the Russian State*. Ed. Michael, H. N. London: The Arctic Institute of North America.

Chapter 3

Birket-Smith, K. (1960) 'The Lapps'. *Primitive Man and His Ways, Patterns of Life in Some Native Societies*. Translated by R. Duffell. London: Odham's Press.

Bogoras, W.
   — (1904–9) 'The Chukchee'. *Jesup North Pacific Expedition*. **XI**, Pt. 1. Leiden: E. J. Brill Ltd; New York, G. E. Stechert.
   — (1909) 'The Chukchee'. *Memoirs of the American Museum of Natural History*. (11) 2–4.

Brandon-Cox, H. (1969) *The Trail of the Arctic Nomads*. London.

Collinder, B. (1949) *The Lapps*. Princeton: Greenwood Press.

Erixon, S. (1937) 'Some Primitive Constructions and their Types of Layout, with their Relationship to European Rural Building Practice'. *Folkliv*.

Forde, C. D.
— (1952) 'The Northern Tungus and other reindeer herders of Siberia'. *Habitat, Economy and Society. A Geographical Introduction to Ethnology*. London: Methuen.
— (1952) 'The Yukaghir: reindeer herders in the Siberian Tundra'. *Habitat, Economy and Society*. London: Methuen.

Hatt, G. (1919) 'Notes on reindeer nomadism'. *American Anthropological Association.* **6** (2), April–June.

Lindgren, E. J. (1930) 'North-western Manchuria and the reindeer-Tungus'. *The Geographical Journal* **LXXV** (6), June.

Jochelson, W.
— (1928) *Peoples of Asiatic Russia*. New York: American Museum of Natural History.
— (1926) 'The Yukaghir and the Yukaghirized Tungus'. Publications of the Jesup North Pacific Expedition, *Anthropological Memoirs, American Museum of Natural History.* **IX** Pt. 3. New York: G. E. Stechert.
— (1933) 'The Yakut'. *Anthropological Papers, American Museum of Natural History.* **33** Pt. 2 New York: G. E. Stechert.

Kharuzin, N. N. (1893) *Etudes Sur les Anciennes Eglises Russes aux Toits en Forme de Tentes*. Nogent-le-Rotrov. Daupeley-Gouverneur Societe Nationale des Antiquaires de France. Memoirs. 6th series **3**.

Koechlin, B. (1974) 'Abris et habitations pour humains et Dieux chez les Vezo, semi-nomades marins de Madagascar'. *L'Architecture d'Aujourdhui.* (175), Sep-Oct.

Levina, M. G. and Potapova, L. P. (1961) *Istoriko-Ethnografichesky Atlas Sibiri*. Moscow and Leningrad: N. N. Miklukho – Maklay Institute of Ethnology.

Mirow, N. T. (1974) 'Notes on the domestication of reindeer'. *American Anthropologist.* (47).

Popov, A. A. (1949) 'The ancient Yakut birchbark tent'. *Sbornik Muzeya Anthropologii i Etnografii.* **10,**

Sirelius, U. T. (1906–9) 'Uber die Primitiven Wohnungen der Finnischen und Ob-Ugrischen Völker'. *Finnisch- Ugrische Forchungen* **6–9**.

Chapter 4

Birket-Smith, K.
— (1929) *The Caribou Eskimos, Material and Social Life and their Cutural Position*. Translated by W. E. Calvert. 2 Vols. Copenhagen. Report of the fifth Thule expedition 1921–24. Gyldendalske Boghandel.
— (1959) *The Eskimos*. Translated by W. E. Calvert. London: Methuen.
— (1960) 'Plains Indians'. *Primitive Man and His Ways, Patterns of Life in Some Native Societies*. Translated by R. Duffell. London: Odhams Press.

Boas, F. (1888) *The Central Eskimo*. Washington: Sixth annual report of the bureau of American ethnology, 1884–5.

Cadzow, D. A. (1926) 'The prairie Cree tepee'. *Indian Notes*. **3** American Museum of Natural History.

Campbell, W. S.
— (1915) 'The Cheyenne tepee'. *American Anthropologist.* NS, **17** (4) Oct–Dec.
— (1927) 'The tepees of the Crow Indians'. *American Anthropologist.* NS, (29).

Curtis, E. S. (1973) *In a Sacred Manner we Live*. Barre, Mass.

Driver, H. E. (1961) *Indians of North America*. Chicago and London: University of Chicago Press.

Ewers, J. C. (1944) 'The Blackfoot war lodge: its construction and use'. *American Anthropologist*. NS, **46**.

Forde, C. D.
— (1952) 'The Blackfoot: buffalo hunters of the North American plains'. *Habitat, Economy and Society. A Geographical Introduction to Ethnology*. London: Methuen.
— (1952) 'The Eskimos: seal and caribou hunters in Arctic America'. *Habitat, Economy and Society. A Geographical Introduction to Ethnology*. London: Methuen.

Grinnell, G. B. (1901) 'The Lodges of the Blackfoot'. *American Anthropologist*. NS, **3, 4**.

Honigmann, J. J. (1946) 'Ethnolography and Acculturation of the Fort Nelson Slave'. *Yale University Publication in Anthropology*. (33).

Jenness, D. (1970) *The Life of the Copper Eskimos*. A report of the Canadian Arctic expedition, 1913–18. **XII** Pt. A, New York and London.

Kroeber, A. L. (1939) *Cultural and Natural Areas of Native North America*. Berkeley: University of California Press.

Laubin, R. and G. (1971) *The Indian Tepee; Its History, Construction and Use*. New York: Ballantine Books.

Lowrie, R. H. (1922) 'The material culture of the Crow Indians'. *Anthropological Papers of the American Museum of Natural History*. **XXI** Pt. 3.

Mandelbaum, D. G. (1940) 'The Plains Cree'. *Anthropological Papers of the American Museum of Natural History*. (37).

Mathiassen, T. (1928) *Material Culture of the Iglulik Eskimos*. Report of the fifth Thule expedition, 1921–24, **6** (1). Copenhagen: Gyldendalske Boghandel.

McClintock, W. (1936) *Painted Tepees and Picture Writing of the Blackfoot Indians*. Southwestern Museum Leaflet Series, (6). Los Angeles.

Müller-Beck, H. (1966) 'Palaeohunters in America: Origin and Diffusion'. *Science*. **152**.

Murdock, G. P.
— (1971) 'The Crows of the Western Plains'. *Our Primitive Contemporaries*. New York: Macmillan.
  (1971) 'The Polar Eskimos'. *Our Primitive Contemporaries*. New York: Macmillan.

Nelson, E. W. (1971) *The Eskimo About Bering Strait*. New York and London: Johnson Reprint Corporation.

Speck, F. G. (1940) *Penobscot Man: the Life History of a Forest Tribe in Maine*. Philadelphia: University of Pennsylvania Press.

Spencer, R. F. (1959) *The North Alaskan Eskimo: a Study in Ecology and Society*. Bureau of American Ethnology Bulletin 171. Washington: Smithsonian Institution.

Spencer, R. F. Jennings, J. D., *et. al*. (1965) *The Native Americans*. New York and London: Harper Row.

Steensby, H. P. (1910) 'Contributions to the ethnology and anthropogeography of the Polar Eskimos'. *Meddelser om Grønland*. (7). Copenhagen.

The Plains Indian Tepee. Department of Indian Art, Denver Art Museum. (19). Colorado.

Underhill, R. M. (1971) *Red Man's America, a History of the Indians in the United States*. (Revised ed.) Chicago and London: University of Chicago Press.

Ward, F. (1975) 'The changing world of Canada's Crees'. *National Geographic*.

147 (4), April.

Waterman, T. T. (1924) 'North American Indian dwellings'. *The Geographical Review.* **14** (1), January.

Weyer, E. M. (1969) *The Eskimos, Their Environments and Folkways.* Reprint of 1932 edition. Hamden: Shoestring.

Wissler, C.
— (1966) *Indians of the United States. Four Centuries of their History and Culture.* Ed. Kluckhohn, L. W. Garden City New York: Doubleday.
— (1910) 'Material culture of the Blackfoot Indians'. *Anthropological Papers of the American Museum of Natural History.* **5** Pts. 1 and 2. New York.
— (1912) *North American Indians of the Plains.* American museum of natural history handbook series (1). New York.
— (1914) 'The influence of the horse in the development of plains culture'. *American Anthropologist.* NS. **16** (1), Jan–March. The Collegiate Press.
— (1910) 'Types of dwellings and their distribution in central North America'. *Internationaler Amerikanisten-Kongreb.* **2** (16). Vienna and Leipzig.

Chapter 5

Aeschylus, (1952) *Prometheus Bound.* Translated by Smyth, H. W. London: William Heinemann.

Andrews, P. A.
— (1971) *The Turcoman of Iran.* Kendal: Titus Wilson and Son, Ltd.
— (1973) 'The white house of Khurasan: The felt tents of the Iranian Yomut and Göklen'. *The Journal of the British Institute of Persian Studies.* (11). London.

Atkinson, T. W. (1858) *Oriental and Western Siberia.* London: Hurst and Blackett.

Beazley, E. (1972) 'Tents of the Turkmen'. *Country Life,* Feb. 3.

Czaplicka, M. A. (1973) *The Turks of Central Asia in History and at the Present Day.* London and New York: Curzon Press.

Dawson, C. (1955) *The Mongol Mission Narratives and Letters of the Franciscan Missionaries in Mongolia and China in the 13th and 14th Centuries.* Translated by a nun of Stanbrook Abbey, London and New York: Sheed and Ward.

Fairservis, W. A. Jr. (1962) *Horsemen of the Steppes.* Leicester: Brockhampton.

Howorth, Sir H. n.d. *History of the Mongols from the 9th to the 19th Century.* Pt. 4. New York: Burt Franklin.

Jochelson, W. (1970) *Peoples of Asiatic Russia.* New York and London: American Museum of Natural History.

Karutz, R. (1911) *Unter Kirgisen und Turkmenen.* Leipzig.

Kharuzin, N. N. (1896) *History of the Dwellings of the Turkic and Mongolic Nomads of Russia.* Moscow.

Komroff, M. (1928) *Contemporaries of Marco Polo.* New York: Liverright.

König, W. (1967) *Mongolei.* Leipzig: Museum für Volkerkunde.

Krader, L. (1963) *Peoples of Central Asia.* 3rd ed. Uralic and Altaic series, **26** Bloomington, Indianna: Indianna University Publications.

Lattimore, O.
— (1963) 'Chingis Khan and the Mongol conquests'. *Scientific American.* **209**, (2), August.
— 1938) 'The geographical factor in Mongol history'. *The Geographical Journal.* **XCI** (1), January.

Minns, E. H. (1971) *Scythians and Greeks: A Survey of Ancient History and Archaeology on the North Coast of the Euxine from the Danube to the Caucasus.* First published 1913. New York: Biblo and Tannen.

Opt'land, C. (1966) 'The admirable tents of the Shah Savan'. *International Archives of Ethnography.* **50** (2). Leiden: E. J. Brill.

Phillips E. D.
— (1957) 'New light on the ancient history of the Eurasian Steppe'. American Journal of Archaeology. **61**.
— (1969) *The Mongols, Ancient Peoples and Places*. London: Thames and Hudson.
— (1966) *The Royal Hordes: Nomad Peoples of the Steppes*. New York: McGraw-Hill Book Company; London: Thames and Hudson.

Radlov, V. V. (1884) *Aus Sibirien lose blätter aus dem Tagebuche eines Reisenden Linguisten*. Leipzig.

Rice, T. T. (1957) *The Scythians*. 3rd revised ed. London: Thames and Hudson.

Rockhill, W. W. (Ed.). (1967) *The Journey of William of Rubruck to the Eastern Parts of the World, 1253–55 as Narrated by Himself with Two Accounts of the Earlier Journey of John of Pian de Carpine*. Reproduced by the Hakluyt Society. Nendeln/Lichenstein.

Rona-Tas, A.
— (1961) 'Notes on the Kazak Yurt of West Mongolia'. *Acta Orientalia Hungarica.* **12** (1–3). Budapest: Akademia Kiado, reprinted by 'Kultura' Hungarian trading company.
— (1959) 'Programme for the ethnological and terminological investigation of the Mongolian tent'. *Studia Mongolica.* **1** Pt. 4.

Rostovtzeff, M. (1969) *Iranians and Greeks in South Russia*. Revised ed. New York: Russell.

Strabo, (1954) *The Geography of Strabo*. Translated by Jones, H. L. London: Heinemann.

The Travels of Marco Polo. (1972) Translated and introduced by Latham, R. Harmondsworth: Penguin Books.

Vambery, H. (1885) *Das Turkenvolk in Seinen Ethnologischen und Ethnographischen Beziehungen Geschildert*. Leipzig.

Vambery, A. (1868) *Sketches of Central Asia, Additional Chapters on my Travels, Adventures and on the Ethnology of Central Asia*. London.

Chapter 6

Boucheman, A. de (1934) *Material de la Vie Bedouine recueilli dans le desert de Syrie (tribus des Arabes Sba'a)*. Documents d'etudes Orientales. Damas-Paris: L'Institute Francais de Damas.

Caskel, W. (1954) 'The bedouinization of Arabia'. *American Anthropological Association.* **56** Pt. 2, (2), April.

Dostal, W. (1959) 'The evolution of Bedouin life'. Gabrieli, F. (Ed.) *Ancient Bedouin Society*. Studi Semitici 2, Rome.

Feilberg, C. G. (1944) *La Tente Noire*. Nationalmuseets Skrifter, Copenhagen: Gyldendalske Boghandel.

Patai, R. (1962) *Golden River to Golden Road: Society, Culture and Change in the Middle East*. Philadelphia: University of Pennsylvania.

Chapter 7

Andrews, P. A. (1972) 'Tents of the Tekna, Southwestern Morocco', in Oliver, P. *Shelter in Africa*. New York, Barrie and Rockliff.

Bates, O. (1970) *The Eastern Libyans, an Essay*. London: Frank Cass.

Birket-Smith, K. (1960) 'The Tuareg'. *Primitive Man and his Ways Patterns of Life in Some Native Societies*. London: Odhams Press.

Chapelle, J. (1957) *Nomades Noirs du Sahara*. Librarie Plon-Recherches en Sciences. (10), Paris: Plon.

Gsell, S. (1929) *Histoire Ancienne de l'Afrique Nord*. **5** Paris: Hachette.

Laoust, E. (1930) *L'Habitation chez les Transhumants du Maroc Central et la Tente dans l'Afrique du Nord*. Archives Berberes et Bulletin l'Institut des Hautes-etudes Marocaines. Hesperis, **10**.

le Coeur, C. (1937) *Les 'Mapalia' Numides et leur Survivance au Sahara*. Archives Berberes et Bulletin de l'Institut des Hautes-etudes Marocaines. Hesperis, **24**.

Nicholaisen, J. (1963) *Ecology and Culture of the Pastoral Tuareg with Particular Reference to the Tuareg of Ahaggar and Ayr*. National Museets Skrifter Etnografisk Raekke. Copenhagen: Gyldendalske Boghandel.

Rackow, E. and Uback, E. (1923) *Sitte und Recht in Nordafrika*. **XL** Stuttgart: Zeitschrift für vergleichende Rechtswissenschaft.

Verity, P. (1972) 'Kabish Nomads of Northern Sudan', in Oliver, P. *Shelter in Africa*. New York: Barrie and Rockliffe.

Chapter 8

Burckhardt, J. L. (1830) *Notes on Bedouins and Wahaby: Collected during his Travels in the East by the Late J. L. Burckhardt*. Sir William Ouseley, Ed. London: H. Colburn and R. Bentley.

Dalman, G. (1928–39) *Arbeit und Sitte in Palastina*. **6** Schriften des Deutschen Palastina-Instituts, Gutersloh, reprinted Hildesheim, 1964.

Dickson, H. R. P. (1967) *The Arab of the Desert: a glimpse into Badawin life in Kuwait and Saudi Arabia*. 2nd edition. London: George Allen and Unwin Ltd.

Doughty, C. M. (1921) *Travels in Arabia Deserta*. **1** London and Boston, P. Lee Warner and J. Cape.

Ettinghausen, R. (1962) *Arab Painting*. Geneva: Skira.

Forde, C. G. (1952) 'The Ruwala Badawin: camel breeders of Northern Arabia'. *Habitat, Economy and Society, a Geographical Introduction to Ethnology*. London: Methuen.

Hess, J. J. (1938) *Von den Beduinen des innern Arabiens*. Zurich and Leipzig.

Lane E. W. (1863) *Arabic-English Lexicon*. Book 1, Pt. 1. Lane-Poole, Ed. London.

Marx, E. (1967) *Bedouin of the Negev*. Manchester: Manchester University Press.

Musil, A.

— (1927) *Arabia Deserta*. American geographical society series (2). New York: Oriental Explorations and Studies.

— (1907–08) *Arabia Petraea*. **3** Akademie der Wissenschaften, Vienna: Ethnologischer Reisebericht.

— (1928) *Manners and Customs of the Ruwala Bedouins*. American geographical society series (6). New York: Oriental explorations and studies.

Oppenheim, M. F. von, (1939) 'Die Beduinen', in Braunlicht, E. and Caskel, W., *Die Beduinen Stämme in Mesopotamien U. Syrien*. Leipzig.

Rackow, E. (1938) 'Das Beduinenzelt'. **21** Berlin: *Baessler-Archiv*.

Raswan, C. R. (1935) *The Black Tents of Arabia*. London: Hutchinson; Boston: Little, Brown Co.

Weir, S. (1976) *The Bedouin*. The Department of Ethnography of the British Museum. London: World of Islam Publishing Company.

Chapter 9

Barth, F. (1968) *Nomads of South Persia: the Basseri Tribe of the Khamseh Confederacy*. Boston: Little, Brown and Co.

Bronowski, J. (1973) *The Ascent of Man*. Sydney: Angus and Robertson.

Edmonds, C. J. (1957) *Kurds, Turks and Arabs*. London, New York, Toronto: Oxford University Press.

Ferdinand, K.
— (1959) 'Les Nomades', in Humlum, J. P. C. N. *La Geographie de L'Afghanistan*. Copenhagen: Scandinavian University Books.
— (1956) 'Afghanistans Nomader'. *Fra Nationalmuseets Arbejdsmark*. Henning Haslund-Christensens Minde-Ekspedition, 1953–55. Copenhagen: Dansk Etnografisk Forening.
— (1959) 'The Baluchistan barrel-vaulted tent and its affinities' *Folk*, **1**.
— (1960) 'The Baluchistan barrel-vaulted tent: Supplementary material from Iranian Baluchistan and Sistan'. *Folk*, **2**.

Fisher W. B. (Ed.) (1968) *The Cambridge History of Iran*. Cambridge: Cambridge University Press.

Schurmann, H. F. (1961) *The Mongols of Afghanistan, an Ethnography of the Moghols and related Peoples of Afghanistan*. The Hague: Mouton and Co.

Walton, J. (1958) 'The gypsy bender tent and its derivatives'. *Man*, **LVIII** Journal of the Royal Anthropological Institute.

Chapter 10

Hermanns, M. (1949) *Die Nomaden von Tibet*. Vienna.

Huc, E. R. (1850) *Souvenirs d'un Voyage dans la Tartarie et le Tibet*, **2** (268). Paris.

Rawling, C. G. (1918) *The Great Plateau, Being an Account of Exploration in Tibet, 1903, and of the Gartok Expedition, 1904–5*. London: Edward Arnold.

Rockhill W. W.
— (1894) *Diary of a Journey through Mongolia and Tibet in 1891 and 1892*. Washington, D.C.: Smithsonian Institution.
— (1893) 'Notes on the ethnology of Tibet'. *United States National Museum, Annual Report*. Washington.

Roerich, G. N. (1931) *Trails to Inmost Asia, Five Years of Exploration with the Roerich Central Asian Expedition*. New Haven: Yale University Press.

Stein, R. A. (1972) *Tibetan Civilization*. London: Faber.

Tafel, A. (1914) *Meine Tibetreise*. 2 Vols. Stuttgart.

Chapter 11

Athenaeus, (1933) *The Deipnosophists*. Translated by Gulick, C. B. London: William Heinemann.

Bandinelli, R. B. (1971) *Rome, the Late Empire: Roman Art AD 200–400*. Translated by Green, P. London: Thames and Hudson.

Barnett, R. D. n.d. *Assyrian Palace Reliefs and their Influence on the Sculptures of Babylonia and Persia*. London: Batchworth Press.

Bieber M. (1961) *The History of the Greek and Roman Theatre*. Princeton: Princeton University Press.

Breasted, J. H. (1962) *Ancient Records of Egypt: Historical Documents from the Earliest Times to the Persian Conquest*. New York: Russell and Russell Inc.

Broneer, O. (1944) 'The tent of Xerxes and the Greek theatre'. *University of California Publications in Classical Archaeology.* **1** (12). University of California.

Cariste, A. (1856) *Monuments Antiques a Orange, Arc de Triomphe et Theatre.* Paris: Firmin Didot.

Cichorius, C. (1896) *Die Reliefs der Traianssäule.* Berlin: Reimen.

Contenau, G.
— (1954) *Everyday Life in Babylon and Assyria.* Translated by K. R. and A. R. Maxwell-Hyslop. London: Edward Arnold.
— (1947) *Manuel d'Archeologie Orientale.* 4 Vols. Paris.

Cottrell, L. (1968) *The Warrior Pharaohs.* London: Evans Brothers Ltd.

de Vaux, R. (1973) *Ancient Israel, its Life and Institutions.* Translated by J. McHugh. London: Darton, L and T.

Dio, C. (1954) *Dio's Roman History.* London: William Heinemann.

Erman, A. and Blackman. (1927) *The Literature of the Ancient Egyptians.* London: Methuen.

Euripides *Ion.* (1946) Translated by Way, A. S. London: William Heinemann.

Fraser, P. M. (1972) *Ptolemaic Alexandria.* 2 Vols. Oxford: Clarendon Press.

Graeffe, R. (1972) 'Roman Theatre Velum'. *Convertible Roofs.* Information of the Institute for Lightweight Structures 5. Stuttgart: Karl Kramer Verlag.

Herodotus. (1946) Translated by Godley, A. D. London: William Heinemann.

Herzfeld, E. (1919) 'Das Assyrische Zelt'. *Orientalische Literaturzeitung.* Berlin.

Homer, (1954) *The Iliad.* Translated by Murray, A. T. London: William Heinemann.

Kupper, J. R.
— (1957) 'Les Nomades en Mesopotamie au temps des Rois de Mari'. *Bibliotheque de la Faculte de Philosophie et lettres de l'Universite de Liege. Fasicule CXLII.* Paris.
— (1959) 'Le role des Nomades dans l'histoire de la Mesopotamienne'. *Journal of the Economic and Social History of the Orient.* **2** Leiden.

Layard, A. H.
— (1853) *Discoveries in the ruins of Nineveh and Babylon.* London: John Murray.
— (1849) *Nineveh and its Remains: With an Account of a Visit to the Chaldean Christians of Kurdistan, and the Yezidis, or devil-worshippers; and an inquiry into the Manners and Arts of the Ancient Assyrians.* 2 Vols. London: John Murray.
— (1853) *The Monuments of Nineveh, from Drawings made on the spot.* 1st Series. London: John Murray.

Luckenbill, D. D. (1927) *Ancient Records of Assyria and Babylonia.* 2 Vols. Chicago: University of Chicago Press.

McIntyre, J. and Richmond, I. A. (1934) 'Tents of the Roman Army and Leather from Birdoswald'. *Transactions of the Cumberland and Westmoreland Antiquarian and Archaeological Society.* (34).

Olmstead, A. T. (1968) *History of Assyria.* Chicago and London: University of Chicago Press.

Parrot, A. *Nineveh and Babylon.* Translated by S. Gilbert and J. Emmons. London: Thames and Hudson.

Paterson, A. (1912) *Assyrian Sculptures: Palace of Sennacherib.* The Hague: Martinus Nijhoff.

Pearson, J. (1973) *Arena, the Story of the Colosseum.* London: Thames and Hudson.

Perrot, G. and Chipiez, D. (1884) *Histoire de L'Art dans L'Antiquite.* 2 Vols. Paris: Faber and Faber.

Petersen, E. A. (1896) *Die Marcus-Säule auf Pizaaz Colonna in Rom*. In Domaszewski A. von, and Calderini, G. Munich.

Plutarch, (1950) *Lives*. Translated by Perrin, B. London and Cambridge, Mass.: William Heinemann.

Polybius, (1954) *The Histories*. Translated by Paton, W. R. 6 Vols. London: William Heinemann.

Ringelmann, M. (1907—8) 'Les constructions rurales de la Chaldec et a l'Assyrie'. *Recueil de Travaux relatifs a la Philolgie et a l'Archeologie Egyptienne et Assyriennes*. **29, 30**. Paris.

Pritchard, J. B. (1965) *Ancient Near Eastern Texts*. Princeton: Princeton University Press.

Rothenberg, B. (1972) *Timna, Valley of the Biblical Copper Mines*. London: Thames and Hudson.

Sophocles, (1951) *Ajax*. Translated by Storr, F. London: William Heinemann.

Tacitus, (1951) *The Annals of Tacitus*. 4 Vols. Translated by Jackson, J. Harvard: William Heinemann.

'Tent of Xerxes and Greek theatre'. *American Journal of Archaeology*. **XLVIII** 1944.

Webster, G. (1969) *The Roman Imperial Army of the First and Second Centuries AD*. London: Adam and Charles Black.

Wreszinski, W. (1935) *Atlas zur Altagyptischen Kulturgeschichte*. **2** Leipzig: Hinrichs.

Xenophon
— (1947) *Cyropaedia*. Translated by Miller, W. London and Cambridge: William Heinemann.
— (1952) *The Persian Expedition*. Translated by Warner, R. Harmondsworth: Penguin Books.

Yadin, Y.
— (1966) *Masada, Herod's Fortress and the Zealot's Last Stand*. London: Weidenfeld and Nicholson.
— (1963) *The Art of Warfare in Biblical Lands*. 2 Vols. London: Weidenfeld and Nicholson.

Chapter 12

Anglo, S.
— (1960) 'Le camp du drap d'or et les entrevues d'Henri VIII et de Charles Quint'. Jacquet, J. (Ed.). *Les Fetes de la Renaissance*. **2** (129). Paris.
— (1966) 'The Hampton Court painting of the Field of Cloth of Gold considered as an historical document'. *The Antiquities Journal*. **XLVI**.

Beurdeley, C. and M. (1972) *Giuseppe Castiglione, a Jesuit Painter at the Court of the Chinese Emperors*. Translated by Bullock, M. London: Lund Humphries.

Bishop, M. (1968) *The Horizon Book of the Middle Ages*. London: Cassel.

Blochet, E. (1929) *Musulman Painting XIIth—XVIIth Century*. London: Methuen.

BM MS *Cotton Augustus I* (ii) (76); (iii) (18), 1520.

Castelfranchi, V. L. (1968) *International Gothic Art in Italy*. Translated by B. D. Phillips. London: Thames and Hudson.

Chambers, E. K. (1906) *Notes on the History of the Revels Office Under the Tudors*. London: A. H. Bullen.

Coulton, G. G. (1930) *The Chronicler of European Chivalry*. Studio Special Winter Number. London.

Daniel, G. (1961) *The Seljuks in Asia Minor*. London: Thames and Hudson.

De Montfaucon, B. (1729–33) *Les Monuments de la Monarchie Francoise*. 4 Vols, Paris.

Dunan, M. (Ed.) (1963) *Ancient and Mediaeval History*. Larouse Encyclopaedia. London: Paul Hamlyn.

Formaggio, D. and Basso, C. (Ed.) (1962) *A Book of Miniatures*. Translated by P. Craig. London: Peter Nevill.

Goodwin, G. (1971) *A History of Ottoman Architecture*. London: Thames and Hudson.

Gray, B. (1961) *Persian Painting*. Geneva: Albert Skira.

Grube, E. J. (1966) *The World of Islam*. London: Paul Hamlyn.

Hindley, G. (1971) *Mediaeval Warfare*. London: Wayland.

Joycelyne, G. R. (1969) *The Field of Cloth of Gold, Men and Manners in 1520*. London: Routledge and Kegan Paul.

Knolles, R. *The Turkish History, from the Original of the Nation, to the Growth of the Ottoman Empire, with the Lives and Conquests of their Princess and Emperors, with a continuation to this present year MDCLXXXVII by Sir Paul Rycault*. 6th ed. 3 vols. London: Samsour.

Kubickova, V. n.d. *Persian Miniatures*. Translated by R. Finlayson. London: Spring Books.

La Description et Order du Camp Festive et Joustes. Paris 1520.

Lejeune, R. and Stiennon, J. (1966) *La Legende de Roland dans l'Art du Moyen Age*. 2 Vols. Brussels: Phaidon.

Lillys, W. (1965) *Persian Miniatures*. London: Souvenir Press.

L'Ordonnance et Ordre du Tournoy, Joustes et Combat a Pied et a'Cheval. Paris. 1520.

Mahler, J. G. (Ed.) (1965) *Oriental Miniatures: Persian, Indian, Turkish*. London: Souvenir Press.

Mallet, M. (1974) *Mercenaries and their Masters: Warfare in Renaissance Italy*. London: Bodley Head.

Marek and Knizicova, (1963) *The Jenghis Kahn Miniatures from the Court of Akbar the Great*. London: Spring Books.

Martin, F. R. (1912) *The Miniature Painting and Painters of Persia, India and Turkey from the 8th to the 18th Century*. London: Bernard Quaritch.

Martin, F. R. and Arnold, Sir T. (1926) *The Nizannis Ms. Illuminated by Bihzad, Mirak and Qasim Ali*. Written in 1495 for Sultan Ali Mirza Barbas, Ruler of Samarz. BM (Or. 6810.) Vienna.

Murois, A.

– (1963) *An Illustrated History of England*. Translated by Miles, H. London: The Bodley Head.

– (1960) *An Illustrated History of France*. Translated by Binsse, H. L. and Hopkins, G. London: The Bodley Head.

– (1966) *An Illustrated History of Germany*. London: The Bodley Head.

Norman, V. (1971) *The Mediaeval Soldier*. London: Barker.

Oertal, R. (1968) *Early Italian Painting to 1400*. Translated by L. Cooper. London: Thames and Hudson.

Paccagnini, G. n.d. *Simone Martini*. London: Heinemann.

Pope, A. U. and Ackerman, A. (Ed.) (1967) *A Survey of Persian Art from Prehistoric Times to the Present*. 9 Vols. London and New York: Oxford University Press.

Rice, D. T. (Ed.) (1965) *The Dark Ages, the Making of European Civilization*. London: Thames and Hudson.

Rorex, R. and Fong, W. (Ed.) (1974) *Eighteen Songs of a Nomad Flute: The Story of Lady Wen-Chi*. New York: The Metropolitan Museum of Art.

Sakisian, A. B. (1929) *La Miniature Persane du XII au XVIIIe Siecle*. Paris and Brussels: Guanoesy.

The Accounts of the Treasurer and Receiver-General of the Artillery, which Record the Making and Erection of the French Tents and Pavilions. Bibliotheque Nationale MS *Francais* 10383 (The Original Accounts), Paris 1520.

Trevor-Roper, H. (Ed.) n.d. *The Age of Expansion*. New York: McGraw Hill.

Warner, J. (1975) 'Castiglione and the conquests of the Ch'ien lung emperor'. *Arts in Asia*. **5** (6), Nov-Dec.

Williams, N.
    – (1967) *Henry VIII and His Court*. London: Weidenfeld and Nicholson.
    – (1960) 'The master of the royal tents and his records'. *Journal of the Society of Archivists*. **2** (2), Oct.

Chapter 13

Chandra, S. (1902) *Journey to Lhasa and Central Tibet*. Rockhill, W., (Ed.). John Murray.

Fugl-Meyer, H. (1937) *Chinese bridges*. Shanghai and Singapore, London: Kelly and Walsh Ltd.

Giles, H. A. 1923. *Travels of Fa Hsien, 399–414 AD or Record of the Buddhist Kingdoms*. Retranslated by Giles. Cambridge: Cambridge University Press.

Goodrich, L. C. (1957) 'Suspension bridges in China'. *Sino Indian Studies*. **5** (3–4).

'Inca suspension bridge'. *National Geographic*. **144** (6). December 1973.

Needham, J. (1971) *Science and Civilization in China*. **4** Pt. 3, Cambridge: Cambridge University Press.

Parsons, W. B. (1939) *Engineers and Engineering in the Renaissance*. Baltimore: Williams and Wilkins.

Popper, P. (1948) 'Cane bridges of Asia'. *National Geographic*. **XCIV** (2).

Robins, F. W. (1948) *The Story of the Bridge*. Birmingham.

Sharp, Sir A. (1920) 'The hinterland of Liberia'. *The Geographical Journal*. **LV** (4) April.

Squier, E. G. (1877) *Peru, Incidents of Travel and Explorations in the Land of the Incas*. New York: Harper and Bros.

'Suspension bridge across Pilcomayo river between Sucre and Potosi'. *National Geographic*. **129** (2), Feb. 1966.

Von Fürer-Haimendorf, C. (1938) 'Through the unexpected mountains of the Assam-Burma border'. *The Geographic Journal*. **XCI** (3), March.

Von Hagen, V. W. (1956) *Highway of the Sun*. London: Victor Gollancz.

Ward, F. K. (1923) *The Mystery Rivers of Tibet*. London: Seely Service.

Chapter 14

Andrews, C. B. (1936) 'Early victorian bridges in suspension in the British Isles'. *The Architectural Review*. (80), September.

Beck, T. (1900) *Beitrage z. Geschichte d. Maschinen Baues*. Berlin: Springer.

Beckett, D. (1969) *Bridges*. London: Paul Hamlyn.

Clark, W. T. (1852–3) *The Suspension Bridge Across the River Danube*. London: John Weale.

Gies, J. (1963) *Bridges and Men*. New York: Doubleday.

Hopkins, H. J. (1970) *A Span of Bridges*. Newton Abbot, Devon: David and Charles.

Navier, C. L. M. H. (1823) *Memoire sur les Ponts Suspendus*. Paris.

Plowden, D. (1974) *Bridges: The Spans of North America*. New York: Viking Press.

Pugsley, Sir A. (1957) *The Theory of Suspension Bridges*. London: Edward Arnold.

Seguin, C. (1824) *Des Ponts en Fil de Fer*. Paris:

Steinman, D. B. (1949) *A Practical Treatise on Suspension Bridges: Their Design, Construction and Erection*. 2nd edition. New York and London: John Wiley and Sons.

Sutherland, J. (1966) 'Long span bridges'. *The Architectural Review*. **CXL** (835), September.

Tames, R. (1972) *Isambard Kingdom Brunel*. Aylesbury Bucks: Shire Publications Ltd.

Thompson, D. (1966) *On Growth and Form*. Abridged edition. Cambridge: Cambridge University Press.

Verantius, Faustus, (1617) *Machinae Novae*.

Vicat, L. J. (1831) 'Ponts suspendus en fil de fer sur le Rhone.' *Annals des Ponts et Chaussées (Memoires et Documents)*. (1).

Werner, E. (1973) *Die Ersten Ketten und Drahtseilbrücken*. Technikgeschichte in Einzeldarstellungen. (28), Dusseldorf: VDI Verlag Gmbh.

Chapter 15

Bannister, T. C. (1957) 'Bogardus revisited. Part II: The iron towers'. *Journal of the Society of Architectural Historians*. **XVI**.

Bastlund, K. (1967) *José Luis Sert*. New York, Washington: Frederick A. Praeger. •

Esquillan, N. and Saillard, Y. (Eds.) (1963) *Hanging Roofs*. Amsterdam: North-Holland Publishing Co.

Excerpts from Hanging Roofs. (1967) Bethlehem Steel Corporation Booklet 2319. May.

Immagini e Materiali del Laboratorio Fortuni. Comune di Venezia, Assessorato alla Cultura e alle Belle Arti, 1978. Venice: Marsilio Edifori.

Makowski, Z. S. (1965) *Steel Space Structures*. London: Michael Joseph.

Le Corbusier, My Work (1960) Translated by Palmes, J. London: Thames and Hudson.

Meller, J. (Ed.). (1970) *The Buckminster Fuller Reader*. London: Penguin Books.

Rhodes, R. (1858) *Tents and Tent Life from the Earliest Ages to the Present Time*. London: Smith, Elder.

Schnaidt, C. (1965) *Hannes Meyer, Buildings, Projects and Writings*. London: Alec Tiranti Ltd.

Twentieth Century Engineering. (1964) New York: The Museum of Modern Art.

Chapter 16

'Bicycle wheel roof spans 240 feet'. *Architectural Forum*. **112** (5), May 1960.

'Bicycle wheels'. *Progressive Architecture*. **42** Feb. 1961.

Boyd, R.
— (1963) 'Under tension'. *The Architectural Review*. **134** (801), November.
— (1958) 'The engineering of excitement'. *The Architectural Review*. November.

Cable Construction in Contemporary Architecture. Bethlehem Steel Corporation Booklet 2264-A. Oct. 1966.

Cable Roof Structures. Bethlehem Steel Corporation Booklet 2318-A February 1968.

'Cable-suspended roof construction State-of-the-Art'. *Journal of the Structural Division, Proceedings of the American Society of Civil Engineers.* **97** ST6, June, 1971.

Chelazzi, P. (1957) 'Axially-stressed wide span structures'. *Progressive Architecture.* **28** (12) December.

Engel, H. (1971) *Structural Systems*, New York: Praeger; London: Iliffe.

Expo '58. (1958) *Architectural Review*. **124** (739). August.

'Hammock-type roof for Dulles Airport'. *Architectural Record.* **130** November, 1961.

Hitchcock, H. R. (Introduction). (1967) *Philip Johnson, Architecture 1949–65*. Chicago, San Francisco: Holt, Rinehart and Winston.

Howard, S. (1960) 'Suspension structures'. *Architectural Record.* **128** September.

'Idlewild — Aircraft maintenance and service facilities'. *Architectural Record.* **130** Sep. 1961.

Leonhardt, A. (1957) 'Entwurf eines Leichtbetonhangedaches'. *Bauingenieur.* (9).

Lessing, L. (1957) 'Suspension structures'. *Architectural Forum.* **107** (6), Dec.

Jawerth, D. (1961) 'Stressed steel cable structures'. *L'Architecture d'Aujourd'hui.* AA (99), Dec.

Littlejohn, E. P. (1957) 'Trans world airlines hangar'. *Civil Engineering.* **27** (10), October.

Mainstone, R. J.
 — (1974) *Developments in Structural Form*. London: Allen Lane.
 — (1968) 'Structural theory and design before 1742'. *Architectural Review.* **CXIII** (854), April.
 — (1963) 'The springs of structural invention'. *RIBA Journal.* **70** (2), February.

Nervi's expanding paper mill'. *Fortune.* September 1964.

Nervi gives a factory the grace of a bridge'. *Architectural Forum.* July, 1964.

'New world in the works'. *The Architectural Forum.* **133** (3), October, 1970.

'Parabolic cable roof'. *The Architectural Forum.* **98** (6), June 1953.

'Parabolic pavilion'. *The Architectural Forum.* **97** (4), October 1952.

Paul Rudolph, Buildings and Projects. (1970) Stuttgart, London and New York: Praeger.

Pierce, D. R. (1956) 'Cables support cantilevered hangar roof'. *Civil Engineering.* **26** (12), December.

'Roof raising at New York state's fair pavilion'. *Civil Engineering.* **33** (12), December, 1963.

Sarger, R. 'Valeur plastique des structures a l'Exposition de Bruxelles'. *L'Architecture d'Aujourd'hui.* (78).

Severud, F. N. and Corbelletti, R. G. (1956) 'Hung roof'. *Progressive Architecture.* **XXXVII** (3), March.

Suspended Structures Concepts. United States steel publication AD USS 55-1898. April, 1966.

Tentative Criteria for Structural Applications of Steel Cables for Buildings. American Iron and Steel Institute. New York, 1966.

'TWA hangar at Philadelphia'. *Engineering News-Record.* Dec. 27, 1956.

'US pavilion at Brussels'. *Engineering News-Record.* Sep. 26, 1957.

'US pavilion at Brussels features cable-supported roof'. *Civil Engineering.* **28** (7), July, 1958.

'Utica auditorium features new lightweight roof'. *Civil Engineering.* **30** (6), June, 1960.

Zuk, W. (1963) *Concepts of Structure*. New York: Reinhold Publishing Corporation.

Chapter 17

'A fan in Japan'. *Architectural Forum*. **126** April, 1967.
'Arena suspension roof'. *Architectural Record*. **135** (7), June 1964.
'Big tops by Tange at Tokyo olympics'. *Progressive Architecture*. **45** Dec. 1964.
Boyd, R. (1966) 'Olympic buildings in Tokyo'. *Architectural Review*. **CXXXIX** (830), April.
'Cable-suspended roof for Yale hockey rink'. *Civil Engineering*. **28** (9), Sep. 1958.
'Cable suspended roof, Yale Severud'. *Civil Engineering*. **28** (9), Sep. 1958.
'Clean sweep in olympics'. *Architectural Forum*. **121** Aug/Sep. 1964.
Farrell, T. (1965) 'Two Tange tents in Tokyo'. *RIBA Journal*. **72** (1), Jan. 1965.
Howard, H. Seymour. (1959) 'Prestressing prevents flutter of cable roof'. *Architectural Record*. **126** August.
Kulterman, U. (Ed.) (1970) *Kenzo Tange: Architecture and Urban Design, 1946–1969*. London: Pall Mall Press.
McQuade, W. (1958) 'Yales viking vessel'. *Architectural Forum*. **109** December.
Medlin, R. L. (1965) 'Prestressed membrane tension structures. *Progressive Architecture*. **46** August.
'Music tent'. *Architectural Forum*. **91** (3), Sep. 1949.
Saarinen, A. B. (Ed.). (1968) *Eero Saarinen on his Work*. London: Yale University Press.
Scalzi, J. B., Podolny, W. Jr. and Teng, W. C. (1969) *Design Fundamentals of Cable Structures*. United States Steel Croporation AD USS 55-3580-01. USA.
Schierle, G. G. (Ed.) (1968) *Lightweight Tension Structures*. Berkeley: University of California.
Siegel, C. (1962) *Structure and Form in Modern Architecture*. Translated by Burton, T. E. London: Crosby Lockwood Staples Ltd.
Stromeyer, P. (1968) *Textile Buildings*. Konstanz: Stromeyer and Co.
Stubbins, H. and Otto, F. (1958) 'The congress hall debate'. *The Architectural Forum*. **108** (1), January.
Temko, A. n.d. *Eero Saarinen*. New York: George Braziller.
The Tent: Soft Shell Structures at Expo '70. (1970) Tokyo: Taiyo Kogyo Co. Ltd.
'Yale's Hockey Rink'. *Architectural Record*. **124** Oct. 1958.
Yokoo, Y., Nakamura, T., Hek, K. and Kawamasa, S., (Eds). (1971) *Tension Structures and Space Frames*. Proceedings of the Pacific Symposium Pt. II Tokyo and Kyoto: Architectural Institute of Japan.
Von Eckhardt, W. (1960) *Eric Mendelsohn*. New York: George Braziller.

Chapter 18

Anchored cable nets mesh, German pavilion, Ile Notre-Dame'. *Progressive Architecture*. **XLVIII** (6), June 1967.
Boyd, R. (1967) 'Germany'. *Architectural Review*. **CXLII** (846), August.
Bubner, E. (1972) *Zum Problem der Formfinding Vorgespannter Seilnelflachen*. IGMA Dissertation 2, Stuttgart: Karl Kramer Verlag.
'Convertible roofs.' *Information of the Institute for Lightweight Structures*. (5). Stuttgart 1972: Karl Kramer Verlag.
'Die Drei Pavilions der 'Sonsbeek '71'. *Werk*. **9** (58), Sep. 1971.

Drew, P. (1976) *Frei Otto: Form and Structure*. London: Crosby Lockwood Staples, Ltd.

'Ensemble sportif patinoire — piscine de conflans — Sainte Honorine, France'. *L'Architecture d'Aujourdhui*. (160), Feb-March 1972.

'Expo '67 — a brilliantly ordered visual world'. *Architectural Record*. (142), July 1967.

'Frei Otto designs 1·864 million cubic feet of air.' *Architectural Forum*. **126** April 1967.

Glaeser, L. (1972) *The Work of Frei Otto*. New York: The Museum of Modern Art.

Happold, E. and Dickson, M. (1974) 'The story of Munich: Zodiac 21' *Architectural Design*. **XLIV** (6), June.

IL Expo '67, Montreal: German Pavilion. (1968) Stuttgart: Published in co-operation with the German Ministry of Federal Property.

Middleton, R.
   — (1971) 'Frei Otto at work'. *Architectural Design*. **XLI** March
   — (1972) 'Munich and olympic games'. *Architectural Design*. **XLII** August.

Minke, G. (1968) 'Tensile structures'. *Architectural Design*. April.

Otto, F. (1969) *Tensile structures: cables, nets and membranes*. **2** Cambridge, Mass. and London: MIT Press.

'Pool parti, architect Roger Taillibert has designed a pool complex in Paris that changes the weather'. *The Architectural Forum*. **137** (3), October 1972.

Roland, C. (1970) *Frei Otto — Structures*. Translated by C. V. Amerongen. London: Longman.

'Steel tent in Montreal'. *The Architectural Forum*. **125** Oct. 1966.

'The Munich tensile structures'. *Zodiac 21*. 1972. Milan, Edizioni di Communita.

Index

Heavy type refers to peoples who use tents; figures in italics to illustration numbers.